MEASURING MARKET POWER

CONTRIBUTIONS TO ECONOMIC ANALYSIS

255

Honorary Editors:
D.W. JORGENSON
J. TINBERGEN†

Editors:
R. BLUNDELL
R. CABALLERO
J.-J. LAFFONT
T. PERSSON

ELSEVIER
Amsterdam — Boston — London — New York — Oxford — Paris — San Diego
San Francisco — Singapore — Sydney — Tokyo

MEASURING MARKET POWER

Edited by

Daniel J. Slottje
Department of Economics
Southern Methodist University
Dallas, TX 75275
USA

2002

ELSEVIER
Amsterdam — Boston — London — New York — Oxford — Paris — San Diego
San Francisco — Singapore — Sydney — Tokyo

ELSEVIER SCIENCE B.V.
Sara Burgerhartstraat 25
P.O. Box 211, 1000 AE Amsterdam, The Netherlands

First edition 2002

Library of Congress Cataloging in Publication Data
Measuring market power / edited by Daniel J. Slottje.
     p.cm. -- (Contributions to economic analysis ; 255)
  Includes bibliographical references and index.
   ISBN 0-444-51156-3 (alk. paper)
    1. Consolidation and merger of corporations--Case studies. 2. Industrial concentration--Case studies. I. Slottje, Daniel Jonathan, 1957- II. Series.

  HD2746.5 .M4 2002
  338.8--dc21

                                  2002033870

British Library Cataloguing in Publication Data
A catalogue record from the British Library has been applied for.

ISBN: 0-444-51156-3
ISSN: 0573-8555 (Series)

Introduction to the series

This series consists of a number of hitherto unpublished studies, which are introduced by the editors in the belief that they represent fresh contributions to economic science.

The term "economic analysis" as used in the title of the series has been adopted because it covers both the activities of the theoretical economist and the research worker.

Although the analytical methods used by the various contributors are not the same, they are nevertheless conditioned by the common origin of their studies, namely theoretical problems encountered in practical research. Since for this reason, business cycle research and national accounting, research work on behalf of economic policy, and problems of planning are the main sources of the subject dealt with, they necessarily determine the manner of approach adopted by the authors. Their methods tend to be "practical" in the sense of not being too far remote from application to actual economic conditions. In addition they are quantitative.

It is the hope of the editors that the publication of these studies will help to stimulate the exchange of scientific information and to reinforce international cooperation in the field of economics.

The Editors

Contents

Contents

Contributors

Andrew Abere
Princeton Economics Group
707 State Road
Princeton, NJ 08544

Oral Capps Jr
Department of Agricultural Economics
Texas A&M University
College Station, TX 77810

Edward K.Y. Chen
Department of Economics
Lingnan University
Tuen Mun, Hong Kong

Jeffrey Church
Department of Agricultural Economics
University of Calgary
Calgary, Alberta
Canada T2N 1N4
E-mail jrchurch@ucalgary.ca

William S. Comanor
Department of Economics
UCSB
Santa Barbara, CA 93106–9210
E-mail comanor@econ.ucsb.edu

Michael J. Doane
PM KeyPoint LLC
Emeryville, CA 94608

Luke Froeb
Owen Graduate School of Management
Vanderbilt University
Nashville, TN 37203
E-mail luke.m.froeb@vanderbilt.edu

Chantal Grandchamp
Institut d'économie et management de la
    santé
Champ de l'air
Rue du Bugnon 21
CH-1005 Lausanne

Dwight R. Lee
Terry School of Business
University of Georgia
Athens, GA 30602

John P. Lenich
University of Nebraska-Lincoln
Lincoln, NE 68588–0902

Ping Lin
Department of Economics
Lingnan University
Tuen Mun, Hong Kong
E-mail plin@ln.edu.hk

Alan Love
Department of Agricultural Economics
Texas A&M University
College Station, TX 77840

Esfandiar Maasoumi
Department of Economics
Southern Methodist University
Dallas, TX 75275

Richard B. McKenzie
Graduate School of Management
University of California
Irvine, CA 92697
E-mail mckenzie@uci.edu

Jeffrey Perloff
University of California, Berkeley
Department of Agricultural and Resource
	Economics
207 Giannini Hall
Berkeley, CA 94720–3310

Stephen D. Prowse
KPMG, LLP
200 Crescent Court
Suite 300
Dallas, TX 75201
E-mail sprowse@kpmg.com

Jon M. Riddle
University of California
Los Angeles, CA 90095–1477

David I. Rosenbaum
Professor of Economics
University of Nebraska-Lincoln
Lincoln, NE 68588–0489
E-mail drosenbaum1@unl.edu

F.M. Scherer
Department of Economics
Harvard University
Cambridge, MA 02138
E-mail mike_scherer@harvard.edu

David S. Sibley
John Michael Stuart Centennial
University of Texas
Austin, TX 78712
E-mail sibley@eco.utexas.edu

Robin C. Sickles
Rice University
Department of Economics
MS22
Houston, TX 77005–1892
E-mail rsickles@rice.edu

Professor Daniel J. Slottje
Department of Economics
Southern Methodist University
Dallas, TX 75275

Steven Tschantz
Department of Mathematics
Vanderbilt University
Nashville, TN 37203

Jesse C. Weiher
FDIC Division of Research and
	Statistics
550 17th St., NW
Washington, DC 20429

Gregory J. Werden
Senior Economic Counsel
Antitrust Division
US Department of Justice
Washington, DC 20530
E-mail gregory.werden@usdoj.gov

Lawrence J. White
Stern School of Business
New York University
44 West 4th Street
New York, NY 10012–1126
E-mail white@stern.nyu.edu

Peter Zweifel
Socioeconomic Institute of the University of
	Zurich
Hottingerstrasse, 10, CH-8032 Zurich
E-mail pzweifel@soi.unizh.ch

Editor's Introduction

The purpose of this book is to introduce the reader to a comprehensive analysis of issues in measuring market power across a variety of countries and for industries within those countries. Several books exist that deal with the specific issue of how various industries are structured (eg., Adams and Brock (1995) and Deutsch (1993)). There are several books on broader antitrust issues in specific industries, like the ones edited by Kwoka and White (1999) and Weiss (1989). To our knowledge this present book is the first to explicitly deal with the complex matters that abound in actually attempting to measure market power across a set of industries. The authors are a group of economists with divergent occupations and backgrounds. Some are "pure" academics, some are current and former FTC (Federal Trade Commission) and DOJ (Department of Justice) economists, some are "pure" consultants and several of the authors wear several hats. That is, they work on antitrust matters as economic consultants and also hold down professorships. What all of these contributors bring to bear is expertise in understanding the complex issues that must be understood in order to perform a rigorous analysis where quantifying market power is important.

The question is an important one in determining the economic impact of potential mergers from both efficacy and consumer welfare dimensions. In antitrust litigation the issue also is of paramount importance and in many instances, a case may come down to a finding of whether the firm in question, does in fact, have and exercise market power. Most economists would agree that market power is simply the ability to influence price. How one goes about determining that question, is the interesting part and it is hoped that after reading this book the reader will gain significant insight into how that process works.

Daniel Slottje
Dallas, Texas
2002

REFERENCES

Adams, W., & Brock, J. (1995). *The Structure of American Industry*, 9th edition. Englewood Cliffs, NJ: Prentice Hall.

Deutsch, L. (1993). *Industry Studies*. Englewood Cliffs, NJ: Prentice Hall.

Kwoka, J., & White, L. (1999). *The Antitrust Revolution: Economics, Competition and Policy*, 3rd edition. New York: Oxford University Press.

Weiss, L. (1989). *Concentration and Price*. Cambridge, Mass.: Harvard University Press.

Measuring Market Power
D. J. Slottje (editor)
Published by Elsevier Science B.V.

CHAPTER 1

Assigning Market Shares for Antitrust Analysis

GREGORY J. WERDEN*

Senior Economic Counsel, Antitrust Division, US Department of Justice,
Suite 10000, Bicentennial Building, Washington, DC 20530

Abstract

Economists working on antitrust cases often are tasked with the assignment of market shares. This essay explores issues that raises, making four major points: (1) all options should duly be considered even if some prove impractical; (2) there may be no clearly correct option; (3) the competitive concern has important implications for the proper assignment of market shares; and (4) because market shares never tell the whole market power story, the goal in assigning them should be merely to accurately and usefully describe the size distribution of competitors.

JEL classification: L40, L11
Keywords: Market shares, market power

---

* The views expressed herein are not purported to be those of the US Department of Justice. Norm Familant, Bill Kolasky, and George Rozanski provided helpful comments.

1.1. INTRODUCTION

To assess single-firm market power or determine likely competitive effects of mergers, antitrust law relies heavily on market shares. Economists recognize substantial limits on the utility of market shares, but when they work on antitrust cases, the assignment of market shares is part of the job. This task goes well beyond "calculation" and "measurement" — two terms conventionally used to describe it, and I use the term "assignment" to reflect the wide range of conscious choices economists should make.

This essay explores the issues that arise in the assignment of market shares and offers concrete advice as to how best to assign shares. The most notable prior contributions to the remarkably scant scholarly literature on this subject are those of the ABA Antitrust Section (1986, pp. 153–61) and Areeda, Hovenkamp, and Solow (2002, §§ 532, 535).

This essay has four major themes: first, there always are choices to be made, and all options should duly be considered even if practical considerations ultimately rule some out. Second, there may be no clearly correct, or even best, choice. Third, the nature of a market power concern often has important implications for the proper assignment of market shares. Finally, because market shares never come close to telling the whole market power story, the goal in assigning them should be merely to accurately and usefully describe the size distribution of competitors in the market.

1.2. THE ROLE OF MARKET SHARES IN ANTITRUST ANALYSIS

1.2.1. Structural analysis in antitrust law

Antitrust law borrows the concept of "market power" from industrial organization economics. A fairly standard legal definition, found in the Horizontal Merger Guidelines (1992, § 0.1) promulgated by the Department of Justice and Federal Trade Commission, is "the ability profitably to maintain prices above competitive levels for a significant period of time." Antitrust law also makes extensive use of the purely legal concept of "monopoly power," which is substantial, and especially durable, market power (see Werden, 1998, pp. 374–80).

Apart from some of the conduct deemed per se unlawful under the antitrust laws, e.g., price fixing, essentially all antitrust violations involve the creation or exercise of market or monopoly power. Section 2 of the Sherman Act prohibits both "monopolization," which means the creation or maintenance of monopoly power through improper means, and "attempts to monopolize." Section 1 of the

Sherman Act prohibits agreements that both restrict trading freedom and produce anticompetitive effects, and courts normally require a threshold showing of market power to establish the requisite effects. Section 7 of the Clayton Act prohibits mergers the effect of which is "substantially to lessen competition," which as explained in the Horizontal Merger Guidelines (1992, § 0.1) is understood to mean mergers that "create or enhance market power."

Modern cases endorse the use of direct evidence of market and monopoly power, but the principal mode of analysis for market power issues in antitrust law is structural, with market delineation and market shares playing critical roles. As explained by a recent court of appeals decision (*Rebel Oil*, 1995, p. 1434), the standard approach is to "(1) define the relevant market, (2) show that the defendant owns a dominant share of that market, and (3) show that there are significant barriers to entry."

The Supreme Court held in a leading case (*Grinnell*, 1966, p. 571) that monopoly power "ordinarily may be inferred from the predominant share of the market," and the courts generally require more than 50% market share to establish monopoly power. The Supreme Court fairly recently observed (*Kodak*, 1992, p. 469 n.15) that "market power is often inferred from market share," and the courts generally require more than 30% market share to establish significant market power.

As I have detailed (Werden, 1997b, pp. 364–65), the structural approach to merger analysis was established by the Supreme Court primarily in the early 1960s. As stated by the most recent court of appeals merger decision (*Heinz*, 2001, p. 715, with citations and internal quotation omitted):

> First the government must show that the merger would produce a firm controlling an undue percentage share of the relevant market, and would result in a significant increase in the concentration of firms in that market. Such a showing establishes a presumption that the merger will substantially lessen competition. To rebut the presumption, the defendants must produce evidence that shows that the market share statistics give an inaccurate account of the merger's probable effects on competition in the relevant market.

The courts have not endorsed any method other than structural analysis to establish that mergers violate the antitrust laws, even though a practical alternative often is available in the form of merger simulation, which employs standard oligopoly models to predict the effects of mergers (see Crooke, Froeb, Tschantz, and Werden, 1999; Froeb and Werden, 1994; Werden, 1997a).

1.2.2. Market delineation and market shares

Market delineation normally is the most difficult and contentious step in structural analysis. Having written extensively on the theory and practice of market delineation (especially Werden, 1983, 1992, 1993, 1998, 2000b), I do not revisit those topics here. Consequently, captive production, used durable goods, and recycling are not addressed. It is essential, however, to consider the relationship between market delineation and the assignment of market shares, and in this regard I employ the analytical framework of the Horizontal Merger Guidelines, of which I was a principal architect.

Guidelines' relevant markets consist of collections of products and areas, and not collections of firms. Before shares can be assigned, it is necessary both to delineate the relevant market and separately "identify the competitors" in the market. For the most part, identifying competitors is a straightforward process of enumerating the firms that sell in the relevant market, but firms are also considered competitors if they do not currently sell but could quickly begin to do so without incurring significant sunk costs. The Guidelines (1992, § 1.32) term the latter competitors "uncommitted entrants," but it is most useful to think of them as supply substituters.

Applying the hypothetical monopolist paradigm of the Horizontal Merger Guidelines, the identification of competitors settles the question of market shares for firms not so identified. They are assigned shares of zero. Nothing is settled for firms identified as competitors in the relevant market. Indeed, some could be assigned shares of zero, if for example, they likely would be unable profitably to sell in the relevant market under anticipated future market conditions. Other aspects of the relationship between market delineation and the assignment of market shares are discussed at several points below.

1.3. COMMON DENOMINATORS FOR ASSIGNING MARKET SHARES

Assigning market shares often presents the figurative, or even literal, problem of adding apples and oranges. Some common denominator must be found that permits the aggregation of apples, oranges, and other fruits in the relevant market. Market shares always can be assigned on the basis of revenues, using dollars as a numeraire, and they can be assigned on the basis of a standardized output measure, such as weight, volume, or an efficiency unit reflecting the rate at which products are traded off in use.

1.3.1. Standardized output units as common denominators

Typical problems in identifying a common denominator are illustrated by two familiar consumer products. One is white bread of the sort sold in plastic bags in countless supermarkets (see Werden, 2000a). It comes in standard size loaves weighing 1, 1.25, and 1.5 pounds, and some packages contain two, or even three, such loaves. A common denominator is needed to aggregate various white bread products, and weight is the obvious choice. A case also could be made for using slices as the common denominator. White bread is used for making sandwiches and toast, and two slices may be considered a standard serving in either use, even though white bread slices vary in thickness.

Toilet tissue presents a more difficult problem. It most commonly comes in packages of four rolls, but single rolls are sold, as are packages containing as many as thirty-six rolls. Rolls are not a common denominator for aggregating packages, because there are single, double, and triple rolls. Nor are sheets a true common denominator, because there is no standard sheet size. Although there is a fairly standard roll width, feet of tissue is not a common denominator either, because there is both one-ply and two-ply tissue.

In a host of situations, objectively measurable performance differences among competing products make an efficiency unit the only possible common denominator (other than revenue). For example, the heat content of a ton of high-quality bituminous coal mined in southern West Virginia may be nearly double that of the subbituminous coal mined in the Powder River Basin of northeastern Wyoming. BTUs serve as a common denominator for aggregating coals of a wide range of heat contents, and not surprisingly, coal prices are often stated in terms of dollars per million BTUs.

Sweeteners provide another instructive example. Corn syrup, fructose, high-fructose corn syrup, and sugar differ in sweetness per pound. If all these products were in a single relevant market, a sweetness equivalence unit would prove a useful common denominator. The need for such a common denominator would be especially acute if non-nutritive (i.e., "no calorie") sweeteners were included in a market with the nutritive sweeteners, since aspartame (sold, e.g., as Equal) is nearly two hundred times as sweet as sugar and other sweeteners (including saccharine) are sweeter still.

Heterogeneity in product durability also may suggest the use of an efficiency unit as a common denominator. The most extreme example is a market in which single-use products compete with reusable ones, as may be the case with some medical instruments. Customer experience may suggest that one unit of a reusable product is substituted for dozens, or even hundreds, of units of the single-use product.

Even pronounced differences in product durability, however, do not unambiguously imply that market shares should be assigned on a basis that fully accounts for durability, because a product may become obsolete or be disused long before its useful life expires. Inexpensive ball point pens with extra ink may be no more useful to consumers than those without extra ink, if experience suggests that cheap pens generally are misplaced or discarded long before the ink is exhausted.

Assigning market shares is most problematic when the appropriate efficiency unit would differ across customers. One customer might need hundreds of units of a single-use product to substitute for one unit of the reusable alternative, while another might need only dozens. There is no true common denominator unless all customers on the margin between single-use and resuable equipment trade the two off at the same rate.

1.3.2. Revenue as a common denominator

Shares assigned on the basis of revenues automatically account for efficiency and durability differences *in a way*, since the trade offs made by marginal consumers are among the determinants of relative prices. Consequently, the use of dollar sales may be a simple solution to a complex problem. But this simple solution is often a highly imperfect one.

Price differences among competing products may be based entirely on brands. For example, private labels (store brands), which account for a substantial portion of total sales for many grocery products, often sell for far less than premium brands, although they are not objectively inferior in quality. The market shares of merging sellers of high-priced premium brands of white bread easily could be 50% higher when assigned on the basis of revenues than when assigned on the basis of pounds. Pounds is the proper common denominator, because consumers trade off premium and private label white bread roughly pound-for-pound, or slice-for-slice, rather than dollar-for-dollar.

When significant price differences among competing products are due to significant product differences, the nature of the product differences is critical. For example, a product may come both integrated with an essential complement and separate from it. A quantity unit, rather than revenue, is the proper common denominator if the price difference between the two types of products equals the price of the separate complement. In similar, but more complex, scenarios, there may be no clear preference between revenue and standardized quantity units, as neither is a true common denominator.

Price differences also may reflect differential rents (unless products are sold on a delivered basis). If the local supply of a product is inadequate to meet local demand, substantial locational rents may accrue to local supplies. These rents are not a sound basis for weighing local supplies more heavily than imported production.

There also may be significant temporal variation in the relative prices of products, while rates at which those products are traded off in consumption remain constant. Contrary to common misconception, this is quite possible for such products to be in the same relevant market (see Werden and Froeb, 1993). Hence, revenue-based market shares could paint a false picture of share volatility.

Revenue-based market shares could be justified on the alternative grounds that they appropriately weight products in accord with consumer preferences. The difficulty with this justification is that consumers have widely divergent preferences, and prices reflect the willingness to pay of just marginal consumers. Revenue-based shares are not shares of consumer surplus derived from the consumption of individual products. Moreover, a price increase could increase a product's revenue share, while decreasing the consumer surplus derived from that product.

1.4. STRUCTURAL AND EQUILIBRIUM MARKET SHARES

1.4.1. Market shares in the structure–conduct–performance paradigm

Market shares can describe the market equilibrium or the competitors in the market. The distinction between these alternatives is potentially critical yet generally overlooked. As explained by Froeb and Werden (1991), the distinction can be framed in terms of the traditional structure–conduct–performance paradigm. In this paradigm, the elements of market structure are competitors' cost functions and any other firm endowments. Conduct is the competitive interaction among competitors, and performance is all the prices, quantities, profits, and such resulting from structure and conduct. Structure changes as performance feeds back into it through entry, exit, investment, and innovation.

In antitrust cases and in the business world, market shares most often are assigned on the basis of revenues, production, and the like, which describe the market equilibrium. Such shares are elements of market performance rather than market structure. Structural market shares, by contrast, are based on the endowments of competitors, for example, on their ownership of assets such as productive capacity or reserves of an exhaustible resource. And structural market shares may differ substantially from equilibrium shares.

1.4.2. Market shares for inferring the exercise of substantial market power

The distinction between equilibrium and structural market shares is important primarily because the exercise of market power can significantly reduce equilibrium market shares. A simple dominant-firm model illustrates the point.

Let market demand be $p(X) = a - X$, where p is price and X is total quantity, and assume that both the dominant firm and competitive fringe have marginal cost functions of the form x_i/k_i, where x_i is output and k_i is capital stock. If K is the total capital stock in the market and σ is the dominant firm's share of K, it can be seen that the dominant firm's residual demand is $p(X)[1 + (1 - \sigma)K]^{-1}$. A useful experiment fixes σ at, say, 0.75, which likely would satisfy legal tests for monopoly, while varying K. The two key quantities in this experiment are the dominant firm's equilibrium output share, s, and the Lerner Index of monopoly (price-cost margin), L, which indicates the extent to which market power is exercised. Both are independent of a.

It is not difficult to show that L is an increasing function of K, while s is a decreasing function. And it is easily seen that for $k > 2$, $s < 0.5$, while L > 0.66. Thus, if antitrust law decrees that only $s > 0.5$ can support a finding of monopoly power, the use of the equilibrium share, rather than the structural share, is highly problematic. It results in finding monopoly power when the dominant firm exercises the least market power and in finding no monopoly power when the dominant firm exercises the most market power.

This example makes a strong case for the use of structural market shares when the inference to be drawn from them is whether the defendant is exercising substantial market power. And that is the relevant inference in many monopolization cases. But most antitrust cases use market shares to make a somewhat different inference. Market shares are used to infer the existence of mere market power in many cases involving anticompetitive horizontal or vertical agreements and attempts to monopolize, but mere market power need not cause a substantial divergence between structural and equilibrium shares. In merger cases, the inference is whether the merger would "create or enhance market power," and existing market power has no clear implications for assigning shares.

Bertrand competition among differentiated products presents a scenario comparable to that with the dominant firm model. In equilibrium, the greater a firm's market power, the higher its price will be relative to its marginal cost, and this causes output-based market shares to understate the importance of leading firms. Ordover and Willig (1983, p. 560) suggest the use of revenue-based market shares in this scenario to avoid this understatement. But the more market power a firm has, the less its revenues are apt to fall when its market power is exercised, and if that is the case, revenue-based shares could overstate the market power of leading firms.

It should also be noted that the use of structural market shares is infeasible with differentiated consumer products. Like manufacturing capacity, brand equity is an asset on which shares might be based, but the proper measure of brand equity has nothing to do with the nature and extent of the investment in creating it, but rather is purely a matter of consumer taste and hence is not readily observable.

1.4.3. Market shares for inferring the potential to exercise market power

Consideration of both the foregoing and a very different scenario serves to demonstrate that the specific nature of the market power concern has important implications for the assignment of market shares and that equilibrium shares may overstate as well as understate actual market power. In this alternative scenario, the antitrust concern is not the ongoing exercise of substantial market power, but rather the potential of proposed or recently undertaken conduct to create or enhance market power.

If two producers of a homogeneous product proposed to merge, there could be a concern that the merged firm would restrict output to drive up the market price. The merged firm's ability to restrict output would be indicated by the merging firms' pre-merger outputs, but its ability to drive up price by restricting output would be determined by the elasticity of its rivals' supply at prices near those prevailing pre-merger. Even if the merging firms accounted for a very large portion of pre-merger industry output, the merged firm would have little market power if rivals' supply were highly elastic, and it would have no market power at all if rivals' supply were perfectly elastic.

In this scenario, Landes and Posner (1981, p. 949) among others suggest that the merging firms be assigned "shares" equal to their current outputs divided by the sum of their outputs and their rivals' capacities. This proposal has some merit, but I do not endorse it mainly because it results in "shares" that are not actually shares at all. Moreover, simple modeling with a standard oligopoly model would provide a far better indication of the merged firm's market power.

1.5. ASSET-BASED MARKET SHARES

When competitors' relative abilities to produce are congruent with their relative abilities to sell, as is most likely to be the case with homogeneous products, market shares generally should be assigned on the basis of ownership or control of productive assets. Market power in such circumstances arises from control over sufficient productive assets to be able profitably to drive up price by holding assets out of production.

Asset-based market shares should be assigned on the basis of ownership or control of the critical assets that reflect firms' differential abilities to compete. For example, a multi-stage manufacturing process may have a particularly capital-intensive stage of production involving a substantial portion of total sunk investment. If so, productive capacity at that critical stage of production could be a sound basis for assigning market shares. It is possible that the true bottle-neck, at which asset ownership is significant, is not in production. In exhaustible resource industries, reserves are generally the best basis for assigning shares, and in some industries, intangible assets may be best.

1.5.1. *General Dynamics* **and exhaustible resource industries**

The most notable court case addressing the assignment of market shares certainly is *General Dynamics* (1974). The government challenged the acquisition of stock in one Midwestern coal producer by another, arguing that the acquisition would contribute to an ongoing, substantial increase in the concentration of coal *production*. This challenge was rejected by the district court, and its decision was affirmed by the Supreme Court.

Coal was used principally by electric utilities and purchased under long-term contracts. Current production was the result of past contracts and not indicative of current competition. Under these circumstances, the Supreme Court (p. 502) found that "the best measure of a company's ability to compete" was "uncom-mitted reserves of recoverable coal," because it was those reserves that coal producers could offer to utilities seeking new long-term contracts. The Court found no anticompetitive effect from the merger because the acquired firm's uncommitted reserves were quite limited.

As an alternative to current production, market shares could have been assigned on the basis of recent contract awards. Recent contract awards often are a good predictor of future awards, but they probably were not a good predictor in *General Dynamics* because of the exhaustible nature of coal resources. Each contract award made a block of resources unavailable for future contracts, so there was no reason to believe that recent awards predicted future awards.

Even if sales are not made pursuant to long-term contract, assigning market shares on the basis of resource ownership generally makes sense in exhaustible resource industries. Resource ownership is likely to be relatively unimportant only if the exhaustible nature of the resource is inconsequential because economically mineable resources are abundant, as is the case, for example, with limestone in some parts of the country.

Although generally desirable, assigning shares on the basis of resource ownership may be difficult because there may be no reliable source for the "universe" of reserves in the relevant market. Collecting reserve data from all active producers is likely to be insufficient, since substantial reserves may be owned by ordinary land owners. Publicly available geological data on resources is often sketchy, and thus, may significantly understate the true universe, and such data may not reflect appropriate economic criteria relating to extraction cost. Finally, private resource owners may apply different economic criteria for assessing reserves than are used to compile the universe.

1.5.2. Capacity-based market shares

Capacity-based market shares are commonly used in process industries (e.g., oil refining and chemicals) that produce homogeneous products using equipment for which there is a rated capacity. The electric power industry usefully illustrates several of the issues that arise in assigning market shares on the basis of capacity (see Werden, 1996).

Because electric power generation must continuously be matched with load, which varies substantially over time, the optimal portfolio of generation resources includes units designed for heavy use (base-load units) and units designed for infrequent use (peaking units). Short-run marginal generation costs are much lower for base-load than for peaking units, and cost heterogeneity also arises from differences in fuel choice and unit age. This cost heterogeneity raises the question of whether market shares should be based on just certain capacity with particular cost characteristics.

The marginal kilowatt is generated by mid-marginal-cost capacity most of the time, so an exercise of market power generally would entail a restriction in output from that capacity, which also would be called upon to make up for the restricted output. Thus, it may seem best to assign generation market shares on the basis of just mid-marginal-cost capacity. However, output from infra-marginal capacity also could be restricted, and the ownership of infra-marginal capacity substantially affects the incentive to restrict output from marginal capacity. Moreover, market power concerns are greatest when the industry marginal cost curve is steep, since that is when restricting output has the greatest effect on the market price. The industry marginal cost curve tends to be steep only at high levels of output. Consequently, a firm with no mid-marginal-cost capacity may exercise substantial market power, while a firm with a great deal of mid-marginal-cost capacity may not. Plainly, all generation capacity that may ever be used is relevant to market power issues, and no capacity-based measure of market share is ideal.

Outside the electric power industry, there are many cases in which certain high-cost capacity should be ignored in assigning market shares. The clearest case is that in which an industry has sufficient modern, low-cost capacity to satisfy the entire anticipated demand, even in the event of an exercise of market power. High-cost capacity that never would be used, ought not to be considered in assigning market shares.

Capacity that would be used only in the event of an exercise of market power also might appropriately be ignored in assigning shares. Suppose the concern is that enough modern capacity might be withheld from the market to bring some outmoded capacity back into production and force prices up to the common marginal cost of all the outmoded capacity. The incentive and ability to exercise market power this way depends on neither the amount of outmoded capacity available to the market nor the ownership of that capacity. This conclusion may no longer hold, however, if the outmoded capacity does not all have the same marginal cost, as in the electric power industry.

Capacity-based market shares are most useful when there is a well established and standardized basis for measuring capacity. If machinery associated with a bottleneck manufacturing process has a rated capacity, that provides a useful common denominator for assigning shares. It matters little, and perhaps not at all, how rated capacity relates to actual capacity to produce, as long the assets of all competitors are evaluated on a consistent basis. For example, if rated capacity systematically understates actual capacity by 20%, shares based on rated and actual capacity are precisely the same.

When there is no well-established capacity common denominator, it still may be possible to assign shares consistently on the basis of capacity, but doing so would be costly and time consuming. Moreover, industry participants may not carefully and accurately respond to requests for information that is not readily available.

1.5.3. Market shares based on intangible assets

The ability to compete often is determined mainly by intangible assets. Such assets could be intellectual property rights related to critical technologies, estab-lished brands, or reputations for superior performance. Although there are many scenarios in which it may be appropriate to assign market shares on the basis of intangible assets, in only one special case is that commonly done. That case is what the antitrust cognoscenti refer to as "one-over-n markets."

There are two essential characteristics of such markets: (1) a finite number of entities possess a readily identifiable set of assets essential for successful competition; and (2) the extent of ownership or control over the essential assets does not distinguish among these entities in any important way. In the clearest case, all competitors have the same costs, and each can supply the entire market demand. In markets with these two characteristics, each competitor is assigned the same market share, so with n competitors, their shares are $1/n$. The Horizontal Merger Guidelines (1992, § 1.41 n.15) indicate that the federal antitrust enforcement agencies assign such shares when "all firms have, on a forward-looking basis, an equal likelihood of securing sales." The Guidelines' language reflects the fact that the competitive interaction in one-over-n markets often resembles an auction.

Candidates for the assignment of $1/n$ shares include markets for technology and Schumpeterian industries, in which competition occurs largely through the introduction of new products or technologies and competition is apt to be more "for the market" than "in the market." Each of these would be appropriately treated as one-over-n markets if there were an identifiable set of assets essential for a reasonable prospect of market success and that prospect either were the same for all competitors possessing that asset set, or there were no sound basis for assigning asymmetric shares.

1.5.4. Markets aggregated as a matter of convenience

Asset-based shares are commonly used when there is a high degree of supply substitutability between products in the relevant market and products outside it. This scenario arises under the Horizontal Merger Guidelines because they consider supply substitution in identifying competitors in the relevant market, rather than in delineating the market. Markets delineated for hospital merger cases present a prime example.

From the patient's perspective, hospitals perform thousands of distinct services for which there are no good substitutes, and under the Guidelines, each is a separate relevant market. The Guidelines (§ 1.321 n.14), however, aggregate "as a matter of convenience" products for which a high degree of supply substitutability implies very similar competitive conditions. In the hospital context, this produces aggregations of relevant markets such as "acute, in-patient services."

An important use of asset-based market shares is illustrated by the government's challenge to Georgia Pacific Corp.'s acquisition of Fort James Corp.

(2001). The complaint alleged the acquisition would give Georgia Pacific the incentive to restrict the output of "away from home tissue products," such as toilet tissue used in public restrooms and paper napkins used by fast food restaurants. These products are converted from massive tissue "parent rolls" produced by "tissue machines." Market shares for away from home tissue products were assigned on the basis of tissue machine capacity, since it was tissue machine production the government believed likely would be restricted after the merger. A single set of shares was used for several separate relevant markets because tissue machines are freely substituted among the various away from home tissue products.

Another interesting case in point is banking services. The principal product of concern in bank mergers is loans to small businesses. Market shares could be assigned on the basis of outstanding balances for small-business loans, but that could be misleading. A bank that has incurred the sunk costs associated with making small business loans can freely substitute in supply between small-business loans and other loans. Hence, it might be preferable to assign shares on the basis of total deposits, which indicate relative abilities to lend, but to assign them only to banks already making substantial small business loans. It is also easy to obtain information on banks' deposits.

Another type of aggregation as a matter of convenience involves aggregation over time. Since electric power is not stored to any significant extent, it is appropriate to delineate time-based relevant markets, resulting, for example, in 8,760 hour-long markets in a non-leap year. Over the course of a year, differences in loads and resource availability may present only relatively few distinct competitive scenarios meriting separate analysis. If so, all of the hours in a year are aggregated into these few scenarios, which are the relevant market aggregations. The simplest, and probably best, way to assign market shares for these aggregations is on the basis of generating capacity.

1.5.5. Projecting asset-based market shares into the future

Although some antitrust cases are concerned with backward-looking market power issues, i.e., whether a defendant possessed market or monopoly power when challenged conduct occurred, the market power analysis in most antitrust cases, especially merger cases, is forward looking. And when market shares are assigned on the basis of ownership or control over productive assets, it is often possible to assign market shares on the basis of ownership or control as of some future date. Capacity additions often are announced well in advance of in-service dates, making it feasible and desirable to assign market shares on the basis of capacity ownership or control a year to two years into the future (although capacity retirements may not be as well publicized or determined as far in advance).

When entry or exit has been determined to be highly likely in the near future, with or without the challenged conduct, it should be *appropriately* reflected in market shares. A positive market share should be assigned to an entrant when shares are assigned on the basis of physical asset ownership, since the degree of a firm's future competitive significance is then reasonably ascertainable. But if building a facility only buys an entrant a ticket in the consumer acceptance lottery, as is apt to be the case when shares are assigned on the basis of output, there is no sound basis for assigning any positive share.

Shares also should not reflect mere entry or exit plans, but rather only entry and exit decisions to which firms have committed themselves. The best, and perhaps only reliable, indication of an entry commitment is having already sunk much of the costs required for successful entry. Thus, electric generating plants well along in the construction process generally should be reflected in market shares, while plants that have not broken ground should not.

1.6. OUTPUT-BASED MARKET SHARES

When competitors' relative abilities to produce are not congruent with their relative abilities to sell, as is most likely to be the case with highly differentiated products, market shares generally should be assigned on the basis of output or sales. Though it generally matters little, there are always many alternative measures that can be used. The use of output-based market shares also raises issues, not arising with asset-based shares, relating to sampling error and changing market conditions.

1.6.1. Measures of output

Output-based shares can be focused on any one link in the chain of production and distribution. If a manufacturer produces to inventory, and ships from that inventory, as sales are made, its sales and shipments should be almost exactly the same, while both differ from production by the change in inventories. Production is apt to be inferior to either sales or shipments as a basis for assigning shares, since a firm unwisely producing more than it can sell does not thereby gain market power. Moreover, sales and shipments are more comparable across firms, since all are serving basically the same demand at the same time, while firms' production schedules may differ for idiosyncratic reasons.

Some fraction of production often is not saleable because it is damaged or defective. Damaged and defective units are remanufactured then sold, sold in different markets, or scrapped. Similarly, some fraction of shipments may be returned because of damage or defects, or because distributors fail to sell it. For example, a small fraction of white bread loaves are sold as animal feed because they come out of the ovens misshapen ("cripples"), and a significant fraction of loaves placed on store shelves are reshipped to thrift stores or used as animal feed because they are not sold while fresh ("stales"). When assigning market shares, it is generally best to exclude units not saleable, or not sold, in the relevant market.

When the market power concern most likely relates to competition for new long-term contracts, it may be best to assign market shares on the basis of recent contract awards. However, one also must consider whether recent contract awards make firms less able to compete for future contracts by tying up productive capacity. And when well-established relationships between customers and suppliers last longer than their contracts, shares might best be assigned on the basis of just the acquisition of new customers.

Some customized products must be ordered well in advance of delivery. Recent orders, like recent contract awards, reflect the current competition in the market, while deliveries reflect conditions at some point in the past, possibly even the distant past. A good case can be made for assigning shares on the basis of orders, provided that they are likely to translate into eventual deliveries. Between the order and delivery date, there likely are penalties for canceling orders commensurate with the costs that have already been incurred to fulfill the orders. If such penalties are relatively low, cancellations are likely to be common, and shipments are apt to be the best basis for assigning shares.

1.6.2. Sampling error

The number of transactions on which market shares are based tends to vary with the frequency of market transactions, which may range from less than one per year to thousands per day. Market shares based on a relatively small number of transactions may raise significant questions.

Illustrative is *Baker Hughes* (1990), a merger case involving producers of hydraulic drilling rigs used in underground hardrock mining. These machines are expensive and infrequently purchased by US mining companies. Indeed, the market is so thin that a single multi-machine purchase could turn the seller into the market leader for an entire year. The government addressed market thinness and share volatility by aggregating sales over a three-year period, but the courts nevertheless found that volatility rendered the government's market shares unreliable.

Table 1.1.   The share of sampled transactions necessary for the
required confidence.

Number of sampled transactions	5	10	25	50	100	1000
Share of sampled transactions necessary for 95% confidence that the true share is at least 50%	100%	80%	68%	62%	59%	52.7%

The courts in *Baker Hughes* overreacted. Volatility surely did not render the government's shares meaningless. The infrequency of machine purchases by individual users meant that only a small fraction of users were sampled each year, and market shares pose a problem of statistical inference when the data on which they are based are essentially a random sample from a population. Since different users obviously had different preferences among suppliers of the machines, *Baker Hughes* presented the classic problem of inferring characteristics of the population from a sample. Standard statistical tools place a confidence interval around market shares subject to sampling error.

Suppose that an alleged monopolist's share is assigned on the basis of a sample of transactions, and the court insists that the evidence demonstrate with 95% confidence that its true share is at least 50% (thus implicating a 90% two-tailed confidence interval, since only the probability in the lower tail of the distribution is of interest). Using the method proposed by Agresti and Coull (1998), Table 1.1 indicates the minimum share of sampled transactions that the alleged monopolist must account for under the test imputed to the court. The table reflects the discrete nature of the data. For example, with 5 sampled transactions, the observed share must be a multiple of 20%, and an 80% observed share is not sufficient for the required level of confidence. Even with such small samples, however, the required degree of confidence can be achieved by a sufficiently large sampled share.

Thin markets need not give rise to sampling error. If a product's users all bought it once a year, the entire population would be observed each year. No matter how small that population, any variation in market shares from year to year would have to stem from variation in supply or demand. Sampling error also does not arise when using asset-based market shares. A form of asset-based shares is likely to be the best approach in the extreme case of highly infrequent transactions and significantly changing market conditions. In such a case, it may be best to identify the competitors and assign each a share of $1/n$.

1.6.3. Time periods for output-based shares

If all intertemporal variation in market shares were due to sampling error or various sorts of extraordinary events, market shares over a longer time period would invariably be preferable to those over a shorter time period. But there is likely also to be market-share variation due to changing market conditions, which presents a variance-bias trade-off in predicting future competitive effects: the further one goes back in time to reduce variance by enlarging the number of observations, the more the data reflect demand and supply conditions significantly different than those today.

The nature of this trade-off varies with the frequency of transactions and the rate of change of market conditions, as reflected by such things as changes in consumer demographics and new product introductions. This trade-off is likely to militate against assigning market shares on the basis of more than about two years of data, and one year commonly may be best. Using more than two years of data probably is best only if transactions are very infrequent (as, for example, are some major defense procurements) and market conditions are quite stable.

Many markets have significant, systematic, seasonal variation in supply or demand. Seasonal variation in market shares might accompany seasonal variation in supply or demand. Out of caution, it is wise to base shares in seasonal markets on data spanning time periods that are integral multiples of one year. If, for example, data are compiled quarterly, one would use the most recent four, eight, etc. quarters.

Output-based shares are commonly used for customized products traded through auction-like procurements. Different firms win different auctions largely because of differing costs of satisfying, or differing abilities to satisfy, the particular demands of individual customers. Under the Horizontal Merger Guidelines (1992, §§ 1.12, 1.22), each procurement may be considered a separate price discrimination market, since the price in each is independent of prices in others. When markets are delineated in this way, they are aggregated as a matter of convenience, just as with supply substitution. Hence, "market shares" are likely to be based on outputs or revenues from procurements over the recent past. Such shares are predictive of the future to the extent that future procurements have characteristics similar to recent past procurements. In most cases, there is no reason to believe otherwise, provided that the recent past is long enough to include a representative sample from the population of procurements.

1.6.4. Projecting output-based market shares into the future

Although entry, exit, investment, and changing market conditions cause shares of current output to predict future competitive strength imperfectly, it is commonly best not to attempt adjustments in the shares to reflect anticipated changes in market conditions. Output-based shares are commonly used with highly differentiated consumer products, and reliable predictions are infeasible for such products. Every year, thousands of new grocery store products fail to attract significant market shares and are discontinued, and there is not likely to be a basis for reliably predicting success for one particular product.

Extrapolating market share trends into the future also is generally unwarranted. Unless the cause of a market share trend is both self-evident and immutable, the current output share of a product is most likely to be the best predictor of the output share of that product in the near future. Market share trends may be sufficiently clear and irreversible for products nearing the end of their life cycles and being supplanted by technologically superior substitutes, and for products benefitting or suffering from powerful network effects. But even in such cases, the best course may be to account for misleading impressions from current shares through informed interpretation of the observed shares, rather than directly adjust the shares themselves.

Still, it is best to account for the likely impact of some imminent, substantial changes in market conditions. A prime example is the expiration of an important patent. Particularly when foreign patents have previously expired and entrants quickly gained substantial share, there should be a sufficient basis for projecting future shares.

It is also best not to project the effects of challenged conduct on output-based market shares. When a merger causes the merged firm to restrict output or raise price, it reduces the merged firm's output share. It is imperative to account for this fact if merger effects are predicted using equilibrium conditions from oligopoly models (e.g., Cournot), but there is no need to do so in computing the "Change in the HHI," which is defined as twice the product of the market shares of the merging firms. That quantity indicates how the Herfindahl-Hirschman Index (HHI) of concentration changes when two structural shares are combined. When equilibrium shares are used, the Change in the HHI is merely an index of the size of the merger (see Werden, 1991).

1.6.5. Innovative approaches in special cases

The proper assignment of market shares depends on the specific competitive concerns and facts presented by each particular case, and special cases may call for innovative approaches. In *Microsoft* (1999), market shares in PC operating systems were assigned on the basis of current sales, but the powerful network effects in that case suggest the possibility of assigning them on the basis of network size, e.g., on the basis of installed user base. Microsoft's far larger installed base and far larger base of compatible applications programs were what allowed it to maintain its market dominance (see Werden, 2001).

It is also interesting to consider an industry in which buyers have an acute need to diversify or even duplicate sources of supply. In the simplest case, each customer would buy one unit from each of two suppliers. If there were only two suppliers, each would be a monopolist in a very real sense, so it would make sense to assign each a "share" of 100%. Similarly, if one supplier was a must-buy and many others competed to be the second supplier, the must-buy supplier could be assigned a 100% "share" reflecting its monopoly as the first supplier, while the other suppliers could be assigned "shares" totaling 100% and reflecting their relative importance in competing to be the second supplier.

1.7. IMPORTS AND EXPORTS

With imports and exports, the assignment of market shares is inextricably inter-twined with the delineation of the relevant market. If, as often presumed, the geographic dimensions of a relevant market denote the location of the consumers in the market, market shares must tend to include imports and exclude exports. If the geographic dimensions of the market denote the location of production facilities in the market, market shares must tend to include exports and exclude imports. Both scenarios arise in practice, and shipments crossing national bound-aries raise special issues.

1.7.1. Assigning shares based on the location of production or consumption

The Horizontal Merger Guidelines delineate markets using the hypothetical monopolist paradigm, asking whether a hypothetical monopolist over a candi-date market would impose a significant price increase. The hypothetical monopolist could charge all customers the same price, or systematically discrim-inate, depending on the locations of customers or other customer characteristics. The Guidelines take two divergent analytical paths depending on how the monopolist prices. One path leads to the assignment of market shares on the basis of the location of production, while the other leads to the assignment of market shares based on the location of consumption.

Under the Guidelines, markets are first delineated under the assumption that there is no price discrimination. Since prices then directly correspond to points of production, the geographic scope of the market refers to locations of production. The competitors in the market are firms that produce in the relevant area or could easily begin doing so without incurring significant sunk costs. Market shares are assigned to firms on the basis of the location of their productive assets, without regard for the geographic disposition of their outputs. A firm that sells in a market's geographic area, but does not produce within it, is not a competitor in the market and must be assigned a share of zero. If, however, a firm is an important competitive force, its location must be included in the relevant market.

If arbitrage would not prevent significant price discrimination in the exercise of market power, additional markets may be delineated. These price discrimination markets consist of groups of products and sets of customers that can be discriminated against. A customer set, which could contain a single element, most often is described by the geographic area in which the customers are located. Competitors in price discrimination markets are firms that currently sell to the relevant set of customers and those that could easily begin doing so without incurring significant sunk costs. Thus, market shares are assigned on the basis of the location of consumption.

The foregoing greatly narrows the issues relating to imports and exports. In price discrimination markets, which are very commonly delineated, especially in consumer goods industries, shares are typically assigned on the basis of consumption in the market, measured in terms of revenue or units. In the event that shares are assigned on the basis of ownership or control of assets, the universe of assets in the market consists of those positioned to supply it economically. For markets not delineated on the basis of price discrimination, the universe for market share calculations consists of the assets located in the market, the output produced by those assets, or revenues generated by that output.

1.7.2. The Landes and Posner argument

In a famous article, Landes and Posner (1981, p. 963) argued that "if a distant seller has some sales in a local market, *all* its sales, wherever made, should be considered a part of the local market for purposes of computing the market share of a local seller." The Guidelines' approach to market delineation and market shares makes a similar result possible, but the suggested asymmetric treatment of local and distant producers is not.

The relevant market absent price discrimination can be properly delineated to exclude the location of a distant producer only if that producer is unable to prevent the exercise of market power by local producers. But if so, that distant producer must be assigned a market share of zero. Landes and Posner plainly have in mind the case in which the distant producers can prevent the exercise of market power by local sellers. In that event, the relevant market absent price discrimination is delineated to encompass the location of the distant producer. This is not the market Landes and Posner presume, but the resulting market shares easily could be roughly the same with their approach.

If the local market is delineated on the presumption of price discrimination, and market shares are assigned on the basis of asset ownership because the product is undifferentiated, the Guidelines' result could closely resemble the Landes and Posner result. But their result would not be obtained in the likely event that much of the distant producer's output is in some sense committed outside the market (see section 1.8.2). Moreover, price discrimination markets are most commonly delineated for highly differentiated consumer products, and for such products, shares are properly assigned on the basis of sales in the relevant market. There is no reason to credit the distant producer alone with a special ability to increase its local sales substantially.

1.7.3. Special factors affecting foreign firms

It has often been argued that special treatment is appropriate when assigning shares for a domestic market that includes foreign-based competitors. Because firms producing outside the United States and shipping into the country are subject to exchange rate fluctuations and other vagaries of international commerce, it has been suggested that such firms be discounted. Doing so does not seem appropriate as a matter of course, but it would be best, for example, if recent exchange rates and other conditions conducive to imports cannot be expected to persist. More difficult to account for is the possibility that foreign suppliers compete passively out of fear that trade restraints may be imposed.

A quite different situation arises when imports are subject to voluntary or mandatory quotas. A binding absolute quota prevents any increase in output in response to an exercise of market power and hence may make a foreign seller less competitively significant than a domestic seller with the same sales. That fact ought to be accounted for, but not in the assignment of market shares. In contrast, the volume of imports subject to percentage quotas must be contracted in the event of an exercise of market power by domestic firms. Percentage quotas normally should be accounted for in assigning shares, perhaps by assigning shares of zero to firms that are subject to them.

1.8. THE PROBLEM OF ATTRIBUTION

The foregoing has addressed mainly the assignment of market shares to products, but the economist's task is to assign them to firms. Normally, there is a an obvious one-to-one correspondence between the two, but that is not always the case. When it is not, the attribution of shares to firms should be keyed to specific market power concerns.

1.8.1. Productive assets owned by competitors

Attribution issues arise when different assets associated with the production and distribution of a single product have different owners. A useful case in point is, again, white bread. For many premium brands and some private labels, the owner of the brand bakes and sells its brand of bread. Bread sold under many private labels, however, is baked under contract by firms that sell premium brands in competition with the private labels. And some brands are licensed from other bakers or non-baking companies. These brands are used by different firms in different parts of the country.

How product shares should be attributed to firms in the bread industry depends on the market power concern. The main concern with a merger of leading bakers is likely to be that the merging firms would raise prices for their brands as they internalized the competition between them (see Werden, 2000a). In addressing this concern, the market shares assigned to private labels should be attributed to the retail chains that own those labels, even if they contract out their baking. The retailers are the strategic decision makers for pricing the private labels, and in the competitive interaction among brands, their contract bakers participate in the relevant market much like the suppliers of flour, although contract bakers selling premium brands may price them somewhat higher as a consequence of their contract baking. As they raise prices for their brands, some consumers substitute to the private labels they bake, and they may earn additional profits from their contract baking.

Licensed labels present different issues, depending on the nature of the license. The simplest case is that of a paid up and perpetual license, which is tantamount to brand ownership and should be treated as such. Also fairly simple is a long-term license with a per-unit royalty, which is just an element of marginal cost to the licensee, like the plastic bag the bread is packaged in. Less clear cut is a license with an ad valorem royalty, but even if a substantial royalty is paid to a competitor in the market, it probably is best not to attribute any of the brand's share to the licensor. A final issue is that licenses may be transferred, and in some situations there may be no assurance that a current licensee will control a brand for long. In such a case, it may be appropriate to attribute a licensed brand's share to the brand's owner rather than to its licensee.

A bread merger also could lead to an exercise of market power by contract bakers. In addressing that concern, market shares assigned to private labels clearly should be attributed to the bakers, be they the retailers themselves or contract bakers. Indeed, shares probably should be assigned on the basis of ownership and control of baking assets, since it is the increase in concentration of baking assets that could create market power.

Producer goods generally present issues relating to control over manufacturing assets rather than brands. In *Archer-Daniels-Midland* (1991), a thirteen-year lease on a competitor's manufacturing facilities with an option to purchase was sensibly treated as the acquisition of the facilities. The apparent rationale is that the lessee controlled production from the facilities and was the residual claimant from them.

Various forms of contract production arise in manufacturing industries, including tolling arrangements in which one firm delivers a raw material or intermediate good to another, which is paid a fee to deliver back to the first firm a refined or manufactured product. Production under a tolling arrangement may appropriately be attributed to the owner of the producing assets (or capacity-based shares be used) if control over capacity is central to competition and the owner of tolling capacity is contractually free to restrict output from that capacity. In other cases, control over capacity is not so important, and output should be attributed to its owner, even if that firm does not produce the output.

A final scenario of interest is that in which "integrators" combine purchased components into final products. If these integrators uniquely possess technology or other assets essential to the production of the final products, the market shares associated with the final products should be attributed to the integrators. But if the integrators' task could just as easily be performed by the component manufacturers or the final customers, the final products' shares should be attributed to the component manufacturers.

1.8.2. Contractual commitment and high opportunity costs

Producer goods and exhaustible resources raise issues relating to the commitment of productive assets. For example, long-term supply contracts for coal raise the issue of whether the reserves committed to the contract should be attributed to their current owner, to the contracting purchaser, or to no one at all. The usual practice in the coal industry has been the third option, because the coal under contract is unlikely ever to be available to any other user. In other industries, it may be best to attribute contracted production to contracting purchasers, because they may make the contracted production available to other potential buyers.

High opportunity costs raise issues similar to contractual commitment, and the Horizontal Merger Guidelines (1992, § 1.41) address both together, providing that, in assigning a firm's market share, its "sales or capacity" is not counted "to the extent that the firm's capacity is committed or so profitability employed outside the relevant market that it would not be available to respond to an increase in price in the market."

A firm selling in two locations may be freely able to shift production between them but not be so willing to do so because it earns significantly different margins in the two locations. For example, a foreign firm exercising market power in its home market would not readily divert production to the United States, where prices were lower, especially since it may have cost or other disadvantages in the United States. A firm capable of substituting in supply also may not be so willing to do so because it earns significantly different margins in two applications of its equipment. Lower-profit business may be taken on only to the extent specialized equipment cannot be fully occupied by the more-profitable uses for which the equipment was designed. In both cases, the opportunity cost of shifting production is irrelevant to the extent that the firm can draw on excess capacity.

1.8.3. Partial ownership, contractual control, and joint ventures

Attribution issues also arise with shared ownership or control, and with ownership divorced from control. Two paradigm cases are a firm partially owned by, or in some way controlled by, a competitor, and a joint venture owned by competitors of the venture or of each other.

If firm A has an equity interest in its competitor, B, that interest necessarily affects A's incentives and, hence, its strategic decisions. But that equity interest affects B's strategic decisions only to the extent that it permits A to influence or control B. A's control over B normally is essentially complete if A owns a majority of the voting shares in B, although the ability to control might be contracted away, as Northwest Airlines claimed to have done while it owned a majority of the voting shares in Continental Airlines. Ownership of a substantial minority interest frequently confers effective control if other ownership interests are widely dispersed. Partial equity interests are conventionally reflected in market shares only when control can be inferred, in which case, the controlling firm is assigned the shares associated with both firms. This is a reasonable approach, even though control through partial equity interests can result in both more and less intense competition than a merger of the two firms.

Control through partial ownership is illustrated by *General Dynamics* (1974, pp. 488–90, 504). In that case, one company acquired all of the stock in another, but it did so in stages over a thirteen-year period. A year after the last of the stock was acquired, the government filed a complaint alleging that an antitrust violation occurred eight years earlier when 34% of the stock had been acquired and control was established. The defendant and the Supreme Court both agreed with the government as to when the acquisition occurred.

Contracts may confer control without an ownership interest. Illustrative is *Whirlpool* (1985), which involved a challenge to the merger of competing manufacturers of dishwashers. Whirlpool Corp. originally proposed to acquire the KitchenAid brand and associated manufacturing assets, and to sell the latter assets to Emerson Electric Co., which would manufacture for Whirlpool under a cost-plus contract. Because the contract prohibited Emerson from competing for the private label business of any other brander, the court initially attributed to Whirlpool the market share associated with the manufacturing assets Emerson was to acquire. When the contract was amended to give Emerson considerable freedom to compete in the private label supply market, the court attributed the market share associated with the manufacturing assets to Emerson.

The proper attribution of market shares associated with joint ventures depends in the first instance on whether the joint venture acts as an independent market participant. In that event, a joint venture should be treated accordingly and assigned a market share. A joint venture plainly is not an independent market participant when a single participant in the venture effectively controls it. In that case, the market share associated with the joint venture should be attributed to the controlling participant.

A joint venture is also not an independent market participant when its participants separately control production and prices for portions of the joint venture's capacity or output. That is the arrangement with some oil pipelines, and it could be appropriate to treat them for competitive purposes if they consisted of several, entirely separate, straws within the pipeline. In such a case, the share associated with the joint venture should be attributed to its separate participants. On the other hand, an evaluation of the joint venture agreements, and operations under it, may reveal substantial limits to competition among joint owners, and the share associated with the joint venture may be best attributed to the venture itself.

1.9. CONCLUSIONS

Because market shares are used by courts to make inferences about market power, considerable care should be taken in their assignment. But market shares still are just descriptive statistics for an industry, intended to describe usefully the size distribution of competitors in the relevant market. Consequently, market shares should be shares of some real and measurable industry quantity that reasonably serves as a common denominator for the array of products in the relevant market.

Some sort of analysis, possibly a highly sophisticated one, should be employed to interpret market shares and accurately assess market power issues. As the Horizontal Merger Guidelines (1992, § 2.0) appropriately state, "market shares and concentration provide only the starting point for analyzing the competitive impact of a merger." Since market shares should not be the embodiment of the competitive analysis, they should not be subject to all manner of adjustments to make them better indices of market power at the expense of making them no longer market shares at all.

Since market shares are not meant to be indices of actual or potential market power, there is considerable scope for letting practicality limit the choices, especially for private parties lacking the government's power to compel the production of the necessary data. To paraphrase Bismark, assigning market shares is "the science of the possible." Since even the best market shares imperfectly reflect market power, imperfections in market shares certainly should not prevent their use. Several of the alternatives discussed above undoubtedly would prove impractical in some cases.

It is not possible in this essay to address the assignment of market shares in every conceivable case. The specific competitive concerns and facts presented by a particular case may call for an approach that differs materially from what is described here. And there is always room for innovation.

REFERENCES

ABA Antitrust Section (1986). Monograph No. 12, *Horizontal Mergers: Law and Policy.* Chicago: American Bar Association.

Agresti, A. & Coull, B. A. (1998). Approximation is better than "exact" for interval estimation of binomial proportions, *American Statistician, 52,* 119–126.

Areeda, P. E., Hovenkamp, H., & Solow, J. L. (2002). *Antitrust Law,* Vol. 2A (2nd edn) Boston: Little, Brown and Co.

Crooke, P., Froeb, L. M., Tschantz, S., & Werden, G. J. (1999). The effects of assumed demand form on simulated postmerger equilibria, *Review of Industrial Organization, 15,* 205–217.

Froeb, L. M., & Werden, G. J. (1991). Endogeneity in the concentration-price relationship: causes and consequences, US Department of Justice, Economic Analysis Group Discussion Paper, 91–97.

Froeb, L. M., & Werden, G. J. (1994). The effects of mergers in differentiated products industries: Logit demand and merger policy, *Journal of Law, Economics, & Organization, 10,* 407–426.

Landes, W. M., & Posner, R. A. (1981). Market power in antitrust cases, *Harvard Law Review*, *94*, 937–996.

Ordover, J. A., & Willig, R. D. (1983). The 1982 Department of Justice merger guidelines: An economic assessment, *California Law Review*, *71*, 535–574.

US Department of Justice and Federal Trade Commission, Horizontal merger guidelines, 1992 (rev. 1997), reprinted in 4 Trade Reg. Rep. (CCH) § *13*, 104.

Werden, G. J. (1983). Market delineation and the Justice Department's Merger Guidelines, *Duke Law Journal*, 514–579.

Werden, G. J. (1991). Horizontal mergers: Comment, *American Economic Review*, *81*, 1002–1006.

Werden, G. J. (1992). The history of antitrust market delineation, *Marquette Law Review*, *76*, 123–215.

Werden, G. J. (1993). Market delineation under the merger guidelines: A tenth anniversary retrospective, *Antitrust Bulletin*, *38*, 517–555.

Werden, G. J. (1996). Identifying market power in electric generation, *Public Utilities Fortnightly*, 15 February, 16–21.

Werden, G. J. (1997a). Simulating the effects of differentiated products mergers: A practitioners' guide. In: Julie A. Caswell & Ronald W. Cotterill (eds), *Strategy and Policy in the Food System: Emerging Issues* (pp. 95–110). Food Marketing Policy Center.

Werden, G. J. (1997b). Simulating the effects of differentiated products mergers: A practical alternative to structural merger policy, *George Mason Law Review*, *5*, 363–386.

Werden, G. J. (1998). Demand elasticities in antitrust analysis, *Antitrust Law Journal*, *66*, 363–414.

Werden, G. J. (2000a). Expert report in *United States v. Interstate Bakeries Corp. and Continental Baking Co.*, *International Journal of the Economics of Business*, *7*, 139–148.

Werden, G. J. (2000b). Market delineation under the merger guidelines: Monopoly cases and alternative approaches, *Review of Industrial Organization*, *16*, 211–218.

Werden, G. J. (2001). Network effects and conditions of entry: Lessons from the *Microsoft* case, *Antitrust Law Journal*, *69*, 87–111.

Werden, G. J., & Froeb, L. M. (1993). Correlation, causality, and all that jazz: The inherent shortcomings of price tests for antitrust market delineation, *Review of Industrial Organization*, *8*, 329–353.

Eastman Kodak Co v. Image Technical Services, Inc., 504 US 451 (1992).

FTC v. H.J. Heinz, Co., 246 F.3d 708 (D.C. Cir. 2000).

Rebel Oil Co. v. Atlantic Richfield Co., 51 F.3d 1421 (9th Cir. 1995).

United States v. Archer-Daniels-Midland Co., 781 F. Supp. 1400 (S.D. Iowa 1991).

United States v. Baker Hughes, Inc., 731 F. Supp. 3 (D.D.C. 1990), *aff'd*, 908 F.2d 981 (D.C. Cir. 1990).

United States v. General Dynamics Corp., 415 US 486 (1974).

United States v. Georgia Pacific Corp., Federal Register, Feb. 6, 2001, pp. 9096–9107 (complaint and competitive impact statement).

United States v. Grinnell Corp., 384 US 563 (1966).

United States v. Microsoft Corp., 84 F. Supp. 2d 9 (D.D.C. 1999) (Findings of Fact), 87 F. Supp. 2d 30 (D.D.C. 2000) (Conclusions of Law), *aff'd in part rev'd in part and remanded*, 253 F.3d 34 (D.C. Cir. 2001).

White Consolidated Industries v. Whirlpool Corp., 612 F. Supp. 1009 (N.D. Ohio 1985), *vacated*, 619 F. Supp. 1022 (N.D. Ohio 1985).

Measuring Market Power
D. J. Slottje (editor)

CHAPTER 2

Mergers Among Bidders with Correlated Values[†]

LUKE FROEB[a,] * and STEVEN TSCHANTZ[b]

[a] *Owen Graduate School of Management, Vanderbilt University, Nashville, TN 37208*
[b] *Department of Mathematics, Vanderbilt University*

Abstract

In the private-values, second-price auction framework, we propose a simple parametric model to analyze the effects of mergers when bidders' values are correlated. Correlation is induced by allowing bidders to draw from a mixture of distributions belonging to a power-related family. For example, if two bidders draw from "high" distributions at the same time, then their values are positively correlated. The dominant strategy equilibrium of second-price auctions implies that if bidders draw correlated values from a mixture of power-related distributions, then winning bids can be expressed as a mixture over auctions in which bidders draw from independent power-related distributions. The closed-form expressions of power-related auctions facilitate estimation and analysis.

Keywords: Correlated private-values, merger, antitrust, second-price auctions
JEL Classifications: D44: L41: horizontal anticompetitive practices

---

* Corresponding author. We wish to acknowledge useful comments from Mikhail Shor.
† Support for this project was provided by the Dean's fund for faculty research.

2.1. INTRODUCTION

In recent years, economists have begun to assess the effects of mergers using formal models of competition. The development is attributable in large part to the ascendancy of noncooperative game theory as the dominant framework for analyzing competition. Merger effects are modelled as the difference between two Nash equilibria, one in which the merging products are priced independently, and one in which they are priced jointly (Werden and Froeb, 1994; Hausman et al., 1994).

In these models, merger effects are likely to be large if two firms sell products that are good substitutes. In differentiated products industries, we can determine whether products are good substitutes by estimating demand models that can accommodate large or small cross-elasticities. For example, in the WorldCom-Sprint merger case, estimated demand for residential long distance phone service showed that WorldCom was a closer substitute to Sprint than it was to AT&T or to other "unbranded" providers (Hausman, 2000). WorldCom abandoned its acquisition plans when the Justice Department challenged the merger.

Although it was not the focus of the merger investigation, WorldCom and Sprint also compete against one another in auctions to supply telephony services to businesses. We can model this competition by specifying cost distributions out of which suppliers draw costs for serving specific clients. The low-cost supplier wins the auction by just outbidding rival suppliers so that the winning bid or "price" is just below the second-lowest cost. In such auctions, a merger, or bidding coalition, will affect price only when the merging firms draw the two lowest costs, and price rises to the third-lowest cost. The frequency of a one-two finish times the magnitude of the resulting price change determines the expected merger price effect, which obviously depends on the characteristics of bidders' joint cost distribution. If two bidders' costs are positively correlated, the frequency of a one-two finish is larger which leads to a larger merger effect.

Despite their obvious importance to policy, models that can accommodate correlated costs are not widely used for analyzing auctions because of their complexity. They are difficult to estimate and analyze for the same reason that probit models are difficult to estimate — the multiple integrals that determine the distribution of winning bids are not easy to work with. The problem is exacerbated for the merger application because economists must work with available data, and within the time constraints of the merger statutes (Section 7A Clayton Act, 15 U.S.C. Section 18a.). To be useful for policy, a model must be tractable, and easily calibrated to available data.

Independent distributions are easy to work with, but independence implies (i) that a firm's market power is related to its "share" or probability of winning, and (ii) that merger effects are closely related to the shares of the merging firms (Tschantz et al., 2000; Waehrer and Perry, 1998). When two bidders' costs are correlated, however, the link between merger effects and shares is weakened. Holding shares constant, mergers have a larger price effect when bidders' costs are positively correlated, and a smaller effect when they are negatively correlated.

In this paper, we propose a simple oral or second-price private-values auction model to analyze the effects of mergers when bidders' costs are correlated. Correlation is induced by allowing bidders to draw from a mixture of independent distributions belonging to the same power-related family. For example, if two bidders draw from "high" distributions at the same time, then their costs are positively correlated. The dominant strategy equilibrium of a second-price auction implies that if bidders draw correlated costs from a mixture of power-related distributions, then winning bids can be expressed as a mixture over auctions in which bidders draw from independent power-related distributions. The closed-form expressions of power-related auctions facilitate estimation and merger analysis.

To illustrate the idea behind mixing, imagine two firms who bid against each other in two different areas, and that their cost distributions are different in each of the areas. If we could match the data to the area that generated it, we would estimate two different models, one for each area. However, if we cannot tell from where the data come, then we say that observable distributions are "mixtures" or weighted sums of the distributions in the two areas. If both bidders have costs that are high in one area, and low in the other, then their observed costs are positively correlated. On the other hand, if one bidder draws cost from a high distribution while his rival draws from a low distribution, and vice versa, then their costs are negatively correlated.

This heuristic should not be taken literally. We are not suggesting that bidders' distributions literally "shift" from auction to auction. Rather we are assuming that bidders each draw from a mixture of two different distributions. The mixing allows us to approximate more general joint value distributions with mixtures of independent distributions and to generalize the IPV framework to admit correlations between bidder values (Froeb et al., 2002). The same kind of mixing has allowed researchers to approximate more general qualitative choice models with mixtures of simple logit choice models (McFadden and Train, 1999).

In what follows, in section 2.2, we characterize the properties of power-related distributions. They have closed-form expressions for winning bid distributions that can be used to construct maximum likelihood estimators, and closed-form expressions for merger effects. Then in section 2.3, we show how to extend the class by mixing, illustrate the effects of correlation on mergers, and suggest estimation strategies.

2.2. FAMILIES OF MIXING DISTRIBUTIONS

2.2.1. Power-related distributions

In this section, we consider the private-values, second-price auction model analyzed by (Waehrer and Perry, 1998) and (Froeb et al., 2002). We use their framework due to its tractability and ease of estimation. In addition, second-price auction outcomes approximate first-price auction outcomes when bidders are not too asymmetric (Maskin and Riley, 1996; Tschantz et al., 2000).

Again, we assume that bidders draw costs or values out of a joint distribution. In a cost or procurement auction, bidders draw costs, the low bidder wins at the second-lowest cost, and mergers raise price. In a value or selling auction, bidders draw values, the high bidder wins at the second-highest value, and mergers reduce price. In what follows we will assume a value auction because the notation is slightly easier. However, everything that follows can be easily generalized to accommodate cost auctions.

Let X_i be the private value of bidder I where $(X_1, \ldots, X_n)$ are mutually independent. We define families of what we call "power-related" distributions.

Definition 1. *The random variables X_1 and X_2, having cumulative distribution functions F_1 and F_2, respectively, are* **power-related value distributions** *if there is some positive number s, such that $F_2(x) = [F_1(x)]^s = F_1^s(x)$, for all x.*

Definition 2. *A* **family of power-related value distributions** *generated by a cumulative distribution function (CDF) $F(x)$ is the set of distributions $\{F^s(x): s \in \mathbb{R}^+\}$.*

For power-related families, the maximum of bidder values is in the same power-related family as the variates from which the maximum is drawn (Waehrer and Perry, 1998).

Lemma 1. *If $X_{\max} = \max\{X_1, X_2, \ldots, X_n\}$, then $X_{\max}$ has CDF $F^{s_{\max}}(x)$ where $s_{\max} = \sum_{i=1}^n s_i$.*

The idea behind using power-related distributions as mixing distributions is to generate asymmetry among bidder value distributions without sacrificing tractability. To do this, we allow bidders to take different numbers of draws from the same base distributions. If s_i is a positive integer, then $F^{s_i}(x)$ can be interpreted as the distribution of the maximum of s_i draws. A bidder taking a large number of draws will have a higher mean than those taking fewer draws. And for auctions among bidders who draw from the same power-related family each bidder wins in proportion to the number of draws he takes from the distribution, i.e., the probability that bidder I wins the auction is

$$p_i = \text{Prob}\,(X_i = X_{\max}) = \frac{s_i}{s_{\max}} = \frac{s_i}{\displaystyle\sum_{j=1}^{n} s_j}. \tag{1}$$

Any distribution in a family of power-related distributions can serve as the base distribution for the family. If $F_{\max}(x)$ is the base distribution for the family, then the individual distribution functions can be expressed as $F_i(x) = F_{\max}^{p_i}(x)$ where $p_i = s_i/s_{\max}$, and $F_{\max}(x) = [F(x)]^{s_{\max}} = F^{s_{\max}}(x)$. The family is parameterized in terms of the observable shares or winning probabilities p_i, and the distribution of the maximum value, $F_{\max}(x)$. The ability to express the distribution in terms of shares facilitates estimation or calibration to observable data.

For procurement auctions, where the low cost bidder wins, we define power-related cost distributions.

Definition 3. *The random variables X_1 and X_2, having cumulative distribution functions F_1 and F_2, respectively, are* **power-related cost distributions** *if there is some positive number s, such that $F_2(x) = 1 - [1 - F_1(x)]^s$, for all x.*

The Gumbel distributions of the logit auction model (Tschantz et al., 2000; Brannman and Froeb, 2000) are from a family of power-related distributions:

$$F_i(x) = e^{e^{-\mu(x - \eta_i)}} = F^{s_i}(x) \tag{2}$$

where $F(x) = e^{-e^{-\mu x}}$ and $s_i = e^{\mu \eta_i}$. Winning probabilities take the familiar logit form

$$p_i = \frac{e^{\mu \eta_i}}{\displaystyle\sum_{j=1}^{n} e^{\mu \eta_j}}.$$

Note that the maximum of independent draws from a power-related family of Gumbel variates has the same variance as the random variables from which the maximum is drawn. It is the only power-related family with this property. In an example below, we will mix over Gumbel distributions when we induce correlation among bidder values.

2.2.2. Prices and shares

Independent power-related auctions have a closed-form relationship between shares and prices. We can derive the relationship from the distribution of the second-highest value, which can be expressed as the weighted sum of the distribution of the maximum and the distribution of the maximum of the losing bidders (Froeb et al., 2000). We introduce some notation for the case of n bidders, drawing random values, $X_1, X_2, \ldots, X_n$.

Definition 4. *The* **symbol**, $X_{-i} = \max\{X_j : 1 \leq j \leq n, j \neq i\}$, *denotes the maximum value among the bidders, excluding bidder i.*

The random variable X_{-i} has CDF $F^{s_{-i}}(x)$, where

$$s_{-i} = \sum_{\substack{j=1 \\ j \neq i}}^{n} s_j.$$

The distribution of the second-highest value given that $X_i = X_{max}$ is,

$$F_{X_{-i}|X_{-i}<X_i}(x) = \left(\frac{1}{p_i}\right) F_{-i}(x) + \left(1 - \frac{1}{p_i}\right) F_{max}(x). \tag{3}$$

The symbol $X_{-i}|X_{-i} < X_i$ denotes the second-highest value given that bidder i has the highest value, and thus wins the auction. Equation 3 can be used to construct maximum likelihood estimators to recover the underlying value distributions from data on winning bids and on who wins each auction (Froeb et al., 2000; Brannman and Froeb, 2000). From the distribution of the second-highest value we can also compute the means and variances of observed bids in terms of the means and variances of the underlying value distributions. Letting $\mu(s)$ and $\sigma^2(s)$ be the mean and variance of the distribution with CDF $F^s(x)$, we obtain

$$\mathrm{E}(X_{\sim i} \mid X_i > X_{\sim i}) = \left(\frac{1}{p_i}\right) \mu(s_{\sim i}) + \left(1 - \frac{1}{p_i}\right) \mu(s_{\max}) \qquad (4)$$

$$\mathrm{Var}(X_{\sim i} \mid X_i > X_{\sim i}) = \left(\frac{1}{p_i}\right) \sigma^2(s_{\sim i}) + \left(1 - \frac{1}{p_i}\right) \sigma^2(s_{\max})$$

$$+ \frac{1}{p_i}\left(1 - \frac{1}{p_i}\right)\left(\mu(s_{\max}) - \mu(s_{\sim i})\right)^2. \qquad (5)$$

To illustrate the price-share relationship implicit in Equation 4, suppose one bidder takes eight draws from a *Uniform*(0, 1) distribution, and another takes two draws from the same distribution. The first bidder will win 80% of the time at a price of 0.61 and the second bidder will win 20% of the time at a price of 0.81. Bidders taking more draws win more frequently and at better prices because when a strong bidder wins, the losing bidders are relatively weak by virtue of the fact that the strong bidder is not among them. Consequently, they are easier to outbid, on average. Thus, larger firms pay lower prices, on average, than smaller firms.

The price-share relationship of Equation 4 will be used to construct a predictor of merger price effects and both Equations, 4 and 5, can be used to construct method-of-moments estimators (Froeb et al., 2002).

2.2.3. Merger price effects

In this section, we use the price-share relationship to derive an expression for merger effects in much the same way that the margin-share relationship is used to derive an expression for merger effects in Cournot models.

To model merger effects, we assume that bidders draw values from independent power-related distributions and that the value of the merged firm is the maximum of its coalition member values. This merger characterization has been used by the antitrust enforcement agencies to model the effects of mergers between hospitals, mining equipment companies, defense contractors, and others (Baker, 1997). From Lemma 1, we know that the value distribution of the merged firm is from the same power-related family as its coalition members. This property means that post-merger expected winning bids lie on the same price-share relationship as the pre-merger expected winning bids. To compute merger effect we need only compare the average of the pre-merger prices to the aggregate post-merger price using the same price-share relationship.

The expected profit to bidder i, since bidder i wins only a fraction p_i of the auctions is

$$E(\text{profit}_i) = p_i E(X_{\max} - B_i)$$

$$= p_i \left[\mu(s_{\max}) - \left(\left(\frac{1}{p_i} \right) \mu(s_{\sim i}) + \left(1 - \frac{1}{p_i} \right) \mu(s_{\max}) \right) \right] \qquad (6)$$

$$= \mu(s_{\max}) - \mu\big(s_{\max}(1 - p_i)\big).$$

A bidder's profit is simply a function of p_i.

Definition 5. *The expected profit to a bidder with winning probability p is* $h(p) = \mu(s_{\max}) - \mu(s_{\max}(1 - p))$.

The total expected profit to all bidders is

$$E(\text{profit}) = \sum_{i=1}^{n} E(\text{profit}_i) = \sum_{i=1}^{n} h(p_i). \qquad (7)$$

If bidders i and j with winning probabilities p_i and p_j merge, then their share after the merger is $p_i + p_j$. Because the auction is efficient, the increase in the expected profit to the bidders is equal to the loss in revenue to the auctioneer. Thus, the expected merger price effect is

$$\Delta E(\text{profit}) = h(p_i + p_j) - h(p_i) - h(p_j). \qquad (8)$$

Equation 6 should look familiar to students of antitrust as it resembles the *Herfindahl-Hirschman Index* or HHI. Similarly, the change in the index, Equation 8 determines the change in expected revenue (price) due to a merger. Unlike the HHI, however, Equation 8 predicts merger effects exactly because the post-merger share is equal to the sum of the pre-merger shares. In Cournot models, shares change from pre- and post-merger, so the predictors are not exact (Froeb and Werden, 1998).

In Figure 2.1, we illustrate the price-share relationship of Equation 7 for a family of power-related Gumbel distributions, estimated from Forest Service Timber auction data (see Brannman and Froeb, 2000 for details). Winning probabilities from the logit estimation are plotted on the horizontal axis and expected winning bids on the vertical axis. In this auction, each bidder's expected price and estimated probability of winning (share) is denoted by a dot. We compute

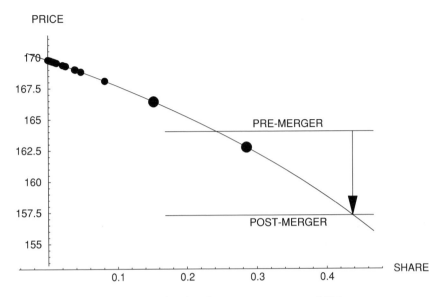

Figure 2.1:   Simulated merger among two bidders.

the effects of a merger between the two best bidders — those closest to the timber tract — which are denoted by large dots. The merger effect of Equation 8 is computed as a movement along the price-share relationship, as the merged entity moves from the average of its pre-merger shares, 45.2% and 20.7% to its post-merger aggregate share, 65.9%. This decreases the expected price paid by the merging firms, from about US$183 to US$176 per thousand board feet, a change of about 3.6%.

2.2.4. Examples of power-related families

In this subsection, we consider two power-related families with closed-form expressions for the mean, variance, and merger price effects. Later, when we use linear combinations of power-related distributions to approximate more general value distributions, the resulting distributions and moments will be linear combinations of the formulas below.

2.2.4.1. *Uniform power-related families*

For a uniform power-related family, we have

$$F(x) = \begin{cases} \frac{x-a}{b-a}, & \text{if } x \in [a, b] \\ 0, & \text{otherwise.} \end{cases}$$

The moments for the family are

$$\mu(s) \quad = \frac{a + bs}{s + 1} \tag{9}$$

$$\sigma^2(s) \quad = \frac{(b - a)^2 s}{(s + 1)^2 (s + 2)} \tag{10}$$

so that profit is given by the function

$$h(p) = \frac{p(b - a)s_{\max}}{(1 + s_{\max})(1 + (1 - p)s_{\max})}. \tag{11}$$

2.2.4.2. *Gumbel power-related families*

The Gumbel power-related family is the only one for which variance is constant,

$$F(x) = \exp\left[-\exp\left(\frac{\pi(\mu - x) - \sqrt{6}\,\sigma\gamma}{\sqrt{6}\,\sigma}\right)\right] \quad \text{for } x \in (-\infty, \infty). \tag{12}$$

The moments for the family are

$$\mu(s) \quad = \mu + \sigma\frac{\sqrt{6}}{\pi}\log(s) \tag{13}$$

$$\sigma^2(s) \quad = \sigma^2 \tag{14}$$

so that profit is given by the function

$$h(p) \quad = -\sigma\frac{\sqrt{6}}{\pi}\log(1 - p). \tag{15}$$

2.3. MIXTURES OF POWER-RELATED DISTRIBUTIONS

2.3.1. Mergers among bidders with correlated values

The biggest drawback to using power-related distributions is the restrictive way that joint bidder value distributions are modelled. In this section we apply the closed-form expressions for the distributions and estimators to linear combinations of power-related distributions,

$$f_i(x) = \sum_{j=1}^{m_i} w_{ij} g_{ij}(x) \tag{16}$$

where $f_i(x)$ is the marginal distribution of bidder i's value expressed as a discrete mixture over power-related distributions $\{g_{ij}\}, j = 1, \ldots, m_i$ with mixing weights $\{w_{ij}\}$. The weights can be thought of as the proportion of time that each bidder draws a given distribution out of an urn. A joint distribution of values, e.g., for bidders i and j, would specify how frequently various combinations of the $g_{ik}(x)$ and $g_{jm}(x)$ are drawn together for all k and m. The joint bidder distribution for all bidder values, $f(x_1, x_2, \ldots, x_n)$, can be specified as a mixture over a set of power-related distributions,

$$f(x_1, x_2, \ldots, x_n) = \sum_{m=1}^{M} w_m g_{1i}(x_1) g_{2j}(x_2) \cdots g_{nk}(x_n). \tag{17}$$

Independence across bidder values implies that $w_m = g_{1i} g_{2j} \cdots g_{nk}$ or that the weight given to the joint occurrence of a particular combination of power-related distributions is proportional to the product of their weights in Equation 15. Correlation among bidder values is induced by choosing the mixing weights, $\{w_m\}$, so that some combinations of power-related distributions occur together more frequently than would be implied by independence.

The key result is that the joint distribution of bidder values can be interpreted as a mixture over $M = \prod_{i=1}^{n} m_i$ power-related auctions in Equation 17. Since all base distributions are power-related to one another, the observed price distribution can be expressed as a mixture over independent power-related auctions. Mixtures of the closed-form expressions for the distribution of price in section 2.2.2 can be used to construct maximum likelihood estimators (Froeb et al., 2002), and the expected merger effects can be expressed as a mixture of the merger formulas of section 2.2.3.

In Figure 2.2, we consider a merger in a three-firm industry where the firms have shares of (30%, 30%, 40%) and the third firm's value is uncorrelated with

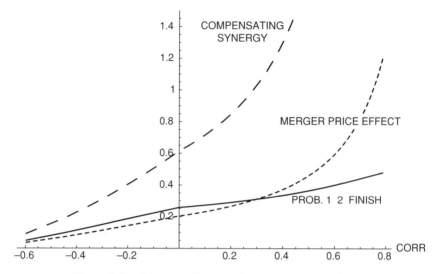

Figure 2.2:   Merger effects vs. bidder value correlation.

the values of the other two. If the first two firms merge, then the post-merger structure is (60%, 40%). We allow the two merging firms to mix over two independent power-related Gumbel distributions, i.e., with the same variance but different means. The third firm draws from a single (fixed) Gumbel distribution from the same power-related family. We suppose the three bidders meet in only two different auctions, and we induce a correlation between the merging firms by adjusting the means of the Gumbel distributions over which they mix. Let μ_{ij} be the mean of the i-th bidder's value distribution in the j-th auction. If $Sign(\mu_{11} - \mu_{12})$ is the same as $Sign(\mu_{21} - \mu_{22})$ then the bidders' values are positively correlated. If they are different, then the bidders' values are negatively correlated.

Holding shares constant, we vary the correlation from -0.6 to 0.8 by changing the means of one of the mixing distributions for one of the merging firms. In Figure 2.2, we plot variables that describe merger effects against correlation. The probability of a one-two finish for the merging firms, necessary for a merger effect, increases from less than 10% to over 40%. As the frequency of one-two finishes increases, so does the expected merger effect of Equation 8. This is a value auction, where the high-bid wins, so mergers reduce price. For display purposes, we plot the absolute value of the expected industry price change. The units of the price change are arbitrarily scaled so only the qualitative changes are meaningful. We see that merger effects increase linearly with correlation until a correlation of about 0.4. Then they accelerate, and seem to increase exponentially.

We also plot the compensating merger synergies that offset the merger effects (Tschantz et al., 2000; Brannman and Froeb, 2000). These are computed by setting the post-merger industry price equal to the pre-merger industry price to solve for the reduction in mean costs, or increase in mean value, sufficient to keep industry price constant. Since price is set by the losing bidder, merger synergies do not affect the price paid by merging firms. However, by making the merged firm a more aggressive losing bidder, merger synergies do raise the prices paid by non-merging firms.

We see that the magnitude of these "compensating" merger synergies are about three times the expected industry price effect they are designed to offset, similar to the magnitudes of compensating marginal cost reductions found in Cournot (Froeb and Werden, 1998) and Bertrand (Werden, 1997) models. Like the price effects they offset, they increase linearly with correlation until a correlation of about 0.2. Then they accelerate, and seem to increase exponentially. When the merger price effect becomes too large, no amount of merger synergies can offset the effect. Recall that merger synergies affect price by making the merged firm a better loser. As synergies increase, the expected benefit of making it a better loser becomes small because the merged firm loses less frequently.

2.3.2. Estimation with mixtures of power-related distributions

One of the advantages of working with a parametric model like this one is that the complexity of the model can be matched to the quality and amount of available data. With abundant data, you can choose a large number of mixing distributions, and the model can be interpreted as a nonparametric kernel density estimator (Froeb et al., 2002). Different power-related families may match the data better than the Gumbel family. In addition to the uniform and Gumbel families, the Weibull (Type I extreme value), and Frechet (Type II) families have closed-form expressions for the mean, standard deviation, and merger effects, and may be more appropriate for certain types of applications (Froeb et al., 2002).

Conversely, nonparametric identification of correlated private values models requires data on losing as well as winning bids, in addition to data on bidder identities (Athey and Haile, forthcoming). However, when working on merger cases, there is rarely enough data, and typically not enough time, to estimate a non-parametric model. In these cases, the parametric models set forth in this paper may be more useful, particularly if the data comes from different sources, like interviews, price-cost margins, or frequency of one-two finishes.

2.4. CONCLUSION

Quantitative benefit-cost analysis of mergers has several advantages over an approach based on shares in a delineated market. Most importantly, it focuses the merger investigation on the effects of the mergers and gives the enforcement agencies a way to explicitly weigh the benefits of a merger against its costs. Under a conventional approach based on market shares alone, there is no way to trade off a change in the industry structure against a reduction in the costs of the merging firms.

REFERENCES

Athey, S., & Haile, P. (forthcoming). *Identification of Standard Auction Models*. Econometrica.

Bajari, P. (1996). A structural econometric model of the sealed high-bid auction: With applications to procurement of highway improvements. Working paper, University of Minnesota.

Baker, J. B. (1997). Unilateral competitive effects theories in merger analysis. *Antitrust*, *11*(2), 21–26.

Brannman, L., & Froeb, L. (2000). Mergers, cartels, set-asides, and bidding preferences in asymmetric second-price auctions. *Review of Economics and Statistics*, *82*(2), 283–290.

Brownstone, D., & Train, K. (1999). Forecasting new product penetration with flexible substitution patterns, *Journal of Econometrics*, *89*(1), 109–129.

Crooke, P., Froeb, L., Tschantz, S., & Werden, G. (1999). The effects of assumed demand form on simulated post-merger equilibria. *Review of Industrial Organization*, *15*(3), 205–217.

Dalkir, S., Logan, J., & Masson, R. T. (1999). Mergers in symmetric and asymmetric non-cooperative auction markets: The effects on price and efficiency. *International Journal of Industrial Organization*, *18*, 383–413.

Froeb, L., Tschantz, S., & Crooke, P. (2002). Second-price auctions with mixtures of power-related distributions. Working paper, Vanderbilt University.

Froeb, L., & Werden, G. J. (1998). A robust test for consumer welfare enhancing mergers among sellers of a homogeneous product. *Economics Letters*, *58*, 267–269.

Hausman, J. (2000). Declaration of Professor Jerry A. Hausman before the FCC in the matter of WorldCom's proposed acquisition of Sprint. February 16.

Hausman, J., Leonard, G., & Douglas, Z. J. (1994). Competitive analysis with differentiated products. *Annales d'Economie et Statistique*, *34*(2), 159–180.

Maskin, E., & Riley, J. (1996). Asymmetric auctions. Working paper, UCLA.

McFadden, D., & Train, K. (1999). Mixed MNL Models for discrete response. *Journal of Applied Econometrics, 89*(1), 109–129.

Tschantz, S., Crooke, P., & Froeb, L. (2000). Mergers in sealed vs. oral auctions. *International Journal of the Economics of Business, 7*(2), 201–213.

US Department of Justice and Federal Trade Commission. (2 April 1992). Horizontal merger guidelines.

Waehrer, K., & Perry, M. K. (1998). The effects of mergers in open auction markets. Working paper, Rutgers University.

Werden, G. J. (1997). A Robust test for consumer welfare enhancing mergers among sellers of differentiated products. *Journal of Industrial Economics, 44*, 409–413.

Werden, G. J., & Froeb, L. M. (1994). The effects of mergers in differentiated products industries: Logit demand and merger policy. *Journal of Law, Economics, and Organization, 10*, 407–426.

Werden, G., & Froeb, L. (1996). Simulation as an alternative to structural merger policy in differentiated products industries. In: M. Coate and A. Kleit (eds), *The Economics of the Antitrust Process* (pp. 65–88). New York: Kluwer

Measuring Market Power
D. J. Slottje (editor)

CHAPTER 3

Measuring the Effect of Cartelization in Medicine: An International Study

PETER ZWEIFEL* and CHANTAL GRANDCHAMP

Socioeconomic Institute of the University of Zurich, Hottingerstrasse. 10, CH-8032 Zurich

Abstract

This contribution builds on knowledge about the power of medical associations in several industrial countries to measure the effects of cartelization. Countries with strong medical associations are predicted to have a slower increase in medical density than others. Failing to control access, a cartel may still be able to limit the effect on members' incomes. In these countries, an increase in provider density should have a smaller impact on relative medical incomes. Both predictions are tested using data from OECD countries. They receive a good deal of empirical support, nevertheless the United States seems to be an outlier in our analysis.

JEL classification: I11, L12
Keywords: Medical association, cartelization, residual demand, medical density, physician income

* Corresponding author.

3.1. INTRODUCTION

Ever since Reuben Kessel's (1958) seminal article, economists have been fascinated with the issue of monopoly power in medicine. The exercise of such power can occur at two levels. At the level of an entire group of suppliers, firms can hold monopoly power collectively by forming a cartel. However, in the case of physicians, the single supplier may also exercise some monopoly power, mainly due to asymmetry of information between patient and physician. This has spawned a string of theoretical and empirical studies focusing on search processes (Dranove and Satterthwaite, 1992; Wolinsky, 1993; Kenkel, 1990; for a survey of the industrial organization of medical markets, see Gaynor (1994)).

The present study belongs to the first camp: it takes as given that physicians' services differ from many others in that they are differentiated, characterized by asymmetry of information, and prevalence of ethical concerns. These characteristics set them apart from others in a given country, creating the scope for the exercise of monopoly power. However, there are also important differences between countries. This paper seeks to exploit these differences by deriving indicators of power for the medical associations of six industrial countries.

The plan of this contribution is as follows: in the next section, the different theories regarding the nature of the market for physician services are reviewed and three common objectives of medical cartels derived, viz. increasing the residual demand for their members, making it less price elastic, and safeguarding cartel discipline. Indicators of institutional features that facilitate the attainment of these objectives are introduced for a ranking of these countries in terms of power. Finally, this ranking is tested using data from OECD countries on the development of physician densities and the response of relative physicians' incomes to the development of medical densities.

3.2. THEORETICAL CONSIDERATIONS

The precise nature of medical markets is a matter of continued theoretical debate. Kessel's (1958) notion seems to be that physicians potentially are subject to perfect competition. At least there is no mention of product differentiation, suggesting that physicians offer a homogeneous service. Monopoly power thus exclusively derives from their successful cartelization. Early empirical evidence was provided by Friedman and Kuznets (1954), who take barriers to entry as a sign of successful cartelization. They find excess returns to medical education. Later studies tend to confirm this finding (see e.g. Burstein and Cromwell, 1985); however they all use data that do not cover recent periods. The existence of anticompetitive practices such as price discrimination and advertising bans also provides evidence for this model, as does the finding by McCarthy (1985) that individual physician practices are characterized by a price elasticity of demand above one.

At the other extreme, physicians frequently are seen as wielding a local monopoly. This is the assumption typically used in the literature on supplier-induced demand (Evans, 1974; Reinhardt, 1985; Labelle, Stoddart and Rice, 1994). Strictly speaking, a medical association would have no role to play in this model, and indeed it is abstracted from most of the work on demand inducement. However, the cost of finding an alternative provider outside the local market is finite for the great majority of patients. Therefore, a physician who induces demand to an extent that runs counter to the interests of his or her patients faces the threat of patient migration. This means that his or her local monopoly is also limited by a residual demand curve, whose location may be modified by a cartel. The empirical evidence is reviewed e.g., by Labelle, Stoddart and Rice (1994). While it is mixed, they conclude in favor of the supplier-induced phenomenon. However, the tests used may not have much power; specifically, Dranove and Wehner (1993) find evidence of induced demand for childbirths, when applying standard tests.

The middle ground between the two extremes is occupied by the monopolistic competition model. With its emphasis on product differentiation, it provides a credible representation of medical markets. After all, the success of medical treatment crucially depends on the matching of two individuals, the physician and the patient. The only difficulty with this model is its prediction of entry into the market until price is bid down to average cost, pushing economic profit to zero, a condition unlikely to hold true in view of important barriers to entry. As noted by Gaynor (1994), most of the papers are theoretical rather than empirical, applying game theory to represent the relationship between physician, patient and insurer (see Gaynor and Vogt, 1999).

The available empirical evidence clearly is insufficient to discriminate between the three models. However, for present purposes the choice of theoretical models makes little difference. For, they all rely on the concept of a residual demand curve facing the individual physician. And, irrespective of the model, the mission of a cartel is (1) to shift the residual demand curve out for members of the cartel, (2) to make the residual demand curve steeper, i.e., less price elastic in the neighborhood of the current price-quantity combination, and (3) to enforce cartel discipline.

1   Shifting the residual demand curve outward: this allows the supplier affected to increase its price and/or quantity sold. Since just raising price (and hence

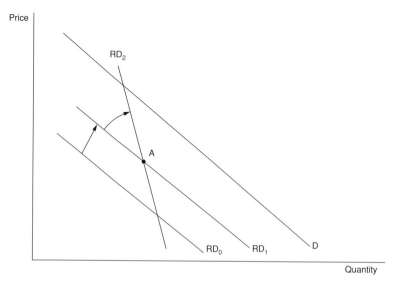

Figure 3.1:   Shifting the residual demand curve as the task of a cartel.

revenue) at an unchanged quantity (and hence cost) is an option, profits (net income in the case of physicians) must rise. In Figure 3.1, let D be total demand and RD_0 a member's residual demand function prior to the cartel's influence (see Noether, 1986a for a similar development). The first task of the cartel is represented by the shift from RD_0 to RD_1. Given a demand increase caused by income growth, enlarged health insurance coverage, and product innovation in medicine, a medical cartel can ensure an outward shift of the residual demand curve by creating or reinforcing barriers to entry. This can be achieved by limiting access to medical school, making medical education more costly in terms of money, required academic achievements, likelihood of failure in exams, and getting the government to curtail immigration of foreign medical graduates.

2   Making the residual demand curve less price elastic: the objective is to increase marginal revenue at the going quantity of services provided and thus to increase (net) income. In Figure 3.1 this corresponds to the rotation around point A. A medical association may not be powerful enough to prevent an inward shift of the residual demand curve, i.e., to prevent an increase of provider density. However, it may still be successful in decreasing its price elasticity, thus insulating its members' incomes from the effect of shrinking

demand at least to some extent. Increased product differentiation (e.g., by creating new specialty) and getting health insurers to cover additional medical procedures or to increase coverage generally are examples.

3 Enforcing cartel discipline: as is well known, members of a cartel have an incentive to chisel because the marginal revenue of additional sales exceeds marginal cost. Chiseling physicians in fact add to the competitive fringe, causing the residual demand functions of loyal members to shift inward. They also undermine the cartel's attempt to reduce the price elasticity of residual demand functions because they must emphasize substitution possibilities to attract additional patients.

A well-known approach to the measurement of monopoly power is to interpret the observed price-quantity combinations as a mixture of demand function and marginal revenue function observations. The optimal quantity has to satisfy

$$P + \lambda \cdot MR = MC$$

where P: price
        λ: parameter, $0 \leqslant \lambda \leqslant \infty$
        MR: marginal revenue
        MC: marginal cost.

If $\lambda = 0$, the supplier is a price taker ($P = MC$); if $\lambda \to 0$, it becomes a monopolist (Scherer and David, 1990, p. 230; for an application to the US market of physician services, see Noether, 1986b).

However, the implementation of this approach requires knowledge of the price elasticity of the (residual) demand curve $\eta = 0$ to determine MR through the formula $MR = p(1 + 1/\eta)$ and of marginal cost MC. Outside the United States, estimates of _ are hardly available, while for a physician, the opportunity cost of time largely determines the marginal cost of providing service — a quantity not easily measured.

In view of the unavailability of data for estimating λ in several countries, a simpler alternative was chosen in this paper. It amounts to relating developments over time in national markets to the power of the respective medical association. In a dynamic context, the following testable implications emanate from the preceding theoretical considerations:

H1:   The more powerful a country's medical association, the less should physician density have increased during the period of observation (shifting out the residual demand curve).

H2:   The more powerful a country's medical association, the smaller should be
       the effect of a given increase of physician density on physician income
       (rotating the residual demand curve).
H3:   The more powerful a country's medical association, the higher should be
       the degree of cartel discipline, and the more marked the effects predicted
       in H1 and H2.

3.3. INDICATORS OF POWER

The "power of organized medicine" is an established theme in medical sociology
(Mechanic, 1991). For present purposes, the concept of power is narrowed down
to mean a medical association's ability to manipulate the residual demand curve
of its members in the aim of increasing and/or protecting their incomes. Due to
lack of data, only a few factors (which however should be particularly relevant
for medical markets) can be studied here.

3.3.1. Power to shift out the residual demand curve

3.3.1.1. Comprehensive social insurance

A somewhat indirect way for a medical cartel to increase the quantity of services
demanded at the going fee level is to have a large population covered by health
insurance. Given that an insured person has to pay only a fraction of the true
cost of medical care, he or she is more likely to demand some care. More individuals covered therefore result in an outward shift of total demand (and residual
demand for cartel members, ceteris paribus). (The effect on price elasticity will
be discussed in section 3.3.2.)

As long as it is private health insurance that expands, the power of a medical
association is of little relevance because private insurers will decide their amount
of business in the light of profit considerations. This changes when the issue is
to bring an even greater share of the population under the purview of social (or
public) health insurance. In that case, a powerful medical association can help
formulate and pass bills that aim to make health insurance compulsory for most
or all residents of a country.

Among the six countries considered, the United States has by far the
lowest degree of comprehensiveness of health insurance (45%, according to
OECD 2000). In Germany, some 8% of the population have opted out of

social insurance, resulting in a rate of coverage of 92%. France follows with 99.5% whereas in Sweden, Switzerland and the United Kingdom, the entire population is covered by social health insurance or a national health service.

On this score, the power ranking is US < D < F, CH, S, UK. (US: United States, D: Germany, F: France, CH: Switzerland, S: Sweden, UK: United Kingdom).

3.3.1.2. Controlling access to medical markets

The residual demand facing a physician importantly depends on the number of practitioners around him or her. A medical association can try to stabilize this residual demand rather directly by making access to the market for medical services costly. If sufficiently powerful, it will push through exceedingly high standards of academic achievement or outright admission quota for medical faculties. In addition, a medical education entails considerable financial outlays, especially in the United States. In the other five countries considered here, tuition is negligible; however, students still face opportunity costs in terms of alternative use of their productive time.

At the low end of the scale, Switzerland does not restrict access to its medical schools, and tuition is very low. Moreover, after completion of their training, physicians can work in charge of public health insurance without delay. In Sweden, access to medical schools is only slightly restricted; some predetermined conditions (schooling, professional experience, grades) and an aptitude test serve to choose future students (see Zweifel, Lyttkens and Söderström, 1998). France is the first country in the list considered here to officially have implemented a nationwide restriction of access to medical education. On the other hand, tuition is nominal and establishment of a practice unregulated. Similar conditions govern admission to medical school in Germany; however, graduates may have to wait to open a practice and must conform to a plan administered by the regional medical association. Next, it is in the United Kingdom where the whole process, starting from access to medical school and ending with a contract with the National Health Service, is administered by the government. Still, the British Medical Association lacks immediate influence over it. Finally, the United States, while not restricting access to medical schools by administrative fiat, is characterized by high barriers in that applicants must have an academic degree prior to taking up medicine. Also, tuition is very considerable. The American Medical Association, with its authority over medical accreditation, directly controls the number of school places as well as the number of schools. Noether (1968a) reviews the evidence and finds a decline of power, which may reflect a change in US antitrust enforcement (Lin et al., 2000).

According to these arguments, the ranking is: CH < S < F < D < UK < US.

3.3.1.3. *A combined partial ranking*

Inspection of the two rankings derived in the preceding subsections reveals several contradictions. In particular, the United States ranks lowest with regard to comprehensiveness of social insurance but highest with regard to control of access. This contradiction can be resolved by noting that comprehensive social insurance shifts out the residual demand curve only if its effect is not neutralized by an influx of additional suppliers. Control over access to medical markets therefore is of more decisive importance. This argument causes the United Kingdom and the United States to form a top group (albeit for different reasons). At the low end of a combined ranking, one may put Germany and Switzerland, with the remaining falling in between: CH,D < F, S < UK, US.

3.3.2. Power to rotate the residual demand curve

3.3.2.1. *Controlling access to medical markets*

An important objective of any cartel is to reduce price competition among its members. This means pushing the price elasticity of the residual demand curve towards zero. This elasticity is roughly the *n*-fold of the market price elasticity, with *n* the number of competitors (Carlton and Perloff, 2000, Ch. 3). Keeping the stock of providers low thus contributes to reducing the price elasticity as well. Therefore, the ranking derived in subsection 3.3.1.2 applies here once more: CH < S < F < D < UK < US.

3.3.2.2. *Ample insurance coverage*

One important additional factor that serves to diminish price elasticity under rather general conditions is insurance coverage, both public and private. Being protected from the financial consequences of their choice, patients have little incentive to seek out physicians who compete in terms of the money price of treatment (for the different forms of moral hazard in health insurance, see

Zweifel and Manning, 2000). This also means that buyer resistance against a high fee level caused by cartelization is minimal. Therefore, the percentage of health care expenditure covered by insurance is used as an indicator. According to OECD (2000), the United States stands out at the low end of the range with 61% coverage of both ambulatory and hospital care, followed by Switzerland, Sweden, France and Germany, while the United Kingdom marks the other extreme with almost 100% public coverage. This gives rise to the partial ranking: US < CH < S, F < D < UK.

3.3.2.3. Differentiation of product

Product differentiation contributes to reducing the price elasticity of the residual demand curve in two ways. First, a strong medical association can help to differentiate medical services from those of other providers of health care. One means for attaining this objective is quality assurance, which serves to distinguish physicians favorably from competing professions such as healing practitioners and psychotherapists that have been unable to enforce a comparable quality standard. This achievement has paid off handsomely in that private and social health insurers in most industrialized countries do not include the services of healing practitioners and psychotherapists in their benefits. Since this exclusion applies to all countries considered here, this point does not result in a ranking of countries.

Second, a medical association may decrease the degree of substitution among its members by creating more and more specialties and subspecialties. In this regard, the United States stands out because it is usually the first country to adopt an innovation in medical technology. On the official AMA Internet page, 126 specialties and subspecialties are listed compared to e.g., 38 on the website of the French Health Ministry (www.sante.gouv.fr). Casual empiricism suggests that the degree of specialization is roughly comparable in the European countries sampled. Therefore, only an extremely partial ranking seems justified: CH, D, F, S, UK < US.

3.3.2.4. A combined partial ranking

Once more, the rankings derived in the three preceding sections are conflicting and partial. It seems that merely the following statements with regard to rotating the demand curve can be made. First, Switzerland (CH) should be placed at the low end. The next lowest position should be assigned to Sweden (S) because control over access (where Sweden ranks low according to subsection 3.3.1.2) has a very direct effect on the steepness of the residual demand curve while the high degree of public coverage conveys to the Swedish national health insurance scheme a measure of monopsony power that could not be neutralized by the Swedish medical association through political lobbying (Immergut, 1992). The rankings indicate that France (F) should be next, followed by Germany (D). They also suggest that one of the most powerful (if not the most powerful) medical associations should be the one of the UK. The ranking of the US is once more uncertain. Two of the three indicators suggest a maximum degree of power to rotate the residual demand curve, one of them (insurance coverage), a minimum degree. It does not seem possible to resolve this contradiction. Therefore, the partial ranking excludes the US, being limited to CH < S < F < D < UK.

3.3.3. Maintaining cartel discipline

According to hypothesis H3, a strong medical association should be particularly effective in both shifting and rotating the residual demand curve, as described in the two preceding subsections. A precondition for success in both domains is the ability to form and maintain a cartel. The economic theory of cartels was developed by Stigler (1964) and Hay and Kelley (1974). Applying this theory to the case of physician services, Zweifel and Eichenberger (1992) studied the costs and benefits of forming and maintaining a medical cartel. However, this material will not be used here because H3 speaks of a reinforcement effect, and the present data set is too limited to permit testing for reinforcement effects. Thus, H3 will not be tested in the following section.

3.4. TESTING THE HYPOTHESES

3.4.1. Differences in the development of physician density

According to the first hypothesis (H1), a powerful medical association should be able to control physician density better than a less powerful one. The data set, "OECD Health Data 2000" contains density data for the six countries for which indicators of power are available: France, Germany, Sweden, Switzerland, United Kingdom, and the United States. The variable is defined to include all practicing physicians, with the exception of the UK where it is restricted to general practitioners. The observation period is 1960 to 1998 for all countries. For each country, a time trend was estimated:

$$\text{Density}_t = \alpha_0 + \alpha_1 \, \text{Time}_t + \varepsilon_t \quad \text{with} \quad \varepsilon_t = \rho\varepsilon_{t-1} + u_t \tag{1}$$
$$u_t \sim N(0, \sigma^2).$$

OLS residuals $\hat{\varepsilon}_t$ exhibited positive serial correlation, according to the Q statistic (Hamilton, 1994). The Prais-Winsten (1954) regression estimator was used for the resulting AR(1) model, which preserves the first observation, in contra-distinction to the Cochrane-Orcutt procedure. After the transformation, the $\hat{u}_t$ residuals could not be distinguished from white noise for all countries.

Estimation results are displayed in Table 3.1. To simplify comparisons, the United States is used as a benchmark and T-tests (assuming independence of coefficients) are performed to assess statistical significance.

The first thing to note is that the United States has a clearly increasing medical density, amounting to 3.6 more physicians per 100,000 population annually (1.8% of the mean value 1960–1998) on average. Thus, the power of the American Medical Association to shift out the residual demand curve for their members seems to be somewhat limited.

The regression coefficient for time (α_1 in equation (1)) is significantly smaller in the case of the UK. Since the UK data cover general practitioners (GPs) only, it is appropriate to calculate the implied annual percentage change to make a comparison with the US estimate possible. Calculated at the means, this amounts to 1.4% annually, clearly less than the US figure. This points to a considerable degree of power of the British Medical Association to shift the residual demand curve, as predicted in subsection 3.3.1.3.

Moreover, France and Germany are very much in the same camp, with signif-icantly higher $\hat{\alpha}_1$ values (0.056 and 0.057) than the United States (0.036). The similarity with Sweden (0.058) was not predicted, however. At first, Switzerland looks like the country with the highest degree of market power of organized medicine, with $\hat{\alpha}_1 = 0.024$; however, this translates into a high rate of change of 1.95%.

The results of Table 3.1 are also displayed in Figure 3.2. For the UK, two graphs are shown. One, labeled UK, reflects the fact that the data cover GPs only. For the other, labeled UK*, the estimated constant $\hat{\alpha}_0$ was increased, shifting the regression equation up so that its predicted value coincides with the one available figure for total physician density. Figure 3.2 confirms the predic-tion of subsection 3.3.1.3 that Germany (D) should be characterized by a limited amount of power to shift out the residual demand curve. It also confirms the

Table 3.1: Results for equation 1 (dependent variable: physician density, 1960–1998).

	Coefficient	Std error	T-stat	Difference from US		Adjusted R^2	Transformed Durbin-Watson	Mean value
				Coefficient	T-stat			
US								
constant	1.246	0.074	16.87	1.246		0.76	2.07	1.97
time	0.036	0.003	11.30	0.036				
France								
constant	0.812	0.089	9.10	−0.434	−3.70	0.80	2.29	1.90
time	0.056	0.004	15.39	0.019	3.95			
Germany								
constant	1.226	0.143	8.59	−0.020	−0.12	0.67	2.02	2.28
time	0.057	0.005	10.98	0.020	3.29			
Sweden								
constant	0.894	0.149	6.01	−0.352	−2.09	0.52	2.04	2.06
time	0.058	0.006	10.45	0.022	3.36			
Switzerland								
constant	0.820	0.192	4.27	−0.426	−2.04	0.53	2.41	1.23
time	0.024	0.006	4.00	−0.012	−1.81			
UK[1]								
constant	0.370	0.029	12.64	−0.875	−10.87	0.61	1.92	0.50
time	0.007	0.001	5.36	−0.030	−8.57			

Note. [1] General practitioners only.

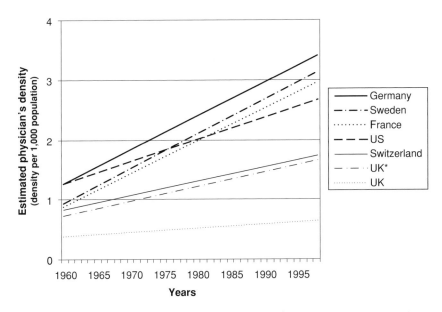

Figure 3.2: Simulation of physician's density[1], based on the results of equation 1.

Note. [1] UK*: all physicians (comparable to the other countries).

predicted similarity of France and Sweden as well as the prediction that both the US and the UK should be characterized by a comparatively slow increase of physician density. The one contradiction is Switzerland, whose rate of increase should have been comparable to that of Germany according to subsection 3.3.1.3 but turns out to be much slower.

Conclusion 1: The six countries studied display differences in terms of their trends in physician density largely as predicted by the partial ranking of subsection 3.3.1.3.

Therefore, hypothesis H1, predicting a negative relationship between the power of organized medicine and the development of physician density, receives some empirical support.

3.4.2. Differences in the development of medical incomes

According to the argument in section 3.2, strong medical associations should be able to insulate their members' incomes from increasing provider density (H2).

This hypothesis cannot be tested directly because it refers to the incomes of cartel members whereas data are only available for all physicians. However, the error incurred should be minor because the overwhelming majority of physicians belong to a medical association in the countries considered. In the case of the United Kingdom, the income figure again relates to general practitioners. Observation periods differ and contain gaps, resulting in a minimum of seven observations for Germany, scattered between 1974 and 1992. The results and comparisons for this country are thus subject to caution. In addition, comparing incomes across countries poses problems. To the extent that physicians use their income on non-traded goods and services, a readily available deflator is the yearly wage or average earnings of a production worker in their own country. Therefore, the dependent variable in equation (2) is physician income relative to average earnings,

$$\text{Income}_t = \beta_0 + \beta_1 \text{Pdensity}_t + \nu_t \quad \text{with} \quad \nu_t = \delta \nu_{t-1} + w_t \qquad (2)$$
$$w_t \sim N(0, \sigma^2).$$

As the explanatory variable, Pdensity rather than Density enters, with Pdensity symbolizing the predicted value from Equation (1). This choice can be justified as a proxi of the density that would result from the interaction of long-run supply and demand schedules (which are not modeled here).

Results are given in Table 3.2. They reveal the startling fact that physician density and relative medical income are positively rather than negatively related in the United States and in the United Kingdom. In the case of the UK, this can be interpreted as an extreme manifestation of the power ranking derived in subsection 3.3.2.4 where the UK occupies first place. In the case of the US, the empirical finding resolves the conflict between the three indicators of power that prevented a ranking. Now one can say that the effects of control over access to the market and product differentiation (single or combined) apparently outweigh the effect of comparatively low insurance coverage. However, in view of the comparatively high mobility of US medical graduates, reversed causality (high relative income attracting additional physicians) cannot be entirely ruled out because correcting for endogeneity using a time trend, as attempted here, may not be sufficient.

For ease of comparison, the estimated relationships of Table 3.2 are again displayed graphically in Figures 3.3 and 3.4; Figure 3.3 documents the fact that

Table 3.2: Results for Equation 2 (dependent variable: relative physician income).

	Coefficient	Std error	T-stat	Difference from US		Adjusted R²	Transformed Durbin-Watson	Mean value Period
				Coefficient	T-stat			
US								
constant	−0.384	1.079	−0.36	−0.384		0.86	1.64	7.80 1974–1996
Pdensity	3.685	0.500	7.37	3.685				
France								
constant	3.770	0.359	10.49	4.153	3.56	0.95	1.96	3.67 1974–1997
Pdensity	−0.033	0.161	−0.21	−3.718	−6.91			
Germany[1]								
constant	13.518	0.760	17.78	13.901	10.09	0.93	–	6.72 1974–1992
Pdensity	−2.641	0.293	−9.02	−6.327	−10.51			
Sweden								
constant	5.856	0.439	13.35	6.239	5.23	0.96	2.14	3.07 1974–1995
Pdensity	−1.117	0.191	−5.83	−4.802	−8.75			
Switzerland								
constant	13.002	1.905	6.82	13.386	5.98	0.83	2.20	4.86 1974–1998
Pdensity	−5.584	1.334	−4.19	−9.269	−6.36			
UK								
constant	2.148	0.446	4.81	2.532	2.12	0.58	1.24	3.32 1974–1998
Pdensity	2.116	0.814	2.60	−1.569	−1.61			

Note. [1] Since data for Germany consists only of seven observations, a Prais-Winsten regression could not be performed. This equation was then estimated by OLS, resulting in too low standard errors of coefficients in the presence of autocorrelation in the error term.

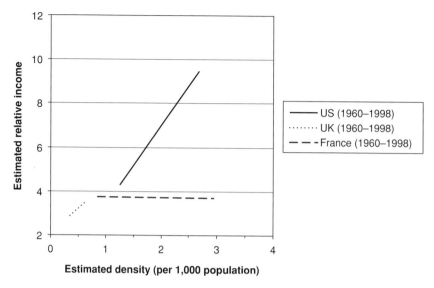

Figure 3.3: Relationship between estimated relative income and estimated density (US, UK, F).

Note. UK: general practitioners only used in the regression.

France (F) also belongs to the camp of countries where an increase of medical density fails to depress relative physician incomes. This does not agree with the ranking of subsection 3.3.2.4 where France occupies a middle position.

This should hold true of Germany (D) as well; however, Figure 3.4 demonstrates that this country has witnessed a marked reduction of relative physician incomes in response to the increase in density of supply. Finally, Sweden and Switzerland should form a group characterized by rather limited power of medical associations to rotate the residual demand curve. As evidenced in Table 3.2, their estimated $\hat{\beta}_1$ coefficients for Equation (2) are indeed negative, implying a reduction of relative physician incomes when (predicted) medical density increases. While this is in accordance with the predictions of subsection 3.3.2.4, a given increase in provider density seems to cause a smaller decrease of relative income in Sweden than in Switzerland. In view of the small standard errors of the $\hat{\beta}_1$ estimates in Table 3.2, this difference is statistically significant. Figure 3.4 confirms the impression of differences between slopes, with Switzerland featuring the strongest negative relationship between density and income in the entire sample.

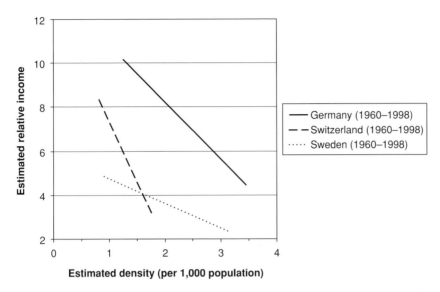

Figure 3.4:   Relationship between estimated relative income and estimated density (D, CH, S).

Conclusion 2:   The six countries studied display differences in terms of their relationships between medical density and relative physician income that partly conform with the partial ranking of subsection 3.3.2.4.

Therefore, hypothesis H2, predicting an attenuation of the effect of an increase in medical density on relative physician income thanks to cartelization in medicine, receives but limited empirical support.

3.5. DISCUSSION AND CONCLUSION

Among the results presented in the preceding section, those for the United States are puzzling. The two indicators available for the American Medical Association's power to shift out residual demand curves were conflicting, and only after a weighting of the evidence was it possible to come up with a prediction of the development of US medical density. Actual observations covering 1974 until the mid-1990s reveal that its medical density increased more slowly than that of France, Germany and Sweden (in spite of the fact that Germany and France officially restrict admissions to medical schools). Therefore, the loss of control over access found by Noether (1986a) for the American Medical Association may be less impressive when put in international perspective. Next, the three indicators of power to rotate residual demand curves were again conflicting — and the United States turns out to be the country where relative physician incomes strongly increase in the face of a growing density of supply. One possible explanation of this difference is that it was the individual American physician who successfully insulated himself or herself from the increased competitive pressure by continuously upgrading his or her practice and skills, as argued by Gaynor (1994).

On the other hand, this "perverse result" should not be over-interpreted to mean that market forces fail generally when it comes to medical care. Switzerland, a country where physician incomes are as little controlled by public regulation as in the United States, displays the strongest negative relationship between medical density and relative physician income of the entire sample (see Figure 3.4). Conversely, government involvement does not guarantee more "reasonable" outcomes. For one, the United Kingdom with its National Health Service constitutes the one instance apart from the United States where relative physician incomes increased in spite of a (albeit small) growth of supply. In addition, they remained stable in spite of sizable supply growth in France (see Figure 3.3), a country where the government negotiates fees for ambulatory care services (Döhler and Hassenteufel, 1995). This stability points to a failure of the French government to take advantage of its monopsony power in its dealings with several competing medical associations.

In conclusion, the present attempt to identify the effects of cartelization of medicine using international comparisons must be deemed a mixed success. The idea was to split up a medical association's market power into its ability to shift out the residual demand curves of its members and to rotate them in order to reduce their price elasticity. The first corresponds to the endeavor to close the market, the second to insulate association members' incomes from competitive preserves that might develop. The search for indicators that would permit to differentiate a set of industrial countries in these two aspects of power proved difficult. In particular, they are conflicting with regard to the United States and hardly give rise to the expectation to find an outlier in the following sense. Whereas US medical density increased in step with other countries from the mid-1970s to the mid-1990s, its relative physician incomes did not decline but actually continued to grow. As to the remainder of the sample, the available indicators permitted a rather successful ranking for the relative development of medical densities (power to shift residual demand curves) but a less successful ranking for the relative impacts of density of supply on relative physician income (power to rotate residual demand curves).

In future work, the channels through which medical associations influence the residual demand curves of their members need to be analyzed in greater detail. Moreover, influences competing with that of medical associations, such as development of demand, health policy initiatives by the government, and the spreading of new settings in the provision of medical care will have to be taken into account.

REFERENCES

Burstein, P. L., & Cromwell, J. (1985). Relative incomes and rates of return for US physicians. *Journal of Health Economics*, *4*, 63–78.

Carlton, D. W., & Perloff, J. M. (2000). *Modern Industrial Organization*, 3rd edition. New York: Harper Collins.

Döhler M., & Hassenteufel, P. (1995). Les politiques de régulation de l'assurance maladie en France et en Allemagne. *Revue française d'administration publique*, *76*, 549–560.

Dranove, D., & Satterthwaite, M. (1992). Monopolistic competition when price and quality are imperfectly observable. *Rand Journal of Economics*, *23*(4), 518–534.

Dranove, D., & Wehner, P. (1993). Physician-induced demand for childbirths. Unpublished manuscript, Evanston: Department of Management and Strategy, Kellogg Graduate School of Management, Northwestern University.

Evans, R. G. (1974). Supplier-induced demand: Some empirical evidence and implications. In: Mark Perlman (ed.), *The Economics of Health and Medical Care* (pp. 162–173). London: MacMillan.

Friedman, M., & Kuznets, S. (1954). *Income From Independent Professional Practice*. New York: National Bureau of Economic Research.

Gaynor, M. (1994). Issues in the industrial organization of the market for physician services. Working paper series, NBER 4695.

Gaynor, M., & Vogt, W. B. (1999). Antitrust and competition in health care markets. Working paper series, NBER 7112.

Hamilton, J. D. (1994). *Time Series Analysis*. Princeton NJ: Princeton University Press.

Hay, G. A., & Kelley, D. (1974). An empirical survey of price fixing conspiracies. *Journal of Law and Economics*, *17*(1), 13–38.

Immergut, E. M. (1992). *Health Politics: Interests and Institutions in Western Europe*. Cambridge: Cambridge University Press.

Kenkel, D. (1990). Consumer health information and the demand for medical care. *Review of Economics and Statistics*, *72*(4), 587–595.

Kessel, R. (1958). Price discrimination in medicine. *Journal of Law and Economics*, *1*(2), 20–53.

Labelle, R., Stoddart, G. G., & Rice, T. (1994). A re-examination of the meaning and importance of supplier-induced demand. *Journal of Health Economics 13*(3), 347–368.

Lin, P., Raj, B., Sandfort, M., & Slottje, D. (2000). The US antitrust system and recent trends in antitrust enforcement. *Journal of Economic Surveys*, *14*(3), 255–306.

McCarthy, T.R. (1985). The competitive nature of the primary-care physician services market. *Journal of Health Economics, 4*(2), 93–117.

Mechanic, D. (1991). Sources of countervailing power in medicine. *Journal of Health Politics, Policy and Law, 16*(3), 485–498.

Noether, M. (1986a). The effect of government policy changes on the supply of physicians: Expansion of a competitive fringe. *Journal of Law and Economics, 29*(2), 231–262.

Noether, M. (1986b). The growing supply of physicians: Has the market become more competitive? *Journal of Labor Economics, 4*(4), 503–537.

Prais, S. J. & Winsten, C. B. (1954). Trend estimators and serial correlation. Cowles Commission discussion paper, no. 383, Chicago.

Reinhardt, U. (1985). The theory of physician-induced demand: Reflections after a decade. *Journal of Health Economics, 4*(2), 187–193.

Scherer, F. M., & David, R. (1990). *Industrial Market Structure and Economic Performance.* Boston: Houghton Mifflin Company.

Stigler, J. G. (1964). The theory of oligopoly. *Journal of Political Economy, 72.*

Wolinsky, A. (1993). Competition in a market for informed experts' services. *Rand Journal of Economics, 24*(3), 380–398.

Zweifel, P., & Eichenberger, R. (1992). The political economy of corporatism in medicine: Self-regulation or cartel management? *Journal of Regulatory Economics, 4*(1), 89–108.

Zweifel, P., Lyttkens, C. H., & Söderström, L. (eds) (1998). *Regulation of Health: Case Studies of Sweden and Switzerland.* Boston: Kluwer Academic Publishers, Developments in Health Economics and Public Policy, no 7.

Zweifel, P., & Manning, W. G. (2000). Moral hazard and consumer incentives in health care. In: A. J. Culyer and J. P. Newhouse (eds), *Handbook of Health Economics 2000* (ch 8). Amsterdam: North Holland Press.

Measuring Market Power
D. J. Slottje (editor)

CHAPTER 4

Spatial Economics and Market Definition

F. M. SCHERER

Department of Economics, Harvard University, Cambridge, MA 02138

Abstract

This chapter contains extracts from testimony I presented in April 1972 in connection with a proposed brewing company merger that had been challenged under the antitrust laws. The testimony is noteworthy because, to the best of my knowledge, it was the first application of an approach to market definition adopted a decade later in new "Merger Guidelines" issued by the Antitrust Division of the Department of Justice.[1] Whether my testimony was considered by the DoJ staff in the deliberations that led to the 1982 Guidelines, or whether we converged independently on an approach that in my opinion is essentially correct, I do not know.

Keywords: Market definition, brewing industry
JEL Classification: L40, L66

---

[1] US Department of Justice, *Merger Guidelines* (Washington: June 14, 1982).

4.1. INTRODUCTION

This chapter contains extracts from testimony I presented in April 1972 in connection with a proposed brewing company merger that had been challenged under the antitrust laws. The testimony is noteworthy because, to the best of my knowledge, it was the first application of an approach to market definition adopted a decade later in new "Merger Guidelines" issued by the Antitrust Division of the Department of Justice. Whether my testimony was considered by the DoJ staff in the deliberations that led to the 1982 Guidelines, or whether we converged independently on an approach that in my opinion is essentially correct, I do not know.

The approach taken in my testimony was rooted in the logic of spatial economics — an area seldom covered in any depth by graduate economic theory courses. I for one was largely innocent of the subject as I began work on a major research project, supported by the National Science Foundation, attempting to explain why business firms often operate numerous plants, many or all of which are too small to realize known economies of scale.[2] It was clear from the outset that solving the puzzle required strong foundations in the logic of plant location in geographic space, to which the most important early contributions were made by Johann Heinrich von Thünen, Alfred Weber, and August Lösch. I gave myself a crash course in the subject and applied the theory to the evidence collected through our research, including interviews with 125 companies operating in twelve industries and six nations — the United States, Canada, Germany, the United Kingdom, France, and Sweden. Twenty-seven of the interviews were accompanied by on-site plant inspections, contradicting Wassily Leontief's definition, in a 1961 lecture at Harvard, of an industrial organization economist as a person who has never been inside a factory.

One of the twelve industries covered by our research was the brewing industry. Among the companies we visited was the Associated Brewing Company, whose headquarters were located in Detroit, not far from my Ann Arbor, Michigan, home. It was clear from the interview that Associated's plants were too small to be efficient and also technologically obsolescent. The two attributes were related, since the newest brewing technology required plant scales much larger than Associated could achieve, given its brand mix and geographic reach. One of the most important findings from our research was that brand-specific production volumes were often at least as important to the realization of minimum costs as

---

[2] The principal outcome was a book, co-authored with Alan Beckenstein, Erich Kaufer, and R. Dennis Murphy, *The Economics of Multi-Plant Operation: An International Comparisons Study* (Harvard University Press: 1976).

were plant scales. Associated's brand mix was highly fragmented, again causing a loss of scale economies. Not surprisingly, the company was doing poorly financially. I felt sympathy for the chief executive officer, Herb Epstein, who had inherited his position from his father and who, it seemed to me, would have been happier working in philosophy, in which he had a master's degree from the University of Michigan, than as head of a failing brewing enterprise.

It was therefore gratifying to read in the newspaper a year after my interview that Associated planned to merge with the G. Heileman Brewing Company, which was one of the most successful "second-tier" US brewers at the time. But a few weeks later my pleasure turned to anger when I read that the merger was being challenged by the Department of Justice. I promptly wrote a letter to Herb Epstein telling him that I thought the government's challenge must be ill-founded and asking whether I could be of help. Remarkably, the letter was delivered the next day, and on that afternoon, I received a telephone call from Herb saying in effect, "Yes, you can help us. We're in preliminary injunction hearings before Judge DeMascio right now. Could you testify the day after tomorrow?" I visited an Ann Arbor supermarket that evening to compile price information, drove to Detroit the next day to plan my testimony with Associated's attorneys, and the day after that was on the witness stand for my first testimony ever in an antitrust case, or, for that matter, any legal proceeding. Preparing to testify was quick and easy because, through my research, I already had extensive information on brewing costs, US brewery locations and new construction trends, and transportation costs. And equally importantly, my research had disclosed the appropriate conceptual framework.

The central question of market definition for the purpose of analyzing mergers under antitrust law is, "What if the merger increases the pricing discretion of the merger partners? By how much might they increase their prices before their price-raising efforts would be rendered unprofitable because they induce competition from more distant producers who, at the higher prices, can afford to bear the costs of transporting product into the affected territory?" Government witnesses had attempted to define the relevant market as individual states within which Associated or Heileman made sales and also as an eight-state area within which their principal breweries were located. My analysis showed that just outside the areas encompassed by the government's proposed market definitions were large, efficient breweries that could, in the wake of increased local prices, ship large quantities of beer into the those areas. Thus, the geographic areas proposed by the government were too narrowly drawn to be relevant markets for the purposes of assessing the state of actual and potential competition.

In previous cases the US Supreme Court had adopted what might charitably be called a cavalier approach to market definition, observing in one brewing merger case that "Congress did not seem to be troubled about the exact spot competition might be lessened" and accepting in that case, followed by a district court in another brewing merger challenge, state boundaries as relevant market delineators.[3] In the Heileman–Associated case, Judge DeMascio bestowed upon me a "nice try" prize for offering "sophisticated economic testimony," but bowed to the weight of precedent and adopted as relevant markets both individual states and the entire eight-state area.[4] Concluding that market shares in individual states were sufficient to find the merger contrary to Clayton Act Section 7, he nevertheless rejected the government's plea for a preliminary injunction because Associated's economic viability (a point on which I also testified) was deemed to be "negligible" and the company might fail while an injunction was binding. He therefore urged the parties to negotiate an asset divestiture plan that would preserve competition and Associated's competitive presence. Token brand divestitures were agreed upon and Heileman was then allowed to acquire Associated's plants and most of its brands. A change in the Supreme Court's membership two years later led to new decisions placing more emphasis on careful economic analysis in market delineation questions,[5] setting the stage for the Department of Justice Merger Guidelines in 1982.

My theoretical and empirical research on the economics of multi-plant operation revealed that ascertaining the intensity of competition among physically differentiated *brands* was conceptually similar to ascertaining the intensity of competition among plants separated from another by geographic distance. These insights were incorporated in the 1980 revision of my industrial organization textbook.[6] For plants separated by geographic distance, the variable determining the degree to which they compete is transportation cost. For products distinguished by differences in physical attributes and/or brand image, the analogous variable is the willingness of consumers to substitute one variant for the other. Drawing upon the insights from my multi-plant research, my 1980 textbook revision used rather similar diagrams to illustrate these two facets of new entrant competition. Steeply sloping functions across either geographic or product characteristics space imply low substitutability; "flat" functions imply high substitutability. The 1982 Department of Justice Merger Guidelines recognized

---

[3] *US v. Pabst Brewing Co.*, 384 US 546, 549 (1966); and *US v. Joseph Schlitz Brewing Co.*, 253 F. Supp. 129 (1966).

[4] *US v. G. Heileman Brewing Co.* et al., Civil Action No. 38162, US District Court for the Eastern District of Michigan (1972).

[5] Notably, *US v. General Dynamics Corp.* et al., 415 US 486 (1974); and *US v. Marinebancorporation*, 418 US 602 (1974).

[6] F. M. Scherer, *Industrial Market Structure and Economic Performance* (2nd edition; Chicago: Rand McNally, 1980), especially pp. 252–258 and 393–398.

similarly that determining which plants competed in a meaningfully defined geographic market was conceptually identical to determining which differentiated products should be included within a meaningfully defined product market. In each case, one asked, "What if the merger makes it possible to implement price increases? Will such price increases nullify transportation or substitution 'frictions' sufficiently to stimulate inroads from 'more distant' sources that undermine the profitability of the price increase?"

Implicit in this formulation of the question, seldom if ever made explicit, is a basic value judgment: how large a price increase can the merging parties implement before they run afoul of either antitrust constraints or inroads from more "distant" competition? In my *Associated Brewing* testimony, I answered the question arbitrarily, without addressing the value tradeoff explicitly, by focusing on the shipping costs over a 350-mile radius, i.e., eight cents for beer sold previously at a dollar, or 8%. The 1982 Department of Justice Merger Guidelines also resolved the question arbitrarily, announcing that "as a first approximation, the Department will hypothesize a price increase of 5% and ask how many buyers would be likely to shift to the other products (or how many [more distant] sellers could sell the product to localized customers) within one year."[7] What this says is that a value judgment has been made allowing the merging firms to be sufficiently unconstrained by more distant competition that they can raise their prices by up to 5%, but that the ability to effect price increases in excess of 5% without outside competitive constraint constitutes an unacceptable degree of merger-attributed monopoly power. Ideally, the decision would weigh the consequences of permitting mergers which in fact enhance monopoly power significantly against the consequences of erroneously prohibiting mergers that pose no serious monopoly problem and might (but might not) have efficiency advantages. But this was not done in the 1982 Merger Guidelines and is still done at best imperfectly.

That the price elevation value judgment might be resolved differently is shown by an experience I had in a 1981 merger antitrust case. Mobil Oil Corporation proposed to acquire Marathon Oil — a merger Marathon opposed. I was witness for Marathon in the preliminary injunction hearing before the Federal District Court in Cleveland. The key issue again was, how should the relevant geographic markets be defined? George Stigler, testifying economist for Mobil, favored a nationwide market definition; I argued for localized markets surrounding petroleum product pipeline terminals. Drawing circles around hypothetical localized markets and calculating the transportation costs from sources on the periphery

---

[7] *Merger Guidelines*, pp. 4 (for product markets) and 8 (for geographic markets).

of those circles, as I did in the Associated Brewing case, was infeasible, because the principal means of petroleum product transportation is the pipeline, the network of pipelines is much less extensive than the network of highways connecting breweries to their potential markets, and transportation costs vary widely with the size of the available pipeline. What the evidence showed was that price differentials between major metropolitan areas of one to two cents per gallon, or a bit less than 1 to 2% of retail gasoline prices, persisted for substantial periods of time.[8] Larger differentials, it appeared, could not persist because product would be shipped from low-price to higher-price territories and arbitrage away the differentials. The question presented to the court was therefore, is the ability to sustain prices 1 or 2% higher in one locality (because of local market structural conditions) than in another sufficient to be of concern from the perspective of the anti-merger laws? The district court concluded that price differences of this magnitude were economically significant, weighed in comparison to petroleum refiners' profit margins (two to four cents per gallon in good years). The court concluded tentatively that markets should be defined at the state level rather than nationally, and, pending a full hearing on the merits, that the merger should be preliminarily enjoined.[9] Thus, in the Mobil–Marathon case, a tougher price increase threshold was accepted than the one I used in the Associated Brewing case and the one accepted in the Merger Guidelines a half year later.

The excerpts from my testimony in the Associated Brewing case follow. They begin with a "balloon" question from the attorney for Associated.

4.2. TESTIMONY

Q: [Mr Cutler] Can you tell us your view of the state of competition in the brewing industry?

A: Let me point out one absolutely important economic fact about the brewing industry. Beer is unfortunately about 90% water. In order to get it to market you have to ship it. Compared to most industrial commodities it is expensive to ship. ... I have developed fairly extensive data on the cost of transporting various commodities. Suppose we wanted to transport an

---

[8] See F. M. Scherer, "Merger in the Petroleum Industry: The *Mobil-Marathon* Case," in John E. Kwoka Jr, and Lawrence J. White, eds, *The Antitrust Revolution* (Glenview: Scott, Foresman, 1989), pp. 19–45.

[9] *Marathon Oil Co. v. Mobil Oil Corporation* et al., Northern District of Ohio, 530 F. Supp. 315, 322, 326 (1981).

average shipment of beer say from Chicago to Cleveland. That is a distance of about 350 miles. This is in 1963. For a dollar's worth of beer at the brewery door it would cost you eight cents to ship it in a truckload quantity to Cleveland. . . . If you wanted to ship it to New York, you incur much more substantial transportation cost, about 17 cents on the dollar.

Q: There is a map over on the board that has not been marked. May we have that marked as an exhibit?

Judge DeMascio: All right. Received.

Q: What does that map tell us? Tell us what you have done.

A: What I have done is indicated with solid triangles the locations of all the plants of the defendants.

Q: What is the hatched line around there?

A: The hatched line designates the eight-state territory about which the government in its various briefs has talked — i.e., Minnesota, Wisconsin, Iowa, Illinois, Michigan, Indiana, Ohio, and Kentucky.

Q: You have read the government's briefs and affidavits by Mr. Dobson?

A: Yes. I have indicated, as stated before, with solid triangles the breweries of the defendants. [*Indicating on map*] We have for Associated Evansville, Indiana; and St. Paul, Minnesota. For Heileman we have Newport, Kentucky; LaCrosse, Wisconsin; and Sheboygan, Wisconsin.

I wanted to give the general feeling for the geographical layout of the plants. And I refer to the new ultra-modern breweries of the national companies. Important plants are shown by dotted circles. We all know that Schlitz has its home brewery in Milwaukee; Pabst is there; Miller is there; and Anheuser-Busch has its home brewery, the biggest in the United States, in St. Louis. OK, what about the new breweries? Here is Winston-Salem, with 4.4 million barrels of capacity. Here is a new brewery in Memphis, Tennessee. . . . Here we have Anheuser-Busch in Columbus, Ohio, 2 million barrels capacity; the Pabst brewery in north central Georgia, with I believe one and one half million barrels capacity. These are 1969 figures. Pabst has enlarged it since then.

But here is the key point. The new breweries of Schlitz, Anheuser-Busch and Pabst are very efficient relative to old traditional breweries, and they are in a very good striking distance relative to the territories that are served by the defendants.

Q: Those breweries, at least some of them, are outside of your hatched area?

A: That's right. Let me make a mark here. [*Indicating on map*] To ship a dollar's worth of beer from the back door of the brewery to, let us say, 350 miles would cost about eight cents. Now, that is a transportation cost that any good efficient brewery can easily afford. It is quite easy when you have a premium price image.

Let's see what Schlitz can do beginning with 1969. That was when Winston-Salem was opened. . . . I am drawing a radius of 350 miles, Your Honor, indicating a 350-mile shipment. They clearly can ship more from Winston-Salem; they can penetrate more than half of Ohio very strongly, and they expand to bracket the Heileman plant and most of eastern Kentucky. Indeed, they can ship farther if they want to, and they can quite easily with eight cents on the dollar ship in large quantities to southern Ohio and eastern Kentucky.

Now, Columbus for Anheuser-Busch has a radius that covers Ohio, most of Michigan, and most of Illinois, and gives it a good low-cost delivery.

Q: As I understand, neither Associated nor Heileman has a plant in Ohio?

A: No. Heileman has a plant south of Cincinnati at Newport, Kentucky.

Finally, let's look at the Memphis plant of Schlitz. That is opening this year. We haven't seen what it can do, except that we know about its efficiency.

Q: That is 4.4 million —

A: 4.4 million barrels per year, yes. Memphis can cover the southern half of Illinois and bracket Associated's Evansville brewery, and can ship beer inexpensively into eastern Kentucky, where Associated is very strong. It can ship beer inexpensively into southern Indiana. It is going to be a tremendous competitive threat when it moves into this territory, into which previously Schlitz could not ship as readily.

Now, 4.4 million barrels of capacity are suddenly becoming available in this area. What can you expect? You can expect a very intensive advertising campaign, beginning probably about the time of the Olympics, sponsored by Schlitz, and you can expect Old Milwaukee to move into the market, below the sub-premium brand price level, so that the older high-cost breweries cannot make beer and deliver it at that price.

There is a further aspect. Schlitz used to ship fair amounts of beer from Milwaukee into these territories, but now it has a nice efficient brewery in Memphis for the territory, so Milwaukee will be freed up in its capacity.

Q: What do you mean?

A: I would start shipping and advertising the Schlitz brand heavily in the St. Paul area and Iowa area and again selling my fighting brand, Old Milwaukee. I will be selling that vigorously in terms of price competition. I would expect Schlitz, which has not done very well in the Minnesota area thus far, to increase marketing in Minnesota and Iowa to the detriment of

Heileman and Associated and other regional breweries such as Hamms and Grain Belt.

. . .

A: One obvious aspect of [the market definition question] is just to look at this map. If you look at this map, what you find is —
Q: Let's put it up.
[The map is put up.]
A: It is a very curious thing. One curious thing is that the defined markets are all said to be states. But geography suggests that it can't be. By some odd quirk of nature, almost all of these breweries are on state lines. . . . As we have seen, the brewery business is a business of transporting products. Efficient plants can transport products at least 500 miles, while a plant with high cost has trouble transporting more than 250 miles. All of these markets cover state lines. St. Paul, right near state lines; Heileman at LaCrosse, right near a state line; South Bend and Detroit not far from state lines; Heileman brewery just south of Ohio; Evansville brewery north of Kentucky and across the border from Illinois. The obvious ranges of shipment for these plants are multi-state. When we define markets in economics we take into account the ability to interpenetrate each others' territories, and these circles show that there is a great deal of actual and potential interpenetration. Both have importance. Actual penetration may be shown by the kinds of [state] concentration figures Mr Dobson presented. At some moment in time somebody is going to be number one and somebody is going to be number two and three and so on. The brewing industry tends to lead to large shares. The key factor is this: as long as all of these companies, and I have counted 15 sizeable companies operating large numbers of breweries in this territory — 15 not counting the defendants — operate breweries here, all with intersecting shipment radii, the companies have an opportunity to interpenetrate each others' markets.
Q: You have to consider all of that to determine what is competition?
A: You have to consider actual and potential interpenetration, and it so happens that the breweries are arranged over the map in such a way that almost all penetrate several different state "markets." I think there is one further very important point. What after all is Section 7 of the Clayton Act all about? It is trying to preserve competition and prevent monopoly. What is monopoly?
Mr Dobey: Objection, Your Honor. I don't think he should be permitted to testify as to what Section 7 means.

[Procedural squabbling]

Q: What does an economist look at when he is trying to evaluate the nature of competition?

Judge DeMascio: Incidentally, I know what you are getting at. That is the reason I sustained the objection prior to the break.

Q: Strictly from an economist's standpoint, not a lawyer's standpoint?

A: What an economist looks at when he examines a situation that may contain a monopoly is the ability to raise prices; that is, to raise prices above the costs of doing business. That is what the whole thing is about.

Q: How does that tie into our case?

A: In trying to define what the relevant market is one has to ask the question, does a seller in some territory, or do a group of sellers in some territory, have the ability to raise prices above their cost of doing business and keep those prices there? That is the relevance to the question of market definition. That is what we are interested in. We are interested in defining the market in such a way as to answer the question: can the sellers in this territory, if they get a large enough share of the territory's sales, can they, by virtue of their large share of those sales, raise prices above the cost of doing business? That is the key question.

Q: How did you answer that question in relation to what the government has defined as the geographic market?

A: The relevance is this. At any moment in time, say the year 1971, which I believe was the year on which Mr Dobson's memorandum focused, it may well be that certain sellers have a large share of some state's sales. That is an important thing to look at. That is an interesting thing to look at. But the problem of market definition is this: suppose they do get a large share of the sales in, let us say, a state. Does that give them the ability to raise prices above the cost of doing business? That is what market definition is all about. It seems to me that the state-wide market definition is really too narrow in this case.

Consider, for example, the state of Illinois. I don't know who the leading sellers are in the state of Illinois. I suspect from Mr Dobson's memorandum that whoever the top four are, they have a pretty high share of the "market." What if they tried to exploit their high share of Illinois sales by raising prices? That is the key question.

Here we have 15 companies all pretty well able to penetrate various states in this whole eight-state area in response to some kind of price stimulus. If the price is raised, that will stimulate, let us say, Memphis to start shipping beer more and more to the north in response to the profit opportunity. That will stimulate Falstaff on the far border of Iowa to ship beer into Illinois. It will certainly stimulate Duquesne or Pittsburgh Brewing Company to begin shipping more beer westward in response to that price stimulus.

Thus, in that critical respect, when there are brewers with quite feasible shipping radii who are able, even though they don't sell currently, as soon as firms try to raise the price, the Illinois sales territory becomes interesting, and one transports beer in response to that price stimulus.

As soon as somebody tries to raise the price, that will bring beer flowing toward the raised price and create a competitive situation that will make it difficult to sustain the increased price.

Q: Do I understand that potential competition keeps the lid on prices?

A: That's right. If someone tries to raise the price significantly above the cost, then that will make it feasible for other companies who may not be doing much in the particular area at the specific moment in time, but that will enable them to absorb additional transportation cost to bring their products to bear in that territory. That is the reason that I counted 15, not including the defendants; 17 in all. There are many sellers in a position by virtue of their ability to transport beer at least 350 or 400 miles, if the stimulus is there, to be competitive in these various state territories. Therefore I believe in general that the state market definition tends to be too narrow and has to be broadened.

I have not done a sufficient study to tell you positively what the relevant market ought to be, but I believe that in most cases the state market definition is too narrow and does not reflect the full potentialities of competition.[10]

---

[10] US Department of Justice, *Merger Guidelines* (Washington: June 14, 1982).

Measuring Market Power
D. J. Slottje (editor)

CHAPTER 5

Market Power and Simultaneous Recoupment in the Maryland: Medical Electronic Claim Submission Market

DAVID I. ROSENBAUM* and JOHN P. LENICH

University of Nebraska-Lincoln, Lincoln, NE 68588–0489

Abstract

Physicians use electronic connectivity services (ECS) as an intermediary to facilitate the filing of medical claims with insurance companies. Traditionally ECS providers charge both doctors and insurers to recover their total costs. In 1993, EDS purchased Blue Cross Blue Shield of Maryland's ECS business. Soon after its purchase, EDS began a pricing campaign that would allow it to capture the growing Maryland ECS market for itself. It did so by charging doctors nothing for ECS and by charging Blue Cross, the primary insurer in the state, a fee well above cost. This high fee was not available to any other ECS provider. The effect of this pricing scheme was to foreclose other ECS providers from the market. Information from a private antitrust case supports the conclusion that EDS had market power. Further, that information supports the conclusion that EDS's pricing scheme was exclusionary. EDS was clearly selling below cost and such selling only made sense if EDS made appreciable gains in market share.

JEL Classification: K21, L41, L89
Keywords: Market power, Medical claims, Healthcare industry

* Corresponding author.

5.1. INTRODUCTION

When a physician serves a patient covered by insurance, the physician may submit a claim to the insurance company for payment. One option available for submitting claims is electronic submission. An electronic claims submission (ECS) vendor provides the physician's office with the software necessary to connect the physician with the vendor's claim clearinghouse. The physician's office enters data about a claim into its computer and electronically sends that data to the clearinghouse. The clearinghouse ensures that a claim is valid, checks that all the requisite information is present, formats the claim as required and submits it to the intended insurance provider. The insurer replies to the clearinghouse about the claim, and the clearinghouse redirects the payment to the original physician.

Electronic connectivity service involves, among other things, establishing a computer connection between a physician's office, the clearinghouse and the various payers. It also involves either selling software to physicians who do not have practice management systems, or specifying to practice management vendors the formats they need to incorporate into their practice management systems to allow the provider to transmit claims from desktop to clearinghouse. Because the electronic submission of claims reduces errors, paperwork and copying, it reduces both the physicians' cost of submitting claims and the third party payer's cost of processing and paying claims.

In the early 1990s, a number of firms, including Blue Cross Blue Shield of Maryland (BCBSM), provided electronic connectivity service (ECS) in Maryland. Blue Cross was the largest ECS provider in the state at that time.[1] In 1993, EDS purchased Blue Cross's ECS business. Soon after its purchase, EDS adopted a new pricing strategy and provided its services to physicians free of charge. It was able to do this and still turn a profit because BCBSM agreed to pay EDS an inflated fee for many of the claims that were filed through EDS. EDS's pricing strategy — which we call "simultaneous recoupment" — was not predatory pricing in the classical sense; EDS did not initially incur losses by providing its services to physicians at no cost. But EDS's strategy was arguably anticompetitive nonetheless.

We will explain how that strategy allowed EDS to eliminate its competitors and obtain market power in the growing Maryland ECS market. We will first discuss the market, EDS's entry into the market, and EDS's pricing strategy. We will then discuss the private antitrust case that Herbert Martello, one of EDS's

---

[1] Amended Complaint, Notice to Plead & Amended Prayer, § 6, *Marello v. Blue Cross and Blue Shield of Maryland, Inc.*, No. 94 CV 9007 (Md. Cir. Ct. Balt. County).

competitors has, so far unsuccessfully, brought against EDS and BCBSM. Martello raised a number of claims in that case, including claims for conspiracy to restrain trade and for conspiracy to monopolize. We believe that these may be the most promising claims for challenging agreements that facilitate simultaneous recoupment.

Although conspiracy to restrain trade and conspiracy to monopolize are legally distinct claims, they nevertheless raise similar issues. Those issues include, among others, market power and anticompetitive effect. After briefly summarizing the law, we will discuss the relevant product and geographic markets. We will then turn to market power. Courts and economists generally define market power as the power to raise price above a competitive level.[2] Courts define monopoly power (which is a high degree of market power) as the power to control price and exclude competition.[3]

The evidence available to us suggests that EDS has a high degree of market power. We will first discuss intrinsic barriers to entry into the ECS market and then look more closely at EDS's power in the market by discussing the number of competitors in the market and EDS's share of the market. We will then address EDS's power to raise prices and to exclude competitors.

We will turn to the issue of anticompetitive effects in the last section of this chapter. We believe that simultaneous recoupment is a form of predation. Normally, predation involves short-run losses to exclude competitors and gain market power and with it, the ability to recoup long-run excess profits. In this case, EDS could indefinitely exclude competitors and simultaneously garner excess profits. The model developed in the appendix supports the conclusion that both the purpose and effect of EDS's pricing strategy was to gain control of the Maryland ECS market.

5.2. BLUE CROSS BLUE SHIELD OF MARYLAND AND EDS

Blue Cross Blue Shield of Maryland (BCBSM) provides, among other things, health insurance and claim handling (or processing) services for other third party payers. Claim handling involves determining whether a medical services provider has a valid claim for payment by a specific third party payer and the amount for which the third party payer is responsible. For example, when a

---

[2] *See, e.g., CDC Techs., Inc. v. IDEXX Labs., Inc.,* 186 F.3d 74, 71 (2d Cir. 1999); *Angelico v. Lehigh Valley Hospital, Inc.,* 184 F.3d 268, 276 (3d Cir. 1999); Campbell R. McConnell & Stanley L. Brue, *Economics* 170 (11th edn. McGraw Hill: 1990).

[3] *See, e.g., United States v. E.I. duPont de Nemours & Co.,* 351 US 377, 391 (1956).

physician files a Medicare claim, the third party administrator first determines if the service is covered by Medicare, correlates the service to a Health Care Financing Administration (HCFA) fee schedule for that Medicare region, verifies the eligibility of the insured, arranges payment to the physician, and then informs the insured of the payment.

In 1993, BCBSM was the third party payer for HCFA. HCFA Medicare payments at the time accounted for approximately 25% of all the revenue physicians nationwide earned from the practice of medicine.[4] In 1993, BCBSM processed claims for HCFA that totaled approximately US$2.5 billion.[5] Over the period 1990–1993, BCBSM earned annual revenues of approximately US$22.3 million in return for the third party administration services it provided to HCFA.[6]

BCBSM was also among the largest suppliers of private health insurance and private third party administrative services in Maryland in 1993. The GAO reported in April 1994 that BCBSM had a 35.2% share of the Maryland private insurance market as of June 30, 1993.[7] As a result of BCBSM's strength in these businesses and its role as the third party administrator for HCFA, physicians who practiced in Maryland could expect to submit claims to BCBSM and to earn a substantial share of their revenues from the claims BCBSM processed.

Prior to 1993, LifeCard, a BCBSM subsidiary, was in the business of providing electronic connectivity services. Although BCBSM withdrew from that business after incurring significant losses, it had an interest in continuing to encourage physicians to submit their claims electronically because electronic claims reduce an administrator's cost of processing (as well as a physician's cost of submitting) claims.[8]

EDS is a multi-product firm that provides, among other things, electronic connectivity services and third party claims administration for HCFA in many other geographic locations throughout the United States. EDS provides a variety of services including systems support, systems integration and management including network management, systems development and electronic commerce. It provides services to many state Medicaid programs, major insurance companies and similar type entities, public and private employer groups, pharmaceutical management firms and Medicare programs in a number of states and

---

[4] See *Physician Marketplace Statistics 1993*, Table 91 (Martin L. Gomez, ed., American Medical Association, 1993).

[5] *BCBSM 1993 Annual Statement.*

[6] Affidavit of Cindy Chandler, March 18, 1999, *Martello v. Blue Cross and Blue Shield of Maryland*, No. 94 CV 9007 (Md. Cir. Ct. Balt. County).

[7] US General Accounting Office, *Blue Cross and Blue Shield: Experiences of Weak Plans Underscore the Role of Effective State Oversight* 35 (GAO/HEHS-94–71 April 13, 1994).

[8] Cost savings related to electronic submission are discussed in section 5.5.

other geographical areas. The latter includes administrative program management services and Medicare Part B services for entities in a number of states.

In February of 1993 EDS purchased BCBSM's LifeCard business. This made EDS the largest ECS provider in Maryland. As part of that purchase agreement, BCBSM agreed to pay EDS 65¢ for every BCBSM and Medicare part B claim that was filed with BCBSM via the EDS system. The 65¢ was well above EDS's average total cost and well above prices in other regional markets.

But that was not the only positive development from EDS's standpoint. In July of 1993 the Maryland Legislature passed a law mandating that health care practitioners in Maryland submit claims electronically rather than by paper.[9] The law empowered the Maryland Health Care Access and Cost Commission (HCACC) to establish a target date for implementation. HCACC established the first target date as July 1, 1995.[10] Therefore, EDS could expect significant growth in the number of claims filed between 1993 and July 1, 1995.

Consider EDS's position in September of 1993. EDS was being paid 65 cents by BCBSM for every BCBSM and Medicare part B claim that was filed. It expected the Maryland market to grow significantly in the next two years. EDS could have increased its short-run profits by charging Maryland physicians for every claim submitted via ECS. If EDS had charged a competitive price to physicians, EDS would have lost some of the growing market to other ECS providers. Instead, beginning September 1, 1993, EDS charged Maryland physicians a price equal to zero for every BCBSM and Medicare part B electronic claim the physicians submitted to EDS. This had two effects. First, by charging physicians a price equal to zero, EDS had the best chance of capturing all physicians converting to electronic submission. Second, a price equal to zero would be the most effective price in forcing all other ECS providers out of the market.

Under a classical predation scheme, a firm begins by pricing below cost. This forces competitors to exit and allows the firm to capture most if not all of the market. The predator then raises price and recoups forgone profits. EDS's pricing strategy was different. Its zero price to doctors allows EDS to capture the market, while the 65¢ payment from BCBSM allows EDS simultaneously to recoup profits forgone from doctors. EDS had no need to raise price in the future because it simultaneously recouped from BCBSM the revenues forgone with its zero pricing to doctors. In essence, the zero pricing/simultaneous recoupment strategy was an equilibrium long-run strategy for EDS to pursue. The zero price allowed EDS continually to have the best chance to expel competitors and capture market

---

[9] Md. Health-Gen. Code Ann. § 19–135 (a)(5)-(6) (2000).
[10] Maryland Health Care Commission, *2000 Electronic Data Interchange Progress Report 3* (available at www.mhcc.state.md.us).

growth. The 65¢ payment from BCBSM allowed EDS simultaneously to recoup revenues forgone from physicians.

5.3. THE MARTELLO LITIGATION

In 1994, Herbert Martello, one of EDS's competitors, filed suit against EDS in Maryland state court. After some initial skirmishing, Martello filed an amended complaint in which he asserted a state law tort claim and three antitrust claims: horizontal market allocation, conspiracy to restrain trade, and monopolization. He asserted those three claims under the Maryland antitrust laws,[11] which, like many state antitrust laws, are worded differently than the federal antitrust laws but are construed much the same way.[12] The cases under the federal antitrust laws therefore provided the analytical framework that the Maryland courts used in evaluating Martello's claims.

Martello's horizontal market allocation claim was based on the noncompetition clause in the 1993 contract for the sale of LifeCard. Martello alleged that EDS agreed not to compete with BCBSM in the market for the third party insurance administration services and that BCBSM agreed not to compete with EDS in the market for electronic connectivity services. In other words, Martello alleged that they allocated the market for third party insurance administration services to BCBSM and allocated the market for electronic connectivity services to EDS.

Martello's restraint of trade claim was based on BCBSM's refusal to deal with Martello on substantially the same terms that it dealt with EDS. Martello alleged that the refusal to deal was not a unilateral decision on the part of BCBSM but was instead the result of a concerted decision on the part of BCBSM and EDS. According to Martello, BCBSM agreed to pay EDS 65¢ for each claim it submitted to BCBSM and not to pay anything to other providers of electronic connectivity services. BCBSM also agreed to provide EDS with computer access and linkage at or above industry standards but not to provide the same to other firms offering electronic connectivity services.

The effect of BCBSM's refusal to deal was to eliminate competition in the market for electronic connectivity services, primarily because it allowed EDS to offer its services to medical providers at a price that none of its competitors could match: zero. EDS was therefore able to engage in what effectively amounted to

---

[11] Md. Comm. L. Code Ann. §§ 11–201 to 11–213 (2000).
[12] Md. Comm. L. Code Ann. § 11–202(a)(2) (2000); *see Natural Design, Inc. v. Rouse Co.*, 485 A.2d 663, 666 (Md. 1984).

a predatory pricing campaign subsidized by BCBSM. BCBSM provided that subsidy, Martello alleged, as the quid pro quo for EDS's agreement not to compete with BCBSM in the market for the third party insurance administration services.

The same conduct formed the basis for Martello's monopolization claims, of which there were actually three: monopolization of the market for electronic connectivity services, attempted monopolization of that market and conspiracy to monopolize that market. These claims were based squarely on the theory that EDS engaged in predatory pricing when it offered its electronic connectivity at no cost. Even though BCBSM was not a participant in the market for electronic connectivity services, Martello alleged that BCBSM profited from its relationship with EDS and therefore had an economic stake in the market.

The trial court dismissed Martello's antitrust claims. On appeal, the Maryland Court of Special Appeals affirmed parts of the trial court's decision and reversed others. The Court of Special Appeals held that the trial court properly dismissed Martello's horizontal market allocation claim. While the agreement to allocate markets may have eliminated competition between BCBSM and EDS, it did not injure Martello. Therefore, he lacked standing to challenge the agreement.[13]

The Court also held that the trial court properly dismissed Martello's monopolization and attempted monopolization claims. The Court noted that both claims were based on the theory that EDS engaged in predatory pricing. Predatory pricing has two key elements: (1) the defendant priced its products below cost; and (2) the defendant has a reasonable prospect of recoupment. The Court rejected Martello's theory of simultaneous recoupment and held that his claim was insufficient because he failed to allege recoupment in the classical sense.[14]

In doing so, the Court relied heavily on the United States Supreme Court's decision in *Brooke Group, Ltd. v. Brown & Williamson Tobacco Corp.*[15] The Supreme Court in *Brooke* held that recoupment is a necessary element of a predatory pricing claim and described predatory pricing as a two-step process: (1) pricing below cost; and (2) subsequently raising prices to a supracompetitive level to recover the losses sustained earlier. The Maryland Court of Special Appeals assumed that the Supreme Court's description of predatory pricing as a two-step process meant that all predatory pricing must occur in two steps. That assumption is questionable, however. The claim at issue in *Brooke* involved the

---

[13] *Martello v. Blue Cross and Blue Shield of Maryland, Inc.*, No. 1837, slip op. at 39–40 (Md. Spec. App. Sept. 23, 1997).

[14] *Id.* at 60.

[15] 509 US 209 (1993).

issue of subsequent recoupment in a traditional two-step predatory pricing claim. Therefore, the issue of simultaneous recoupment was not before the Supreme Court.

Even though the Maryland Court of Special Appeals rejected Martello's monopolization and attempted monopolization claims, Martello's two conspiracy claims survived. The Court noted that neither Martello's restraint of trade claim nor his claim for conspiracy to monopolize required proof of recoupment in the classical sense.[16] On remand, however, the trial court made the mistake of believing that they did and therefore entered summary judgment against Martello.[17]

5.4. THE LEGAL STANDARDS

We do not agree that recoupment in the classical sense is necessary to support a claim of monopolization or attempted monopolization based on predatory pricing. But we will leave that matter for another day. Our purpose here is to show how agreements that facilitate simultaneous recoupment can be challenged as conspiracies in restraint of trade (Section One of the Sherman Act or its state law equivalents) and as conspiracies to monopolize (Section Two of the Sherman Act or its state law equivalents).

Section One of the Sherman Act prohibits agreements that unreasonably restrain trade. Some agreements — for example, horizontal market allocation agreements — are deemed unreasonable per se. Most are not. They are instead evaluated under the Rule of Reason. Under the Rule of Reason, an agreement is unlawful if it has substantial anticompetitive effects that outweigh its presumptive effects. Because competitive effects cannot be assessed in a vacuum, Rule of Reason analysis normally involves defining the relevant market, assessing the characteristics of the market, and evaluating the defendant's market power.[18]

Section Two of the Sherman Act prohibits among other things conspiracies to monopolize. There is some disagreement among the courts as to what has to be shown in order to establish a conspiracy to monopolize. At the very least, the parties must have: (1) entered into an agreement with the specific intent of obtaining a monopoly: and (2) committed an overt act in furtherance of a

---

[16] *Id.* at 40–43 (restraint of trade), 62 (conspiracy to monopolize).

[17] *Martello v. Blue Cross and Blue Shield of Maryland, Inc.*, No. 94 CV 9007 (Md. Cir. Ct. Balt. County March 26, 2001).

[18] For further discussion of the Rule of Reason, see William C. Holmes, *Antitrust Law Handbook* § 2:10, at 193–215 (West Group 2001).

conspiracy.[19] Many, but not all, courts require proof of the relevant market as well as proof of anticompetitive effects.[20] Although not necessary, proof of market power is relevant to the issues of specific intent and anticompetitive effect.

Agreements that facilitate simultaneous recoupment can have significant anticompetitive effects because they may allow a firm to eliminate its current competitors and to erect entry barriers against potential competitors. The likelihood of the agreement producing those effects (and thereby running afoul of the antitrust laws) depends to a great extent on the characteristics of the market and the power that the firms have. In the following sections, we will use the *Martello* case as a vehicle to illustrate the role of market definition and market power in assessing anticompetitive effects. For purposes of this discussion, we assume the existence of the agreements between BCBSM and EDS as alleged by Martello.

5.5. RELEVANT MARKET

An antitrust market can be defined as a group of goods or services that a hypothetical monopolist would need to control in order profitably to raise the price of those goods or services by a small but significant amount — perhaps 5 or 10% for a non-transitory period of time — without losing appreciable sales to competitors.[21] Antitrust markets have both a product and a geographic dimension. The product dimension encompasses all of the products that a monopolist would have to control in order profitably to raise the price without losing customers to similar alternatives the monopolist does not control. The geographic dimension encompasses all of the locations a monopolist would have to control in order profitably to raise the price without losing customers to geographically near competitors.

5.5.1. The relevant product market

After they treat insured patients, physicians submit claims for payment to third party payers such as Medicare, Medicaid, BCBSM, other private insurers, or

---

[19] *E.g., Intergraph Corp. v. Intel Corp.*, 195 F.3d 1346, 1363 (Fed. Cir. 1999); *AD/SAT v. Associated Press*, 181 F.3d 216, 233 (2d Cir. 1999).
[20] *See* 2 Julian O. von Kalinowski, Peter Sullivan and Maureen McGuirl, *Antitrust Laws and Trade Regulation* § 26.02[4], at 26–41 to 26–42 (2d ed. LexisNexis 2001).
[21] *See* United States Department of Justice, *1992 Merger Guidelines* § 1.10.

self-insured employers. Claims can be submitted either electronically or by hard copy. An ECS provider equips physicians with the software necessary to connect electronically with the ECS's central clearinghouse facilities. It then charges the physician a fee per claim to receive the claim from the physician, check it, format it accordingly and send it on to the proper insurance provider.

Claims submitted using electronic connectivity services rather than hard copy are estimated to save physicians and payers between 25¢ and US$1 per claim according to Maryland's Health Care Access and Cost Commission.[22] Electronic claim submission results in fewer errors, less administrative cost and a quicker return of fees to physicians for services rendered. In Maryland, where 7,873,908 electronic claims were processed by EDS alone in 1993, this resulted in a savings to physicians and payers of between US$1,968,500 and US$7,874,000.[23]

EDS documents show that in 1993 it had revenues from physicians on ECS services of US$740,523.[24] A 5% increase in price would increase revenues to EDS and consequently costs to physicians by approximately US$37,000. This is less than a 2% loss in the cost savings from using electronic rather than paper submission. It is doubtful that loss in cost savings would force physicians to switch back to paper submission.

EDS data show that for the first three months of 1995, EDS averaged approximately 374,000 Medicare part B claims per month.[25] At that time EDS was charging physicians nothing for each Medicare part B claim filed. In April of 1995 EDS increased its price to physicians for Medicare part B claims from zero to 32¢ per claim. Yet for the last nine months of 1995, physicians filed an average of 442,000 Medicare part B claims per month.[26] That is an increase of 18%.[27] If filing via paper were a viable alternative, EDS's sales should not have increased when it increased the price to physicians.

More to the point, in July of 1993 the Maryland Legislature passed a law mandating that health care practitioners in Maryland submit claims electronically rather than by paper.[28] Once the law went into effect, it ruled out paper submission as an alternative to electronic submission.

---

[22] *Daily Record*, March 9, 1999.

[23] EDS-provided data.

[24] *See* Joint Record Extract at E. 882, *Martello v. Blue Cross & Blue Shield of Maryland, Inc.*, No. 1837 (Md. Spec. App. Sept. Term 1996) (hereinafter cited as "Joint Record Extract").

[25] *Id.*

[26] *Id.*

[27] Note that the increase in number of claims with an increase in price does not necessarily violate the law of demand. Rather it indicates that the demand curve is shifting outward.

[28] Md. Health-Gen. Ann. Code § 19–135(a)(5)–(6) (2000).

In conclusion, a small price increase would not offset the cost savings from using electronic submission. A significant price increase was accompanied by a significant *increase* in demand. If paper submission were a likely substitute, neither of these conditions should exist. Furthermore, the Maryland Legislature removed paper submission as even an inferior alternative. Therefore, it seems reasonable to conclude that electronic connectivity service is the relevant product market.

5.5.2. The relevant geographic market

For an area to be a relevant geographic market, a hypothetical monopolist would have to be able to raise price by some small amount and not lose significant trade to firms that are located nearby.[29] That means that for Maryland to be the relevant geographic market, a hypothetical monopolist would have to be able to raise prices by 5 or 10% and not lose a significant number of physicians to an electronic connectivity service provider located in another part of the country.

Physicians' offices tend to be small and widely dispersed throughout an area. Traditionally ECS providers seek out physicians. ECS providers travel to a physician's office to explain their products. They display their products at trade shows attended by physicians. They send mailings to physicians' offices.[30] Hence, rather than physicians travelling to seek out ECS providers, ECS providers travel to a geographic market to seek out doctors.

While electronic claim submission does save physicians money, the overall expenditures on electronic connectivity services are modest in comparison to other costs and revenues. If ECS prices were to go up by say 5%, it is doubtful that a Maryland physician would spend the time and expense necessary to travel to another state to seek ECS services.

The 1988 report of LifeCard International (BCBSM's ECS division) is illustrative of the geographic scope of the market.[31] LifeCard was the predecessor of EDS's clearinghouse. The report says:

> At the inception of the Provider Network, LifeCard grossly misunderstood the marketplace. Since no research or market

---

[29] *See* United States Department of Justice, *1992 Merger Guidelines* § 1.21.

[30] In March 1993, for example, BCBSM sent a letter presumably to several physicians touting EDS's MHIN ECS service. *See* Joint Record Extract at E. 109.

[31] *See id.* at E. 311.

examination took place, the original business plan overestimates the market size. Estimates were based on total number of doctors in Maryland and did not clearly delineate non-office based physicians as well as Montgomery and Prince George counties physicians (who primarily do business with the D.C. Blue Cross Blue Shield plan). Based on the inflated figures of 15,000 physicians and lack of market understanding, LifeCard projected sales of 1500 Provider Network units in 1987 and a total of 5000 by the end of 1989.

In reality, there are approximately 1500 to 2000 potential customers in the immediate market for Provider Network. This number assumes the following:

7500 Non-Federal Office Based Providers

4700 of these physicians are in [LifeCard] primary market area (which excludes [Prince Georges] and Montgomery counties)

BCBSM's initial thought was to include all Maryland physicians in the geographic market. Upon later analysis, BCBSM itself refined its own geographic definition of the market to Maryland minus Montgomery and Prince George counties.

In conclusion, ECS providers normally travel to doctors. The savings associated with switching vendors are not great enough to warrant extensive travel and search. BCBSM itself concluded that the market consisted of Maryland minus two counties. Therefore, it seems reasonable to conclude that Maryland is certainly the outside boundary of a relevant geographic market.

5.6. BARRIERS TO ENTRY

5.6.1. Efficiencies from using one ECS provider

The typical physician's office has a computer system to facilitate practice management. Among other things, it is used for record keeping, scheduling, bookkeeping and submitting electronic claims. To submit a claim, someone in the physician's office enters the relevant data and then electronically transmits the data to a clearinghouse. Since claims to any third party payer can be submitted via one clearinghouse, a physician's office typically will have only one computer system and one ECS provider. It makes little economic sense to have a separate computer system and/or separate software so that some claims can be filed with one clearinghouse and other claims filed with a second clearinghouse. There is a cost to having a second computer. There may also be training costs for the second software system.

Electronic connectivity service providers typically charge a minimum and maximum, or a monthly or annual fee for claim submission and processing.[32] A physician's office would not want two ECS providers if one were used infrequently. In that situation, the office would pay a high average cost per claim for the infrequently used provider and could save money by converting those claims to the more generally used provider. Similarly, once the physician entered sufficient claims to reach the maximum fee from one provider, the extra cost of each additional claim filed through that provider would be zero. In that case, the physician would not want to use a second provider. As a consequence, physicians will only use one provider.

5.6.2. Specific barriers

In perfectly competitive markets it is relatively easy for firms to switch their suppliers. However, if barriers to entry exist, switching may not be so easy. The following factors are barriers to entry in this market.

1 Switching costs
If a physician's office uses electronic claims submission, then all of its insurance-related revenues are generated via its ECS system. Once an office has a system that works well, there is a risk of a disruption in revenue flows by switching to another provider. Hence, a physician's office typically will stay with its initial provider unless there is a significant cost saving associated with switching providers or the alternate provider offers some other compensating benefit to offset the risk. If the market price is near zero, there may not be enough compensation to induce physicians to switch ECS providers.

2 Format compatibility
Practice management software does a myriad of things, including formatting claims for submission to a clearinghouse. Practice management software transmits claim information in the format loaded into the management software. Although there has been movement toward a universal format, there still is no single universal format for claim submission. Therefore, an ECS provider can make its product work with a physician's practice management system only if

---

[32] Joint Record Extract at E. 266–7. Also see B.2744.

the system formats the claim in a manner that the ECS provider's clearinghouse software understands.

If the practice management system and the clearinghouse formats are incompatible, then an ECS provider has a few alternatives. None of them are realistic, however. One alternative is to convince the practice management software developer to change its proprietary software to mirror the ECS's format. This is not likely, especially if the ECS provider is a relatively small firm. A second alternative is to convince the physician's office to switch to practice management software that has a compatible standard. The cost of switching to a new practice management system, however, makes this unlikely. A third alternative is for the ECS provider to change its format to mirror the format in the practice management software. However, since there is no universal standard, this makes little sense.

Once a physician's office has a practice management system, it is unlikely to switch to a clearinghouse with an incompatible format. Even if a particular practice management system software vendor has software for another clearinghouse, there is generally a charge (about US$300 to US$1,000) for that module. Moreover, paying that additional charge rarely gives the physician the ability to submit to multiple clearinghouses simultaneously because the rest of the software package generally has to be configured to the requirements of the clearinghouse when the module is installed.

In response to this situation, some clearinghouses distribute at little or no cost to the physician software that will create electronic claims in the clearinghouse special format. However, for a physician using practice management software, the use of clearinghouse software is impractical since it requires that his/her staff enter the claims data twice — once for the clearinghouse software and once for the practice management system.

Other clearinghouses have produced software that can directly or indirectly capture the claims information from a limited number of practice management systems without the need for double entry. However, even when such clearinghouse software is successful, the practice management software must generally be configured in a way that practically limits the office from transmitting to any other clearinghouse. Therefore, format compatibility can be a potentially serious barrier to entry.

5.6.3. Conclusion

At least two barriers exist for new entrants into the Maryland ECS market. First, switching costs make physicians hesitant to change providers. Second, format compatibility may prevent a new entrant from acquiring physicians with incompatible practice management software.

5.7. MARKET POWER

5.7.1. Market competitors

Before EDS purchased LifeCard, BCBSM policy was that all claims destined for BCBSM had to be filed with LifeCard. Martello was the only Maryland clearinghouse to bypass that requirement and not file claims destined for BCBSM through LifeCard. When EDS purchased LifeCard, Martello continued to be the only clearinghouse filing BCBSM claims independent of EDS. All other BCBSM claims went through EDS.

The evidence suggests, however, that by end of 1994, EDS and Martello were the only ECS providers left in the Maryland market.[33] The 1998 report of the Maryland Health Care Access and Cost Commission (HCACC) indicates that in 1998, six ECSs, including EDS, were certified to operate in Maryland. However, the report also indicates that none of them were certified *before* February of 1997. Hence, there is no way to tell for sure if any of them, other than EDS, were operating in the Maryland market during the period in question.

The Faulkner & Gray *Health Data Directory* shows 88 companies providing electronic claims processing in the US in 1997. However, this does not indicate how many were processing claims in 1993 and of those, how many were processing claims in Maryland. With entry barriers as described above, a firm processing claims in some other part of the country would not necessarily be a competitor in the Maryland market in 1993.

5.7.2. Market shares

EDS records indicate that in December of 1994, EDS filed 681,895 private and Medicare claims with BCBSM and 63,853 claims with other private insurers. In January of 1995, BCBSM lost the Medicare part B contract. EDS records indicate that in January of 1995, it filed 380,007 claims with BCBSM and 407,839 other claims which include claims filed for Medicare part B and other private insurers. If the number of claims filed with other private insurers was the same

---

[33] *See* Joint Record Extract at E. 141–2.

over those two months, it implies that in January of 1995, EDS filed 380,007 claims with BCBSM and 343,986 claims for Medicare part B. Therefore, BCBSM claims made up approximately 52.5% of combined BCBSM/ Medicare part B claims.

In 1993, EDS filed 7,476,038 electronic claims with BCBSM. If the ratio of BCBSM private claims to Medicare part B claims holds from the paragraph above, 52.5% of those 7.5 million claims (which equals 3.9 million claims) were for BCBSM private claims and the other 47.5% (which equals 3.6 million claims) were for Medicare part B. Historically BCBSM had 35% of the private insurer market in Maryland.[34] If the 3.9 million claims submitted to BCBSM for BCBSM private insurance payment represent 35% of the private claim market, then in 1993 there must have been 11.2 million private electronic claims in all. (35% of 11.2 million is 3.9 million.)

Adding the 11.2 million private claims with the estimated 3.6 million Medicare claims gives a total market of 14.8 million electronic claims in 1993.[35] EDS had a total of 7.9 million claims in 1993 so its implied market share was 53.4% of the market. Another way to interpret this data is that 53 out of every 100 electronic claims were destined for processing by EDS.

5.7.3. Ability to raise price

Over the 24-month period from January 1989 through December 1990, BCBSM's subsidiary clearinghouse, LifeCard, charged BCBSM from 10¢ to 30¢ per claim. Over the entire period, LifeCard charged BCBSM an average fee of 16¢ per claim. Once EDS took over LifeCard's operations, EDS increased the fee it charged BCBSM from 16¢ to 65¢ per claim. This is an increase of over 300% and demonstrates EDS's ability to raise price.

The November 6, 1993 issue of *Automated Medical Payments News* indicates that a "pricing survey of 40 claims clearinghouses and third-party processors reveals the average per-claim processing fee is 47¢ and dropping (p. 1)". EDS's fee to BCBSM of 65¢ was 38% higher than the national average fee of 47¢.[36]

---

[34] The GAO reported that as of June 1993, BCBSM's market share was 35.2%.

[35] All but Martello's Medicare part B claims had to go through EDS. Therefore, EDS's Medicare part B claims approximately equal the entire number of Medicare part B claims.

[36] In 1994, HCFA reviewed the costs for BCBSM's electronic claims business. In its report HFCA indicated the market rate for claim processing is "$.30 – $.40 per claim". *See* Joint Record Extract at E. 411. Hence, HFCA data also indicate that EDS's fee to BCBSM was well above the market rate.

Although the agreement between BCBSM and EDS provided that BCBSM could renegotiate the 65¢ fee charged by EDS, the renegotiation could only happen if BCBSM "determines that any healthcare insurer or administrator competing with BCBSM is receiving electronic connectivity services from a third party vendor which are comparable to the total portfolio of electronic connectivity services BCBSM is then receiving from EDS at a cost that is at least 35% less than the current cost to BCBSM".[37] In other words, even if the contract was renegotiated, EDS was still guaranteed a fee at least 35% in excess of fees charged by a competitor.

The foregoing demonstrates two things. First, EDS was able to increase significantly the fee paid by BCBSM for clearinghouse services. Second, EDS was able to increase the fee well above the national average market price and could be guaranteed a premium of at least 35%. If market power is demonstrated by the ability to raise price above the competitive level, then EDS clearly had market power.

5.7.4. Ability to exclude competitors

As discussed above, doctors will only use one ECS provider. The only reason to switch from EDS to some new provider is if the new firm provides some benefits not available from EDS. The only benefit an equally efficient competitor can normally offer is a better price. However, EDS was already charging doctors nothing for BCBSM and Medicare part B claims and 35¢ for all other private claims. The best an entrant could do was meet EDS's zero price on BCBSM and Medicare claims and set some price below 35¢ for all other private claims. Such pricing would not generate enough sales or revenues to make entry worthwhile. Yet the 65¢ payment from BCBSM exclusively to EDS made the same strategy profitable to EDS.

The market share discussion above indicates that over half of all electronic claims went to BCBSM. A physician would not be interested in using an ECS provider that did not file claims with BCBSM. As a result, a new entrant would have to offer filing for BCBSM claims. Yet EDS was the only ECS provider that received 65¢ per claim from BCBSM. Therefore, on approximately half of its claims, a new entrant would receive no revenue from BCBSM and, because it would have to meet EDS's zero price, no revenue from physicians.

---

[37] This is on page 18 of the contract which is page E. 358 of the Joint Record Extract.

Table 5.1:   EDS claims and costs.

	1993	1994	1995
Number of claims	7,873,908	9,943,823	9,836,138
Total cost (US$)	2,696,244	4,917,791	4,053,108
Cost per claim (¢)	34.2	49.5	41.2

The only way to justify entry would be by making up the revenues forgone on BCBSM claims with excess revenues generated on claims to other private insurance companies. That would not have been possible, however, even for an equally efficient firm. Table 5.1 shows EDS's number of claims filed, total costs and the resulting average cost per claim for the years 1993, 1994 and 1995. The average cost varied from 34.2¢ to almost 50¢. Over the three-year period as a whole, the average cost was 42¢ per claim. Yet EDS charged physicians 35¢ per claim for non-BCBSM private claims.

For a potential entrant to attract customers, it would have to charge a price less than 35¢ per claim. This would not even cover costs for the non-BCBSM claims. Furthermore, it would leave no excess revenues to cover the losses on the BCBSM-destined claims. EDS, on the other hand, generated an average profit of 23¢ from BCBSM on each BCBSM-destined claim. Since EDS's pricing strategy generated excess revenues, it could indefinitely charge a zero price and prevent entry. EDS's pricing strategy therefore created a barrier to entry. Other competitors had no incentive to enter because physicians had no incentive to deal with them. For example, here is what one medical claims specialist had to say in her affidavit in the Martello litigation.[38]

> 3. As part of my business, I make arrangements for physicians' claims to be electronically processed and submitted through clearinghouses to insurance companies such as Blue Cross and Blue Shield of Maryland.
> 4. Since August, 1993, Herbert H. Martello, whom I know as an electronic claims clearinghouse, has made repeated bids to provide my firm with clearinghouse services. In evaluating his proposals and those of other companies, I have repeatedly decided to award the contracts to the Maryland Health Information Network ("MHIN"). [Maryland Health Information Network is

---

[38] *See* Joint Record Extract at E.141–2.

the name EDS gave the LifeCard clearinghouse after EDS purchased LifeCard from BCBSM.]

5. The primary reason I have awarded the business to MHIN and not to Herbert Martello or other companies is that the MHIN has offered to process Blue Cross and Medicare claims free and that the other companies, including Herbert Martello, have not made that offer.

6. My experience has been that in Maryland only MHIN now makes proposals to process physicians' electronic claims and that except for Herbert Martello the other companies which used to submit bids no longer do so.

7. I anticipate that I will continue to award my clearinghouse business to MHIN and deny business to Herbert Martello because I do not anticipate that his company will match MHIN's offer to process Blue Cross and Medicare claims free of charge.

This illustrates in very practical terms that EDS had the power to exclude, and did exclude other clearinghouses from the Maryland ECS market.

EDS's ability to exclude competitors came at an important time. As previously discussed, the Maryland Legislature had mandated the conversion from paper to electronic filing. EDS's pricing strategy would allow it to capture all of these new ECS users. EDS's zero pricing combined with switching costs would make it difficult for an entrant to capture these new physicians once they developed a relationship with EDS.

In this respect, it was very important for EDS to eliminate Martello as a competitor. Martello's was the only clearinghouse that could submit BCBSM and Medicare part B claims directly to BCBSM. All other clearinghouses had to submit those claims through EDS. Hence, EDS collected 65¢ on all BCBSM-related claims, even if they originally were filed with another clearinghouse. On Martello's claims to BCBSM, however, EDS made no revenue. Therefore, Martello was the one competitor that most impacted EDS's revenue per claim from BCBSM.

It is also interesting to note that because of EDS's agreement with BCBSM, health consumers were injured in at least two distinct ways. First, BCBSM policyholders absorbed the charge for all BCBSM-destined claims, including all Medicare claims in 1993 and 1994. In a memo dated February 16, 1994, BCBSM officials indicated that "Medicare will not pay [65 cents] and base business will have to subsidize Medicare claims submitted through MHIN".[39] Secondly, there

---

[39] Joint Record Extract at E.453–5.

was double payment for the BCBSM claims captured initially by other clearinghouses. In other words, there is nothing to indicate that BCBSM extracted a promise from any other clearinghouse than EDS to charge physicians zero if the claim were submitted to BCBSM through MHIN. All indications are to the contrary. For example, in August 1994, Professional Office Systems was charging 29¢–35¢ per claim to the physician and then BCBSM was paying 65¢ when the claim was eventually submitted by BCBSM.[40] Hence consumers ultimately ended up paying from 94¢ to US$1.00 for claim processing with a market price of approximately 40¢. Other clearinghouses such as Keystone Medical Systems, Systems Architects, Inc., and Cydata had a per-claim charge as well.[41]

5.7.5. Conclusion

In 1993, EDS controlled an estimated 53% of the Maryland ECS market. Upon entering the market EDS raised its fee to BCBSM by 300% to a level 38% above the national average fee. It had the power to raise price. EDS also had and exercised the ability to exclude competitors as demonstrated by economic reasoning and the evidence from medical providers. Based on EDS's market share and its ability to raise its price and exclude competitors, it seems reasonable to conclude that EDS had market power.

5.8. THE PREDATION SCHEME

5.8.1. Description of EDS's pricing strategy

In many ways, EDS's market power flowed from the favorable 65¢ payment from BCBSM. That payment allowed EDS to charge physicians nothing for claims to BCBSM, which in turn allowed EDS to exclude equally efficient competitors from the market. EDS's pricing strategy therefore had anticompetitive effects.

Those effects were much like the effects of a classical predatory pricing scheme. Under a classical predatory pricing scheme, a firm begins by pricing

---

[40] *Id.* at E. 267.
[41] *See* Joint Record Extract at E. 265–67 (Maryland Medicare Preferred Vendor List, August 1994); *Processors Maintain an Even Pricing Keel*, Automated Medical Payments News 1, 2 (December 6, 1994).

below cost. This forces competitors out and allows the firm to capture market share. The predator then raises price and recoups forgone profits. EDS's pricing strategy was slightly different. Its zero price to doctors allowed EDS to capture the market. The 65¢ payment from BCBSM, however, allowed EDS to simultaneously recoup profits forgone from doctors. EDS had no need to raise price in the future because it simultaneously recouped from BCBSM the revenues forgone with its zero pricing to doctors.

In essence, the strategy was an equilibrium long run strategy for EDS to pursue. The zero price allowed EDS continually to have the best chance to expel competitors and capture market growth. The 65¢ payment from BCBSM allowed EDS simultaneously to recoup revenues forgone from physicians. That is the functional equivalent of predatory pricing.

5.8.2. Predatory pricing

When a firm begins to produce it incurs two types of costs, fixed costs and variable costs. Fixed costs represent the costs of assets that are required even before a firm actually begins production. Variable costs represent the costs that a firm incurs only once it actually begins production. If a firm shuts down, it incurs its fixed costs but avoids all of its variable costs. However, if it shuts down, it generates no revenues. Hence, by shutting down a firm loses all of its fixed costs. Therefore, it is profit maximizing or loss minimizing to stay open in the short run so long as price covers all of the variable costs and even a small portion of the fixed costs of production. After all, producing and covering at least some fixed costs is better than shutting down and covering no fixed costs.

When price is greater than average variable cost, the revenue received from each unit produced covers all of the variable costs associated with the unit and there is still some revenue left over on each unit to pay toward fixed costs. Hence, in the short run, it is worthwhile for a firm to stay open as long as price is greater than average variable cost. When price is less than average variable cost, revenues are less than variable costs. The firm cannot cover all of its variable costs and there is nothing left over to cover any fixed costs. In this situation, the firm is better off shutting down. If it shuts down, it has no variable costs and only loses its fixed costs. Hence, average variable cost forms the threshold for prices that warrant short-run production. A price below average variable cost makes production uneconomical. A price above average variable cost makes production viable at least in the short run.

When a firm engages in predation and sets a price lower than average variable cost, it is forcing its competitor from the market. The competitor may be just as efficient as the predator. It may have identical costs. It may produce a product of equal or better quality to the predator. Even so, if price is below average variable cost, the most profitable thing for the competitor to do is stop production. A firm has to cover all of its costs to maintain viability over time. Therefore, over a long period of time price has to be greater than average total cost. If price is below average total cost and a competitor expects it to remain there for a long time, the most profitable thing for the competitor to do is leave the market.

Every claim filed with EDS required some resources for processing. Therefore, every claim that a physician filed with EDS had a marginal cost. By charging physicians a price equal to zero, EDS had to be pricing below marginal cost. Because marginal cost is difficult to measure, economists sometimes substitute average variable cost for marginal cost in pricing standards.[42] EDS-provided data show a "Breakdown of Operating Costs by Year". The breakdown shows the "Total Cost", "Variable Costs" and "Fixed Costs" associated with ECS in each of the year 1993 through 1995. Those figures are shown in Table 5.2.

Table 5.3 repeats the EDS-provided total variable costs shown above, shows the number of claims per year as reported by EDS and calculates the average variable cost per claim. EDS's average variable cost was between 3.1¢ and 3.8¢ per claim. A price of zero was clearly below EDS's average variable cost.

In this particular case, EDS's price of zero was clearly below average variable cost and average total cost. If competitors cannot sell at a price at least equal to average variable cost, the most profitable thing to do is stop producing. If competitors cannot sell at a price at least equal to average total cost, and they expect this condition to extend into the indefinite future, the most profitable thing to do is leave the market.

EDS's predation strategy called for zero pricing to doctors over an indefinite period of time. A zero price is below average variable cost and average total cost. Such a price will force competitors from the market. That is the effect of such a price. As explained in the next section, that is also the likely purpose of such a price.

---

[42] That is the approach advocated by Phillip Areeda and Donald F. Turner, the authors of the most influential legal article on predatory pricing, *Predatory Pricing and Related Practices Under Section 2 of the Sherman Act*, 88 Harv. L. Rev. 697 (1975). For further discussion of the legal aspects of predatory pricing, see III Phillip E. Areeda and Herbert Hovenkamp, *Antitrust Law* §§ 723–49 (rev. ed. Little, Brown & Co. 1996).

Table 5.2: EDS's variable, fixed and total costs.

	1993	1994	1995
Variable costs (US$)	240,321	378,058	356,425
Fixed costs (US$)	2,455,923	4,539,733	3,696,683
Total costs (US$)	2,696,244	4,917,791	4,053,108

Table 5.3: EDS's total variable costs, number of claims and average variable costs.

	1993	1994	1995
Variable cost (US$)	240,321	378,058	356,425
Number of claims	7,873,908	9,943,823	9,836,138
Average variable cost (¢)	3.1	3.8	3.6

5.8.3. Predatory intent

Except in exceptional situations, firms typically do not have a pro-competitive reason to price below average variable cost. When a firm sets a price below average variable cost, it is necessarily imposing losses on itself. Under normal competitive conditions, there is no reason to do this. The firm is better off shutting down. Therefore, the general conclusion is that there must be some non-competitive reason for pricing so low. If a firm is purposely imposing losses on itself, it must be expecting to recoup those losses somehow. When below average variable cost pricing is combined with the other features of predation, it is reasonable to conclude that the intent of such pricing is to force a competitor from the market. Absent the predatory effect, there is no reason to price below average variable cost.

This does not exactly describe the EDS predation scheme. BCBSM was paying EDS 65¢ for every claim EDS submits to BCBSM. Hence, even when EDS priced its electronic connectivity service to doctors at zero, it still covered all of its costs. However, using economic reasoning similar to the reasoning used above, it can still be shown that EDS's likely intent in pricing at zero was to exclude competitors and capture the entire market for itself.

Suppose EDS were to price ECS to doctors right at average variable cost. An equally efficient competitor could remain in the market, at least in the short run. EDS could cover all of its variable costs with the revenues it generated from prices charged to physicians. EDS could cover its fixed costs with the 65¢ it generated from BCBSM. An equally efficient competitor could cover all of its variable costs with the revenues it generated from physicians. It would cover none of its fixed costs, however.

Now suppose EDS lowers its price below average variable cost. On its original customer base, price is below average variable cost. Hence, the revenue it generates from those physicians does not cover all of the variable costs of providing service to those physicians. EDS would have to use the 65¢ from BCBSM not only to cover its fixed costs, but to cover some of its variable costs as well. If EDS were to keep its original customer base, it would make no sense to price below average variable cost. Therefore, the only reason it makes sense for EDS to price below average variable cost is if EDS gains sales beyond its original share of the market. Hence EDS's intent had to be to gain a larger share of the market.

Normally, gaining market share is not an antitrust violation. In fact, one of the goals of the antitrust laws is to promote competition. Firms that produce better products or are more efficient or have visionary managers should be allowed to gain market share at the expense of their weaker rivals. But when a pricing scheme makes no economic sense *except* if it drives equally competent, equally efficient, equally well-managed competitors from the market, then it has to be viewed as exclusionary, i.e., predatory.

More telling information also reveals EDS's predatory intent. In January 1995, BCBSM lost the Medicare part B contract. Since BCBSM was no longer the Medicare part B administrator, EDS could no longer collect 65¢ for each Medicare part B claim it filed with the new Medicare part B administrator. However, for the next 15 months, until April 1996, EDS continued to charge physicians nothing for Medicare part B claims. In other words, EDS was collecting *no* revenue on every Medicare part B claim it filed. It collected nothing from the new Medicare part B administrator and nothing from the doctors. During that 15-month period, EDS records indicate that it filed approximately 5 million Medicare part B claims.[43] Hence over a 15-month period, EDS earned no revenues on over 400,000 claims per month. Yet it still continued to zero price. There is no economic reason for EDS to zero price, absent zero pricing's ability to increase EDS's market share.

---

[43] Joint Record Extract at E. 882.

As the discussion in the Appendix further explains, EDS's pricing strategy makes sense if it allows EDS to capture most of the growing ECS market. It makes no sense, however, if EDS captures only approximately 60% of the market. Since EDS voluntarily initiated and sustained such a pricing scheme, it must have been EDS's expectation that it would capture a significant part of the growing ECS market in Maryland. Hence, at the time it adopted the strategy, EDS must have expected to capture a significant share of the market.

EDS's quest to gain sales apparently was successful. From February to August of 1993, EDS averaged 15 new sales to physicians' offices per month. It estimated a monthly average of 81,000 yearly claims from new sales. EDS averaged 13 new installations, 20 pending installations and 16 forecasted new installations per month over that same seven-month period. In September 1993 EDS began its zero pricing campaign. From September 1993 through January 1994 EDS averaged 35 new sales to physicians' offices, an increase of 131%. It estimated a monthly average of 169,000 yearly claims from new sales, an increase of 107%. From September 1993 through January 1994 EDS doubled its average new installations. Its pending installations increased by 270%. Forecasted new installations increased by 167% from the previous average.[44] Clearly EDS's predatory actions increased its output in the Maryland ECS market.

EDS-provided data indicate that from February through August of 1993, EDS averaged 689,000 electronic claims per month. Once EDS began its zero pricing campaign, its average jumped to 763,000 claims per month in the remaining four months of 1993. This is an increase of almost 11%. In 1994 EDS averaged 829,000 claims per month. This is a 20% increase in claim volume over the pre-predatory pricing period.[45]

Based on the results of the model, EDS's pricing below average variable cost, its forgoing of revenues on over 5 million claims, and its significant increases in customers and claims following the introduction of its zero pricing campaign, it seems reasonable to conclude that EDS's intent was to eliminate equally efficient competitors and capture most, if not all, of the growing Maryland ECS market.

5.9. CONCLUSION

Even if simultaneous recoupment is insufficient to support a claim for predatory pricing, it may be sufficient to support claims for conspiracy to restrain trade

---

[44] Joint Record Extract at E. 462.
[45] Joint Record Extract at E. 882.

and conspiracy to monopolize. An agreement that facilitates simultaneous recoupment may have serious anticompetitive effects. Those effects include the elimination of equally efficient competitors, the creation of entry barriers, and the enhancement of market power.

It is possible that there may be legitimate business justifications for such an agreement. For example, a firm like BCBSM may choose to deal exclusively with a firm like EDS in order to achieve various efficiencies. But it is also possible that a firm may choose to subsidize another firm, not to achieve efficiencies but to protect itself from competition. The agreement would most likely be illegal in such a case because there would be no procompetitive effects to offset the anticompetitive effects of the agreement.

APPENDIX: A MODEL TO SHOW SIMULTANEOUS RECOUPMENT

A.1. INTRODUCTION

Under a standard predation scheme, a firm begins by pricing low and driving out its competitors. Over this predatory period, the firm is sacrificing revenues to gain market share. A measure of the sacrificed revenue is the difference between the amount the firm earned under predation and the amount it could have earned absent predation. Eventually the firm raises its price and recoups the forgone profits. A measure of the recoupment is the difference between the amount the firm earns once it gains market power and the amount it would have earned had it not engaged in predation to begin with. Predation is profitable if the recoupment is greater than the initial sacrifice.

An identical measure of the profitability of predation is the following. Measure the stream of profits earned from the entire predation scheme. This includes the profits made during the predatory period and the profits available after the firm raises its prices. Then measure the entire stream of profits the firm would have earned if it had not predated. Compare the streams. Predation is worthwhile if the profits earned from predation are greater than the profits earned from the alternative.

A.2. MODEL

Let t represent a period of time equal to a month. Let N_0 represent the total number of claims filed through an electronic clearinghouse in September of

1993. From September of 1993 through June of 1995, the expected number of claims would grow quickly as the law mandating electronic filing came into effect. Let N_t represent the total number of claims filed through an electronic clearinghouse in month t, and define N_t as $N_t = N_0 e^{n_1 t}$, where n_1 is the exponential growth rate in electronically filed claims over that period. Using this formula, by July 1, 1995 the number of claims filed through an electronic clearinghouse would be $N_{22} = N_0 e^{n_1 22}$. Starting July 1995, let the number of claims filed through an electronic clearinghouse equal $N_{22+t'} = N_{22} e^{n_2 t'}$ where n_2 is a slower exponential growth rate once the law has been fully implemented and $t' = t - 22$.

Let P_t^{BCBS} equal the price EDS gets from Blue Cross Blue Shield for each claim filed in period t. Let P_t^{DR} equal the price EDS gets from the physician for each claim filed in period t. If EDS predates, P_t^{DR} is equal to zero. If it does not, P_t^{DR} is some positive number.

Let VC_t equal the variable cost of each claim filed in period t. Let FC_0 equal EDS's fixed costs in September 1993. The data show that while variable costs remained constant over time, fixed costs were falling. Hence let EDS's fixed costs in period t be defined as $FC_t = FC_0 e^{c_1 t}$, where c_1 is the exponential rate of change in fixed costs over time. The rate of change should be negative.

Let S_0 equal EDS's market share in September 1993. Generally, its market share in period t can be defined as $S_t = S_0 e^{s_1 t}$, where s_1 is the exponential rate of change in market share over time. If EDS's strategy is effective, its market share should grow as it captures the growth in claims between September 1993 and July 1995. Therefore, $s_1 > 0$ until all new claims are added and EDS's market share reaches its equilibrium level. After that s_1 may equal zero. If EDS does not predate it should lose market share and s_1 should be negative. Eventually the market should reach some equilibrium level. Then EDS's market share should stabilize. With either a positive or a negative s_1 let T^* be the period when EDS's market share stabilizes. EDS's market share before that time can be described as $S_t = S_0 e^{s_1 t}$. After period T^*, its market share should equal $S_{T^*} = S_0 e^{s_1 T^*}$.

The number of claims filed through EDS in any period t equals $N_t S_t$, the total number of claims filed times EDS's market share. EDS's profit in any period t equals $N_t S_t (P_t^{BCBS} + P_t^{DR} - VC_t) - FC_t$, the number of claims filed times revenue net of variable cost per claim, minus fixed costs. If r is the discount rate, the present discounted value of profits EDS earns over any period T_1 to T_2, $\Pi_{T_1}^{T_2}$, can be defined as:

$$\Pi_{T_1}^{T_2} = \int_{t=T_1}^{T_2} e^{-rt} \{ N_t S_t (P_t^{BCBS} + P_t^{DR} - VC_t) - FC_t \} \, dt.$$

Recall that the market was expected to grow quickly from September 1993 through June 1995. If T^* comes before July 1995, EDS's profits through some ending period, T^{end} would equal:

$$\int_{t=0}^{T^*} e^{-rt} \{N_0 e^{n_1 t} S_0 e^{s_1 t} (P_t^{BCBS} + P_t^{DR} - VC_t) - FC_0 e^{c_1 t}\}\, dt +$$

$$\int_{t=T^*+1}^{22} e^{-rt} \{N_0 e^{n_1 t} S_{T^*} (P_t^{BCBS} + P_t^{DR} - VC_t) - FC_0 e^{c_1 t}\}\, dt +$$

$$\int_{t=23}^{T^{end}} e^{-rt} \{N_{22} e^{n_2 t'} S_{T^*} (P_t^{BCBS} + P_t^{DR} - VC_t) - FC_0 e^{c_1 t}\}\, dt.$$

If T^* comes after July 1995, EDS's profits through some ending period, T^{end} would equal:

$$\int_{t=T^*+1}^{22} e^{-rt} \{N_0 e^{n_1 t} S_0 e^{s_1 t} (P_t^{BCBS} + P_t^{DR} - VC_t) - FC_0 e^{c_1 t}\}\, dt +$$

$$\int_{t=23}^{T^*} e^{-rt} \{N_{22} e^{n_2 t'} S_0 e^{s_1 t} (P_t^{BCBS} + P_t^{DR} - VC_t) - FC_0 e^{c_1 t}\}\, dt +$$

$$\int_{t=T^*+1}^{T^{end}} e^{-rt} \{N_{22} e^{n_2 t'} S_{T^*} (P_t^{BCBS} + P_t^{DR} - VC_t) - FC_0 e^{c_1 t}\}\, dt.$$

A.3. DATA

As described previously, EDS's market share in September 1993 was estimated to be 53.4%. Hence, $S_0 = 0.534$.

EDS's data show that in September of 1993, EDS processed 747,966 electronic claims through its clearinghouse. If EDS's 747,966 claims equaled 53.4% of market claims, then total September claims, N_0, would be equal to 747,966/0.534 = 1,400,685.

In February 1995, The Gallup Organization released a report entitled *Physician Office Automation & Billing Practices Survey*. Table 21 of the report indicates that in 1994, 46% of solo practitioners' claims and 65% of group practices' claims that were submitted electronically were done so via a clearinghouse. The table also indicates that 63% of all claims that were submitted electronically were submitted via a clearinghouse. Thus 0.46 times solo practice claims plus 0.65 times group practice claims must equal 0.63 times all claims submitted electronically. Since the percentage of group practice claims equals one minus the percentage of solo practice claims, it must be that $0.46X + 0.65(1 - X) = 0.63$, where X is the percentage of solo practice claims. Solving this equation, $X = 0.105$. So roughly 10% of electronic claims submitted via a clearinghouse were from solo practitioners.

The Gallup report's Table 18 indicates that 40% of solo practitioner's claims and 42% of group practices' claims were submitted electronically. Multiplying these percentages by the percentages of electronic claims filed via a clearinghouse (from the paragraph above), implies that 18% of solo practitioners' and 27% of group practices' *total* claims were submitted electronically via a clearinghouse in 1994.

Eighteen percent of solo practitioner's claims were submitted electronically via a clearinghouse. That makes up a total of 10% of all claims filed electronically through a clearinghouse. The other 90% were the 27% of claims filed electronically through a clearinghouse by group practices. Therefore, in total, 26% of all claims were filed electronically through a clearinghouse in 1994. In September of 1993 it was already estimated that 1,400,685 claims were filed electronically through a clearinghouse. If this makes up approximately 26% of all claims, then approximately 5.4 million claims were submitted either electronically or on paper in September 1993.

In July of 1993 the Maryland State Legislature passed a law mandating that all claims eventually were to be filed electronically. The first proposed target date was July 1, 1995.

US Department of Commerce, Bureau of the Census estimates show that in 1980 Maryland had a population of 4.217 million people. By 1990 that number had grown to 4.727 million people. This implies a monthly exponential growth rate of 0.00095. If an estimated 5.4 million claims were filed either electronically or on paper in September of 1993, and if claims grow in direct proportion to the population, then an estimated 5.5 million claims would be filed by July 1995. This means that N_{22} is estimated to equal 5.5 million claims.

If N_0 is equal to 1.4 million claims and N_{22} is equal to 5.5 million claims then the growth rate in claims filed over that period is $n_1 = \ln(N_{22}/N_0)/22 = 0.06$. So from September 1993 through July 1995 the total number of claims filed electronically via a clearinghouse would have been expected to grow at about 6% per month. After that time, the number of claims would grow as fast as the population grew. From the population figures above, $n_2 = 0.00095$.

The following table shows EDS's estimated variable cost per claim, the number of claims filed in the years 1993 through 1996 and the implied variable cost per claim. EDS provided the data. Variable cost averaged 3.5¢ per claim. Hence, $VC_t = 0.035$.

	1993	**1994**	**1995**
Total variable cost (US$)	240,321	378,058	356,425
Number of claims	7,873,908	9,943,823	9,836,138
Cost per claim (¢)	3.1	3.8	3.6

Other EDS data show the total cost and the number of claims processed in each month from September 1993 through June 1998. Multiplying the variable cost of 3.5¢ per claim times the number of claims and subtracting that from total costs gives fixed costs per month. These data can be used to run the regression $\ln(FixedCosts_t) = \ln(FC_0) + c_1 t$, where FC_0 is the measure of fixed costs in the initial month and c_1 is the exponential decay rate of fixed costs. When the regression is corrected for first order autocorrelation, the results are $FC_0 = 376,122$ and $c_1 = -0.0094$.

Blue Cross Blue Shield agreed to pay EDS 65¢ per claim. Therefore, $P_t^{BCBC} = 0.65$. Under its predation scheme, EDS's price to doctors for BCBSM and Medicare part B claims is equal to zero. For all other private payer claims, the price to doctors was 0.35¢. If EDS were not to predate it would set a positive price to doctors for all claims. One alternative is for EDS to set its price to doctors for BCBSM and Medicare part B claims equal to the price for all other private claims, 0.35¢. As a second alternative, in 1993 Martello was charging a price of 10¢ per claim. EDS could match that price.

The November 6, 1993 issue of *Automated Medical Payments News* was a special issue addressing pricing by clearinghouses. Page 2 of that issue contained the following: "automated medical payments processing executives do agree on one major pricing trend: Within five years . . . the average claim processing fee will be 25 cents or less". As a third alternative, if EDS does not predate, it will set $P^{DR} = 0.25$¢.

Previous discussion indicates that EDS filed 747,966 claims in September 1993. Total claims in September 1993 and July 1995, respectively, were estimated to be 1,400,685 and 5,400,000. This implies the market would grow by about four million claims over that period. Under EDS's pricing scheme, if it kept all of its initial claims and captured all of the growth in the market, its July 1995 market share would be $(4,000,000 + 747,966)/5,400,000 = 88\%$ of the electronic claims market. If EDS captured all of the growth in the market, kept all of its initial claims, and captured half of the claims previously filed by other clearinghouses that were forced out of the market by EDS's pricing actions, then its market share in July 1995 would be 93%. An 88% market share in July 1995 implies that $s_1 = \ln(88/53.4)/22 = 0.023$. A 93% market share implies that $s_1 = \ln(93/53.4)/22 = 0.025$.

If EDS did not use its pricing strategy, its market share could evolve in a number of ways. Suppose EDS kept its September market share so that in July 1995 it maintained 53.4% of the market. Alternatively, if firms like Martello were to grow at EDS's expense, EDS could lose perhaps 5 or 10 percentage points in market share.

Results are initially generated estimating profits over a period of ten years ($T^{END} = 120$) and using an annual discount rate of 10% ($r = 0.10/12$). Once the initial results are presented, discussion will focus on the implication of varying the time period and the discount rate.

A.4. RESULTS

Results of the model are presented in Table A.1. The first part of the table estimates EDS's discounted profits over ten years if it engages in its preferred pricing strategy. Under this scenario, EDS is not charging physicians for BCBSM and Medicare part B claims. EDS is recouping those revenues by collecting 65¢ from BCBSM on every BCBSM and Medicare part B claim. Row (1) shows EDS's profits if it captures all of the expected growth in the market. Under this scenario, EDS captures an eventual 88% of the market and its profit over the ten-year period equals US$173 million. Row (2) shows what happens if EDS captures all growth as well as capturing share from other competitors. Its market share grows to 93% and its profit over the ten-year period is US$183 million. If EDS's market share were to rise above 93%, profit would be greater than US$183 million.

The second part of the table examines EDS's profits over the same period of time if it does not zero price doctors. Rows (3), (4) and (5) show EDS's estimated profits if it continues to get 65¢ for each BCBSM claim *and* charges doctors

David I. Rosenbaum and John P. Lenich

Table A.1: EDS profits as a function of its price expected eventual market share and time to reach new market share.

EDS price to physicians	I. PROFITS (in million US dollars)			

Under predatory pricing

    EDS's eventual market share

    $P^{DR} = 0¢$

(1) 88% EDS profit	173			
(2) 93% EDS profit	183			

	Months to reach new market share			
	10	**20**	**40**	**80**

Under non-predatory pricing

    EDS's eventual market share

    $P^{DR}=10¢$

	10	20	40	80
(3) 53% EDS profit		119		
(4) 48% EDS profit	106	106	113	116
(5) 43% EDS profit	93	94	101	105

    $P^{DR} = 25¢$

	10	20	40	80
(6) 53% EDS profit		147		
(7) 48% EDS profit	132	132	135	137
(8) 43% EDS profit	116	117	120	125

    $P^{DR} = 35¢$

	10	20	40	80
(9) 53% EDS profit		166		
(10) 48% EDS profit	149	149	149	152
(11) 43% EDS profit	132	133	133	138

10¢ for every BCBSM and Medicare part B claim. Row (3) shows that if EDS were to maintain its beginning market share of 53% over the ten-year period, its profit under this non-zero pricing scheme would be US$119 million.

Row (4) shows EDS's expected profit over the ten-year period if its market share falls by five percentage points over a number of months. If it takes ten months for EDS to lose market share, its profit is US$106 million. If it takes 80 months for EDS's market share to go from 53 to 48%, its profit over the ten-year period would be US$116 million. Row (5) shows EDS's expected profit over the ten-year period if its market share falls by ten percentage points over a number of months. The discounted value of profit ranges between US$93 and US$105 million, depending upon how long it takes EDS to lose market share.

Rows (6), (7) and (8) show EDS's estimated profits if it charges doctors 25¢ for every BCBSM and Medicare part B claim. Depending on its ending market share and the time it takes EDS to lose market share, the present value of profits discounted over the ten-year period, ranges from US$116 to US$147 million.

Rows (9), (10) and (11) show EDS's estimated profits if it charges doctors 35¢ for every BCBSM and Medicare part B claim. Depending on its ending market share and the time it takes EDS to lose market share, the present value of profits discounted over the ten-year period, ranges from US$132 to US$166 million.

Comparing the results from the zero pricing scheme to those under a non-zero pricing scheme, it is clear that charging doctors nothing makes sense. If EDS zero prices, it earns between US$173 and US$183 million dollars. If it does not, even if it maintains its market share, receives 65¢ from BCBSM for every BCBSM and Medicare part B claim and charges 35¢ to doctors for every claim, regardless of its source, EDS makes only US$166. Zero pricing carries a bonus of at least US$7 million. Under alternative pricing schemes, zero pricing carries an even larger bonus. EDS earns more profit by capturing most of the market than it does by setting a competitive price to doctors and sharing the growing market with other ECS providers.

Increasing the period of time for calculating discounted profits does not change the results qualitatively. It is still more profitable for EDS to zero price doctors than to charge a positive price. Changing the discount rate does not qualitatively change the results either. Even with an annual discount rate ranging anywhere between zero and 25%, zero pricing is still the most profitable strategy. Clearly when zero pricing allows EDS to capture most of the growing Maryland ECS market, it is preferable to competition.

Table A.2 shows results when EDS captures less of the growing Maryland ECS market. The first part of the table again estimates EDS's discounted profits over ten years if it zero prices. Again, EDS is not charging physicians for

Table A.2:   EDS profits as a function of its price expected eventual market share and time to reach new market share.

EDS price to physicians	II. PROFITS (in million US dollars)			
Under predatory pricing				
EDS's eventual market share				
$P^{DR} = 0¢$				
(1) 60% EDS profit	114			
(2) 70% EDS profit	135			

	Months to reach new market share			
	10	**20**	**40**	**80**
Under non-predatory pricing				
EDS's eventual market share				
$P^{DR} = 10¢$				
(3) 53% EDS Profit		119		
(4) 48% EDS Profit	106	106	113	116
(5) 43% EDS Profit	93	94	101	105
$P^{DR} = 25¢$				
(6) 53% EDS Profit		147		
(7) 48% EDS Profit	132	132	135	137
(8) 43% EDS Profit	116	117	120	125
$P^{DR} = 35¢$				
(9) 53% EDS Profit		166		
(10) 48% EDS Profit	149	149	149	152
(11) 43% EDS Profit	132	133	133	138

BCBSM and Medicare part B claims. EDS is collecting 65¢ from BCBSM on every BCBSM and Medicare part B claim. Row (1) shows EDS's profits if it captures an eventual 60% of the market. Its profit over the ten-year period equals US$114 million. Row (2) shows what happens if EDS captures an eventual 70% of the market. Its profit over the ten-year period is US$135 million.

The second part of Table A.2 is identical to the second part of Table A.1. It shows EDS's estimated profits if it sets a competitive price to physicians rather than a zero price. Again, EDS is still collecting 65¢ on every BCBSM-related claim.

Compare the first part of Table A.2 to the second part. If EDS expected zero pricing eventually to earn it only 60% of the growing Maryland ECS market, it would be worth it only if the alternative were to charge physicians 10¢ per claim. If EDS could charge physicians more, it would be more profitable for EDS to continue collecting 65¢ from BCBSM and collect 25¢ or 35¢ from physicians. Zero pricing would not be worth it.

If EDS expected predation eventually to earn it 70% of the growing Maryland ECS market, the situation changes somewhat. When EDS charges physicians 10¢ or 25¢, if the alternative were to lose market share, zero pricing is the more profitable strategy. However, when EDS charges physicians 35¢, it would be more profitable for EDS to continue collecting 65¢ from BCBSM and collect 35¢ from physicians. Zero pricing would not be worth it.

Comparing Tables A.1 and A.2, the implication is that EDS's pricing strategy makes sense only if EDS expects the strategy to gain it a dominant share of the market. Since EDS chose to pursue the predation strategy, it must have intended to dominate the Maryland ECS market.

Measuring Market Power
D. J. Slottje (editor)

CHAPTER 6

Measuring Market Power in the Steel Industry

ESFANDIAR MAASOUMI[a], STEPHEN D. PROWSE[b,*],
and DANIEL J. SLOTTJE[a,b]

[a] *Department of Economics, Southern Methodist University, Dallas TX 75275*
[b] *KPMG LLP, 200 Crescent Court, Suite 300, Dallas TX 75201*

Abstract

This chapter describes a mode of economic analysis one can use to measure market power in the context of antitrust litigation in the steel plate industry. We describe our framework of analysis, our method of defining the relevant market and the indicia we examine to evaluate the degree of market power exercised by the Defendant in this market.

Keywords: antitrust, market power, steel industry
JEL classification: L41, L12, L61

---

* Corresponding author.

6.1. INTRODUCTION

One area of economics that receives significant attention is the measurement of market power in the context of antitrust litigation. The purpose of this chapter is to give an example of how economists actually analyze the issue of market power in a real world situation. In particular, this chapter describes a mode of economic analysis that can be performed to measure market power and determine the effects of certain alleged anti-competitive acts in an antitrust litigation in the steel plate industry. In this chapter, we describe the framework of analysis, the method of defining the relevant market and the indicia one can examine to evaluate the degree of market power exercised by the Defendant in the relevant market. To keep the names of the parties confidential, we refer to them merely as "Plaintiff" and "Defendant".[1]

We were retained by a steel manufacturing company in an antitrust litigation. Plaintiff alleged that the Defendant had engaged in anti-competitive acts starting in late 1997 that had the intent and effect of eliminating competition for the sale of steel plate products in North America. Plaintiff claimed that the agreement restrained competition between Plaintiff and Defendant in the market for steel plate products in North America. Counsel for Defendant asked us to evaluate the antitrust allegations by Plaintiff in this matter. To do so, we performed an economic analysis of the relevant market and determined the degree to which Defendant exerted market power in a manner detrimental to consumers as a result of the alleged anti-competitive acts.

In this chapter we describe the framework we used to evaluate the nature of the relevant product and geographic market for steel plate products, the degree of competition in that market and the effects of the alleged anti-competitive acts on the degree of competition in that market. In addition, we perform an empirical examination of these issues using data and information on the number of sellers in the marketplace, market shares, measures of market concentration, the degree of market contestability, the level of profitability in the market, the elasticity of supply in the market, the elasticity of demand faced by an individual firm, and how price is determined in this market.

6.2. A FRAMEWORK FOR MEASURING MARKET POWER

In examining an allegation of anti-competitive behavior, it is necessary to define

---

[1] In addition, we omit certain analyses we performed on the market share and financial performance of the Defendant in this matter.

and study the market in question. The steps involved in this analysis include defining the market, evaluating the competitive nature of that market and examining whether Defendants did indeed attain market power by virtue of the alleged anti-competitive act and if they have exercised this market power in a manner that is detrimental to consumers.

Defining the market includes assessing the relevant "product" market and the relevant "geographic" market. It is well known by economists that the appropriate definition of a market must take into account substitution possibilities in both consumption and production. Evaluating substitution on the consumption side involves assessing the extent to which there are firms in the market that produce competing products. Products are competitive with each other if they are perceived to be substitutes in the eyes of buyers. The existence of substitutes is important because if there are close substitutes for a firm's product, any effort by the firm to increase price would not be profitable because buyers would have an opportunity to quickly switch to these cheaper comparable products. Such products should generally be included in the definition of the relevant market.

Substitution on the production side must also be considered. Groups of firms making products that are not substitutable for the relevant product may nevertheless be meaningful competitors if they employ essentially similar skills and equipment and if they could move quickly into the production of the relevant product should the possibility of profit lure them in that direction. This concept is known in the industrial organization literature as "contestability." Given a long enough time interval and sufficient investment, shifts in production activity — more accurately described as new entry than substitution — can occur. Ease of entry is important because if enough firms can enter an industry by constructing new facilities or converting existing ones, any effort to increase price would not be profitable because other firms would have the incentive to enter and compete prices down.

In evaluating the degree of competition in a market and whether a firm (or firms) have market power, an economist looks at a number of indicia that relate to market structure, firm conduct and firm performance. Market structure indicia include the number of sellers in the market, their respective market shares, measures of overall market concentration, the extent of significant barriers to entry and the degree of market contestability and new entry, how elastic supply is in the market and the elasticity of demand faced by the individual firm. Analyzing firm conduct in the relevant market involves evaluating how a firm sets price and whether any of its actions have an anti-competitive effect on the market that is detrimental to consumers. Finally, analyzing firm performance involves evaluating how firms are performing, whether they are earning normal or supernormal profits, and how they are responding to competitive pressures in the market.

We analyze these indicia under the market definition that we propose. In addition, we evaluate whether or not these indicia of competition changed significantly after the date at which the alleged anti-competitive acts began.

6.3. GEOGRAPHIC AND PRODUCT MARKET DEFINITION

As noted above, the first step in analyzing antitrust allegations is to properly determine the relevant product market and to carefully define the relevant geographic market. To do so first requires an understanding of the overall steel industry and market structure for steel products and their substitutes.

6.3.1. Background on the steel industry

There are a number of important characteristics of the steel industry. First, there are about 10,000 distinct iron and steel products, including unfinished products (such as pig iron), semi-finished products (including steel billets, blooms and slabs), finished or rolled steel products (including bars, rods, plates, structurals and sheets), and finally high unit value steel products such as forgings and castings.[2]

On the supply side, the steel industry consists of five major classes of producers: large integrated US companies, reconstituted steel mills, minimills, overseas steel producers and a specialty steel segment. The integrated US companies produce most of their steel from scratch in large "integrated" mills. They typically use a step-by-step manufacturing process that involves converting raw materials such as coke, iron ore and limestone first into molten pig iron, then into steel ingots or slabs, and finally into finished steel products such as steel plates and sheets. Integrated mills use an oxygen furnace for steel making. The number of integrated mills has declined steadily since World War II. Currently they include Bethlehem Steel, Geneva, National, Ispat Inland, LTV Steel, AK Steel, Weirton Steel, Acme Steel, Rouge Steel, WCI Steel and US Steel. These integrated companies produce a variety of steel products.[3]

Reconstituted steel mills are typically smaller steel plants that were either originally sold off by the integrated companies as part of their restructuring process

---

[2] See Adams and Mueller (1990).
[3] See www.business.com – integrated steel producers.

in the 1970s and 1980s or went through bankruptcy: they typically have lower costs than the integrated companies and are a source of intense competition for the integrated companies. Some reconstituted steel mills include Geneva Steel and California Steel Industries.[4] They typically produce various forms of finished steel including steel plates.

Minimills are nonintegrated steel producers. They do not produce finished steel from scratch but convert scrap steel directly into finished products including bars, rods and small structural shapes and plates. They have substantially lower costs than the integrated companies and since the 1960s have dramatically increased their market share of finished steel products. Currently, they make up about 48% of total production in the steel market in the US.[5] Some minimill companies are Nucor, IPSCO and Oregon.[6] In all there are over a hundred minimill companies in existence in the US today.[7] Minimills have recently become a fast growing source of steel plate. For example, IPSCO's first minimill plant set up to produce steel plate was brought on line in November 1997.[8] In addition, Nucor started up a minimill in the third quarter of 2000 and Ipsco opened a second minimill in 2001.

Overseas producers play a major role in supplying US finished steel demand today, including steel plates. For example, the market share of steel plate products comprised by imports grew significantly over the relevant time period. Imports accounted for 26% of steel plate in the US in 1997 and grew to 38% in 1998.[9]

Finally, specialty steel producers are a relatively small niche market and focus on the production of high unit value alloy, stainless and tool steels.

On the demand side, steel in various forms is used in the construction and production of roads, buildings, bridges, automobiles, appliances, farm equipment and machinery. In 1998, construction and automobile manufacturers accounted for approximately 13% of total US shipments of steel, with the remainder spread across various machinery, rail equipment, appliances, packaging and energy markets.[10] Demand for steel plate comes mainly from the durable capital goods sector. Plate is used in shipbuilding and the construction of bridges, pipe, tanks, and vessels as well as rail cars, barges, and offshore platforms. It is also used in the manufacture of tractors, combine harvesters and fork lift trucks.

---

[4] See the testimony of Richard K. Riederer, President and CEO, Weirton Steel Corporation Before The Senate Steel Caucus, November 30, 1998: Hearing on "The Steel Import Crisis".
[5] See www.environmentaldefense.org
[6] See www.business.com – minimill steel producers.
[7] See www.environmentaldefense.org
[8] See *Metal Center News*, "Ipsco's New Plate Mill in Iowa," May 1999.
[9] See the American Iron and Steel Institute, Annual Statistical Report.
[10] See *New Steel*, "Strong Fundamentals Continue," January 1999.

After a review of the structure of the steel industry, including the facts discussed above, we concluded that the appropriate market definition to use in this matter was the *global market for steel plate products*. The large share of overseas production in total US steel plate consumption argues for inclusion of overseas producers in the market definition and is supported by survey evidence found in the International Trade Commission ("ITC") report on the cut-to-length ("CTL") plate market. For example, the ITC report on the cut-to-length plate market found that plate imports competed with domestic plate products in the US. Additionally, in the ITC survey of steel plate purchasers, 83% of purchaser responses indicated that imports were always or frequently interchangeable with domestically-produced steel plates. In addition, the ITC Report states "CTL plate produced in the United States is shipped nationwide. Imported CTL plate from the subject countries is marketed in most areas of the United States."[11]

It is obvious from the ITC report and the numerous complaints filed by US steel companies and from the empirical evidence available in this matter that international borders do not inhibit the flow of steel plate into the US. While transportation costs are of course important, they are not a barrier to entry of foreign steel into the US. The study by Adams and Mueller notes that a steel user "in San Francisco is economically (that is, in terms of freight costs) closer to Japan than to Pittsburgh."[12] Given the ITC survey data, actual empirical data from the American Iron and Steel Institute ("AISI") that is corroborated by the ITC, and standard economic theory, we concluded that the relevant geographic market for steel plate is the world.

6.4. ASSESSING THE DEGREE OF COMPETITION AND MARKET POWER

The next step in the analysis is to evaluate the competitive nature of the steel plate market. In order to perform these evaluations, we first provide an overview of the steel plate market in the late 1990s.

6.4.1. Background on the steel plate product market in the late 1990s

The steel industry in the late 1990's was characterized by intense competition between suppliers (both domestic and overseas) and falling prices for steel

---

[11] See ITC Publication 3273, p. 17.
[12] See Adams and Mueller (1990) p. 74.

products, including steel plate. The poor market conditions for steel producers were reflected in their deteriorating financial condition, sharply falling profits and numerous bankruptcies. These conditions have prevailed in virtually all niches of the steel market, from unfinished to finished steel products (including steel plate) and affected virtually all types of steel producers, from the integrated mills to overseas producers to the minimills.

The proximate cause of much of this weakness in the steel industry was the increased supply of steel products (including steel plate) from two sources: overseas producers and domestic steel manufacturers. For cut-to-length steel plate, as noted in the ITC report, imports grew from approximately 1.4 million tons in 1997 to almost 2.2 million tons in 1998, a 53% jump in imports in one year. Over that same period, US plate mills increased cut-to-length plant capacity from about 6.7 million tons to 8.6 million tons, a 28% increase.[13] Combined, it is clear that the increase in the supply of steel plate for 1998 was substantial.

For example, starting in the second half of 1998, the supply of low priced imports of steel products into the US from overseas producers in Japan, Russia, Korea and Brazil increased dramatically. Steel imports in the US reached an all-time high in the second half of 1998. The reason for the flood of imports into the US lay in the economic downturns in Asia, Russia, and Brazil (all associated with financial crises in these countries) that started in late 1997 and meant that the demand for steel in these countries plummeted with the result that domestic steel producers in Japan, Korea, Russia and Brazil looked for other foreign markets in which to sell their steel.[14] Given the relatively stable demand for steel in the US and the US market's unprotected status (relative to other developed steel markets such as the European Union), the US became the destination of much of these countries' excess steel production.[15] As noted above, much of this imported steel was in the form of steel plate products. The increase in steel plate imports between 1997 and 1998 illustrates the ability of foreign plate producers to supply the US market at will.

Increases in domestic steel capacity in the US also contributed to the steel glut in the US in the late 1990s. As a result of expectations of strong and growing demand for steel in the mid-1990s, many domestic US steel producers — particularly steel plate producers — had committed to an expansion of their capacity

---

[13] See ITC Publication 3273, page IV–10 and III–5.

[14] See "New Crisis in Steel", A Report submitted to The House Ways and Means Trade Subcommittee and The Senate Finance Committee, by Dewey Ballantine LLP, April 1999.

[15] Much of these imports were found by the International Trade Commission to be in violation of anti-dumping laws which make illegal the export of goods at below fair value prices. See ITC Publication 3273.

Table 6.1:   Domestic steel plate production.

Group	1995	1996	1997	1998	1999
Bethlehem Steel[1]	1,350,000	1,430,000	1,360,000	1,700,000	1,700,000
Lukens	590,000	650,000	755,000		
CitiSteel	250,000	268,000	260,000	221,000	200,000
Geneva	575,000	650,000	720,000	1,068,000	575,000
Gulf States	420,000	424,000	380,000	390,000	333,200
Inland Steel	250,000	–	–	–	–
IPSCO	–	–	100,000	480,000	700,000
Jindal	–	–	–	197,511	244,107
Letourneau	150,000	170,000	150,000	150,000	100,000
Oregon	295,900	280,000	195,000	350,000	450,000
Tuscaloosa	425,000	425,000	350,000	575,000	575,000
USS	1,040,000	1,125,000	1,200,000	1,165,000	822,892
Total	5,345,900	5,422,000	5,470,000	6,296,511	5,700,199

Note. [1] Bethlehem Steel acquired Lukens in 1998.

Source. AISI and Company Reports.

to come on-line in the mid- to late 1990s and early 2000s. As a result, domestic production capacity of steel plate increased sharply during this time period.[16] New, expanded, or restarted plate capacity grew from 1994 through 1998 by 2.8 million tons.[17] Domestic production of steel plate in turn increased, from 5.5 million tons in 1997 to almost 6.3 million tons in 1998, as shown in Table 6.1. The growth in capacity for plate continued into the year 2000. For example, during 2000, IPSCO Steel constructed a new minimill in Mobile County, Alabama, which added an additional 1.25 million tons of capacity to the plate market.[18] Nucor also built a new plate mill during 2000 in Hertford County, North Carolina, adding capacity of 1 million tons to the plate market.[19]

---

[16] This is consistent with the findings of ITC Publication 3273 (page 20), which reports that the US domestic industry's capacity to produce CTL plate increased by over 6% in 1997, 21% in 1998, and over 6% in the first half of 1999.

[17] See *American Metal Market: Mini-Mill Steel Supplement*, November 26, 1996 which shows new capacity in tons over this period to be 350,000 for Tuscaloosa Steel, 1,250,000 for Ipsco, 400,000 for Geneva Steel, 60,000 for Citisteel, and Thin-Slab mini-mills added 750,000 tons of capacity.

[18] See *New Steel*, IPSCO, September 2000.

[19] See *New Steel*, Nucor, September 2000.

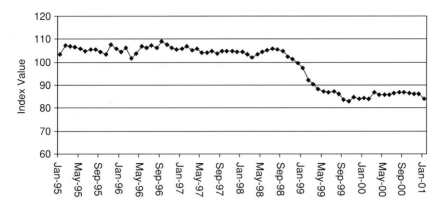

Figure 6.1:   Producer price index blast furnaces and steel mills – plates, carbon.

Source. Bureau of Labor Statistics, Series ID: pcu3312#412.

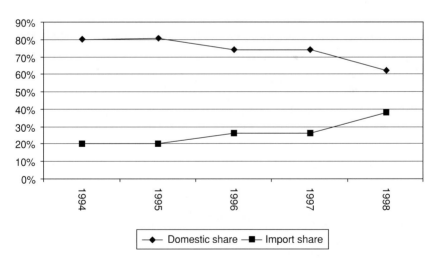

Figure 6.2:   US steel plate market share.

Note. Domestic share includes plate mills and strip mills.

Sources. AISI and Company data.

As a result of increased imports and domestic production, the US steel plate market suffered a classic case of "oversupply" of steel. Prices of steel products consequently fell dramatically in 1998 and 1999 as steel plate producers competed intensely to maintain their market share. Figure 6.1 illustrates the movement of the producer price index for carbon steel plate from January 1995 through January 2001. It shows a steady decrease from July 1998 through October 1999, reflecting steel plate producers attempting to maintain market share in the face of increased supply from domestic and foreign sources. Despite their willingness to cut prices as evidenced by the falling steel plate producer price index, US steel producers nevertheless lost significant market share to overseas producers in 1998 as depicted in Figure 6.2.[20]

Capacity utilization rates for US steel plate producers consequently fell dramatically. Many US steel plate producers were forced to lay off workers, and experienced sharply falling profits or dramatically increased losses over this period as shown in Table 6.2.

There were several steel producers who declared bankruptcy in the late 1990s and early 2000s. Both Geneva Steel and Gulf States Steel were steel plate producers who entered Chapter 11 during this period.[21] In addition to these plate producers, many steel companies declared bankruptcy during this period, including CSC Ltd., Acme Steel, GS Technologies Operating Co., Northwestern Steel & Wire Co., Trico Steel, Republic Technologies International, LTV Corp., J&L Structural Corp., Qualitech Steel Corp., and Wheeling-Pittsburgh Steel Corp.[22] Steel industry analysts were virtually unanimous in their description of the poor market conditions in the late 1990s, as evidenced by the following excerpts from an analyst's report on the steel industry:

> **1998: A "Death Spiral" for global steel prices.** Prices for steel sheet on the world market have plummeted to the lowest levels relative to costs since World War II, and possibly, in the history of the industry. Profits in the fourth quarter should be sharply lower.

> **1999: A likely "Death Valley" for global steel prices.** Next year is shaping up as an even more troubling year than 1998. Profits

---

[20] This market share calculation is based upon imports and domestic production and the resulting apparent domestic consumption.

[21] See *American Metal Market*, "Geneva Steel Awaits Loan Decision," May 22, 2000 and "Gulf States Steel Set to Bite Bullet on Costs," July 11, 2000.

[22] *American Metal Market*, "Banks Wary on Steel Loans Despite Federal Guarantee," June 5, 2001 and *Purchasing*, "Bankrupt Trico Steel Closes Alabama Mini-Mill," May 3, 2001.

Table 6.2:   Results of operations of US producers in the production of CTL plate.

Ratios to net sales (percent)	Fiscal year			January–June	
	1996	**1997**	**1998**	**1998**	**1999**
Gross profit (%)	8.7	7.2	8.3	9.2	0.5
Operating income/(loss) (%)	4.9	3.0	4.0	5.4	(5.2)
Net income/(loss) (%)	2.9	1.0	0.5	2.4	(9.4)
Number of firms reporting	23	24	25	25	25

Source. US International Trade Commission Report dated January 2000, Table VI-1, page VI-2.

> are likely to plummet. World steel export prices are likely to remain depressed at least for the first half of 1999.
>
> **2000: Recovery hopes.** Price improvement is possible by 2000.[23]

Other published sources characterized the state of the steel industry in the late 1990s in the following manner:

> The severe economic problems that roiled the Asian countries beginning in 1997, together with global overcapacity, precipitated a global "steel crisis" in 1998, with continuing consequences for US steel producers in 1999.[24]

In short, the steel plate market in the middle of 1998 was characterized by intense price competition between domestic and overseas steel producers with excess plate production capacity that led to falling prices, falling profits, and rising bankruptcies. These characteristics prevailed throughout the entire steel industry and affected virtually all steel producers, regardless of their specialty or focus.[25] The steel plate market in particular was severely

---

[23] See *Global Steel Finance: Shake Out*, PaineWebber, December 23, 1998.

[24] See *Steel Mill Products: US Industry and Trade Outlook, 2000*.

[25] Mr. Duane Dunham, president and CEO of Bethlehem Steel, speaking to the Congressional Steel Caucus (Sept. 14, 2000), stated "Our consumers are today blessed with having a revitalized, internationally competitive domestic steel industry." He went on to state "Unsold steel at docks, e.g., rebar and hot rolled coil, is again reaching overflow levels in Houston."

affected.[26] The existence of such conditions makes it unlikely that the steel plate market was subject to the exercise of market power by one or a number of firms. In the following sections, we explicitly consider the degree to which the steel plate market in this period was subject to market power exercised by the Defendant.

To do so, we analyze a number of indicia economists typically look at to evaluate the degree of market power exercised by a firm and its impact on consumers. These indicia include the number of sellers in the market, their respective market shares, measures of overall market concentration, the degree of market contestability and new entry, the elasticity of supply for the market as a whole, the elasticity of demand faced by the Defendant, the profitability of firms and how they respond to competitive pressures in the market and price determination in the market. We analyze these indicia under the market definition proposed earlier. In addition, we evaluate whether or not these indicia of competition changed significantly after late 1997 — the date at which the alleged anticompetitive acts began.

6.4.2. Number of sellers in the market

Under the definition of the market used in this paper, there do not appear to be competitive concerns raised by the number of firms in the marketplace. Suppliers consist of all producers of steel plate products, including domestic integrated companies, reconstituted mills, strip mills, minimills, and overseas producers. It is clear there are a very large number of such suppliers. In 1997, the total number of just domestic cut-to-length plate suppliers totaled at least 43, while there were at least 57 overseas steel producers that imported steel plate into the US that year.[27] No competitive concerns are raised by the number of firms existing under this market definition.

6.4.3. Market shares

Market share data is another indicator used by economists when evaluating the competitiveness of a market. It provides information on the extent to which a

---

[26] The International Trade Commission determined that the steel plate industry was materially injured by reason of imports from a number of countries, including France, Japan, India, Indonesia, Italy and Korea. See ITC Publication 3273.

[27] ITC Publication 3273 lists 20 US mills and 23 US processors that produce CTL steel plate; it also lists 57 foreign companies that imported CTL plate into the US between January 1996 and June 1999.

firm or group of firms dominate the total sales in a market and therefore provides insight into their potential market power. We calculate market share data for the US steel plate market in Table 6.4 for the years 1997, 1998 and 1999 for the 11 major steel plate producers, US strip mills (in aggregate) and imports by country. For this calculation, we divided each domestic producer's production, and each country's import tonnage, by total US production plus total shipments into the US. Table 6.4 shows the results of our calculations. We note that no individual producer in this market appears to have sufficient market share to raise competitive concerns — the highest individual firm's market share is Bethlehem Steel/Lukens at just under 17% in 1999.

6.4.4. Market concentration

Economists often use a Herfindahl-Hirschman Index ("HHI") as a measure of the concentration of a market that incorporates information about the number of firms in the market as well as each firm's market share. The HHI is calculated as the sum of the squared market shares for each firm in the market. When one firm makes up the entire market (a pure monopolist), the HHI attains its maximum value of 10,000. The HHI declines as the number of firms in the market increases, and rises with rising inequality of market shares among a given number of firms. As a benchmark, the Department of Justice considers a market with an HHI below 1000 to be unconcentrated and unlikely to be subject to any adverse competitive effects. A market with an HHI between 1000 and 1800 is considered to be moderately concentrated. Markets with an HHI above 1800 are considered to be highly concentrated. The Justice Department considers a change in market share producing an increase in the HHI of less than 100 points in a moderately concentrated (1000–1800) market not to raise significant competitive concerns depending on certain other factors such as the degree of contestability, the existence of barriers to entry, price determination in the market, etc.

We calculate the HHI value for the relevant market for each of the years 1997, 1998 and 1999 using the market share data in Table 6.4. Since we do not have data for individual foreign companies' market shares, we count each country's exports as if they came from one firm.[28] This is a conservative assumption which serves to inflate the calculated HHI above its true value, since most foreign countries have more than one firm which imports steel plate into the US.[29] Similarly,

---

[28] In this sense we have chosen a "group level" calculation of HHI, thereby ignoring "within group" dispersion.

[29] ITC Publication 3273 for example, lists 11 Japanese, 5 German, 3 Korean, and 3 U.K. firms that imported steel plate into the US in 1998.

Table 6.4:   HHI for global carbon cut-to-length and coil plate suppliers.

Plate supplier	Market share			HHI: Times 100 and squared		
	1997 (%)	1998 (%)	1999 (%)	1997	1998	1999
Mexico	0.38	0.72	1.02	0.142	0.511	1.032
Canada	3.64	3.03	3.82	13.233	9.165	14.565
Guatemala	0.00	0.00	0.00	0.000	0.000	0.000
Venezuela	0.40	0.51	0.60	0.159	0.261	0.366
Peru	0.00	0.01	0.00	0.000	0.000	0.000
Brazil	0.48	0.89	0.51	0.229	0.787	0.260
Argentina	0.00	0.00	0.16	0.000	0.000	0.027
Sweden	0.42	0.33	0.45	0.173	0.110	0.204
Finland	0.01	0.24	0.22	0.000	0.057	0.050
Denmark	0.04	0.02	0.00	0.001	0.000	0.000
United Kingdom	0.22	0.87	0.41	0.047	0.765	0.169
Netherlands	0.50	0.73	1.16	0.251	0.535	1.336
Belgium	0.14	0.37	0.23	0.019	0.140	0.053
Luxembourg	0.02	0.02	0.00	0.001	0.000	0.000
France	2.07	2.21	2.13	4.282	4.868	4.535
Federal Republic of Germany	0.72	0.53	0.41	0.524	0.286	0.171
Austria	0.13	0.19	0.02	0.018	0.035	0.001
Spain	0.00	0.01	0.00	0.000	0.000	0.000
Portugal	0.00	0.00	0.00	0.000	0.000	0.000
Italy	1.02	0.88	0.13	1.041	0.782	0.018
Norway	0.00	0.00	0.01	0.000	0.000	0.000
Czech Republic	0.77	0.42	0.32	0.587	0.178	0.102
Slovakia	0.08	0.17	0.07	0.006	0.028	0.006
Hungary	0.06	0.11	0.22	0.003	0.012	0.046
Switzerland	0.02	0.04	0.02	0.000	0.001	0.001
Latvia	0.16	0.02	0.00	0.024	0.001	0.000
Lithuania	0.00	0.24	0.00	0.000	0.056	0.000
Poland	0.04	0.00	0.00	0.002	0.000	0.000
Russia	7.19	10.77	0.25	51.668	115.986	0.064
Ukraine	2.05	1.52	0.26	4.213	2.296	0.067
Kazakhstan	0.03	0.24	0.45	0.001	0.056	0.202
Slovenia	0.00	0.00	0.03	0.000	0.000	0.001
Macedonia	0.41	0.45	0.24	0.164	0.206	0.058
Romania	0.36	0.60	1.56	0.130	0.364	2.422

Table 6.4:   *(continued)*

Plate supplier	Market share			HHI: Times 100 and squared		
	1997 (%)	1998 (%)	1999 (%)	1997	1998	1999
Bulgaria	0.33	0.18	0.19	0.107	0.034	0.038
Turkey	0.14	0.02	0.17	0.019	0.000	0.029
Cyprus	0.00	0.02	0.00	0.000	0.001	0.000
India	1.32	1.44	2.19	1.739	2.071	4.778
Thailand	0.00	0.26	0.16	0.000	0.068	0.027
Malaysia	0.00	0.12	0.00	0.000	0.013	0.000
Indonesia	0.47	1.24	1.06	0.222	1.542	1.127
China	1.51	1.28	1.41	2.274	1.630	2.001
Republic of Korea	0.22	2.68	1.94	0.049	7.179	3.756
Taiwan	0.00	0.09	0.56	0.000	0.008	0.312
Japan	0.55	4.65	0.62	0.307	21.586	0.385
Australia	0.00	0.04	0.29	0.000	0.002	0.084
New Zealand	0.16	0.09	0.17	0.026	0.008	0.029
Republic of South Africa	0.10	0.26	0.58	0.011	0.069	0.342
Import total	26.15	38.51	24.06	683.973	1483.243	579.062
Bethlehem Steel (a)	12.72	12.98	16.89	161.733	168.555	285.412
Lukens	7.06	0.00	0.00	49.844	0.000	0.000
CitiSteel	2.43	1.69	1.99	5.911	2.849	3.950
Geneva	6.73	8.16	5.71	45.330	66.525	32.652
Gulf States	3.55	2.98	3.31	12.627	8.871	10.964
IPSCO	0.94	3.67	6.96	0.874	13.438	48.392
Jindal	0.00	1.51	2.43	0.000	2.275	5.885
Letourneau	1.40	1.15	0.99	1.967	1.312	0.988
Oregon	1.82	2.67	4.47	3.325	7.145	19.999
Tuscaloosa	3.27	4.39	5.71	10.712	19.283	32.652
USS	11.22	8.90	8.18	125.916	79.158	66.874
Strip mills	22.70	13.40	19.29	515.151	179.578	372.076
Total	100.00	100.00	100.00	1015.062	720.690	918.504

Note. [1] Bethlehem Steel acquired Lukens in 1998.

Source. AISI and company reports.

since we do not have individual strip mill company data on steel plate production we assume that all strip mill plate production came from one company.
Again this is a conservative assumption that serves to inflate our calculated
HHI's above their true value, since there is more than one strip mill company
that produces plate.

In calculating the HHI for the plate market, we include both carbon and
alloy cut-to-length and coil plate. We utilize production data from domestic
plate mills and strip mills, as well as import data. The results are shown in
Table 6.4.

The HHI values are 1015, 721, and 919 for 1997, 1998 and 1999, respectively.
These calculated HHI values for 1997 through 1999, which as described earlier
are likely to be above the true HHI values, indicate a market that is unconcentrated and therefore unlikely to be subject to anti-competitive effects. Further
there is little change in the HHI values from 1997 to 1999, indicating that
whatever the alleged anti-competitive acts by Defendant, it did not result in an
increased concentration of the market that would be considered significant.

6.4.5. Market contestability and new entry

The market for steel plate products is clearly contestable and subject both to new
entry and significant capacity expansion of existing firms in the market.[30] These
are characteristics that are inconsistent with a market subject to anti-competitive
forces. The massive expansion of capacity of domestic steel plate producers in
the mid 1990s, and the diversion of overseas producers' steel plate products to
the US market in 1998 and 1999 described in detail earlier in this chapter are
examples of how the steel market is subject to new entry and capacity expansion. As noted earlier, IPSCO added a new plate facility in Mobile, Alabama
that will increase capacity by 1.25 million tons.[31] Nucor also built a new plate
mill during 2000 in Hertford County, North Carolina adding capacity of
1,000,000 tons to the plate market.[32] Therefore, much of this new entry and
capacity expansion occurred subsequent to the alleged anti-competitive acts by
Defendant starting in late 1997, again suggesting that these acts had no anti-
competitive effects on the steel plate market.

---

[30] See for example the discussion in the previous section on the state of the steel plate industry in
the late 1990s.
[31] See IPSCO press release 3/27/2001.
[32] *New Steel*, Nucor, September 2000.

6.4.6. Elasticity of supply

The elasticity of supply of a product measures the percentage change in aggregate supply of that product resulting from a 1% change in its market price. It is a potentially important measure of how price competitive a market is. For example, in a market where the elasticity of supply of product was zero, a firm would be able to raise price for the product without facing any subsequent increase in supply of that product from other firms looking to take advantage of the increase in market price. In other words, a firm would likely be able to raise price profitably. However, in a market where the elasticity of supply was very high, then any firm that raised price would immediately face increased output from other firms which would defeat the attempt to raise price.

While there are no studies that estimate the elasticity of supply for the steel plate market, there are some studies which estimate the supply elasticity for the steel industry as a whole. These include Matthews (1993) and Cima (1996), both of which present supply elasticities that are high (between 2.0 and 5.9). In addition, the low capacity utilization in the steel plate industry over the relevant time period for this matter (discussed in the previous section) suggest that the elasticity of supply in the steel plate market was high: it would have been relatively easy for domestic steel plate firms to expand output in response to any increase in price. In addition, the collapse in demand for steel plate from Asia and other parts of the world and the increased volume of steel plate imports to the US over this period suggest that foreign manufacturers of steel plate also exhibited low capacity utilization and would have been able to respond to any increase in steel plate prices in the US with significantly increased output. Given the likelihood of high supply elasticities for steel plate over this period, it is unlikely that any steel plate producer (or group of producers) would have had sufficient market power to raise prices.

6.4.7. Elasticity of demand faced by the Defendant

The elasticity of demand faced by an individual firm is measured as the percentage change in the quantity demanded of that firm's product in response to a 1% change in the price charged by the firm, given constant prices charged by the firm's competitors. If a firm's elasticity of demand is very high, then it will be unable to raise price profitably because doing so will result in its customers switching their demand to the firm's competitors.

While we do not estimate the elasticity of demand faced by the Defendant firm, we can draw conclusions about the elasticity of demand likely to be faced by any individual firm in the steel plate market over this period. In a simplified world, where all firms are the same size, the elasticity of demand faced by an individual firm is given by the formula:

$$E = n \cdot e + (n - 1)N$$

where E is the elasticity of demand for an individual firm,
       n is the number of firms in the market,
       e is the market elasticity of demand,
       N is the elasticity of supply of a competitor firm.[33]

Given the relatively large number of firms in the market (n), and the relatively high supply elasticities discussed above, it is likely that the elasticity of demand faced by any individual firm (E) is relatively high, thus implying that there would be little chance that any individual firm would have been able to profitably raise price in the steel plate market over this period.

6.4.8. Profitability of firms in the market

Economists often look at the financial performance of firms in an industry as an indicator of market power. In a competitive market, firms are unable to charge prices significantly above their costs. Thus the industry as a whole does not make an above normal return, and in particular, individual firms that do not have cost advantages over their rivals cannot make above normal profits.

Examination of the profits of the cut-to-length steel plate firms over the period 1997 through 1999 do not indicate market power in the industry as a whole. Indeed, while the industry as a whole was making an operating profit in 1997 (equal to 3% of net sales), by the first half of 1999, this had turned into a substantial operating loss (of 5.2% of net sales). Our analysis of Defendant's profitability indicated a similar trend, again implying a lack of market power.

6.4.9. Price determination in the market: Can a firm (or firms) exercise market power?

An important indicator of the competitiveness of a market is whether or not any firm in that market can influence price. In a competitive market, firms are price

---

[33] See Carlton and Perloff (1994), pp. 100–103.

takers (i.e., the price is determined by market forces) and must pass changes in industry wide costs onto buyers of their product.

In Figure 6.3 below, we present a time series for prices of steel plate in the US. Note that prices declined dramatically in 1998 and midway through 1999. This is not generally consistent with the exercise of market power by firms in the market or an adverse impact on consumers. In particular, it is not consistent with Defendant acquiring market power as a result of its alleged anti-competitive acts. After the alleged acts started, prices for steel plate peaked in May 1998 at about US$437 per ton and then declined continuously to under US$300 per ton by October 1999.

Particular pricing practices in the steel plate market appear to vary from firm to firm. But no firm appears to have the power to set prices and maintain them independent of market conditions. For example, the International Trade Commission notes that most producers of steel plate price on a transaction-by-transaction basis.

6.4.10. Industry response to competitive pressures

Another (indirect) indicator of competitiveness in a market is the response of firms to competitive pressures. In a competitive market, some firms will respond to competitive pressures by increasing productivity through innovation and other

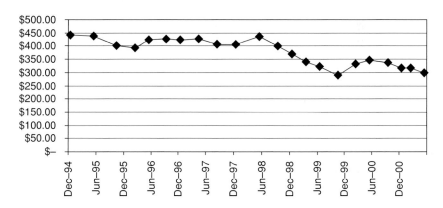

Figure 6.3:   Steel plate price per net ton.

Source. World Steel Dynamics.

means, while other firms that do not will exit the market (either through bankruptcy or merging with another firm). The background to the steel industry in general and the steel plate industry in particular in the late 1990s — discussed at length in previous sections — appears to be a prime example of these two different types of behavior. While many firms downsized in an effort to increase productivity and brought newer plants on line with innovative techniques, others failed or shut down their older, poorly performing plants.

6.5. CONCLUSION

After defining the relevant market and evaluating all the indicia of market power discussed above, it is our conclusion that the market for steel plate in the late 1990s was not subject to anti-competitive forces to any material degree, and that the alleged anticompetitive acts by the Defendant could not have resulted in the Defendant attaining sufficient market power to raise price and hurt consumers.

REFERENCES

Adams, W. and H. Mueller, (1990), "The Steel Industry," in *The Structure of American Industry*, 8th Edition, Adams and Mueller (eds.), New York: MacMillan.
Carlton, Dennis W. and Jeffrey Perloff (1994), *Modern Industrial Organization*, New York: Addison-Wesley.

CHAPTER 7

Measuring Market Power and Competition Policy in Hong Kong

PING LIN[a] and EDWARD K. Y. CHEN[b]

Department of Economics, Lingnan University, Tuen Mun, Hong Kong

Abstract

Unlike most other advanced countries, Hong Kong does not yet have a comprehensive competition law. Yet lack of competition and abuse of market power exist in many important sectors, as found by a series of studies issued by the Hong Kong Consumer Council in the 1990s. We describe in detail the approach of the Consumer Council in measuring market power in various markets, particularly its use of the conventional structure-conduct-performance paradigm combined with the unique roles of land scarcity and market contestability. The second part of the chapter provides an evaluation of the current competition policy in Hong Kong, which came into effect in 1998 as a result of the Consumer Council's studies.

Keywords: Competition policy, market power
JEL Classification: L10, L60

---

[a] Corresponding author.
[b] Served as the Chairman of the Hong Kong Consumer Council between 1991 and 1997.

7.1. INTRODUCTION

Antitrust or competition policy is a relatively new concept in Hong Kong. The government of Hong Kong did not have a competition policy until early 1998. Historically, the government has adopted a positive non-intervention policy toward market activity, a philosophy that has dominated almost every aspect of its policy making. Laissez-faire has been treated with great respect, and market forces have been regarded as the best way of allocating resources. Many people in Hong Kong, including government officials, still regard antitrust as another way for the government to intervene with the free market system. Given such an environment, systematic studies of market power are rare in Hong Kong. In this chapter, we review the studies conducted by the Hong Kong Consumer Council in the early 1990s on measuring market power in major industries, focusing on the methodologies used. These studies raised the public's attention to market power in Hong Kong and paved the way for the establishment of Hong Kong's competition policy in 1998. We also provide an evaluation of the current competition policy by pointing out two fundamental drawbacks of its sectoral approach: distortion of resources in the long run and the government's inability to convey to the public the impartiality of its competition decisions.

7.2. THE CONSUMER COUNCIL'S STUDIES OF MARKET POWER

The Hong Kong Consumer Council ("the Council") is a statutory body established in 1974. In the early 1990s, the Council, under the chairmanship of one of the authors of this chapter, developed a keen interest in studying the anti-competitive behavior of firms in many service sectors in Hong Kong. In October 1992, the Council launched a series of studies on market competitiveness and its impact on consumer welfare. The sectors covered included the markets for bank deposits, supermarket retailing, gas supply, telecommunications, radio broadcasting, and residential property market, among others. "Low levels of competition" were found in most of the sectors studied.

In assessing competition issues and measuring market power, the Council adopted the conventional "structure-conduct-performance" paradigm. In applying this standard methodology, the Council paid great attention to two important factors that are unique to Hong Kong and have strong implications for industrial structure and firm conduct: (A) limited supply of land and (B) market contestability.

A *The land factor*

For a city like Hong Kong where land is perhaps the most scarce resource, availability of land determines to a great extent important aspects such as entry cost, supplier–customer relationship, product substitutability, pricing, and so on. For instance, in the residential property market, limited access to and higher costs of land directly pose a huge entry barrier to new entrants. In the energy market, limited land supply implies that it is more economical for new firms to lease storage capacity from established firms, rather than build their own facilities. Since the major operators in this market are vertically integrated, this determines the ease of entry as well as post-entry conduct at both the wholesale and retail levels. Also, the inability to obtain favorable land sites was a major reason for the recent close-down of its Hong Kong branches by the French-based supermarket chain store company, Carrefour, which entered into the Hong Kong market in 1996 and managed to open up only four branches before it exited in late 2000. In its studies, the Council paid great attention to the land factor and its crucial roles in determining industry structures and firm conduct in Hong Kong.

B *Market contestability*

Another key factor the Council emphasized was contestability of market. Given its thin size, it is often the case that there are only a few firms actually competing with one another in many sectors in Hong Kong, especially in the non-tradable sectors. The role of potential competition is therefore very important. For markets that are contestable (and thus entry is easy and does not involve a large amount of sunk cost), even monopoly firms are disciplined by the threat of potential entrants. If existing firms were earning above normal rates of return, entry would occur in contestable industries. The degree of contestability thus affects firm market power and conduct in an important way. The emphasis and application of the contestable market theory can be seen in almost every single study of the Consumer Council, as well as in its final competition report published in 1996 (see section 7.3).

In the following section we draw on case studies of the markets for energy, housing, and banking deposits to illustrate the approach used by the Council in measuring market power. As we will see, the methodologies used are not technically sophisticated, involving mostly scrutiny of rather basic aspects of market structure, firm conduct and performance. One reason for this is that there is a lack of statistics on industrial organization in Hong Kong, presumably due to the fact that market power and antitrust have not been regarded as significant issues by government authorities. For example, basic information such as four-firm concentration ratios simply does not exist for most industries in Hong Kong, not to mention the Herfindahl-Hirschman Indices. The lack of basic statistics rendered the Council's task quite difficult. The Council sometimes was forced to infer the underlying market structure and firm conduct from information about firm performance (profitability, corporate growth, etc.). To accomplish this, the Council often needed to conduct international comparisons using indicators of firm performance in other countries/regions as benchmarks for "reasonable rates of return" in Hong Kong. Despite the data limitations, however, the findings of the Council's studies were pioneering and are, to date, perhaps the only set of systematic studies of market power in Hong Kong. It provided valuable information about market power and anti-competitive practices.

7.2.1. The domestic water heating and cooking fuel market

In 1995, the Council provided a detailed study of competition in the market for domestic water heating and cooking fuel (Consumer Council, 1995). Domestic consumers of water heating and cooking fuel in Hong Kong were, and still are, served by three main alternatives, namely town gas, cylinder and bulk liquefied petroleum gas (LPG), and electricity. By examining the regulatory environment of these markets, the Council found that the existing regulatory framework, technical and cultural factors created a significant competitive advantage and a resultant market dominance for the Hong Kong and China Gas Company Ltd. (HKCG), the sole supplier of town gas in the market.[1]

7.2.1.1. Regulatory factors

In order to safeguard public safety, Section 17(4) of the Gas Safety (Gas Supply) Regulation prescribes that "No person shall install a gas main for the conveyance of liquefied petroleum along or across a road." This regulation directly affects developers' choices of energy supply. Since transmission of LPG under public roadways was banned by regulation, a new housing development can only secure a central LPG supply by building special storage depots in the vicinity of the development to supply the fuel to the entire development. Further, no residential structure should be built on top of, or within a defined distance from the storage depot. Town gas, on the other hand, does not face similar constraints. Since land must be earmarked for the storage depot within the development, LPG

---

[1] HKCG manufactures town gas using naphtha as a feedstock. By contrast, six major oil companies supply LPG to Hong Kong. Natural gas is used for power generation in Hong Kong. In 1997, town gas accounted for 74% of the total fuel gas sold in energy terms, while LPG accounted for the remaining 26% (Lam, 2000, p. 304).

must pay a premium to developers to compensate for the loss of space which could otherwise be used for other profitable purposes. Under such circumstances, town gas clearly has a competitive advantage over LPG.

7.2.1.2. Cultural and technical factors

Town gas also enjoys a competitive advantage over electricity in the market. The use of electricity for cooking is confined mostly to appliances such as electric kettles, rice cookers, and microwave ovens. For Chinese cuisine preparations, "flame cooking" of gas fuel is preferred by consumers. "Flame cooking" is a critical ingredient in the preparation of any Chinese meal and is thus crucial to the daily life of Chinese consumers. The availability of gas for cooking is almost taken for granted by consumers. With over 90% of the Hong Kong population being ethnic Chinese, private developers would hesitate to not supply gas for cooking purposes. For water heating, gas fuel is also preferred to electricity because the former can provide a continuous supply of heated water whereas the majority of electric water heaters installed in Hong Kong are of the storage type, which naturally limits the amount of heated water.[2]

7.2.1.3. Evidence of market dominance

The council examined the relative market share of different suppliers in both the gas market as well as the broader market including electricity. In the market for gas fuel, HKCG in 1993 had the largest market share of 66% whereas the remaining 34% was distributed among five LPG suppliers. When electricity was included in the market for water heating and cooking, HKCG remained the largest player with the estimated market share ranging from 51% to 40% for 1992.

7.2.1.4. Barriers to entry

The Council also argued that the market for water heating and cooking fuel is not contestable and that HKCG is likely to maintain its market dominance. This

---

[2] A more viable alternative to the gas water heater is the instantaneous type of water heater. However, this type of water heaters can only be installed where electricity supply is boosted with a three-phase electrical installation, which is not available in most small and medium size apartments in Hong Kong.

is so mainly because building a new gas transmission network poses great difficulty. First and foremost, due to the high initial investment required, it is unlikely
that a competitor can enter the industry and be able to compete with the incumbent who already enjoys the economies of scale. Second, Hong Kong's highly
congested underground traffic may not be able to accommodate another gas
transmission network. Thus, threat from potential entrants to challenge HKCG's
position in the town gas market is remote. Competitive pressure from LPG and
electricity is also limited since they are not perfect substitutes for town gas.

7.2.1.5. Market conduct

In terms of pricing, the Council found that price increases of town gas since
1985 have been below increases in the Consumer Price Index ("CPI"). In fact,
the inflation-adjusted price of town gas for 1994 was only 71% of the 1985 price
level. However, the levels of price increases have been well above the increase
in costs and price increases for town gas have been higher than those for electricity. These findings reflect the fact that HKCG has enjoyed a dominant
position in its market.

The Council also looked at alleged anti-competitive practices by HKCG aimed
at preventing potential entrants. An established electricity provider, China
Light&Power (CLP) has been attempting to penetrate the water heating market
in Hong Kong since early 1990. To promote the use of its water heaters to
consumers, CLP negotiated with private developers for "the supply and installation of 18 kW instantaneous water heaters free of charge" and to provide to
the developers financial assistance needed for such installation. To defend its
market share HKCG countered this promotion initiative by charging developers
a much higher project cost for the gas supply if developers opted for gas supply
for cooking purposes only, CLP claimed that by this action HKCG had abused
its monopoly position in the market. The Council held the view that such an
action constituted an unfair trade practice. It argued that given the fact that gas
is the preferred cooking fuel for the preparation of Chinese cuisine, developers
couldn't afford to refrain from supplying gas cooking facilities in their developments.

7.2.1.6. Performance

Among other profitability indicators, the Council compared the returns on assets
of HKCG with those of other energy companies both in Hong Kong and abroad.

For the period from 1985–1994 the ten-year average returns on asset was 14.1% for HKCG, compared to 11.8% and 11.9% for CLP and Hong Kong Electric, respectively. The average returns for the five largest US electric and gas companies, the most profitable in the world, ranged from 2% to 5%, with the average of 3.6% for the same period.

Based on its analysis, the Council concluded that HKCG had attained a position of market dominance in the residential water heating and cooling fuel supply market, due to the lack of effective competition. It made five recommendations to the government in order to safeguard competition in the market. One of the recommendations was to establish an Energy Commission which would serve as an umbrella organization to monitor and regulate the energy industry in relation to competition issues. This recommendation has not been followed by the government.

7.2.2. The motor gasoline, diesel and LPG markets

In 1998, shortly after the Hong Kong economy was hit by the Asian financial crisis, there was a growing panic concern about the "reasonableness" of fuel prices in Hong Kong, which had maintained levels familiar to them before the financial crisis, whereas prices in other sectors had plunged. It was conjectured that oil companies in Hong Kong had been collusively setting prices for motor vehicle fuels. In late 1998, the Consumer Council launched a study on the markets for motor gasoline and diesel in Hong Kong as well as the markets for cylinder LPG and piped LPG (for use as a domestic hot water and cooking fuel). (See Consumer Council, 2000.)

The study found that the three industries were highly concentrated, with three leading oil companies holding over 70% of the piped and wholesale cylinder LPG market, 90% of the motor gasoline market, and 80% of the diesel market. The degree of vertical integration was also judged to be high in these industries. In particular, all five oil-and-LPG importing companies (Shell, Caltex, Mobil, Esso, and CRC) engage in wholesale and retailing business. The five wholesalers all have their own storage facilities in Hong Kong. Given the small land area and high rental cost in Hong Kong, potential entrants into the markets face substantial investment costs in setting up adequate storage facilities. If they choose to lease storage capacities from the vertically integrated competitors, it is likely that they would face discriminatory treatments.

The Council conjectured that such highly concentrated industries with substantial entry barriers are conducive to collusive behavior. However, lacking the legal power, the Council was unable to obtain critical importing and cost information from the oil companies. Based on second-hand information, the Council found no direct evidence of explicit collusion in these markets, although it discovered that uniform pricing was used in gasoline retailing and cylinder LPG wholesale markets. The Council thus relied on comparison of prices with cities in other countries and regions in order to infer about "collusive pricing" in the Hong Kong markets. Specifically, the Council found that the price of LPG in Hong Kong (exclusive of taxes) was about 60% higher than that in Singapore and about 4.5 times higher than that in Malaysia and Shenzhen.

Along with abnormal price levels, the Council was particularly concerned with the apparently high entry barriers to the industries. As noted earlier, one main form of entry barrier is the high degree of vertical integration among existing firms from wholesale to retailing, which makes it difficult for new competitors to enter into either the wholesale or retailing market. Another related factor is the government restrictions on those who can bid for petrol filling sites on offer by the government. Existing regulations require that a bidder either hold a license to import oil or be able to have guaranteed supply from a licensed supplier. This restriction, argues the Council, tends to favor the existing players against potential competitors who do not have the wholesale storage facility of the oil companies. For making a bid, a potential entrant would have to obtain essential qualification from the parties it would eventually be bidding against for a specific site.

7.2.3. The residential property market

The Council's study of the residential property market in 1996 seeks to (1) assess the degree of competition in the private residential property market; (2) examine restrictive practices, if any, in the market which may affect the consumer; and (3) make policy recommendations, if necessary, to promote competition and protect consumer interests. It found that there are two crucial factors affecting the functioning of the housing market in Hong Kong: (1) the role of government as monopoly provider of new land, and regulator of building development; and (2) the high market concentration of developers of private housing (Consumer Council, 1996).

The market for new residential property is highly concentrated. For the period from 1991 to 1994, 70% of the total new private housing was supplied by the top seven developers, 55% by the top four developers, and one developer consistently supplied over 25% of new housing units. The Council then looked at how "contestable" the market is. Although there are no legal barriers to entry, potential new entrants have the following major disadvantages compared to existing firms. (1) higher land costs: due to historical reasons, the incumbents were able to acquire "cheap" land and build a stock of land bank. Potential developers, on the other hand, must pay a much higher land price to the government in land auctions; (2) limited access to land resources: new entrants are largely dependent on the amount of government land released each year, and suffer from tendering procedures which were restricted to holders of Letters A and B at some sites.[3] Land banks also enable major developers to maintain smooth production levels regardless of government supply. Given these factors, the Council then noted that whilst new entrants have emerged since 1981, no new firm has become a major player (i.e. capable of producing 5% or more of the annual supply of new private housing). The greatest obstacle has been the hefty entry costs and limited availability of land (Consumer Council, 1996a, p. 4). The Council then concluded that there was little competitive pressure from potential new entrants to the market.

With regard to the market behavior of major developers, the Council conducted various case studies. In three case studies over the period 1990–1995 from developments in Tseung Kan O, Ma On Shan and Lam Tin, the developers put their finished units on competing sites for sale in alternate order. According to the Council, these marketing strategies meant less choice, higher prices, and reduced ability to make price comparisons for consumers. They may also have enabled the developers to influence the market atmosphere. (The developers contend that such techniques were the results of heated competition.) Another set of case studies covering the years 1994 to 1996 considering developments in Tai Po, Yuen Long and Shatin, found that apartments in different developments were generally released for sale at different times, even though they varied in terms of location and size. Apartments were also released in batches. While the developers regarded this as a means to test the market, the Council considered it as a form of price discrimination or "regulating supply".[4]

To estimate firm profitability, the Council conducted further case studies. In five case studies involving 13 residential developments and covering the period 1985–1995, the Council estimated that profits were particularly high for

---

[3] Letters A and B mean a land exchange entitlement granted by the Government in consideration of the surrender of any agricultural or building land in the New Territories to the Government. Most of the Letters A and B were acquired by a handful of developers in the 1970s and 1980s.

[4] The Council also found in its study that long-term vacancy rates (the proportion of apartments vacant two years after completion) were significantly higher among apartments owned by developers than those in the overall market: 11% of 17,300 new units compared to 4% of 885,700 housing stock in 1995.

developments on land acquired through Letters A and B. They ranged from 77% to 364% of the total estimated development costs. For lots obtained from public land auction, the estimated profit margins ranged from 6% to 109%.

7.2.4. Measuring the monopolistic rent of the interest rate cartel

After a period of bank runs in the late 1970s, banks in Hong Kong formed an interest rate cartel, with the goal of preventing "cut-throat" competition in the markets for deposits. The cartel, under the umbrella of the Hong Kong Association of Banks (HKAB), set interest rates on deposit accounts for all member banks, prior to its dismantling in 2001 by the government.

Based on a consulting project undertaken for the Consumer Council by the Department of Economics & Finance at the City Polytechnic (now called City University) of Hong Kong, the Council issued a report entitled "Are Hong Kong Depositors Fairly Treated?" in 1994.[5] In addition to assessing competition in the banking market in general, the report focused much attention on the measurement of the monopolistic rent extracted by the interest rate cartel among the licensed banks in the deposit markets.

With the help of the Hong Kong Monetary Authority, the Central Bank of Hong Kong, the Council calculated the Herfindahl Indices for the banking industry. For the market for Hong Kong dollar demand deposit, the HHI index in the licensed bank category ranged from 1000 to 1200 for the period 1988–1992. The HHI indices for savings deposits ranged from 1600 to 1700 during the same period. These indicated a relatively high degree of concentration, considering that there were about 155 to 161 licensed banks in that period.

To come up with a measure of the monopoly rent created by the interest agreement, the Council compared the interest-rate spreads of Hong Kong banks with those in other countries such as Japan, the United States, Singapore, UK, Australia and Malaysia. Three categories of deposits were considered: demand deposits (checking accounts), saving accounts and time deposits (CD accounts). Under the rules of the HKAB, demand deposit accounts were not permitted to pay interest. For saving and time deposit accounts, the HKAB set the maximum interest rates that its member banks could offer. Using data for the period from 1978 to 1992, the Council found that the annual interest spreads in Hong Kong were consistently higher than those in other countries during the period examined. In particular, the prime-CD interest spread ranged 0.71% to 2.04% higher

---

[5] See Consumer Council (1994). See also Chan and Khoo (1998) for an updated version of the consulting report.

than ADD comparisons in Hong Kong, with an average of 1.65%. The prime-saving rate spreads ranged from 0.26% to 3.07% higher, with an average of 1.79%. Based on these differences in interest rate spreads, the Council estimated that the monopoly rents earned by Hong Kong banks were about 5.17 billion HK dollars for 1991, representing about 0.8% of the GDP (Consumer Council, 1994).[6] For the period of 1987–1994, the estimated rents were 1.05% of the respective GDP (Chan and Khoo, 1998).[7]

Based on its study, the Consumer Council recommended that the government abolish the interest rate cartel over a number of years. The government followed this recommendation and started removing the interest rate restrictions on demand deposits and short-term time deposits in 1997. The interest rate cartel was completely removed in July 1 2001.

7.3. HONG KONG'S COMPETITION POLICY

Based on its studies, the Consumer Council published a report, entitled *Competition Policy: The Key to Hong Kong's Future Success*, in November 1996 (Consumer Council, 1996b). In this report, it strongly recommends the adoption of a comprehensive competition law, which should at a minimum contain the following:[8]

a) Article 1: to prohibit explicit agreements between firms that are intended or have the effect of preventing, restricting or distorting competition. These include horizontal agreements such as those involved in price-fixing cartels, bid-rigging, etc., and vertical agreements such as retail price maintenance, exclusive dealership, tie-in sales, long-term supply contracts, etc.

---

[6] US$1 is worth about HK$7.8 under the current linked exchange rate regime.

[7] Since the checking accounts did not pay interest rate, Chan and Khoo (1998) proposed that the interest spread that should have been paid to those accounts is the savings rate less 1%. The rent for each category of deposits was estimated by multiplying the respective interest spread and the annual balance of that category.

[8] The proposed competition law also included articles controlling the abuse of collective dominance, and the control of mergers and acquisitions. The Council, however, noted the desirability of deferring the introduction of these two articles due to technical reasons, arguing that "the issues raised in cases involving complex monopoly are best addressed when experience has been cumulated. Decisions relating to mergers and acquisitions also raise difficult technical issues, which must be resolved within a strict time table if the ordinary conduct of business is not to be impeded" (Consumer Council, 1996b, p. 76).

b) Article 2: to prohibit any abuse by one or more undertakings of a dominant position that prevents, restricts or distorts competition. This would address monopoly pricing, and vertical restraints such as tie-in sales enforced through market dominance.

The Council also recommended that an independent Competition Authority be established with the power to investigate possible breaches of the law, and that an Appeal Body be set up to hear appeals against decisions by the Competition Authority.

One year after the publication of the Council's report, the government responded by first establishing a Competition Policy Advisory Group (COMPAG) in December 1997, chaired by the Financial Secretary. Then in May 1998 it issued a formal policy statement, which stated that instead of introducing an overall competition law, the government had decided to set up a sector-specific competition policy framework.[9] The essence of the sectoral approach is to identify anti-competitive behavior and to initiate pro-competition measures, on a sectoral basis, through administrative or legislative measures. Put differently, instead of establishing an overall legal framework for the entire economy, the government proposed to set different rules for different sectors to govern competition within the sectors concerned, with the administration of these sector-based rules being carried out by relevant sector-specific agencies.[10] In the policy statement, the government declared that the objective of its competition policy was "to enhance economic efficiency and free flow of trade, thereby also benefiting consumer welfare." The government recognized that restrictive practices are detrimental to the overall interests of Hong Kong, and included two types of business practices, horizontal restraints and abuse of market position.[11,12]

---

[9] The policy statement is available at: http://www.info.gov.hk/tib/roles/index%5fmain.htm.

[10] For example, the *Telecommunications Ordinance of Hong Kong* and the *Broadcasting Authority Ordinance* specify the competition principles to be followed in promoting competition in the telecommunications industry and the broadcasting industry. The enforcement bodies are, respectively, the Telecommunications Authority and the Broadcasting Authority.

[11] For horizontal restraints, the following practices that have the effect of impairing economic efficiency or free trade or are intended to distort normal market operations were listed in the statement "for illustrative purpose only": (1) price-fixing; (2) bid-rigging, market allocation, sales and production quotas; (3) joint boycotts; and (4) unfair or discriminatory standards among members of a trade or professional body (intended to deny newcomers a chance to enter or contest in the market).

[12] The government also set out the following examples of conduct that might involve an abuse of market position: (1) predatory pricing; (2) setting retail price minimums for products or services where there are no readily available substitutes; and (3) conditioning the supply of specified products or services to the purchase of other specified products or services or to the acceptance of certain restrictions other than to achieve assurance of quality, safety, adequate service or other justified purposes.

7.4. AN ASSESSMENT OF HONG KONG'S COMPETITION POLICY FRAMEWORK

Since the establishment of its competition policy, the government has dealt with a number of competition cases in various sectors. For instance, in the telecommunications sector, the Telecommunication Authority, the agency responsible for enforcing the competition rules set for the industry, considered about 81 cases since late 1997. In this section, we provide a brief assessment of the current competition policy in Hong Kong.

Before adopting this policy, the government was aware of the advantages and disadvantages of a sectoral approach. For instance, according to the Consumer Council, a sectoral approach is "piece meal" and fails to provide comprehensive guidelines in a consistent manner; competition provisions in different sectors may be subject to different interpretations and carry different penalties; further a sectoral approach may be prone to the capture of regulators by interest groups.[13] The government, on the other hand, stressed that a sectoral approach is less expensive to set up; it can take into account industry specifics and thus provides greater certainty to the business community; it helps avoid "over-kills." The government further stated that it does not see the need to introduce a competition law to Hong Kong at this stage.

We agree with the Consumer Council and support a broad competition law approach. In addition to the arguments made by the Council, we identify two more, fundamental, drawbacks of the sectoral approach.

7.4.1. Distortion of resource allocations in the long run

From a general viewpoint, a sectoral approach may hinder the efficient allocation of resources across different sectors of the economy. In choosing which sectors to invest in, private agents follow not only price signals, they also consider the "institutional costs" of operating in different environments. Under a sectoral approach, different sectors will inevitably have different sector-specific rules of the game. These rules are enforced by different regulatory agencies which may interpret the rules differently, follow different criteria, and have different enforcement experiences. One may then expect that, other things being equal, "fair players" and/or weak players would prefer to enter sectors where competition rules are perceived as complete and fair, so that they are less likely

---

[13] Consumer Council (1996b), p. 32.

to be "bullied" by dominant firms, whereas "nasty players" would choose sectors where competition rules are either absent or lenient so that they would face less disciplinary restrictions. Different "institutional environments" therefore imply different rates of return on investment, which will unavoidably affect private investors' decisions as to which sectors to enter. In the long run, the potential distortion of a sectoral approach on resource allocation across sectors should not be ignored.[14]

7.4.2. Dual roles of competition enforcers

Under the current sector-based competition policy, various government regulatory agencies must perform dual roles. On the one hand, as regulators of natural monopolies, these agencies must fulfill their traditional regulatory duties, such as issuing and administrating business licenses, and reviewing and monitoring the prices and qualities of regulated firms. On the other hand, these agencies are the judges when competition complaints and allegations are brought *against* the firms they regulate.[15] For simplicity, we name these two roles as regulator and enforcer, respectively. In other antitrust jurisdictions, these two roles are generally performed by separate agencies.

An effective enforcement of competition rules requires fair and independent decisions on competition complaints. But to act fairly and independently is a separate matter from being able to convince the concerned parties and the public that one has done so. The ruling in a competition case affects not only the parties concerned in the case, but it also influences the future behavior of other firms. It is therefore extremely important for the enforcer to make sure not only that justice is done, but also that justice is seen to be done. However, when the very same agency is responsible for two inter-related duties, it is difficult for outsiders

---

[14] The arguments provided here are analogous to those often made regarding the relationship between foreign direct investment and competition policy. When considering investment options in different markets, foreign companies place a high premium on the country that has the most developed legal system in terms of allowing access and protection to the investment, reducing administrative burdens and addressing the distortions of competitive process.

[15] For example, competition provisions in the telecommunications and the broadcasting industries are enforced, respectively, by the Telecommunications Authority and the Broadcasting Authority. The TA's responsibilities include economic regulation, technical regulation, enforcing fair competition rules, setting technical standards, coordinating the development of the telecommunications infrastructure, investigating consumers' and industry complaints, managing the radio spectrum, providing advice to the Government on telecommunications matters and representing Hong Kong in international telecommunications organizations.

to believe that decisions concerning one such duty are made independent of considerations of the other duty. The dual roles often conflict with one another. The enforcers under a sectoral approach face an information problem in communicating their impartiality to the public.

An information problem arises because the general public, as well as the parties to a competition case, do not have access to comprehensive information regarding the regulator's decision making in performing either of its roles.[16] Although a competition case can be open to the public throughout, it is impossible for the public to know exactly how a regulator interacts with the firms it regulates on a daily basis, especially with long-time incumbents with which regulators often have close working or even personal relationships. It is, then, natural for the public to presume biased decisions by the enforcer/regulator. The burden of proof lies with the regulator.[17] Unless it acts *solely* as an enforcer, it is difficult for the agency to prove it behaves independently in making competition rulings.

The information problem can be illustrated by recent merger and acquisition cases in the mobile phone service industry. In December 1997, the Telecommunication Authority (TA) approved the application by Hong Kong Telecom CSL to acquire "Pacific Link". Prior to the case, both companies participated in a bidding process organized by the TA for mobile phone service licenses in Hong Kong. While Pacific Link won a license, Hong Kong Telecom CSL was not successful. The TA was criticized in the acquisition case for having compromised the regulatory environment by allowing the loser in a license bidding process to buy back a license.[18] The TA was having difficulties defending its position because it was unable to convince critics that it had acted fairly in both granting mobile phone licenses and in approving the acquisition. Similarly, the TA was unable to establish that its approval of the transaction was independent of its on-going negotiation with HK Telecom (CSL's parent) on termination of HK Telecom's exclusive licensing contract in the international calls market. Since the government had to compensate HK Telecom for early termination of its monopoly status, questions were raised as to whether the TA's approval of CSL's acquisition of Pacific Link was related to the terms of the

---

[16] The standard information problem pertaining to regulation refers to the difficulty of obtaining (cost) information from the regulated firm. (See Laffont and Tirole, 1993). Here we emphasize the difficulty for the enforcer to explain to the public its independent decision-making when it also serves as a regulator.

[17] The tendency to presume biased decisions is certainly strong when the competition decisions concern an incumbent firm versus newcomers, or domestic firms versus foreign firms.

[18] In a subsequent case involving acquisition of P Plus by Smartone Telecommunications Limited, approved by the TA in March 1998, exactly the same criticism was raised once again.

negotiation. Specifically, it was asked whether the approval of HKT's acquisition was a part of the "compensation package" for the early termination of the monopoly contract.[19] In cases like these, the dual roles of the TA provide the very cause of the criticisms and the obstacle for the TA to prove its innocence. Had an independent authority approved the acquisition and the TA been responsible for making license decisions only, there probably would not have been such criticisms. We are not claiming, nor do we believe, that the TA was "captured" by any interest groups. Our point is that, empowered with its dual roles, the TA actually suffers from its inability to *convince* the public that its decisions on competition issues are independent from those related to its traditional regulatory duties.

In our view, the foregoing criticisms of the TA's dealing are not specific to these individual cases. Rather, they reflect the general drawback of a sectoral approach that stems from the presence of asymmetric information, and will likely arise in other sectors as well. Having to perform traditional regulatory duties hinders a government agency's ability to establish itself as an independent competition policy enforcer. Consequently, the agency's reputation and effectiveness in performing either role may be undermined.

In addition to the above-mentioned two fundamental drawbacks, the current sectoral approach of the government suffers also from other problems, such as narrow coverage and lack of public enforcement. Specifically, the current competition policy of Hong Kong covers only a small number of industries (telecommunications and broadcasting); most industries do not yet have competition provisions set for them. On the enforcement side, the government and various enforcement agencies mainly depend on complaints from plaintiffs to open up competition cases. They seldom initiate competition investigations themselves. Moreover, the burden of proof is on the complainants under the current rules. A more detailed assessment of this approach can be found in Chen and Lin (2002).

7.5. CONCLUDING REMARKS

Studies on market power in Hong Kong are rare. This is so primarily because of the government's long-time positive non-intervention policy and the misconception that antitrust is another type of regulation and thus necessarily intervenes

---

[19] In January 1998, shortly after its approval of the acquisition case, the TA announced that it would compensate Hong Kong Telecom with about US$858.97 million (net of tax) for surrendering this exclusive right.

with market activity. The Consumer Council's studies reviewed here, although technically not sophisticated, represent, to date, the first set of comprehensive studies of market power in Hong Kong. The conventional structure-conduct-performance approach combined with emphasis on unique features in Hong Kong, namely the limited size of land and a low level of market contestability, was shown to be fruitful in producing information about market power measurement. It is fair to say that the Consumer Council's studies have dramatically changed many people's views on the existence of market power in Hong Kong and the extent to which it is abused. The Consumer Council's studies have also influenced the general attitude towards antitrust. The newly established competition policy of the government was entirely triggered and based on these studies.

Relative to the current sectoral approach, we believe that a comprehensive competition law with an independent enforcement body can better promote competition and economic efficiency in Hong Kong, as the Consumer Council has been advocating since the mid-1990s.[20] First, the consistency of competition provisions for all sectors of the economy should not be undervalued, especially in an era of rapid technological change which blurs the boundaries of traditional markets. The government should consider how to better balance consistency of rules (and avoidance of misallocation of resources in the long run) against simplicity and sector specifics. Second, having an independent enforcement body that is unrelated to any traditional regulatory duties can overcome the information problem inherent in the sectoral approach. Lessons should be drawn from international antitrust experience. To avoid "over-kill", a system similar to the one in the European Community is perhaps most suitable for Hong Kong.

REFERENCES

Chan, Bob Y., & Khoo, Terence. (1998). An analysis of the deposit-taking market of Hong Kong. *Review of Industrial Organization, 13,* 651–667.

Chen, Edward K. Y., & Lin, P. (2002). Competition policy under laissez-faireism: Market power and its treatment in Hong Kong. *Review of Industrial Organization,* forthcoming.

Cheng, Leonard K., & Wu, C. Q. (1998). *Competition Policy and Regulation.* Hong Kong: Commerce Press.

Consumer Council. (1994). *Are Hong Kong Depositors Fairly Treated?*

Consumer Council. (1995). *Assessing Competition in the Domestic Water Heating and Cooking Market.*

---

[20] Cheng and Wu (1998) also argue that a competition law is a necessary underpinning for a comprehensive competition policy in Hong Kong.

Consumer Council. (1996a). *How Competitive Is the Private Residential Property Market?*
Consumer Council. (1996b). *Competition Policy: The Key to Hong Kong's Future Success.*
Consumer Council. (2000). *A Study of Motor Gasoline, Diesel and LPG Markets in Hong Kong: Findings and Recommendations.*
Laffont, J. J., & Tirole, J. (1993). *A Theory of Incentives in Procurement and Regulation.* The MIT Press.
Lam, Pun-lee. (2000). Dominance in Hong Kong's gas industry. *Review of Industrial Organization, 16,* 303–312.

Measuring Market Power
D. J. Slottje (editor)
© 2002 Elsevier Science B.V. All rights reserved

CHAPTER 8

Staples–Office Depot and UP–SP: An Antitrust Tale of Two Proposed Mergers

LAWRENCE J. WHITE

Stern School of Business, New York University, 44 West 4th Street,
New York, NY 10012–1126

Abstract

This paper examines two proposed mergers of the 1990s: the Staples proposal to merge with Office Depot, and the Union Pacific railroad's proposal to merge with the Southern Pacific. Though the two mergers appeared to be quite different on the surface, closer analysis indicates that they were surprisingly similar: both involved a merger of two of the three firms in their respective markets; and both involved significant issues of market delineation. However, the two proposals received quite disparate treatment by different antitrust regimes: the former was blocked by the FTC, while the latter was approved by the STB. The former was a sensible decision; the latter had disastrous consequences for freight shipments in the American southwest in the late 1990s.

Keywords: Mergers, antitrust, office super stores, railroads
JEL classification: K21, L40, L81, L92

8.1. INTRODUCTION

On September 4, 1996, Staples, Inc., announced its intention to acquire Office Depot, Inc. A year earlier, on August 3, 1995, the Union Pacific Corp. announced its intention to purchase the Southern Pacific Rail Corp.

At first glance these were two disparate merger proposals, involving two very different industries. Staples and Office Depot were office super store retailers; the UP and SP were railroads. And, from an antitrust perspective, the disputes surrounding the two mergers appeared to be very different.

But, as this chapter will argue, the two mergers were surprisingly similar: At its core, each involved a merger of two of the three firms in their relevant markets. Also, market delineation was important for the analysis of both mergers. Their outcomes, however, were quite different: The Federal Trade Commission (FTC), with jurisdiction over the Staples–Office Depot merger, challenged the merger and ultimately prevailed in US District Court. By contrast, the Surface Transportation Board (STB), the agency with jurisdiction over railroad mergers,[1] approved the UP–SP merger.

If this were all that was notable about the two mergers, a comparison of the two mergers might warrant a paragraph or two in an antitrust legal textbook, which would remark on the different legal treatment of similar "three-to-two" mergers by different government agencies. The UP–SP merger wasn't just another three-to-two merger, however. Despite the UP's grand promises of efficiencies that would follow from the merger, its implementation initially created such havoc within the merged company that, for over two years, rail freight movements in the American southwest were stalled badly, at a very large cost to shippers and recipients of rail freight in the region.

Accordingly, an examination of the two proposed mergers and how they were treated legally can yield useful insights into public policy in the US and the ways in which its inconsistent treatment of otherwise similar arrangements can lead to unfortunate consequences.

This chapter will proceed as follows. In section 8.2 we will summarize the narrative of the Staples–Office Depot proposed merger and its legal outcome.[2] In section 8.3 we will describe the UP–SP merger and its outcome.[3] Section 8.4 will offer a brief conclusion.

---

[1] The STB came into existence on January 1, 1996, and was the successor to the Interstate Commerce Commission (ICC) as the economic regulator of the railroad industry.
[2] This narrative will draw heavily on Dalkir and Warren-Boulton (1999).
[3] This narrative will draw heavily on Kwoka and White (1999b).

8.2. THE STAPLES–OFFICE DEPOT MERGER

8.2.1. The business context

The "office super store" (OSS) retail concept was pioneered by Staples in 1986, as a large-volume retail outlet for office supplies and other business-related products that focused on small- and medium-sized businesses, home office customers, and individuals. The strategy involved a wide selection of items (5,000–6,000 in a store) and sharply discounted prices (typically 30%–70% below manufacturers' suggested list prices), based on direct-from-the-manufacturer purchases at substantial discounts. Prices at OSSs were often substantially below the prices for the same items that were being sold in local stationery stores and other outlets. Office Depot quickly followed Staples into the OSS category.

This retail concept proved to be a great success. Both chains expanded rapidly. When the merger of the two firms was proposed, Office Depot and Staples were the first and second largest chains of OSSs in the US. As of 1997 (when the case went to trial) Office Depot operated over 500 stores in 38 states; it had worldwide revenues in 1996 of US$7.3 billion and a 1996 year-end stock market value of US$2.2 billion. Staples operated 550 stores in 28 states; it had worldwide revenues in 1996 of US$4.5 billion, and a stock-market valuation of approximately US$3 billion at year-end 1996.

In the decade following Staples' innovation, 23 other OSS chains attempted to replicate these two chains' success. By the time of the proposed merger, however, only OfficeMax, Inc., was a close rival to the two chains. OfficeMax had been spun off from Kmart in 1994. As of 1997 it had 575 stores in 48 states, with 1996 sales of US$3.2 billion.

When the Staples–Office Depot merger was first proposed, most observers believed that it would face few problems in avoiding a legal challenge. After all, both chains primarily sold office supplies and related materials and equipment, and there were tens of thousands of other sellers of such items, from mom-and-pop stationery stores to drug store chains to Wal-Mart and Kmart. The merger's proponents claimed that the two chains accounted for less than 10% of the nation's sales of such items.

Subsequent events showed that this optimism was unfounded. After considering the arguments (presented below), the FTC in April 1997 decided to challenge the merger,[4] which required requesting a preliminary injunction (PI)

---

[4] The FTC initially voted to oppose the merger in March; a subsequent effort to address the FTC's competitive concerns, through a proposed divestiture of 63 stores to OfficeMax, was rejected in April.

in federal district court. The FTC filed its request on April 9, 1997, which (as is usually the case) precipitated an expedited "mini-trial" on the antitrust merits of blocking the merger. The trial began on May 19, 1997.

8.2.2. The legal context

The relevant antitrust law with respect to mergers is the Clayton Act, passed in 1914. Enforced by the Department of Justice's (DOJ) Antitrust Division and by the FTC, Section 7 of the Act instructs the agencies to block any merger "where in any line of commerce in any section of the country, the effect of such acquisition may be substantially to lessen competition or to tend to create a monopoly." In essence, as the Act is currently interpreted, mergers that would likely create or enhance market power are to be blocked.

There are three basic elements to modern antitrust analysis of mergers:[5] (1) the delineation of the relevant market; (2) the determination of the likelihood of post-merger exercise (or enhancement) of market power; and (3) the extent to which any promised efficiencies from a proposed merger should be considered as an offset to any feared market power. The DOJ-FTC *Horizontal Merger Guidelines* have structured these agencies' approach to merger analysis for the past two decades.[6]

8.2.2.1. The relevant market

Since the prevention or inhibition of an increase in market power is the goal of antitrust merger enforcement, the Merger Guidelines define a market as a product (or cluster of products) sold by a group of sellers who, if they acted in concert, could succeed in profitably raising their prices by a significant amount for a significant period of time. In essence, this defines a relevant market as one that can be monopolized. The Guidelines define a significant price increase generally as 5% and a significant period generally as one year. The smallest group of sellers that could exercise market power is generally selected as the relevant market for analysis.

These principles encompass both geographic space and product space. Also, even if a group of sellers could not sustain a significant price increase toward

---

[5] An extended discussion can be found in Kwoka and White (1999a).

[6] The "modern" incarnation of these guidelines was first adopted by the DOJ in 1982, with a modification in 1984 and additional modification and formal joint adoption by both agencies in 1992, and a further modification in 1997.

all of their customers, if they could practice price discrimination toward a significant group of customers, then that customer group constitutes a relevant market.

8.2.2.2. *The likely exercise of market power*

The Merger Guidelines use a number of market factors to indicate the likely post-merger creation or enhancement of market power: (a) the post-merger level of seller concentration (measured by the Herfindahl-Hirschman Index (HHI)[7] and the change in the HHI brought about by the merger; (b) the conditions of entry into the market; (c) the nature of the buyers' side of the market; (d) the characteristics of the product and its market context; and (e) the history of seller behavior in the market.

A merger is more likely to be challenged when the post-merger seller concentration is higher;[8] when the increase in seller concentration brought about by this merger is greater; when conditions of entry are more difficult; when buyers are more numerous and diverse (and thus less able to thwart coordinated behavior through noticeable shopping around and volume purchases); when the characteristics of the product or the market make it easier for sellers to monitor each others' behavior; and when the history of seller behavior indicates that coordinated behavior is more likely.

If the initial structure presented by the merger is likely to raise anti-competitive concerns, divestitures of sufficient assets to third parties, so as to restore a competitive structure, are a common remedy that then permits the (modified) merger to proceed.

8.2.2.3. *Efficiencies*

The Merger Guidelines recognize that mergers can bring significant efficiencies and cost-savings but also that such efficiencies are often easy to promise but may fail subsequently to materialize or they may be achievable without the

---

[7] This is defined as the sum of the squared market shares of all of the sellers in the market.

[8] The Guidelines specify that a post-merger seller HHI level of 1,000 is a level below which mergers will rarely be challenged; a post-merger level of 1,800 is a level above which (if the merger itself causes a change in the HHI of 100 or more) there is a presumption that the merger should be challenged; and intermediate HHI levels warrant further examination. In actual enforcement practice, few mergers with post-merger levels below 2,000 have been challenged, and some mergers with substantially higher levels have been approved, because of other market characteristics.

merger. The Guidelines indicate that a merger will not be challenged where the promised efficiencies are "cognizable" (i.e., merger-specific and verifiable) and of a sufficient magnitude that the merger would (net) not have anti-competitive consequences.

The continuing challenge of the enforcement agencies and of the courts has been to convert these somewhat general principles of merger analysis into specific approval/denial decisions with respect to specific mergers.

8.2.3. The FTC's arguments

The FTC's arguments in opposing the Staples–Office Depot merger tracked the analytical points of the Merger Guidelines: (1) the relevant market was OSSs in individual metropolitan markets (metropolitan statistical areas, or MSAs); (2) within those markets, the merger would reduce the number of competitors from three to two (i.e., the combined firm and OfficeMax), or from two to one (in MSAs where only Staples and Office Depot were present), creating a less competitive duopoly in the former and converting duopolies into monopolies in the latter; and (3) the true efficiencies from the merger would be small.

8.2.3.1. An OSS market

Though the products sold by OSSs were sold by other retail outlets, the pricing data presented by the FTC indicated that OSSs by themselves, in individual MSAs, constituted a relevant market. The data showed that prices of the items sold by Staples or by Office Depot were highest when only one of them was present in a metropolitan area, lower when there were two OSSs in the MSA, and lower still when all three were present. Sophisticated econometric modeling, which controlled for other factors, showed results that were quite similar to the straightforward price comparisons. Further, in the econometric results, the presence of other major sellers, such as Wal-Mart or warehouse price clubs, were not constraints on OSSs' prices when two or three OSSs were in an MSA.

In addition to the price evidence, there were internal documents of Staples and of Office Depot that indicated that each was concerned primarily or exclusively with the rivalry (or its absence) from other OSSs and described MSAs as "competitive" or "uncompetitive" in terms of whether one or more OSS rivals were present or absent.

In sum, since Staples or Office Depot could *and did* charge significantly higher prices in MSAs where it was the sole OSS than it did when two or three OSSs were present, OSSs in MSAs were markets that could be monopolized and thus constituted a relevant market.

8.2.3.2. Anti-competitive effects from the merger

The same evidence that delineated the markets also showed what the effects of the merger would be. When Staples and Office Depot were together in an MSA, prices were 11.6% lower than when only Staples was present in the MSA and 8.6% lower than when only Office Depot was present. When all three OSSs were present in an MSA, prices were 4.9% lower than when only Staples and OfficeMax were present and 2.5% lower than when only Office Depot and OfficeMax were present. The FTC's econometric analysis indicated that the merger would have the effect of raising prices above what they would otherwise have been, on average, by 7.3%.

The FTC argued further that, because of high sunk costs of entry and the apparent "saturation" of most MSAs (according to the defendants' documents), entry by a new OSS was not likely.

8.2.3.3. Efficiencies

While acknowledging that the OSSs had, in the past, been the pioneers in creating the low-cost OSS segment, the FTC argued that the merger was unlikely to create significant economies that could not be achieved by the two OSSs separately. Also, the magnitude of the claimed efficiencies had increased dramatically (almost 500%) between the time that the merger was approved by the Staples board of directors and the time that the parties presented their efficiencies analysis to the FTC, casting some doubt on the accuracy of the latter estimates. The FTC estimated that the merger would bring true efficiencies of only 1.4% of sales and that only a small part (a seventh, or 0.2%, based on an econometric analysis of Staples' costs and prices) of these efficiencies would be passed through to consumers, so that the net effect of the merger would be a 7.1% (= 7.3% − 0.2%) price increase.

8.2.4. The Staples/Office Depot arguments

The merging parties, not surprisingly, argued that the FTC's analysis was incorrect and that the merger's effect would be a *decrease* in prices, not an increase.

8.2.4.1. The market

The parties argued that the FTC's econometric analysis was flawed and offered an alternative analysis that indicated that the presence or absence of another OSS had only a small effect on the price charged by Staples or Office Depot. These results would indicate that OSSs were not a separate market and that their pricing was constrained by a wider set of competitors, especially Wal-Mart, Best Buy, Comp USA, and other large sellers of items that overlapped with those sold by the OSSs.[9] Thus the relevant market was an appreciably wider one (in product space) than just OSSs. The parties agreed, however, that the relevant geographic market was individual MSAs.

8.2.4.2. Competitive effects of the merger

Since Staples and Office Depot were embedded in a relatively wide market, their merger was unlikely to have any significant anti-competitive effects. Their actions were too constrained by other sellers of office supplies. Further, the parties argued, entry was relatively easy; the sunk costs were not large. OfficeMax had increased its planned store openings, and rivals could arise through consolidations of local stationery stores.

8.2.4.3. Efficiencies

The parties contended that the merger-specific efficiencies were considerably larger than was claimed by the FTC — around 4.5% of sales — and that two-thirds of the gains would be passed through to consumers. Since the parties' econometrics estimates showed that the immediate price effects of the merger would be to raise prices by only 0.8%, while the passed-through efficiencies would reduce prices by 3% (= 4.5% × 0.67), the net effect of the merger would be a *reduction* in prices of 2.2% (= 0.8% − 3.0%).

8.2.5. The decision

After a seven-day trial, Federal District Court Judge Thomas F. Hogan, on June 30, 1997, issued his opinion, which found in favor of the FTC's request to block

---

[9] The point-counterpoint as to the merits of the two sets of analyses can be found in Baker (1999) and Hausman and Leonard (no date).

the merger.[10] His opinion was one of regret: "In light of the undeniable benefits that Staples and Office Depot have brought to consumers, it is with regret that the Court reaches the decision that it must in this case."[11] But he found that the relevant market was OSSs in MSAs;[12] that the very high post-merger levels of seller concentration[13] and the likely absence of entry would likely mean anti-competitive effects; and that efficiencies were likely to be modest and modestly passed through to consumers. In sum, he was (albeit, reluctantly) convinced by the FTC's arguments and halted the merger.

8.2.6. Aftermath

In the years following Judge Hogan's decision both Staples and Office Depot continued to expand. Office Depot remains the leading OSS, with Staples second. As of March 2001, Office Depot had expanded to 787 stores in the US, with worldwide sales of US$11.6 billion in 2000. As of February 2001 Staples had expanded to 973 stores (including smaller "Staples Express" stores) in the US, with worldwide sales of US$10.7 billion in 2000. OfficeMax continued as the third OSS, with 953 stores in the US (as of March 2001) and worldwide sales of US$5.2 billion in 2000. There has been no noticeable reduction in the competitive vigor of the OSS market.[14]

8.3. THE UP–SP MERGER

8.3.1. The business context

Mergers have been a way of life in the railroad industry. From 186 major ("class I") railroads in 1920, mergers reduced their numbers to 39 in 1980. The mergers increased the surviving railroads' regional coverage and scope, but no railroad

---

[10] *Federal Trade Commission* v. *Staples, Inc.* 970 F. Supp. 1066.

[11] *FTC* v. *Staples*, 970 F. Supp. 1066, 1093.

[12] He appeared to rely primarily on the simple price differentials among markets that the FTC presented and the documents but did not rely on either side's econometrics.

[13] In 15 MSA markets the post-merger market share of the merged entity would be 100%, and in 27 other MSA markets the market share would be above 45%. The HHI would rise on average by 2,715 points in the relevant MSA markets as a consequence of the merger.

[14] For a more extensive discussion of the post-1997 developments in the sale of office products, as well as a critical view of the case and its outcome, see Grengs (2001).

Table 8.1: The four major western railroads and their characteristics (as of 1994).

Railroad	Track miles	Revenues ($ billion)	Employees
Burlington Northern	22,189	5.0	30,711
Union Pacific	18,759	5.2	29,946
Southern Pacific	17,499	2.9	18,251
Santa Fe	8,352	2.7	15,020

Source. Kwoka and White (1999b, p. 67).

had (or even today has) achieved comprehensive national coverage or even a coast-to-coast route.

Another important feature has been the railroads' century-long losing struggle against other surface freight transportation modes: trucks, pipelines, and ships and barges.[15] As of 1995, rail accounted for 41% of intercity freight tonnage, which was substantially below the railroads' share in the early decades of the century. This decline was partly due to the technological developments of the other modes; but the stultifying regulation of surface transportation, and especially of railroads, by the Interstate Commerce Commission (ICC) also played a major role.[16]

As part of the general deregulation of the 1970s and 1980s, the Congress passed the Staggers Act in 1980, which substantially deregulated the railroad industry, providing it with considerably more flexibility in its operations and in its pricing, up as well as down. And mergers continued apace. Between 1980 and early 1995, mergers had reduced the number of Class I railroads to only eleven, of which only large major railroads operated in the western United States: the Burlington Northern (BN), the Union Pacific (UP), the Southern Pacific (SP), and the Santa Fe (SF). Table 8.1 provides the major characteristics of these four railroads.

In August 1994, the BN proposed to purchase the SF, which would create the largest railroad in the west. The ICC approved the BN–SF merger in August 1995.

---

[15] The struggle for passengers was lost to cars, buses, and airlines and finally abandoned with the Congressional creation of Amtrak in 1971.

[16] For critiques of that regulation, see Meyer et al. (1959), Friedlaender (1969), Friedlaender and Spady (1981), Keeler (1983), and White (1999a, 1999b).

Two weeks before the BN–SF merger was approved, the UP announced its intention to acquire the SP, which would create an even larger railroad and vault the UP–SP into first place. The UP and SP had an intertwined history. The UP and an SP predecessor (the Central Pacific) had been the two railroads commissioned by President Lincoln in 1862 to build the transcontinental railroad (which was completed in 1869). They had sought to combine in the early twentieth century but were rebuffed by the courts on antitrust grounds.

In early August 1995 they again attempted to combine. Their merger proposal immediately sparked considerable controversy. Dozens of interested and affected parties presented formal comments (pro and con) to the ICC/STB (which had jurisdiction with respect to the merger). The commentators included eleven other railroads; 38 individual shippers and 19 trade associations (the largest of which represented 1,400 individual shippers); five federal agencies; 12 state governments, as well as many individual communities within those states; and five labor unions.

8.3.2. The legal context

Despite the considerable deregulation provided by the Staggers Act, the ICC remained as the regulatory agency for the railroads and, most importantly, retained the powers of merger approval or rejection for railroad mergers (rather than these powers devolving to the FTC or DOJ). When the ICC was dismantled at the end of 1995 and the Surface Transportation Board (STB) created to replace, the STB retained the ICC's merger review powers.

The ICC/STB's legislative mandate in assessing mergers is broader than that of Section 7 of the Clayton Act. Rather than focusing just on the competition and efficiency issues and the tradeoffs (if any) between them, the ICC/STB is instructed by legislation also to consider a railroad merger's effects on "the adequacy of transportation to the public" and "the interest of carrier employees," among other things.

Further, even though a major focus of the agency has been on the basic antitrust issues — market power versus efficiencies — the ICC/STB's approach has been much more accommodating toward railroad mergers. An important underlying ethos of the agency has been that the railroads had experienced hard financial times during the late 1960s and the 1970s and that they need all the help that they can get to return to adequate profitably. Consequently, (a) the agency has generally been more accepting of claims of efficiencies than have the FTC or DOJ; (b) it has been less concerned about decreases in the vigor of competition; and (c) where monopoly outcomes would have arisen as a consequence of a merger, the ICC/STB has usually sought to remedy them with modest requirements, such as trackage rights for other railroads,[17] rather than divestitures of track to other railroads. The result has been a strong tendency for the agency to approve railroad mergers.[18]

The UP and SP filed their formal proposal for the merger before the ICC in November 1995. The ICC was succeeded by the STB on January 1, 1996, and the STB assumed jurisdiction and considered the arguments offered by the merging railroads and by other interested parties. Though the ICC/STB did not have the same policy attachment to the Merger Guidelines as did the DOJ and FTC, the arguments offered by the parties tended to follow the structure developed by the Guidelines, albeit in somewhat different orderings.

8.3.3. The UP–SP's case for the merger

8.3.3.1 Efficiencies

The prospective efficiencies of the UP–SP merger were the centerpiece of the merger applicants' arguments. The UP–SP expected efficiencies to arise in a large number of ways. First, by taking advantage of the consolidated track systems, the UP–SP could offer significantly shorter routes between a number of important city pairs, thereby reducing the direct costs of transport and also reducing shipment times. Second, the UP–SP could offer single-line service to shippers for far more destinations, thereby reducing the delays that plague joint-line service.[19] Third, the use of parallel routes of the two carriers would relieve congestion and permit different-speed trains to use different sets of parallel tracks, thereby creating greater flexibility in service; a similar argument was advanced for rail yards and other facilities. Fourth, rolling stock could be used more efficiently on the combined lines. Last, computer systems could be combined, joint purchasing would achieve economies, and corporate overheads generally could be reduced.

The applicants quantified the cost savings from the merger (for themselves and for shippers) at about US$750 million a year, which was slightly less than 10% of the pre-merger UP–SP revenues.

---

[17] Trackage rights allow a second railroad to gain access to otherwise captive shippers over the first railroad's tracks.

[18] The last major rail merger that the ICC had rejected had been the proposed merger of the Southern Pacific and the Santa Fe in 1986.

[19] In essence, the replacement of joint-line with single-line service is a form of vertical integration, since the freight hand-off in a joint line movement (the equivalent of a supplier–customer transaction) is being replaced with a single ownership transaction.

Also, the applicants argued that the SP was an ailing firm with diminishing competitive vigor. It needed a general overhaul, but lacked the resources to accomplish it and would fall further behind in a competitive struggle with the consolidated BNSF and even with an independent UP. The merger was necessary to invigorate the SP.

Finally, the shadow of the merged BNSF loomed large. The applicants repeatedly argued that the UP–SP merger was necessary to allow the merged entity to compete on even terms with the BNSF.

8.3.3.2. Competitive effects of the merger

For many shippers that currently had rail service only through dual access to the UP and the SP, the merger would reduce their access to a single carrier. These were described as the "two-to-one" shippers. Other shippers currently had access to the UP, the SP, and a third rail carrier — typically the BNSF — and they would find their choices reduced to two. These were the "three-to-two" shippers.

For the two-to-one shippers, the merger applicants made extraordinary efforts to assure a continued "two" level of competition through a trackage rights agreement with the BNSF. The latter railroad would have the right to run its trains over the merged UPSP tracks in order to serve these customers. The annual traffic covered by these trackage rights totaled US$900 million (over 10% of the pre-merger revenues of the two merging lines) and about 4,000 miles of track (about 11% of the merged UPSP system). This level of trackage rights in a railroad merger was unprecedented. Further, it would replace an ailing SP with a vigorous BNSF.

As for the three-to-two shippers, the applicants argued that they would be better served by the vigorous competition that would ensue between a more efficient UPSP and the BNSF than they would be by a powerful BNSF, a smaller UP, and a weak SP that would become even weaker. Further, the applicants argued that (a) there was no reliable evidence that showed that a three-to-two merger of rail carriers would cause freight rate increases; (b) existing studies that did predict such an effect suffered from deficiencies that made them unreliable and irrelevant; (c) coordinated behavior among the two sellers in the rail market would be unlikely, since monitoring and policing of each other's actions was difficult, especially since railroads' service dimensions could be extensively differentiated; and (d) many shippers were large and capable entities that could shop around and play off the two rail carriers against each other, in essence holding "auctions" for the rights to carry their freight.[20]

---

[20] See Willig (1995).

In sum, a model of "Bertrand"[21] unfettered price competition, yielding a competitive outcome, would be a reasonable approximation to rail markets with even as few as two carriers.

8.3.3.3. *Market delineation*

Market delineation did not attain the same prominence in the UP–SP merger as it did for the Staples–Office Depot proposal, but it was importantly present. In the UP–SP's designation of which shippers were in the "two-to-one" category, the merger applicants were implicitly making delineations. In some instances they excluded shippers because the UP–SP believed that competition from other modes offered sufficient alternatives (i.e., a wide market); in other instances they excluded shippers because the UP–SP believed that they were served currently by only the UP *or* the SP — i.e., they currently faced a monopoly anyway — and this single-carrier service would not change after the merger (i.e., a narrow market).

8.3.4. The arguments against the UP–SP merger

The opponents of the merger included many (but not all) shippers, other railroads[22] (but not the BNSF), and the US Departments of Justice, Transportation, and Agriculture.

8.3.4.1. *Market delineation*

The merger opponents argued that the applicants had seriously understated the extent of the two-to-one problem, by delineating markets too narrowly so as to portray current monopoly (UP or SP service) situations where there was really actual or potential competition. First, the applicants ignored instances where the shipper (or recipient) might be directly served by only the UP or the SP, but the other carrier was close enough that the threat or actuality of using trucks or barges for short trans-shipments, or the threat of short rail extensions by the other, effectively kept the two lines in competition with each other.

---

[21] I.e., where each competitor chooses its price as its strategic variable and myopically assumes that the other(s) will keep their prices unchanged.

[22] The author filed comments in this case on behalf of the Kansas City Southern Railway Co.

Second, the applicants ignored instances in which only the UP or the SP might serve one end of a shipment but the other was one of the two carriers competing at the other end, and thus inter-line service was currently necessary; recent research showed that the monopoly carrier in such instances did not capture all of the potential rents, but the merger would yield a single-line service monopoly (which would capture all of the rents).

Third, they ignored instances of "source competition" (where two shippers at different locations, served by different railroads, compete to serve a recipient) and "destination competition" (where a shipper has a choice of destinations — e.g., seaports for a shipment destined for overseas — that are served by different railroads) where the UP was the sole carrier on the one route and the SP was the sole carrier on the other route.

In sum, the applicants had defined these markets too narrowly. The aggregate consequences were serious. These unremedied two-to-one situations involved an additional US$1 billion or so of shipments, above the US$900 billion that the applicants had identified, and a 20% increase in freight rates was predicted.[23]

8.3.4.2. The exercise of market power

In the unremedied two-to-one markets, the exercise of market power would be immediate. In the "remedied" two-to-one markets, the trackage rights remedy was wholly inadequate as a device for creating effective competition. A trackage rights arrangement is equivalent to a tenant (the BNSF) competing for the same customers with its landlord (the merged UPSP). By structuring the terms of the tenancy arrangement, the landlord can distort and mute the competitive threat from the tenant. For the trackage rights agreement that had been negotiated with the BNSF, the UP–SP had established fees and other arrangements that put the BNSF at a substantial disadvantage in competing for these customers. In addition, since the BNSF was the "tenant" in nearly all the trackage rights arrangements, the multi-market contacts between the BNSF and the merged UPSP, with their risks of encouraging oligopolistic coordination, would be increased even further than in just the (unremedied) three-to-two markets.

The three-to-two markets involved about US$5 billion in rail freight revenues.[24] Most strands of oligopoly theory predict that a reduction in the

---

[23] This prediction was based on cross-section regressions that compared freight rates on routes with one, two, three, etc., rail carriers, holding constant other important characteristics; see Majure (1996) and Grimm (1996).

[24] Neither the merger applicants nor its opponents devoted much analytical efforts to the four-to-three markets, since they knew from past decisions that the ICC/STB was convinced that the

number of sellers from three to two will reduce the vigor of competition and cause the prices to be higher. Only the Bertrand model of competition, for an *undifferentiated* product, would predict no change in price. But the applicants were simultaneously endorsing a Bertrand outcome while emphasizing the differentiations in the service offerings of the two railroads as the impediment to collusive behavior. However, product differentiation "softens" Bertrand competition, leading to a non-competitive outcome. Further, though the applicants likened rail competition for the shipments of a large customer to an auction, standard auction theory predicts that fewer bidders will mean less favorable prices. And the extensive, repeated contacts of the BNSF and the merged UPSP across all of the two-carrier markets (which would be exacerbated by the trackage rights agreement) would also tend to encourage a less competitive climate.

In addition to theoretical predictions that three-to-two would mean less vigorous competition, there was a large body of empirical literature (including literature on auctions) that indicated that this reduction would mean higher prices.[25] Though most of this literature involved industries other than rail, included were a number of studies of rail freight markets that showed that the number of carriers on a route influenced freight rates in the expected way.[26] A reduction in the number of carriers from three to two was expected to increase freight rates by about 10%. Also, a study of the bids that the Department of Defense (DOD) received for rail freight movements of military equipment showed that the number of bidders mattered in the expected way.[27]

As for the financial health of the SP, though the SP was financially weak, it was not failing. It had successfully raised capital in recent years, and its operations were improving. More important, detailed econometric analysis indicated that its presence made a significant difference in reducing rail rates.

---

reduction in the number of carriers in such markets was irrelevant; even the opponents' efforts with respect to three-to-two mergers was considered an uphill effort, since past ICC rulings had found that such reductions increased competition, so long as merger entailed superior "character of competition," "more competitive routes," "more diverse geographic competition," and stabilizing a weak competitor.

[25] See Bresnahan (1989), Schmalensee (1989), and Weiss (1989); Kwoka (1979) specifically showed that the presence of a sizable third seller in a market caused price-cost margins to decline. And Evans and Kessides (1994) had shown the price-raising consequences of repeated multi-market contacts in another transportation context, airlines.

[26] See Grimm (1985, 1996), MacDonald (1987, 1989a, 1989b), Winston et al. (1990), Grimm et al. (1992), Burton (1993), Wilson (1994), and Majure (1996).

[27] See Ploth (1996).

8.3.4.3. Efficiencies

The merger's critics argued that the promised efficiencies could prove chimerical. First, the merger would yield a larger organization, which unavoidably would be more difficult to manage. Second, the UP had had difficulties in absorbing the operations of the Chicago & North Western Railway, which it had acquired earlier in 1995. Third, some of the applicants' predictions of cost savings were simply a projection of industry trends and would likely occur anyway, even in the absence of the mergers. Fourth, some of the cost savings involved transfers from other parties, which meant no social gains. Finally, some of the single-line integration efficiencies could be achieved through better coordination between the independent UP and SP.

8.3.4.4. A summing up

The merger's opponents argued that the risks of new or enhanced market power were quite high, that the trackage rights arrangement with the BNSF was inadequate as a remedy, and that the promised efficiencies were speculative at best. The opponents urged outright rejection of the merger or, alternatively, a conditioning of its approval on the divestiture of duplicative track into the hands of rival railroads, which would lessen the problems of oligopolistic behavior.

8.3.5. The STB's decision

The ICC and then the STB reviewed a voluminous record in late 1995 and the first half of 1996, including public hearings. On July 3, 1996, the STB issued its decision.

In a lengthy opinion the STB approved the merger, supporting the UP–SP on virtually all of the major issues and making only modest changes in the trackage rights agreement.[28] The Board concluded that the merger would result in superior service, substantial cost savings, enhanced competition, and (because of the trackage rights agreement) adequate protection to "captive" shippers.

> [T]he merger as conditioned [by the trackage rights agreement] clearly will be pro-competitive in the sense that it will stimulate

---

[28] 1 STB. 233 (1996).

price and service competition in the markets served by the merged carriers. The merger will create a more efficient UP/SP system competing head-to-head throughout the West with BNSF. UP/SP customers will benefit from tremendous service improvements brought about by reductions in route mileage, extended single-line service, enhanced equipment supply, better service reliability, and new operating efficiencies.[29]

8.3.6 Aftermath

8.3.6.1. The merged entity

In September 1996 the UP began to implement the merger. By the summer of 1997 it was clear that the company's integration efforts were unraveling. One harbinger was a deterioration of safety, with an extraordinary number of train crashes and crew deaths. Simultaneously, the UP began experiencing congestion problems, as trains and shipments began slowing down and backing up and shippers and recipients began to complain about lost shipments and long delays. "Near gridlock" began to be a common description of the UP system. The company experienced substantial managerial and logistics problems. For example, the UP and the SP had different computer systems and dispatching systems, and workers from one system were unable to adapt readily to the other's computers and operations. Cutbacks in management, crews, and equipment — which had been part of the projected cost savings from the merger — worsened the problems.

Despite the UP's repeated assurances of service improvements, extensive problems continued to plague the UP through 1998 and into 1999, especially in the Gulf Coast area.[30] The UP began sending freight on competing truck and rail carriers, including the BNSF. Only in 2000 did the UP's problems appear to be behind it, although even then critics remained.[31]

As of early 2002 it is too early to tell whether the long-run effects of the merger will meet the rosy predictions of the merger applicants and the STB — substantial efficiencies and no increase in market power — or will be closer to

---

[29] 1 STB. 233, 375 (1996).

[30] Weinstein and Clower (1998) estimate that the losses to Texas shippers in the last half of 1997 alone were over US$1 billion.

[31] See Schmeltzer (2000).

the dire warnings of the merger's critics — heightened market power and few net efficiencies. But the short-run consequences of the merger are all too clear: the costs to rail freight shippers and recipients in the southwestern US have been substantial.

8.3.6.2. The industry

Three months after the STB approved the UP–SP merger, the managements of the CSX railroad (one of the two major railroads in the southeast) and of Conrail (the sole major railroad in the northeast) announced an agreement to merge Conrail into CSX. A week later the other major southeastern railroad, the Norfolk Southern (NS), made a higher offer for Conrail. After a few months of further offers and counter-offers and legal wrangling, the three parties agreed that CSX and the NS would jointly buy Conrail and split its route structure and equipment between themselves. This transaction was approved by the STB in June 1998. Despite extensive planning, so as to avoid the problems experienced by the UP, both acquirers experienced significant service disruption problems in absorbing their respective Conrail pieces that lasted for over a year.

Further consolidation of the US rail system seemed inevitable. The first shoe to drop was the decision of the Canadian National Railway Co. (CN) to purchase the Illinois Central (IC), a major US carrier with north–south routes from New Orleans to Chicago and surrounding communities in the Mississippi Valley. Since these two carriers had few overlapping routes — it was a true "end-to-end" merger — it raised little controversy, and the CN–IC merger was approved by the STB in June 1999.

The next merger proposal, however, proved to be the straw that broke the (STB) camel's back. In late December 1999 the BNSF and the CN proposed a merger that would make the BNSF the first transcontinental US railroad (although its Atlantic terminus would be solely in Canada). The STB, concerned about the service disruptions that had followed the UP–SP merger and the CSX–NS–Conrail transaction and also concerned about what other merger proposals might soon follow, never seriously considered the merger. Instead, the agency proposed and then approved (in March 2000) an unprecedented fifteen-month moratorium on all Class I railroad mergers.

During that moratorium, the STB reconsidered its policy approach to mergers and issued a new policy statement in June 2001.[32] That new statement retained

---

[32] STB Ex Parte No. 582 (Sub-No. 1), "Major Rail Consolidation Procedures," June 11, 2001.

the public interest balancing approach that had traditionally guided the agency but added explicit requirements on merger applicants to provide assurances as to the pro-competitive nature of their proposed transactions, to provide back-up plans in the event of service disruptions following a merger, and to guide the agency as to the likely future course of rail industry mergers.

The new policy statement did not indicate, however, a change in philosophy of the STB with respect to crucial competitive issues, such as market delineation and oligopoly behavior (such as three-to-two concerns), although future mergers might not present such issues in the profusion that was presented in the UP–SP merger. Also, whether the burden on applicants will actually be greater remains to be seen, since applicants — as was the case by the UP–SP — already provide extensive documentation and assurances as to why their merger will be pro-competitive and not create service problems.

In sum, rather than adopting something akin to the stance of the DOJ and the FTC — a positive attitude toward competition, a concern about oligopoly behavior, and a skepticism toward claimed efficiencies — the STB seems (despite its rhetoric to the contrary in its new policy statement) to be continuing along its traditional path. The test of this proposition will occur when, as will inevitably be the case, one of the two remaining eastern rail lines proposes to merge with one of the two remaining western lines.

8.5. CONCLUSION

The proposed mergers of Staples and Office Depot and of the Union Pacific and Southern Pacific railroads appeared, at first glance, to involve quite different issues. On closer examination, however, they involved similar issues: three-to-two mergers, and some crucial questions concerning market delineation.

They received, however, disparate legal treatment. The Staples–Office Depot proposal was rejected by the FTC and the courts; the UP–SP proposal was waived through by the STB. In this author's opinion, the FTC's approach was the correct one, and the STB's approach was flawed; thousands of freight shippers in the southwestern US would surely agree with the latter assessment.

American antitrust policy has historically had a number of industrial exemptions, carve-outs, and special regulatory regimes — e.g., for agriculture, for fisheries, for newspapers, for ocean shipping, for airlines, and for railroads. These alternatives to mainstream antitrust enforcement, in the name of some other social goal, have almost always yielded unsatisfactory results. Unfortunately, the STB's handling of the UP–SP merger was solidly in that tradition.

REFERENCES

Baker, Jonathan B. (1999). Econometric analysis in *FTC v. Staples*. *Journal of Public Policy & Marketing*, *18* (Spring), 11–21.

Bresnahan, Timothy F. (1989). Empirical studies of industries with market power. In: Richard Schmalensee and Robert Willig (eds), *Handbook of Industrial Organization*, vol. 2 (pp. 1011–1057). Amsterdam: North-Holland.

Burton, Mark L. (1993). Railroad deregulation, carrier behavior, and shipper response: A disaggregated analysis. *Journal of Regulatory Analysis*, *5* (December), 417–434.

Dalkir, Serdar, & Warren-Boulton, Frederick R. (1999). Prices, market definition, and the effects of merger: Staples-Office Depot (1997). In: John E. Kwoka, Jr and Lawrence J. White (eds), *The Antitrust Revolution: Economics, Competition, and Policy* (pp. 143–164). New York: Oxford University Press.

Evans, William N., & Kessides, Ioannis N. (1994). Living by the "Golden Rule": Multi-market contact in the U.S. airline industry. *Quarterly Journal of Economics*, *109* (May): 341–366.

Friedlaender, Ann F. (1969) *The Dilemma of Freight Transport Regulation*. Washington, D.C.: Brookings Institution.

Friedlaender, Ann F., & Spady, Richard H. (1981) *Freight Transport Regulation: Equity, Efficiency, and Competition in the Rail and Trucking Industries*. Cambridge, Mass.: MIT Press.

Grengs, Christopher M. (2001). The "best-ever" *Staples* antitrust suit: Hoisted with their own petards, a case of *Hamlet* without the Danish Prince. Ludwig Von Mises Institute Working paper, May 28.

Grimm, Curtis M. (1985). Horizontal competitive effects in railroad mergers. *Research in Transportation Economics*, vol. 2.

Grimm, Curtis M. (1996). Verified statement, on behalf of the Kansas City Southern Railroad, 29 March.

Grimm, Curtis M., Winston, Clifford, & Evans, Carol S. (1992). Foreclosure of railroad markets: A test of Chicago leverage theory. *Journal of Law & Economics*, *35* (October): 295–310.

Hausman, Jerry A., & Leonard, Gregory K. (no date). Documents versus econometrics in *Staples*. Mimeo (accessible at http://www.antitrust.org/cases/staples/hausleon.html).

Keeler, Theodore E. (1983). *Railroads, Freight, and Public Policy*. Washington, D.C.: Brookings.

Kwoka, John E., Jr (1979). The effect of market share distribution on industry profits. *Review of Economics and Statistics*, *61* (February): 101–109.

Kwoka, John E., Jr (1984). Output and allocative efficiency under second degree price discrimination. *Economic Inquiry*, *22* (April).

Kwoka, John E., Jr, & White, Lawrence J. (eds). (1999a.). *The Antitrust Revolution: Economics, Competition, and Policy*, 3rd edition. New York: Oxford University Press.

Kwoka, John E., Jr, & White, Lawrence J. (1999b). Manifest destiny? The Union Pacific and Southern Pacific railroad merger (1996). In: John E. Kwoka, Jr and Lawrence J.

White (eds), *The Antitrust Revolution: Economics, Competition, and Policy*, 3rd edition (pp. 64–88). New York: Oxford University Press.

MacDonald, James M. (1987). Competition and rail rates for the shipment of corn, soybeans, and wheat. *Rand Journal of Economics, 18* (Spring): 151–163.

MacDonald, James M. (1989a). Railroad deregulation, innovation, and competitive effects of the Staggers Act on grain transportation. *Journal of Law & Economics, 32* (April): 63–96.

MacDonald, James M. (1989b). Concentration and railroad pricing. In: Leonard W. Weiss (ed.), *Concentration and Price* (pp. 205–212). Cambridge, Mass.: MIT Press.

Majure, W. Robert (1996). Verified statement, on behalf of the US Department of Justice, 3 June.

Meyer, John R., Peck, Merton J., Stenason, John, & Zwick, Charles. (1959). *The Economics of Competition in the Transportation Industries*. Cambridge, Mass.: Harvard University Press.

Ploth, I. William. (1996). Verified statement, on behalf of the Kansas City Southern railroad, 29 March.

Schmalensee, Richard. (1989). Inter-industry studies of structure and performance. In: Richard Schmalensee and Robert Willig (eds), *Handbook of Industrial Organization*, vol. 2 (pp. 951–1009). Amsterdam: North-Holland, 1989.

Schmeltzer, John. (2000). Merger doubters still stalk Union Pacific deal. *Chicago Tribune*, 2 October.

Weinstein, Bernard L., & Clower, Terry L. (1998). The impacts of the Union Pacific service disruptions on the Texas and national economies: An unfinished story. Mimeo prepared for the Railroad Commission of Texas, 9 February.

Weiss, Leonard W. (1989). *Concentration and Price*. Cambridge, Mass.: MIT Press.

White, Lawrence J. (1999a). US public policy toward network industries. AEI-Brookings Joint Center for Regulatory Studies.

White, Lawrence J. (1999b). The deregulation of the telephone industry: Lessons from the US railroad deregulation experience. In: Ryuzo Sato, Rama V. Ramachandran and Kazuo Mino (eds.), *Global Competition and Integration* (pp. 471–506). Boston: Kluwer.

Willig, Robert. (1995). Verified statement, on behalf of the Union Pacific and Southern Pacific railroads, 30 November.

Wilson, Wesley W. (1994). Market-specific effects of rail deregulation. *Journal of Industrial Economics, 42* (March): 1–22.

Winston, Clifford, Corsi, Thomas M., Grimm, Curtis M., & Evans, Carol A. (1990). *The Economic Effects of Surface Freight Deregulation*. Washington, D.C.: Brookings.

Measuring Market Power
D. J. Slottje (editor)

CHAPTER 9

How Digital Economics
Revises Antitrust Thinking[†]

RICHARD B. MCKENZIE[a]* and
DWIGHT R. LEE[b]

[a] *University of California, Irvine, CA 92697*
[b] *Terry School of Business at the University of Georgia, Athens, GA 30602*

Abstract

Conventional antitrust thinking developed in the industrial era during which the production of goods was constrained by positive marginal costs. Digital goods (software, e-books, e-music, e-movies, etc.), which are made from 1s and 0s (or electrons), are not so constrained. That is to say that the marginal production costs are zero, or close to zero. Also, digital goods often are subject to network effects. These two market features — zero marginal productions and network effects — change dramatically firms' pricing decisions and their incentives to become the dominant, if not close-to-sole, producers in their markets. These market features, and firm's behavioral responses, require that antitrust thinking on such matters as market dominance, zero and below-zero pricing, above-marginal cost pricing, and entry and exit barriers be revised. The required revision in antitrust thinking is illustrated by the Microsoft antitrust case that began in 1998.

Keywords: Digital economics, antitrust, network effects
JEL Classification: L40, L63

[†] This article is reprinted with permission from *The Antitrust Bulletin*, 46 (2; summer 2001), 253–298.
* Corresponding author.

9.1. INTRODUCTION

Antitrust thinking and enforcement have traditionally been firmly grounded in conventional economic models of monopoly and oligopoly market structures, all fully and inevitably constrained by the "laws" of demand and decreasing returns. The new economics of "digits," encompassing those goods (like software, books, and music) that are capable of being reduced to 1s and 0s (meaning electrons) — or what we call "digital economics" — necessarily changes antitrust thinking and enforcement. This is primarily because of two concepts, and accompanying postulates, discussed below, that have risen to prominence in economics over the past two or three decades, and have played important roles in the Microsoft antitrust trial over the past three years.

In this chapter, we explore various ways digital economics should give rise to revisions in the way antitrust cases against digital firms should be appraised and how antitrust prosecution of digital firms will be restrained. We use the experience with the Microsoft antitrust case to show how errors can be made in antitrust prosecutions when underlying monopoly models are not revised to accommodate these digital economic postulates. Although the thrust of our arguments advises restraint in antitrust prosecution, we also argue that the prospects of effective, anti-monopoly, antitrust prosecution can be seen as beneficial to those firms, like Microsoft, that are subject to digital and network forces and that become dominant, if not "monopoly," producers in their markets.

The analysis clearly has international implications, given that flows of digital goods have no natural national boundaries. Indeed, international flows of digital goods are largely indistinguishable from intranational flows. Furthermore, the cost of shipping digital goods is, for the most part, unaffected by the distance covered, which should mean that cross-national entry barriers in the form of shipping costs are lower for digital goods than non-digital goods. However, as will be seen, the competitive advantages of lower shipping costs can be offset by other forms of entry and exit barriers that, supposedly, come in the form of consumer and producer "lock-ins." To understand these points, we need to lay out a few key concepts.

9.2. KEY CONCEPTS IN DIGITAL ECONOMICS

The first concept central to digital economics is "network effects," or the functional connection between the infra-marginal and marginal value of a digital good, like an operating system, and the number of units of the good that are in use (Arthur, 1989, 1990, and 1996; Katz and Shapiro, 1985). There is, in effect, a form of economies of scale in demand. In the operating systems market, network effects imply that the greater the number of copies of, say, Windows that are in use, the greater the value of that operating system to computer users because the number of applications available for Windows will be positively influenced by the number of Windows users. The interconnectedness between current and future value implies a unique future short-run demand for each level of current consumption that results from a given current price.

The second concept central to digital economics is what might be termed "radical scale economies" in production, meaning that all (or almost all) production costs are upfront costs, making the marginal cost of production zero (or very close to zero), if not below zero [as UCLA economist Benjamin Klein (1999) has postulated when complementary products are involved].[1] Again, in the case of operating systems, the cost to Microsoft of developing even a new version of Windows is substantial, running into the hundreds of millions of dollars. However, the marginal cost of reproducing Windows for original computer manufacturers is, for Microsoft, about as close to zero as imaginable, if not zero. The reason is straightforward: typically, Microsoft sends a master copy of Windows to a manufacturer like Dell that then copies the master onto the computers that are sold. As a condition of its license, Dell is responsible for replicating the operating system and is even responsible for the support of Windows, which mainly involves responding to their computer buyers' calls (Microsoft inevitably gets some service calls on copies of Windows sold by Dell and other computer makers).

Granted, retail copies of software products sold through retail outlets like CompUSA may have positive marginal costs, albeit limited to the packaging and distribution. However, the point is that for most operating system copies sold (and upwards of 90% of copies of Windows are sold with new machines), the cost is viewed as very close to zero. Perhaps as important, the cost remains close to zero through what can be viewed as an unlimited number of copies reproduced, making the economies of scale in production practically unlimited, or, at least, extending beyond the scope of the long-run demand.[2]

---

[1] A graphical model for production of a digital good is much like the usual textbook model for a "natural monopoly." The main difference is that in the conventional natural monopoly model, the long-run marginal cost of production is assumed to decline steadily throughout the relevant range of the market, which gradually pulls the average production cost downward. In the case of a *pure* digital good (one in which all costs are upfront), the average cost, and thereby marginal cost, for the first unit produced initially equals the upfront cost. However, the marginal cost of production from the first unit on is zero, meaning the marginal cost curve runs along the horizontal axis. The average cost curve falls precipitously at first and becomes asymptotic to the horizontal axis.

[2] Brian Arthur, who has written a number of the pioneering articles on network effects and increasing returns has drawn a distinction between goods with diminishing and increasing returns:

These two concepts — economies of scale in demand and supply — have derivative concepts that can feed into antitrust thinking. First, there is the problem of the market "tipping" toward one product, resulting in "winner-take-all" (or most) of the market (Frank and Cook, 1995). When one firm gains market share, the value of the product to consumers in that market increases, which can cause more consumers to join the network resulting in an escalation in the demand for the product and growth in the firm's market dominance. The network effects can be "network externalities," given that consumer purchases increase the gains of other consumers, possibly resulting in market inefficiency.[3] Consumers can also become "locked in" to a given product because of the "switching costs" associated with moving from one network to another. In the case of the operating system market, the cost of switching from Windows to the Apple Mac operating system would entail the purchase of the new program, new equipment, and retraining. The net result of switching costs is that the product technology standard that is adopted can be "path dependent" and, in the end, can mean, so it is argued, that "inferior" products continue to dominate production decisions and consumer purchases. The problems of network externalities, tipping, path dependency, and switching costs (if not lock-ins), all leading to market inefficiency, are, many think, illustrated by the continued use of the QWERTY keyboard that is, supposedly, less efficient than alternative keyboards that have been developed over the last century (David, 1985) [a line of argument that has been severely contested (Liebowitz and Margolis, 1990 and 1995)].

The Microsoft antitrust case has been a laboratory for how digital economics can play out in court. In its original antitrust complaint against Microsoft filed in May 1998, the Justice Department grounded its case in the relatively new digital economics:

> Microsoft has maintained a monopoly share (in excess of 80%) of the PC operating system market over an extended period of time. The durability of Microsoft's market power in part reflects

---

I would update Marshall's insight [that which firm achieves market dominance depends on "whatever firm gets a good start"] by observing that the parts of the economy that are resource-based (agriculture, bulk-goods production, mining) are still for the most part subject to diminishing returns. Here conventional economics rightly holds sway. The parts of the economy that are knowledge-based, on the other hand, are largely subject to increasing returns.

(1990, p. 95)

[3] Not all "network effects" are necessarily "network externalities," as is sometimes suggested in the literature (Katz and Shapiro, 1985). Many networks have sponsors, meaning that the externalities are internalized, meaning there are no resulting market inefficiencies (Liebowitz and Margolis, n.d.).

the fact that the PC operating system market is characterized by certain economies of scale in production and by significant "network effects." In other words, the PC operating system for which there are the greatest number, variety, and quality of applications will be selected by the large majority of PC users, and in turn writers of applications will write their programs to work with the most commonly used operating system, in order to appeal to as many potential customers as possible. Economies of scale and network effects, which reinforce one another, result in high barriers to entry.

(J. Klein, et.al, § 58)

Judge Thomas Penfield Jackson affirmed both the Justice Department's and his own view of scale economies for software developers (which he developed as the trial proceeded) when he found, "What is more, once a firm had written the necessary software code, it could produce millions of copies of its operating system at relatively low cost" (*Findings of Fact*, 1999, § 30).[4] The judge concurred with the Justice Department that Microsoft has a dominant market

---

[4] Judge Jackson also found that network effects pose what he called a "chicken and egg problem" for software developers:

> The ability to meet a large demand [because of scale economies in supply] is useless, however, if the demand for the product is small, and signs do not indicate large demand for a new Intel-compatible PC operating system. To the contrary, they indicate that the demand for a new Intel-compatible PC operating system would be severely constrained by an intractable "chicken-and-egg" problem: The overwhelming majority of consumers will only use a PC operating system for which there already exists a large and varied set of high-quality, full-featured applications, and for which it seems relatively certain that new types of applications and new versions of existing applications will continue to be marketed at pace with those written for other operating systems. Unfortunately for firms whose products do not fit that bill, the porting of applications from one operating system to another is a costly process. Consequently, software developers generally write applications first, and often exclusively, for the operating system that is already used by a dominant share of all PC users. Users do not want to invest in an operating system until it is clear that the system will support generations of applications that will meet their needs, and developers do not want to invest in writing or quickly porting applications for an operating system until it is clear that there will be a sizeable and stable market for it. What is more, consumers who already use one Intel-compatible PC operating system are even less likely than first-time buyers to choose a newcomer to the field, for switching to a new system would require these users to scrap the investment they have made in applications, training, and certain hardware.

> (*Findings of Fact*, § 30)

position, well within the requirements for an antitrust trial to proceed: Microsoft possesses a dominant, persistent, and increasing share of the world-wide market for Intel-compatible PC operating systems. Every year for the last decade, Microsoft's share of the market for Intel-compatible PC operating systems has stood above 90%. For the last couple of years the figure has been at least 95%, and analysts project that the share will climb even higher over the next few years. Even if Apple's Mac OS were included in the relevant market, Microsoft's share would still stand well above 80% (*Findings of Fact*, § 35).

The reason for the existence of the high barriers to entry are, according to the Justice Department (and trial judge), the self-perpetuating nature of sales to build on sales,

> One of the most important barriers to entry is the barrier created by the number of software applications that must run on an operating system in order to make the operating system attractive to end users. Because end users want a large number of applications available, because most applications today are written to run on Windows, and because it would be prohibitively difficult, time-consuming, and expensive to create an alternative operating system that would run the programs that run on Windows, a potential new operating system entrant faces a high barrier to successful entry.
>
> (J. Klein, § 3)

Moreover, the Justice Department found that key Microsoft executives appear to have understood key digital economic concepts and used them in designing the company's monopoly maintenance through winning the "browser battle." According to the Justice Department, two Microsoft executives reasoned that "the 'key factors to keep in mind' were, first, the need to increase browser share and, second, that the way to do that was: 'Leveraging our strong share on the desktop will make switching costs high (if they get our technology by default on every desk then they'll be less inclined to purchase a competitive solution. . . .)'" (J. Klein, § 108).

Hence, the Justice Department concludes, "Indeed, because of the extraordinary growth and importance of the Internet, the Internet browser market is itself a substantial source of potential profits to any company that might achieve a durable dominant position and be able to charge monopoly prices for the efficient use of the Internet or the web. The importance of the Internet and the significant public benefits resulting from its use, make the potential benefit to a monopolist and the potential economic and social cost of monopolization in this market very high" (J. Klein, § 65). Again, according to the Justice Department, the emergence of Netscape's Navigator, used in conjunction with Sun Microsystem's Java programming language that would make for a cross-platform web-based operating environment, threatened "to reduce or eliminate one of the key barriers to entry [the array of 70,000 Windows applications] protecting Microsoft's operating system monopoly" (J. Klein, § 7).

9.3. THE ROLE OF MARKET DOMINANCE

Historically, a firm's market dominance, measured by its share of industry sales (as the "industry" is defined for the particular case), has been an important surrogate for the firm's "market power," or ability to raise its prices to monopoly levels (or above the marginal cost of production). As Hovenkamp (1999) notes, courts have relied "on the fact that there is a positive correlation between market *share* and market power" (1999, p. 80), with "market power" defined earlier as the ability of a firm "to deviate profitably from marginal cost pricing" (1999, p. 79).[5] The courts have reasoned that the ability of a firm to deviate from marginal cost pricing is functionally related to its ability to reduce the market supply of the product below competitive levels. With the curbed supply, the market price will rise, and so will the firm's profits. Of course, if there are no other producers in the market, and none can enter because of prohibitive barriers to entry, the firm is in total control of industry output, which it alone can manipulate to maximize profits.

If the firm is merely the dominant producer, not the sole producer, then the dominant producer's ability to restrict aggregate industry supply is itself restricted by the ability of the other firms in the industry (and those who can enter) to make up for sales not made by the dominant producer. For non-digital goods (those that are material in nature and cannot be reduced to 1s and 0s), the

---

[5] Hovenkamp reports how the Fourth Circuit Court specified the market share requirements in cases involving an attempted monopolization of a market: "(1) claims of less than 30% market shares should presumptively be rejected; (2) claims involving between 30% and 50% shares should usually be rejected, except when conduct is very likely to achieve monopoly or when conduct is invidious, but not so much so as to make the defendant per se liable; (3) claims involving greater than 50% share should be treated as attempts at monopolization when the other elements for attempted monopolization are also satisfied" (*M&M Medical Supplies and Service* v. *Pleasant Valley Hospital* as cited in Hovenkamp, 1999, p. 285). Hovenkamp then cites a number of cases in which "most other courts use numbers in the same range, with a few indicating that a rising market share is a stronger indicator of sufficient market power" (Hovenkamp, 1999, p. 285, notes 35 and 26).

smaller the share of the market supplied by firms other than the dominant producer, the greater the ability of the dominant producer to restrict aggregate industry supply and the greater its market power, ceteris paribus. The market power of the dominant producer in markets for non-digital goods stems in part from the fact that the existing non-dominant producers face positive and increasing marginal costs of production. This means that as the non-dominant producers try to expand sales in response to the dominant producer's curb in sales, the non-dominant producer's expansion in sales is chocked off, eventually, by their rising marginal costs. The result can then be an aggregate net reduction in sales equal to the difference between the dominant producer's curb in sales minus the non-dominant producers' total expansion in sales. The market (monopoly) price charged will be set by the net reduction in industry supply and, presumably, constant demand.

Market share and market power should not have the same "correlation" in markets for digital goods, like operating systems, as in non-digital goods, for example, cereal or microprocessors. The reason is simple, as the Justice Department has found is the case in operating systems: the marginal cost of production is virtually zero, if not zero, and is practically constant for what is likely to be the full scope of the likely market (even when that market might be quite "large"). If the dominant producer tries to restrict production, then the other non-dominant producers can expand output without their marginal production costs ever rising much above zero. (For instance, if Microsoft were to restrict sales of Windows, IBM could easily, with no added costs, expand its output of OS/2 by duplicating Microsoft's license with computer manufacturers, making the computer manufacturers responsible for transferring OS/2 to the computers sold. If the Justice Department starts with the presumption that Microsoft's marginal cost is practically zero, it would have to assume, for sake of consistency, that IBM's marginal cost is also practically zero.) Hence, in the limit cases, the collective expansion of non-dominant producers' output will fully offset the supply curb of the dominant producer, meaning that in such limit cases there would be no correlation between market share and market power. The supply response of the non-dominant producers can be fully offsetting no matter whether the dominant producer's market share is 50%, 80%, or even 99% .

This is to say, in the case of digital goods, the relationship between market share and monopoly power would at best be discontinuous. That is, the dominant producer would have monopoly power if it had 100% of market sales, provided it were protected by prohibitive barriers to entry. It would have no such monopoly power if its market share were lower than 10%, regardless of whether it were protected by prohibitive barriers to entry.

Hovenkamp effectively recognizes this point by citing a formula original with Landes and Posner (1999, note 2, p. 945) that includes the elasticity of supply, as well as the elasticity of demand, as a determinant of a dominant producer's market power.[6] In that formula, as the supply (or demand) elasticity goes to infinity, the firm's market power goes to zero. With constant and virtually zero marginal cost of digital goods, the dominant producer's market evaporates, no matter what its level of dominance is, mainly because the elasticity of supply of the non-dominant producers is infinity when their marginal cost is constant and zero.

The practical consequence of this revised thinking can be seen in the Microsoft case. The Justice Department does not seem to appreciate that its declaration in its complaint that the marginal cost of production of operating systems is practically nil and constant, belies its argument that Microsoft has market power simply because of its more than 80% (really upwards of 95%) market share.[7] The two lines of argument are inconsistent. The existence of one other operating system producer — for example, IBM with OS/2 — can totally undermine Microsoft's market power even if IBM has a trivial portion of market sales, simply because, as indicated, the non-dominant producer could supplant any reduction in sales of the dominant producer.

Perhaps non-dominant producers of a digital good do eventually, within the bounds of total market sales, face somewhat escalating marginal production costs (after all, someone may have to provide customer service, which might only be provided with non-digitized resources that are subject to increasing marginal cost[8]). Still, the point is that dominance per se in markets does not mean as much

---

[6] The Landes/Posner formula for monopoly power is

$$(P_m - P_c) = S_j/(e_m^d + e_j^s(1 - S_j)).$$

Where: P_m = monopoly price e_m^d = market elasticity of demand
P_c = competitive price (marginal cost) e_j^s = elasticity of supply of competing or fringe firms
S_j = firm's market share.

[7] The Justice Department actually represents Microsoft's "market share" at 95% for 1997 through 2000 with the introduction of its exhibit 1, a table titled "Microsoft's Actual and Projected Share of the (Intel-Based) PC Operating System Market [*United States* v. *Microsoft*, Exhibit 1, First District Court, civil action no. 98–1232, nd (http://www.usdoj.gov/atr/cases/exhibits/1.pdf)]. A firm's "market share" is normally viewed as its *sales* divided by industry sales (as the industry is defined for purposes of the case at hand). In the case of Exhibit 1, Microsoft's "market share" is something quite different, the percent of *existing* personal computers (not annual sales) that have Windows installed on them.

[8] Even if Dell provides service support for Windows, any decreasing returns it faces in service can feed into Microsoft's decision making, given the highly competitive nature of the computer manufacturing industry and how Dell's added support costs can reduce the price Dell is willing to pay for Windows.

in digital markets as in non-digital markets (say, markets for industrial goods, like cereal or cars). Put another way, to achieve any given level of monopoly power, a dominant producer in digital markets would have to have a greater market share than a dominant producer in a non-digital market. Hence, there should be less need for antitrust enforcement in digital markets, or fewer antitrust cases should be expected in digital markets, ceteris paribus.

9.4. THE MEASURE OF MARKET SHARE

Stripping "market share" as used in antitrust analysis of all its complexities, real world calculations of market sales are made by dividing the annual sales of a firm by total annual sales within the "relevant market."[9] All sales that are considered are legal sales. If Kellogg has US$5 billion annual sales of cereal with the relevant cereal market defined as US$10 billion of legal sales, then Kellogg has a 50% "market share." There is no reason to consider Kellogg's past cereal sales because cereal is perishable. There is a good reason for not including illegal sales: cereal "pirates" very likely would operate on a smaller scale than Kellogg and would likely face production costs per box much higher than Kellogg's and perhaps rising at a faster rate. As a consequence, it may reasonably be argued that Kellogg's "market share," as computed, can say something about Kellogg's ability to restrict sales within the cereal market and raise the prices it charges.

Digital goods are far from perishable. Indeed, there is no reason that they should ever deteriorate physically, mainly because, at their core, they are not physical. Hence, past sales of digital goods cannot be summarily dismissed as being irrelevant to calculating the market share.

Microsoft might indeed have a 90-plus percent of the operating system market when the "relevant market" is restricted to those operating systems sold each year through retail stores and computer makers for computers that employ Intel-compatible microprocessors. However, does that mean that Microsoft has 90-plus percent of *all* operating system "sales"? The answer is clearly no, as Reynolds (1999) has pointed out, given that the "relevant market" was so narrowly defined in the Microsoft antitrust case that it does not include the Apple Mac (because Apple computers are not Intel-compatible) or Linux (because Linux is not generally installed on computers to be used by single users).

---

[9] Hovenkamp (1999, p. 82) defines the "relevant market" as "the smallest grouping of sales for which the elasticity of demand and supply are sufficiently low that a firm with 100% of that grouping could profitably reduce output and increase price substantially above marginal cost."

However, the answer remains no, even when the relevant market remains restricted to Intel-compatible computers. The reason is that past sales of Windows cannot be dismissed because they have not perished. When buyers do not upgrade their computers, they effectively "buy" their old operating system from themselves, and the price is very attractive, nothing. Their ability to effectively buy their old operating system from themselves is relevant because it is an additional check on the monopoly pricing of a dominant firm like Microsoft. In 1998, when the Justice Department computed Microsoft's market share at 95% (albeit incorrectly[10]), only 16% of personal computer owners had upgraded to Windows 98 (the then latest version of Windows). Consider also that in 1999, there were nearly 113 million desktop computers in the United States. Microsoft sold slightly more than 11 million copies of Windows 98 in 1998, which means there were approximately 107 million US Windows users in 1999 who could have upgraded to Windows 98. These users in effect elected that year to "buy" the old version of Windows they already had installed on their machine from themselves at, of course, a zero price, or they bought (or stayed with) some other operating system, like IBM's OS/2. Hence, Microsoft's sales of Windows 98 in 1999 of under 11 million copies represented a remarkably low share of all operating system "sales" (broadly defined) in the United States, just over 10%.

In other words, Microsoft is in competition with its previous sales, for reasons that Ronald Coase explained in a celebrated article on market power and durable goods.[11] Digital goods have one very important characteristic not fully appreciated in conventional antitrust thinking: they are highly durable. The Justice Department convinced the trial court, and wants the Appeals Court to believe,

---

[10] As noted, the Justice Department's computed market share for Microsoft is the ratio of the existing personal computers with Intel-compatible processors and with Windows installed on them to the total number of personal computers with Intel-compatible microprocessors.

[11] Ronald Coase (1972) wrote a celebrated article years ago in which he pointed out that even a monopolistic producer of a durable good would charge a competitive price for its product. Why? Because no sane person would buy all or any portion of the durable good at a price above the competitive level. He used the example of a monopoly owner of a plot of land. If the owner tried to sell the land piecemeal, he would have to lower the price on each parcel until all the land was bought, which means the owner would have to charge the competitive price: the price where the demand for the land and the supply of the land come together. It might be thought that the sole owner of land would be able to restrict sales and get more than the competitive price. However, buyers would reason that if the monopoly owner eventually wanted to sell the remaining land, it could only be sold at less than the price of land already sold, which means the buyers who bought the land at the high price would suffer a loss in the market value of their land. This means that the buyers would wait to buy until the price came down, but then the owner would sell nothing at the monopoly price, and would only be able to sell the land at the competitive price.

that Microsoft had no good business reason to integrate Internet Explorer into Windows 98 — other than to predate against Netscape. There is one very good reason Microsoft must do something like integrate an important new feature — for example, an Internet browser — every time it comes out with a new version of Windows: it must give its customer base — its network — a good reason to spend even a modest sum of money for the new version. When Microsoft was contemplating the construction of Windows 98, it was obvious to just about everyone in the computer industry, including people at Netscape and Microsoft, that the Internet would play an important role in the future of computing. Microsoft had to move aggressively toward making Windows useful in the emerging Internet world and thereby to give its customer base, and applications developers, a reason to move to Windows 98. Microsoft also had to give its customers a good reason not to move toward rival operating systems that could easily emerge.

In addition to their durability, digital goods are capable of being copied by pirates at small cost. Pirates can also distribute their easily replicated copies electronically. Accordingly, pirated copies of digital goods cannot be dismissed from computing market share as easily as they can be dismissed in computing the market shares of non-digital goods. Pirating can be pervasive in digital goods, and is very pervasive in software markets. The Software Information Industry Association estimates the software "piracy rates" (or percent of software packages in use that have been illegally copied) for nearly ninety countries. In 1998, only five of the countries had piracy rates of less than a third (the United States' piracy rate is 26%, the lowest of all countries), and half of the countries had piracy rates of greater than two thirds (with China's piracy rate at 95%). Pirated copies can impose a significant competitive constraint on digital goods producers. If a digital goods producer, for example, Microsoft, increases its price, it gives pirates an incentive to expand their market sales. Put another way, the pirates add to the elasticity of supply that, when considered in the context of the Landes/Posner equation, lower the market power of firms computed for antitrust purposes.

9.5. DEMAND-SIDE SCALE ECONOMIES

Network effects imply substantial economies of scale on the demand side of the market. The larger the sales, the greater the value of the product to consumers, and the greater the demand. Accordingly, network firms can be expected to favor pricing strategies similar to those adopted by other firms whose market demands over time are interconnected with current sales. For example, producers of addictive products (including cigarette makers and dealers of illegal street drugs) understand that their future demand is a function of current consumption (Becker and Murphy, 1988). The greater the sales today of some street drug like heroine, the greater the future demand and consumption, ceteris paribus, or so "addiction" (or the resulting chemical dependency) implies. Even oil producers can face a lagged-demand link between current and future demand, given that consumers' future value of the good can be affected by capital investments and consumer choice associated with current use (Lee and Kreutzer, 1982).

The link between current and future demand creates an incentive for the producer of network goods (or addictive and lagged-demand goods) to push its price downward. When future demand is positively linked to current consumption, any revenue forgone currently can be made up, possibly, with greater sales and, possibly, higher prices in the future. The main difference between the market for, say, heroine and oil on the one hand and digital goods on the other is that the former is subject, presumably, to positive and rising marginal production costs, which implies that producers of digital goods have a greater incentive to expand current sales than do producers of heroine and oil. Also, to the extent that all production costs are upfront, once the competitive process begins, it is likely to play out with few, if any, holds barred, given that the spoils of the market competition will go to the one that achieves market dominance. In their search for developing dominance through network effects and zero marginal production costs, below-zero prices are not unreasonable, or necessarily predatory.

Regardless of exactly how the competitive process develops, network effects imply that the long-run demand elasticity of network goods will be increased by two factors. The first factor is one that affects the demand for non-network goods as well as network goods, time. The long run provides consumers with more time (or just opportunities) for them to seek out and switch to substitutes, which implies they can be more responsive to a price change of either a digital or non-digital good in the long run than in the short run. The second factor is unique to network goods. The short-run demand for network goods can build as consumption increases, or as the value of the good for consumers also increases, implying that the quantity response to a price change will be much greater in the long run than short run.[12] There is no such presumption of demand building on sales for non-network goods. Again, using the formula Hovenkamp cites for determining the market power of a firm, the long-run market power of firms with a given market share (and given elasticity of supply) should be less for a producer of a network good than a non-network good. The greater the network

---

[12] For more details on the pricing pattern for network goods over time, see Lee and McKenzie (2001).

effects, the greater the elasticity of demand, a conclusion fully in line with Becker and Murphy's conclusion regarding addictive drugs, contrary to what is commonly thought (Becker and Murphy, 1988). This means that the gap between the price a dominant network firm would choose and the competitive price would be lower. The deadweight loss for network goods should also be lower, implying a reduced interest in the prosecution of a dominant producer of a network good (with any given market share).

Network effects, combined with the prospects of market tipping, can also affect both the expectations of consumers and producers. Consumers will want to buy that good that is expected to be dominant, because it will be the good that yields the most consumer value over time. The greater the expectations of a particular firm's dominance in the future, the greater the current demand and consumption, and the greater the likelihood of that firm's eventual market dominance. The prospects of expected future dominance and greater market demand can add to the firm's incentive to suppress its current price in two ways. First, the lower price can lead to greater consumption and greater future demand. Second, the lower current price can be considered a signal of how much the firm understands the interconnectedness of current price with future demand and dominance. It can also signal its interest in achieving future dominance and its willingness to forgo current revenues and profits for future revenues and profits. As a consequence, consumers can be expected to move to network firms that offer relatively lower current prices because of their expectation that that firm will achieve market dominance. Their expectations, encouraged by the firm's pricing strategy, can be self-fulfilling.

The demand-side scale economies embodied in network effects require some revision of antitrust thinking mainly because, conventionally, "'predatory pricing' refers to a practice of driving rivals out of business by selling at a price below cost" with the "intent — and the only intent that can make predatory pricing rational, profit-maximizing behavior — is to charge monopoly prices after rivals have been dispatched or disciplined" (Hovenkamp, p. 335). With network effects, a firm's upfront suppressed prices can only have one *intent*, which is to respond to the nature of the market and price its network good so that other firms are driven out of the market (or to prevent other firms from driving it out of the market). The intent is to make consumers expect that the lower-than-marginal-cost upfront price will contribute to its eventual dominance. The price charged upfront can rationally be zero or, for that matter, negative.

If the upfront pricing strategy leads to a current loss, that loss has to be offset by an improvement in its future profits, which implies rising future prices that are, eventually, above cost. However, it doesn't follow for two reasons that any rise in the future price to points above cost is necessarily a monopoly price, implying the collection of monopoly rents *over time*. First, any excess of the future revenue stream above production costs must be set against the upfront losses from below-cost pricing. Over the course of time, the firm may not make more than a competitive rate of return. Indeed, the firm's upfront pricing strategy, and its upfront losses, can be viewed by the firm not so much as a "loss," but rather as a necessary upfront investment, which implies that its true cost of production must incorporate that fixed investment in order to determine whether the future price is above the *true* production cost, considering all upfront investments, including the upfront loss.

Second, the future price might be rising, but so is demand. As a consequence, it does not follow that a rising future price is further removed from the competitive price, or closer to the monopoly price, than the lower (perhaps zero or negative) upfront price that is charged. Indeed, net consumer surplus available to buyers can be greater at higher future prices (that might give the appearance of monopoly prices, because of the suppressed upfront prices) than at the lower upfront prices. Buyers can benefit from the higher future prices (and give the appearance of charging above-cost monopoly prices) because the future "profit" encourages the network firm to suppress its upfront price and build the network. The greater the potential for future "profits," the greater the upfront investment the network firm would be willing to make in the form of upfront losses. Future profits will also affect the speed with which the network will develop. The greater the speed of network development, the greater the net consumer surplus over time, and the closer the link between suppressed upfront prices and higher future prices.

Conventional antitrust thinking requires that proof of an offense of attempted monopolization contain three elements: "1) specific intent to control prices or destroy competition in some part of commerce; 2) predatory or anticompetitive conduct directed to accomplishing the unlawful purpose; and 3) a dangerous probability of success" (Hovenkamp, 1999, p. 280).[13] The problem with using those criteria in network markets is that such markets will very likely, given the underlying postulates about the market, become dominated by a single firm. In addition, there is a reasonable expectation that the winning dominant firm, whichever firm that might be, will achieve its dominant position (with a greater likelihood than in markets for non-network goods) by lowering its price to below-cost levels for the purpose of building the network, which can be mis-

---

[13] In *Spectrum Sports*, the Supreme Court ruled, "We hold that petitioners may not be liable for attempted monopolization . . . absent proof of a dangerous probability that they would monopolize a particular market and specific intent to monopolize" (*Spectrum Sports, Inc.* v. *McQuillan*, note 8 at 506 US at 459 113 S. Ct. 884, at 892).

construed as "predatory" in the sense that the pricing strategy is used to achieve monopoly power, not just mere market dominance.

Given the implied upfront losses from the adopted initial pricing strategy, there is not just a "dangerous probability" that the dominant producer will raise its price in the future, there is the virtual certainty that the dominant firm will do so in order to achieve the anticipated rate of return on its investment in the long run. Furthermore, the firm that achieves dominance will very likely have had the *intent* of achieving its dominance by eliminating existing competitors with the upfront low prices. Otherwise, the firm could be supplanted by some other firm that also had the intent of wiping out other competitors.

Does that mean that the emerging dominant firm has, by the combination of the low early price and the higher later price, somehow constricted the size of the market for its network good as a monopolist might try to do? Not necessarily. In fact, the pricing combination could enhance market efficiency because the market is actually larger than it would otherwise be, and the "average" price charged by consumers would be lower than it otherwise would be. The reason is that with the early price reduction and the expansion of the demand, the elasticity of the long-run demand can be higher than it would have been if some other more reserved upfront pricing strategy had been used, leading to the long-run price being lower than it would if the elasticity of the long-run demand were lower. However, given conventional thinking about the correlation of market dominance and market power, there is definitely a dangerous probability that dominant network firms will be prosecuted for antitrust violations unjustly, that is to say, they may not have acted any more monopolistically (and may have acted more competitively) than other non-network firms with much lower market shares.

In conventional markets for conventional goods, a finding that a firm was *capable* of raising its price was sufficient to conclude that the firm presented a dangerous probability of raising its price in the future. After all, if a firm could raise its price, it would be losing collectible profits, causing the price of its stock to suffer.[14] However, the theory of networks requires that a distinction be made between the *ability* of a dominant producer to exploit the inelasticity of its short-run demand for greater profits and the *incentive* to do so, given the much higher elasticity of its long-run demand under which the network effects can build — and unravel. A firm producing a network good must fear that an increase in the current price might lead to greater current profits, but also to an unraveling of the network in the long run, causing the firm to gain short-run profits at the

---

[14] If the dominant firm didn't raise the price for its good, then savvy investors could buy up controlling interest in the company, change the firm's pricing policy, and sell the stock at a capital gain.

expense of profits later on. The net effect of the firm seeking to exploit its current *ability* to raise its price could be a reduction in the market value of its stock. In short, the dominant firm might have the *ability* to raise its price — which could erroneously be equated with a "dangerous probability" of the firm raising its price, because it has no *incentive* to do so.

Microsoft has been charged with violating both sections of the Sherman Act mainly because of its predatory pricing of Internet Explorer. It charged nothing for Internet Explorer in spite of having "spent something approaching the US$100 million it has devoted each year to developing Internet Explorer and some part of the US$30 million it has spent annually marketing it," as Judge Jackson found (Findings of Fact, § 140). According to the judge, Microsoft incurred the substantial browser development costs and potential revenue loss from giving away the browser (and then bartering away space on the Windows desktop with Internet service providers in exchange for their willingness to distribute Internet Explorer) for one overriding reason — the protection of the "applications barrier to entry" (*Findings of Fact*, § 141). The array of other complaints against Microsoft, including exclusionary agreements with computer makers and Internet service providers, as well as its pricing of Internet Explorer, "lacked pro-competitive justifications" (Findings of Fact, § 410).

Indeed, the only justification the judge found was to protect the applications barrier to entry by rapidly gaining a substantial market share for Internet Explorer at Netscape Navigator's "expense," making Microsoft's business tactics necessarily "predatory."[15] Hence, the judge concluded that Microsoft posed the "dangerous probability" of achieving monopoly in the browser market.[16] What

---

[15] In the judge's words, "Microsoft also gave other firms things of value (at substantial cost to Microsoft) in exchange for their commitment to distribute and promote Internet Explorer, sometimes explicitly at Navigator's expense. While Microsoft might have bundled Internet Explorer with Windows at no additional charge even absent its determination to preserve the applications barrier to entry, that determination was the main force driving its decision to price the product at zero" (*Findings of Fact*, § 136). The judge concluded, "Microsoft's campaign must be termed predatory," given that "the Court has already found that Microsoft possesses monopoly power," as reflected in its substantial market share (*Conclusions of Law*, p. 18). More generally, the judge concluded, "While the evidence does not prove that they would have succeeded absent Microsoft's actions, it does reveal that Microsoft placed an oppressive thumb on the scale of competitive fortune, thereby effectively guaranteeing its continued dominance in the relevant market. More broadly, Microsoft's anticompetitive actions trammeled the competitive process through which the computer software industry generally stimulates innovation and conduces to the optimum benefit of consumers (*Conclusions of Law*, p. 18).

[16] Judge Jackson wrote, "The Court is nonetheless compelled to express its further conclusion that the predatory course of conduct Microsoft has pursued since June of 1995 has revived the dangerous probability that Microsoft will attain monopoly power in a second market. Internet Explorer's share

is important to note is that Judge Jackson never once indicates that the legal standard for making the "dangerous probability" assessment is affected in the least by the nature of the market for digital goods on which the case is founded. Indeed, the judge does nothing more than cite the relevant cases that lay out the conventional legal standard for "market share" and "dangerous probability."[17]

While it is hard here to take issue with aspects of the judge's ruling against Microsoft (for example, his finding that Microsoft did seek to divide the operating system and browser markets in a meeting that was held June 21, 1995), it is equally clear that using the prism of the two central postulates of digital economics, Microsoft's business tactics could be construed as having a "procompetitive justification," as well as effect. The "effect" of Microsoft's tactics appears straightforward, a reduction in the price of the two leading browsers — Navigator and Explorer — to zero. The intent of the zero pricing of the browser may have been to destroy Netscape, as the Justice Department and judge claim, but it could also be construed as a natural competitive response to the advent of a competitive threat — Netscape — in the form of a new computer platform market that, like Windows, is presumably subject to network effects and zero marginal cost. After all, when marginal cost is zero, competitive, marginal cost pricing would dictate a zero price. Moreover, when a network is threatened, one would expect the ensuing competition to be intense because current *and* future profits, as well as market dominance, are at stake. Microsoft might have an incentive to lower its price to zero (and beyond) just to ensure that its network doesn't unravel as the market tips toward Netscape's platform. The tipping could be the consequence of both applications developers and computer users moving to a new lower priced and superior standard.

Furthermore, Microsoft did not preclude a superior platform from establishing itself as the standard. It could not do so. If Microsoft were restricting sales and pricing its products like a monopolist, the task of a standard takeover by Netscape would be relatively easy, especially if Netscape were truly a superior platform and were being sold at a competitive price. Even if Microsoft had not charged a monopoly price for Windows, but threatened to do so in the future

---

of browser usage has already risen above 50%, will exceed 60% by January 2001, and the trend continues unabated" (*Conclusions of Law*, p. 22).

[17] Judge Jackson quotes approvingly *M&M Medical Supplies & Serv., Inc. v. Pleasant Valley Hosp., Inc.*, 981 F.2d 160, 168 (4th Cir. 1992) (en banc), "'A rising share may show more probability of success than a falling share. . . . [C]laims involving greater than 50% share should be treated as attempts at monopolization when the other elements for attempted monopolization are also satisfied.' (citations omitted); *see also* IIIA Phillip E. Areeda & Herbert Hovenkamp, *Antitrust Law* § 807d, at 354–55 (1996) (acknowledging the significance of a large, rising market share to the dangerous probability element)."

with a "dangerous probability," consumers could be expected to move to the Netscape standard (or some other standard). There might be switching costs for shifting, but there would also be *expected* "staying costs," or consumer surplus that would be surrendered to Microsoft for not making the switch to another operating system. In addition, there is no problem of the network *effects* being network *externalities*. The gains from the switching would be received by Netscape, which could be expected to cover many of the switching costs with the added long-run profits that could be received (especially if Microsoft were to produce and price like a monopolist).

Microsoft may have responded to the Netscape threat "with ferocity" [to use Netscape's founder Jim Clark's phrase (1999, p. 49)], but that is not unexpected in a world of network and digital goods. In fact, it is expected because of the magnitude of the "prize," which is not simply for more sales, but for very possibly most, if not all, of the market that will tip toward the standard setter. Moreover, the additional sales are likely to be lucrative, given that they add nothing (or very little) to cost.[18] To keep the network together, a network sponsor for software like Microsoft has to assure applications developers that it, Microsoft (not Netscape), will continue to be the standard computer platform, thus giving them reasons to continue to refine and upgrade their applications for Windows. The advent of another potentially successful platform can unsettle their expectations, which may only be resettled by the network sponsor (Microsoft) proving that it will remain very competitive. Such proof can take the form of zero prices for product upgrades and strong reactions to competitive threats.

Do such reactions by Microsoft "lack pro-competitive justification"? They could easily be seen as the essence of pro-competitiveness, maybe not in markets for industrial, non-digital goods, but certainly in digital goods markets.

9.6. THE BENEFITS OF SWITCHING COSTS AND LOCK-INS

In the Microsoft case, switching costs and lock-ins are treated by both the Justice Department and Judge Jackson as sources of monopoly power and, hence, market inefficiency. For example, Judge Jackson found,

> Unfortunately for firms whose products do not fit that bill, the porting of applications from one operating system to another is a

---

[18] Besen and Farrell note, "Because the prize (becoming the 'standard') is so tempting, sponsors may compete *fiercely* to have their technologies become the standard, and this competition will generally dissipate part — perhaps a large part — of the potential gains" (1994, p. 119).

costly process. Consequently, software developers generally write applications first, and often exclusively, for the operating system that is already used by a dominant share of all PC users. Users do not want to invest in an operating system until it is clear that the system will support generations of applications that will meet their needs, and developers do not want to invest in writing or quickly porting applications for an operating system until it is clear that there will be a sizeable and stable market for it. What is more, consumers who already use one Intel-compatible PC operating system are even less likely than first-time buyers to choose a newcomer to the field, for switching to a new system would require these users to scrap the investment they have made in applications, training, and certain hardware.

(Findings of Fact, § 30)

Such a view of switching costs might be appropriate for non-digital goods, because their marginal costs are positive and generally rising within the relevant range of the market. However, when the marginal cost is zero and the products exist, perspectives must adjust. This is because the price competition among competitors can drive the price to zero, at which, of course, all existing competitors will incur losses equal to their upfront development costs. Even with only two producers in the market with the same cost structures that equally divide the market, the price would not stop falling at their average costs (which is equal to the development costs divided by the quantity, since there are no reproduction costs). The reason is that their products exist, and it would be beneficial for each producer to lower its price and try for a larger share of the market. With a larger scale, their average cost would fall and some revenues will always reduce their losses. In short, selling some units at any price above zero results in losses that are less than would be incurred if one or both producers dropped out, at which point their losses would equal their development costs.

Potential producers of digital goods like Microsoft and applications developers would want to see some protection against such intense competitive incentives that can result in prices close to zero, if not zero, *before* they incur upfront development costs. Switching costs — and, at the limit, lock-ins — can be the type of restraint producers need to incur the necessary upfront development costs. Consumers need not be worse off because of the switching costs, even when they are later "exploited." The reason is that they get the products they need at levels of development that are greater than they would otherwise and their upfront prices would be lower than otherwise (because of the prospects of higher prices later), points the authors have developed at length elsewhere (Lee and

McKenzie, 2001). Here, we can extend the point by noting that if the prospect of zero pricing is not muted by "natural" switching costs (the kind that Judge Jackson is concerned about), then we would expect the digital producers to seek out "unnatural" forms of protections that come in the form of short and long-term contracts. We might anticipate that the greater the development costs, the closer marginal cost is to zero, and the lower the natural switching costs, the longer the contract that the digital producers would seek with consumers. Hence, antitrust enforcers must tread very carefully in equating switching costs, or long-term contracts, with monopoly power or market inefficiency. Each can be seen as a substitute for the other, and each can give rise to market activity that would not otherwise occur and, as such, could be construed as efficiency enhancing.

9.7. THE DOMINANT PRODUCER'S DEMAND FOR ANTITRUST ENFORCEMENT

Textbook models of monopolies suggest that monopolies — and their legal counterparts, dominant producers — would be opposed to antitrust laws that are effectively enforced. After all, effective antitrust enforcement would mean lower firm prices, rents, and stock values.

However, such a line of analysis is narrowly conceived. It starts with the *existence* of the monopoly, and does not consider the circumstances under which a monopoly (or just dominant producer) might emerge. Firms that produce digital goods with the potential for network effects that might cover almost all, if not all, of the market have good reasons for wanting effective enforcement of antitrust laws. Such firms can reason that their network members can see the potential for the firm's potential market dominance that can give them the power to raise their prices and garner monopoly rents in the future. To build their networks, such firms would have to lower their prices for two reasons. First, they would have to lower their upfront prices to encourage the building of the network effects. Second, they would also have to lower their upfront prices even more to offset the expectation of the later monopoly pricing threat.

In the case of the operating system market, the likely dominant producer would have to temper the fears of both application developers and their software buyers, as well as their own buyers of the operating system. The operating system buyers would fear that they would have to pay monopoly prices for upgrades. Application developers would have to fear that the future curb in sales for the operating system caused by monopoly pricing would undermine their application sales, and undermine the market value of their upfront development investments. Their fear would be all the stronger if the market for the operating system is subject to tipping (which also could mean "un-tipping," or unraveling) as buyers and application developers moved to lower priced computer platforms. Buyers of applications would have to fear that the network effects they garner by joining a particular computer platform would dissipate as application developers withdrew their support. The reduced demand for the platform would mean that the operating system firm that threatens to be a monopoly would have to lower its upfront price by more than would be the case if the operating systems buyers, applications developers, and applications buyers did not fear being subject to future monopoly pricing. Through lower upfront prices, these developers and buyers would effectively demand "pre-payment" of the monopoly rents that they fear will be extracted later.

A firm that has the potential for being a monopoly might try to handle the extant fears by committing itself to competitive, or non-monopoly, prices in the future. However, the developers and buyers have good reasons to doubt the commitment. When a network is in the early stages of development, the verbal or written commitment may not be credible, simply because of the newness of the firms and network. In addition, the developers and buyers can reason that if the commitment to price competitively into the future is honored by the parties making the agreement, then in the future, monopoly rents will be forgone and the company's stock will then be less than it could be if the monopoly rents were then extracted. Savvy investors may be able to buy controlling interest in the firm, institute monopoly prices (in overt or covert ways), generate monopoly rents, and then sell their stock for a capital gain. Realizing the lack of credibility of its commitments not to act monopolistically, the firm would naturally be interested in having third-party enforcement of its commitments that may take the form of contracts. However, contracts are difficult to make foolproof, especially when substantial monopoly rents may be at stake in finding legal ways of skirting the contractual language.[19]

In the incompleteness and other flaws of contracts lie a firm's potential interest in antitrust laws and their effective enforcement. The enforcement of antitrust laws can, in effect, add credibility to a firm's commitment that it will not in the future charge monopoly prices. The firm can say, in effect, to developers and buyers, "You may not believe me when I commit to competitive, non-monopoly prices (and other business practices), but you can take comfort from the fact that antitrust officials are standing watch and will prosecute when you or others complain." Such a statement can carry even greater weight if there is more than one source of antitrust enforcement. The monopoly practices missed by one

---

[19] For a discussion of the problem of incompleteness of contracts, see Milgrom and Roberts (1992, pp. 127–129).

source of enforcement (for example, the Federal Trade Commission) can be caught by the other (the Antitrust Division of the Department of Justice), and the competitiveness of the enforcement sources can add credibility to the firm's commitment not to act monopolistically in the future.

Naturally, if the antitrust laws are never enforced, they may add little to the credibility of the firm's commitment not to act monopolistically. Hence, firms that might become monopolies, or just dominant producers who threaten to achieve monopoly power, can have an interest in active enforcement, especially when the enforcement is against others.[20]

An array of economic and legal critics has argued that the problem with antitrust laws is that their enforcement has been perverse, meaning counterproductive.[21] With the encouragement of less aggressive competitors, antitrust enforcers have all too frequently used the laws to thwart competition, rather than monopoly."[22] If, or when, antitrust enforcement thwarts (contrary to the

---

[20] However, that is not to say that they would not want the laws enforced (at least at some point) against them. Such enforcement could add significant credibility to the firm's commitment to not act monopolistically (at least not for long). As a consequence, a firm that is prosecuted could gain from antitrust actions being taken against it, at least up to some undefined point. The firm might incur legal costs in being prosecuted, and convicted, but it could gain by a greater demand by developers and buyers to join its network, meaning its upfront prices could be higher than they would otherwise be. The result could be that the net revenue gains upfront more than offset its legal costs. Of course, "too many" actions (or any one action being "too severe") can undermine the credibility of its commitment, causing its network to unravel. As in all things, firms would see "optimal" antitrust enforcement (which could be predicated on a host of factors that cannot be considered here). This does not mean that Microsoft should relish intensity of its antitrust troubles with the Justice Department that began in 1998. The penalties could be serious. However, this line of argument suggests that the company's troubles do have some potential hidden benefits, a reactivation of the government's commitment to prevent dominant producers like Microsoft to act monopolistically. Such an outcome could increase (at least marginally) the willingness of applications developers to write for Windows, and operating system and applications buyers to stay with the Wintel computer platform, thus allowing Microsoft to charge (marginally) higher prices than it otherwise would be capable of doing.

[21] Once a critic of antitrust enforcement in the 1970s and before, Bork (1978, p. 63) concludes, "[M]odern antitrust has so decayed that the policy is no longer intellectually respectable. Some of it is not respectable as law; more of it is not respectable as economics; and now I wish to suggest that, because it pretends to one objective while frequently accomplishing its opposite, and because it too often forwards trends dangerous to our form of government and society, a great deal of antitrust is not even respectable as politics."

[22] Baumol and Ordover (1985, p. 247) have observed, "There is a specter that haunts our antitrust institutions. Its threat is that, far from serving as the bulwark of competition, these institutions will become the most powerful instrument in the hands of those who wish to subvert it . . . We ignore it at our peril and would do well to take steps to exorcise it." Later, they add (p. 257), "Paradoxically, then and only then, when the joint venture [or other market action] is beneficial [to consumers], can those rivals be relied upon to denounce the undertaking as 'anticompetitive.'"

presumed intent of antitrust law) the emergence of lower future prices from competition among rivals for the network standard, the conventional model of competition would suggest that antitrust enforcement would lead to higher current prices. However, that would not be the case for producers of network/ digital goods. Developers and consumers would anticipate smaller networks in the future, as the market shares of competitors are prevented from shrinking with the emergence of a dominant (more competitive) producer. To overcome the resistance of developers and buyers, network firms would have to charge, over time, lower prices than they otherwise would. Consumers would be getting lower prices, but it doesn't follow that they would be "better off." This is because their demand for the size networks that are achieved would be lower, leaving them a smaller consumer surplus.

9.8. COMPLEMENTARY GOODS

Conventional models of monopoly that undergird antitrust enforcement start with the presumption that the monopoly good is sold in isolation from all other goods. Indeed, for a pure monopoly, all substitutes are ruled out by assumption. The typical presumption is that the monopoly (or just dominant producer) does not produce complementary products, nor does it have an incentive to produce complementary products that other firms do not have — unless such products can be used to fortify the monopoly. As noted, the trial judge in the Microsoft case has found that Microsoft's development of its browser, which can only be construed as a complementary software product to Windows (given that the browser can be integrated into Windows), had one overriding purpose, to protect the applications barrier to entry into the operating system market. Accordingly, the browser's zero price was declared to be "predatory."

Nothing in the trial was ever said about Microsoft's other, largely complementary products, for instance, Office (Microsoft's suite of productivity applications), which means that the Justice Department did not appear to see a need to link in court the pricing of Windows with the sales and pricing of Office (or any other Microsoft software or hardware product), and vice versa. However, the absence of evidence presented at trial on the market linkages between Windows and Office did not stop the Justice Department from proposing a breakup of Microsoft into two firms, one that would get Microsoft's operating systems and another that would get everything else, including Internet Explorer. By not raising the complementarity of Windows with Microsoft's various other products, the Justice Department and outside supporters of the breakup made the argument that the breakup would lead to more competitive operating systems and applications markets, which, in turn, could potentially lower the price of the products more or less across the board. By splitting off Office from Windows, Microsoft would no longer, so the Justice Department argued, release the application program interfaces early to Office program developers, giving Microsoft a market advantage in the suites market. By leveling the playing field, there would, supposedly, be more effective market competition to Office and lower suite prices. If Office is made the core of a firm that is independent from Windows, then the Office firm could, possibly, form the basis of a new computer platform, given that Office has as high a share of the suites market as Windows has of the operating system market. The owners of Office would be more inclined to develop its applications for alternative operating systems, for example, Linux, or so it has been argued.

Our purpose here is not to contest the theories underlying the proposed breakup that was adopted by the trial judge. Rather, our purpose is to introduce two points about complementary products that were sidestepped in the Justice Department's case against Microsoft, perhaps because the lawyers and economists at the Justice Department hold to conventional antitrust lines of thinking about why firms do what they do.

First, it must be noted that a monopoly (or just dominant producer) in conventional analysis will always produce and price where marginal cost equals marginal revenue, thus extracting monopoly rents. However, that is not necessarily true for a monopoly with complementary products, especially one that dominates the market for complementary products, as does Microsoft.

Granted, the monopoly owner of a digital good will seek to maximize revenues, which in itself will lead to maximum profits, mainly because marginal cost is zero, but this is only when it does not have complementary products. By lowering the price of the monopolized products to some point below the monopoly price, the firm might lose revenues in the market for the monopoly products. However, it will increase the demand for the complementary digital product that can then be sold in greater numbers at a higher revenue-maximizing price. The stronger the complementarity of the products, the lower the price of the monopoly good. The greater the number of complementary products, the greater the incentive the monopoly has to lower the price of its product. Moreover, the greater the concentration of the complementary products market, the greater the incentive the monopoly firm has to lower its monopoly price. (If the market for the complementary products is highly fragmented among a number of producers, the increased sales of the monopoly product will lead to few sales of the monopoly's complementary products.) This means that the greater the monopoly's share of the complementary products market, the greater the increase in demand and price of the complementary products.

In all of the testimony in the Microsoft case, no one on the Justice Department's side thought to suggest that a plausible explanation for why the price of Windows is so low is its complementary products, perhaps most importantly, Office, given its 90% or higher share of the suites market. The Justice Department could have made the point that Microsoft was extracting a monopoly price, not through Windows, but rather through the sales and price of Office (if in fact that was the case).

There is a second, perhaps more important, reason Microsoft has complementary products like Office: network effects. When Windows was first introduced in 1983, there were few Windows applications, and it was unclear that Windows would achieve the market dominance that it now enjoys. Applications developers were understandably leery of joining the Windows network. One practical reason Microsoft had for developing Office (or, rather, its component applications) was to start the network effects rolling. That alone could encourage applications developers to write for Windows. In addition, by developing Office, Microsoft was alerting developers to its own confidence in Windows' market potential and was willing to put its own upfront investment funds at risk, which could also encourage developers to write for Windows.

Moreover, applications developers then had an understandable fear that a dominant producer of an operating system like Microsoft will exploit its monopoly power at some point in the future. The applications developers would have to worry that an increase in the price of Windows in the future will lower the demand for their complementary products that are necessarily complements to the operating system (given that the applications are technologically tied to the operating system). This means the value of their upfront investment in the development of their applications would be lost. The greater the incentive Microsoft has to charge the monopoly price, the greater the risk that the application developers incur. This means, as explained above, the developers' risk costs of writing for the operating system dominant producer is functionally related to how many complements the dominant producer has, how strong the complementary relationship is, and the concentration of segments of the applications market controlled by the dominant producer in the operating system.

In other words, by Microsoft having market dominance in a major software market like productivity suites, the company provides a form of self-enforcing contact to applications developers. Put another way, Microsoft gives applications developers some assurance that it will not exploit any monopoly power it achieves in the operating system market, which is to say that Microsoft's own complementary products reduce the risk cost incurred by applications developers that, in turn, can give rise to more developers being willing to write for Windows and that, in turn again, can translate into a greater demand for Windows.

Consumers may pay higher prices (although this is not certain) for software products, but that does not mean they are worse off. The size of the network can expand with the reduction in the developers' risk cost, as can consumer surplus value. Contrary to conventional antitrust thinking, no monopoly pricing need be involved.

Indeed, the elimination of Microsoft's complementary products through a breakup can have consequences that could be construed as contrary to the purpose of antitrust enforcement. The breakup along the lines that Judge Jackson has ordered could take away Microsoft's incentive to lower the price of Windows below the monopoly price, which is to say that a higher price for Windows would be encouraged. Moreover, the breakup could increase the risk costs incurred by applications developers, reducing their willingness to write for Windows and curbing the network effects and consumer benefits.

Network sponsors like Microsoft must stand ready to defend the network, not only because of their direct interest in retaining control over the standard for, say, operating systems, but also because they must defend the interests of the applications developers who also have an economic interest in a stable standard. The applications developers do not want their investments undercut by destabilizing threats to the network. Seeing the network shrink with the advent of a new entrant (or just the threat of a new entrant), developers will understandably consider redeploying their applications for what looks to be the next new "big thing," or standard. Developers must also be concerned that other developers are thinking the same way and that the cumulative effects of such thinking across applications developers — especially when the number of developers is large (as Microsoft has[23]) — can give rise to an accelerating decline in the network, which can feed on itself. Accordingly, the network sponsor has a strong incentive not only to defend the network with efforts that are in proportion to the threat of entrance, but disproportionately to it. In other words, the network sponsor has an incentive to meet the lighting of a competitive "match" with the lighting of its own "welding torch," just to maintain confidence that it, the network sponsor, will defend the interests of the applications developers.

---

[23] Microsoft estimates that there are 20,000 developers writing for Windows, the source of the 70,000 applications that make up the judge's so-called "applications barrier to entry" (according to Scott Fallon, Microsoft Corporation, as reported to Richard McKenzie in an email exchange from September 13, 2000 through October 5, 2000). McKenzie has questioned the existence of 70,000 applications (2000). Both he and Fallon agree that many of the applications counted in the so-called "applications barrier to entry" have minimal sales and, thereby, are of no consequence to a firm that seeks to take over a portion of the operating system market, especially if Microsoft restricts its sales in order to charge above competitive prices (McKenzie, 2001, epilogue).

This line of argument can be used to reinterpret events at the heart of the Microsoft antitrust case. As the trial evidence shows, the Microsoft Corporation did not recognize the Internet threat, in the form of Netscape's Navigator, to its operating system market until late 1994 or early 1995 (*Findings of Fact*, §§ 17, 71, and 72). In a long May 1995 memorandum to his executive staff ominously titled "The Internet Tidal Wave" that was then marked "confidential," Gates radically upgraded company-wide interest in and commitment to the Internet, outlining both the threats and opportunities the Internet presented Microsoft. He insisted that his executive staff give the Internet the "highest level of importance." Indeed, in that memo, as in his 1995 book, Gates equated the importance of the Internet to Microsoft with the development of the first IBM PC and asked all company divisions to rethink and redesign their products with the Internet in mind, indicating with force the problems Microsoft would face in playing catch-up to existing Internet players and noting that the proposed network computer was a "scary possibility" (Gates, 1995, p. 1). Because Navigator, along with Sun's Java programming language, was at the heart of the Internet threat, Microsoft undertook an intense campaign to develop its own browser with the obvious intent of making sure that Internet Explorer would be technologically superior to Navigator, the purpose of which was, naturally, to gain market share from Navigator. The company then bundled Internet Explorer with Windows, eventually integrating Internet Explorer into Windows. Moreover, it gave away the browsing technology and tried to tie up an array of distribution outlets (computer manufacturers and Internet service providers, for example) to maximize IE's market share.[24]

---

[24] Judge Jackson found:

> As soon as Netscape released Navigator on December 15, 1994, the product began to enjoy dramatic acceptance by the public; shortly after its release, consumers were already using Navigator far more than any other browser product. This alarmed Microsoft, which feared that Navigator's enthusiastic reception could embolden Netscape to develop Navigator into an alternative platform for applications development. In late May 1995, Bill Gates, the chairman and CEO of Microsoft, sent a memorandum entitled "The Internet Tidal Wave" to Microsoft's executives describing Netscape as a "new competitor 'born' on the Internet." He warned his colleagues within Microsoft that Netscape was "pursuing a multi-platform strategy where they move the key API into the client to commoditize the underlying operating system." By the late spring of 1995, the executives responsible for setting Microsoft's corporate strategy were deeply concerned that Netscape was moving its business in a direction that could diminish the applications barrier to entry.
>
> (*Findings of Fact*, § 72)

Were these actions predatory, the natural response of a monopoly trying to protect its market dominance, or were they competitive? The Justice Department and trial judge obviously concluded they were predatory and anti-competitive. However, the perspective we have developed offers a contrary, and more charitable, view of Microsoft's actions: they were pro-competitive, the type of actions that a dominant producer would take to respond to a competitive threat in a market beset with network effects and a minuscule marginal cost of production. Microsoft's tactics were, without question, aggressive, but perhaps also necessary to assure network members, consumers and applications developers, that Microsoft, the network sponsor, stood ready to protect the operating system standard and their interests. The "ferocity" of Microsoft's response was attributable in part to the existence of the 20,000 applications developers (not so much to the count of applications per se). Had Microsoft had far fewer developers, like so many other software firms have, then the competitive response would have been more tempered. However, that would have meant that the price charged would have been higher.

9.9. ROLE OF CARTELS

Conventional cartel models hold that the colluding firms form cartels to restrict production and raise their prices and collective profits. The presumption is that cartels have an interest in hiking prices in both the short and long run. However, according to conventional analysis, cartels have a difficult time holding to their production agreements, as evident in the history of the unstable OPEC cartel agreements. The greater the number of colluding firms, ceteris paribus, the greater the incentive cartel members have to cheat on their production agreements, and the less likely the colluding firms will charge monopoly prices and earn monopoly rents, or the more likely the cartel agreement will break down into competitive pricing.[25]

Network/digital economics forces revisions in the way cartels are expected to behave. Most prominently, with network effects, competitors initially have an incentive to collude with the intent of lowering, not raising, prices in order that the development of the network will be encouraged and the future demand for the product will rise, perhaps along with the price. If there is cheating in this initial period, it will come in the form of members breaking with the cartel, taking advantage of the rising demand from network effects — *and* raising their prices,

---

[25] See Posner (1976, chap. 4).

not lowering them. In the future, the members will then have the standard cartel incentive to restrict sales. However, because the market will have expanded between the short and long run, the incentive to enter the market in the long run will be greater than it was in the short run, especially if the cartel members then restrict sales. In effect, by colluding initially to lower prices and expand the market, the cartel members encourage entry and, hence, they encourage cheating in the short and long run. Their collusive efforts undermine, as in conventional cartel thinking, their incentive to form the cartel in the first place.

In conventional markets, cartels are unambiguously harmful to consumers. That is not necessarily the case in markets for digital/network goods. In spite of higher anticipated prices in the future, consumers could want cartel agreements to stick, mainly because of the lower initial prices and the benefits from a larger network. And because of the problems of cartels holding to their agreements, consumers could prefer the emergence at the start of a single (if only dominant) producer of the network product. With the emergence of such a producer, the more likely the initial price will be lowered and the faster and more complete will be the development of the network, market demand, and consumer surplus. Indeed, the more aggressive a firm is in developing its dominance (say, by charging nothing for its product or paying consumers to take the product), the greater the development of the network, demand, and consumer surplus. However, given the way antitrust enforcers interpret business tactics (as was true in the Microsoft case), the more aggressive the actions of the dominant producer initially, the more likely the dominant firm would be charged with "predation."

9.10. MULTIPLE OUTCOMES

Brian Arthur, whose pioneering work has led to renewed interest in network effects, argues that economists have traditionally founded their economic models on an assumption of diminishing returns for one overriding reason, the theoretical attractiveness of the models: "Diminishing returns imply a single equilibrium point for the economy, but positive feedback — increasing returns — makes for many possible equilibrium points" (Arthur, 1990, p. 92). He has also argued with elaborate mathematical models, "There is no guarantee that the particular economic outcome selected from the many alternatives will be the 'best' one. Furthermore, once random economic events select a particular path, the choice may become locked-in regardless of the advantages of the alternatives" (Arthur, 1990, p. 92).

The feedback effects that can give rise to increasing returns, and multiple outcomes, include anything that can lead to a reduction in production costs, such as "learning by doing" and network effects. And Arthur sees network effects that extend well beyond the interdependency of operating system sales and applications that has been central to the examples we have used. He also sees feedback effects in the markets for typewriter keyboards, which we have considered, and VCR recording formats. According to Arthur, the VCR market started with the VHS and Beta formats. A large number of recorders that used one or the other format would lead to video stores carrying more of those kinds of tapes, which would then feed the demand for recorders for that kind of format. Hence, "a small gain in market share would improve the competitive position of one system and help it further increase its lead" (Arthur, 1990, p. 116). He concludes that the early market gains for the VHS format "tipped" the market toward the VHS format, making it the ultimate dominant format. Not only was it impossible for anyone to know when the competition began which format would ultimately "win," it is possible that the "superior" format did not win the struggle for market dominance. Indeed, Arthur surmises that "the claim that Beta was technically superior is true, then the market's choice did not represent the best economic outcome" (Arthur, 1990, p. 116). Instead of the outcome depending on product superiority, there is a good chance that the outcome will be dependent upon chance events that favor one product or the other, or the outcome favors, as Arthur quotes Alfred Marshall's *Principles of Economics* approvingly, "whatever firm gets a good start" (p. 116).

Because of space limitations, we do not wish to take up the issue of whether Arthur is correct in theory or practice. At the same time, we note that other economists have found serious flaws in the reported history of the two major examples of markets that Arthur and others use, the keyboard and the VCR format (Liebowitz and Margolis, 1990 and 1995). It does not now appear that the products that came to dominate their respective markets, QWERTY in keyboards and the VHS in recording formats, are indeed the inferior products they have been thought to be. For purposes of argument, we accept the contention that increasing returns can yield multiple outcomes and that, from time to time, the competitive process might result in inferior products being selected that have some durability.

The issue of concern for this chapter is how those prospects might affect antitrust thinking and enforcement. This issue is of some concern because antitrust enforcement is grounded in the fear that firms with market dominance will exert their monopoly power on production and prices, and the increasing returns/feedback literature is replete with arguments that those firms that get the better starts will come to dominate their markets. Should antitrust enforcement be used to attack dominant firms with the intent of increasing the frequency with which "superior" outcomes are chosen, or decrease the frequency with which "inferior" outcomes result? Can it be used for that purpose with some probability of success, on balance? To understand the problem, we must first note that while an inferior product *might* become dominant, there is nothing in the feedback/network effects literature that says how frequently inferior outcomes will occur. It might be very infrequent. We must also note that even Arthur starts with a humbling acknowledgement, "Yet it would be impossible at the outset of the competition to say which system would win, which of the two possible equilibria [in the VCR market] would be selected" (Arthur, 1990, p. 116).

The problem of picking the winner in other markets with far more than two possible outcomes would be even more problematic. Then there is the prospect that if an inferior outcome were selected — meaning that the present value of the benefits of switching to a new outcome were greater than the switching costs, properly discounted, for years to come — there are at least some grounds for believing that in some, if not all, of the inferior outcomes, a correction is likely, given that there would be net gains that could be garnered by entrepreneurs who have the foresight to engineer the switchover (Liebowitz and Margolis, 1995).

Still, we might concede the prospects of true market failure, in which the network effects are true network *externalities*. Problems remain with using antitrust enforcement, or any other form of regulation, to improve upon market outcomes, given that antitrust enforcers will have to sort through all the various possible outcomes to select the one outcome that would be superior to the one chosen by market forces. As Hayek (1944) has cautioned, it is doubtful that the enforcers would have the required information to make the assessment of relative merits of outcomes after the fact, but less before the fact. It is hard to know how the enforcers would be able to determine the costs and benefits of outcomes that never occurred. It would appear that any contemplated antitrust attack on a dominant producer because of its dominant winning market position would also have repercussions on how the competitive process would work itself out. Such antitrust prosecutions might in fact deter inferior outcomes from occurring, but given the prospects of antitrust mistakes, they could also discourage superior outcomes from occurring. The firm that expects to be the eventual winner in the competitive process may, fearing antitrust prosecution, temper its competitiveness, thus giving an "inferior firm" a "better start" than it would otherwise have, a greater prospect of being the winner, in spite of the fact that it has an inferior product. If, as Arthur postulates, we cannot know the outcome of a freewheeling competitive process, can we know better the net effect — whether there is, on balance, an improvement or degradation in outcomes — of antitrust enforcement intended to "improve" outcomes?

The Justice Department clearly adopted the theory of "feedback effects" in its antitrust case against Microsoft. It shows signs in its case that it also accepted

Arthur's extension, that a market like the operating systems market, if left alone, could lead to an inferior outcome, especially if a firm like Microsoft with an already "good start" used its market muscle to discourage entry by a competitor like Netscape that might have had a superior product.[26] Throughout its complaint, the Justice Department argued strongly in favor of antitrust violation to ensure that people have choices among alternative computer platforms.[27] Judge Jackson seems to have concurred that absent antitrust action and penalties, there could be no guarantee that the superior computer platform would win, given Microsoft's starting advantages and its aggressive competitiveness.[28] He seems to have dismissed the prospects that if the Netscape/Sun combination had truly

---

[26] In its original complaint, the Justice Department argued:

> Because of its resources and programming technology, Microsoft was well positioned to develop and market a browser in competition with Netscape. Indeed, continued competition on the merits between Netscape's Navigator and Microsoft's Internet Explorer would have resulted in greater innovation and the development of better products at lower prices. Moreover, in the absence of Microsoft's anticompetitive conduct, the offsetting advantages of Microsoft's size and dominant position in desktop software and Netscape's position as the browser innovator and the leading browser supplier, and the benefit to consumers of product differentiation, could have been expected to sustain competition on the merits between these companies, and perhaps others that have entered and might enter the browser market.
>
> *(Complaint, § 11)*

[27] For example, consider these two passages: 1) "Thus, Microsoft began, and continues today, a pattern of anticompetitive practices designed to thwart browser competition on the merits, to deprive customers of a choice between alternative browsers, and to exclude Microsoft's Internet browser competitors" (*Complaint*, § 12). 2) "Microsoft intends now unlawfully to tie its Internet browser software to its new Windows 98 operating system, the successor to Windows 95. Microsoft has made clear that, unless restrained, it will continue to misuse its operating system monopoly to artificially exclude browser competition and deprive customers of a free choice between browsers" (§ 19).

[28] Judge Jackson found:

> Many of the tactics that Microsoft has employed have also harmed consumers indirectly by unjustifiably distorting competition. The actions that Microsoft took against Navigator hobbled a form of innovation that had shown the potential to depress the applications barrier to entry sufficiently to enable other firms to compete effectively against Microsoft in the market for Intel-compatible PC operating systems. That competition would have conduced to consumer choice and nurtured innovation. The campaign against Navigator also retarded widespread acceptance of Sun's Java implementation. This campaign, together with actions that Microsoft took with the sole purpose of making it difficult for developers to write Java applications with technologies that would allow them to be ported between Windows and other platforms, impeded another form of innovation that

been superior, then Netscape/Sun would not have withdrawn from the market. Seeing its superiority, applications developers would switch to the new Netscape/ Sun platform — especially if Microsoft were actually producing and pricing like a monopoly. If the company were not producing and pricing like a monopoly, then the antitrust actions against Microsoft could definitely choke off its compet- itiveness, but there is no guarantee that under those circumstances the "superior" outcome would then emerge.

9.11. CONCLUDING COMMENTS

The advent of network and digital economics poses no threat to conventional microeconomic models of markets. As recognized, demand curves in the network and digital portions of the economy still slope downward with the elas- ticity remaining a function of the number of existing competitors and the openness of markets to entry. The distinction between fixed and variable costs remains valid, implying that profit-maximizing pricing still requires considera- tion of marginal cost. At the same time, network and digital economics does elevate the importance of increasing returns, self-re-enforcing market develop- ment, tipping, and lock-ins in economic models. This means that expectations are of greater importance in network/digital economic analysis than in conven- tional economic analysis. What we have done in this chapter is show how these changes in emphasis of concepts play out in economic theory and how they force revisions in antitrust thinking and enforcement. If antitrust enforcement was often on shaky ground under conventional market analysis, as critics have main- tained, then surely the enforcers will want to tread more carefully in the network/digital sector of the economy.

---

bore the potential to diminish the applications barrier to entry. There is insuffi- cient evidence to find that, absent Microsoft's actions, Navigator and Java already would have ignited genuine competition in the market for Intel-compatible PC operating systems. It is clear, however, that Microsoft has retarded, and perhaps altogether extinguished, the process by which these two middleware technologies could have facilitated the introduction of competition into an important market.

(*Findings of Fact,* § 411)

REFERENCES

Akerlof, George A. (1982). Labor contracts as a partial gift exchange. *Quarterly Journal of Economics, 97* (November): 543–569.

Arthur, W. B. (1989). Competing technologies, increasing returns, and lock-in by historical events. *Economic Journal, 99*: 116–131.

Arthur, W. B. (1990). Positive feedbacks in the economy. *Scientific American, 262*: 92–99.

Arthur, W. B. (1996). Increasing returns and the new world of business. *Harvard Business Review*, 100–109.

Baumol, William J., & Ordover, Janusz (1985). Use of antitrust to subvert competition. *Journal of Law and Economics, 28*: 247.

Becker, Gary S., & Murphy, Kevin (1988). A theory of rational addiction. *Journal of Political Economy, 96*(4) (August): 675–700.

Besen, Stanley M., & Farrell, Joseph (1994). Choosing how to compete: Strategies and tactics in standardization. *Journal of Economic Perspective, 8*(2) (Spring): 117–131.

Bork, Robert H. (1978). *The Antitrust Paradox: A Policy at War with Itself*. New York: Basic Books.

Clark, Jim, with Edwards, Owen (1999). *Netscape Time: The Making of a Billion-Dollar Start-up That Took On Microsoft*. New York: St. Martin's Press.

Coase, Ronald H. (1972). Durability and monopoly. *Journal of Law and Economics, 15* (April): 143–149.

David, P. A. (1985). Clio and the economics of QWERTY. *American Economic Review, 75*: 332–337.

Frank, Robert H., & Cook, Philip J. (1995). *The Winner-Take-All Society: Why the Few at the Top Get So Much More Than the Rest of Us*. New York: Penguin Books.

Gates, Bill (1995). The internet tidal wave. Memorandum, 26 May, Department of Justice's exhibit 20, p. 1 (http://www.usdoj.gov/atr/cases/ms_exhibits.htm).

Hayek, F. A. (1994). *The Road to Serfdom*. Chicago: University of Chicago Press.

Hovenkamp, Herbert (1999). *Federal Antitrust Policy: The Law of Competition and Its Practice*. St. Paul, MN: West Group.

Katz, M. L., & Shapiro, C. (1985). Network externalities, competition, and compatibility. *American Economic Review, 75*: 424–440.

Klein, Benjamin (1999). Microsoft's use of zero price bundling to fight the "Browser Wars". In: *Competition, Innovation and the Microsoft Monopoly: Antitrust in the Digital Marketplace* (pp. 217–254). Proceedings of a conference held by the Progress and Freedom Foundation in Washington, D.C., 5 February 1998. Boston: Kluwer Academic Publishers.

Klein, Joel I., et al. (1998). *United States v. Microsoft, Complaint*, First District Court, civil action no. 98–1232, 20 May 1998.

Klopfenstein, B. C. (1989). The diffusion of the VCR in the United States. In: M. R. Levy (ed.), *The VCR Age*. Newbury Park, Calif.: SAGE Publications.

Landes, William, & Posner, Richard (1981). Market power in antitrust cases. *Harvard Law Review* (94).

Lee, Dwight R., & Kreutzer, David (1982). Lagged demand and a "perverse" response to threatened property rights. *Economic Inquiry, 20* (October): 579–588.

Lee, Dwight R., & McKenzie, Richard B. (2001). A case for letting a firm take advantage of network effects and "locked-in" customers. *Hastings Law Journal, 52*(4) (April): 795–812.

Liebowitz, S. J., & Margolis, S. E. (1990). The fable of the keys. *Journal of Law and Economics, 33*: 1–26.

Liebowitz, S. J., & Margolis, S. E. (1995). Path dependence, lock-in and history. *Journal of Law, Economics and Organization, 11*: 205–226.

Liebowitz, S. J., & Margolis, S. E. (no date). Are network externalities a new source of market failure? Working paper. Dallas: University of Texas, Dallas, http://www.go.com/?win=_search&sv=M6&ud9=IE5&qt=stan + liebowitz&oq=emerging + digital + economy&url=http%3A//wwwpub.utdallas.edu/%7Eliebowit/&ti=Untitled&top=).

McKenzie, Richard B. (2000). Microsoft's "applications barrier to entry": The case of the missing 70,000 programs. *Policy Analysis, 380* (31 August).

McKenzie, Richard B. (2001). Trust on trial: How the Microsoft case is reframing the rules of competition. (Paperback edition) Boston: Perseus Books.

Milgrom, P., & Roberts, J. (1992). *Economics, Organizations and Management.* Englewood Cliffs, NJ: Prentice Hall.

Posner, Richard A. (1976). *Antitrust Law: An Economic Perspective.* Chicago: University of Chicago Press.

Reynolds, Alan (1999). U.S. vs. Microsoft: The monopoly myth. *Wall Street Journal.* (9 April). p. A12.

Shapiro, C., & Stiglitz, J. (1984). Equilibrium unemployment as a worker discipline device. *American Economic Review, 74* (June): 433–444.

Shughart II, William F. (1990). *Antitrust Policy and Interest Group Politics.* New York: Quorum Books.

Measuring Market Power
D. J. Slottje (editor)

CHAPTER 10

Raising the Costs of Unintegrated Rivals

An Analysis of Barnes & Noble's Proposed Acquisition of Ingram Book Company[†]

DAVID S. SIBLEY[a]* and MICHAEL J. DOANE[b]

[a] *John Michael Stuart Centennial, University of Texas, Austin, TX 78712, USA*
[b] *PM KeyPoint LLC , Emeryville, CA 94608, USA*

Abstract

This chapter derives a test expression for vertical foreclosure when the downstream market is monopolistically competitive and the upstream market is a monopoly. We illustrate the use of this test expression in the proposed merger between Barnes & Noble, Inc. and Ingram Book Company. Ingram Book Company is the dominant book wholesaler in the United States. Our analysis presents conditions in which the merged firm would have had the incentive to engage in price and non-price discrimination against rivals in the retail book market. We incorporate an adjustment to our test expression to allow for competitive reactions by rivals of Ingram in the wholesale book market.

JEL classification: D4, L22, L81.
Keywords: Vertical mergers, vertical foreclosure, raising rivals' costs, antitrust, book retailers, book wholesalers

---

* Corresponding author.
[†] The authors thank Ashish Nayyar for insightful comments.

10.1. INTRODUCTION

In November 1998, Barnes & Noble, Inc. ("B&N"), the largest book retailer in the US, announced its interest in purchasing the Ingram Book Company ("Ingram"), the largest book wholesaler in the US.[1] Mr. Leonard Riggio, Chairman of B&N, stated the merger would enable faster and more cost-effective deliveries to on-line and retail customers and would "create a strategic business unit which will revolutionize book distribution in the next century."[2] The proposed merger, however, evoked widespread complaints from independent bookstore owners who expressed concern that the merged firm would possess both the ability and the incentive to raise the costs of its retail rivals through such means as providing B&N preferred access to popular titles and raising wholesale prices.[3] Concerned that the merger would likely be challenged in court by the Federal Trade Commission, B&N withdrew its offer to purchase Ingram, and stated its intention to expand the capacity of its internal distribution centers.[4] This chapter develops a test expression for examining the conditions under which the incentives of the merged firm are to raise the costs of its unintegrated rivals. We illustrate the application of the test expression using the example of B&N's proposed acquisition of Ingram.

This chapter is part of the literature on vertical foreclosure. There are two main ways of modeling monopolistic competition in the downstream industry. One approach assumes a single representative customer that consumes a small amount of every conceivable good, instead of consuming only his preferred product. See Dixit and Stiglitz (1977) and Spence (1978). In this setting, the effects of a vertical merger between an upstream monopolistic and a downstream firm are ambiguous. See Perry and Groff (1985) and Dixit (1983). Recently, Küen and Vives (1999) have shown, in the representative consumer setting, that the welfare effects of such a merger are positive under a plausible assumption on the utility function of the representative consumer. In this literature, different products typically enter the representative consumer's utility function in a symmetrical way.

An alternative approach to characterize differentiated product competition is

---

[1] In 1998, the annual revenues of B&N and Ingram were approximately US$3 billion and US$1.4 billion, respectively. See Hoover's Inc. (1999) and Bianco (1997). Bianco (1997) states Ingram handles about two-thirds of the books that wend their way through wholesalers to bookstores.

[2] See Junnarker (1998).

[3] The American Booksellers association submitted more than 115,00 signatures from the book-buying public on a petition to the Federal Trade Commission. See http://www.bookweb.org/home/news/btw/1820.html.

[4] See Labatan and Carvajal (1999).

in a "smoothed" Bertrand framework in which each firm chooses its price and its demand depending not only on its price but that of other firms. This approach differs from the representative consumer model in that consumers may have different preferences between different products and may choose to purchase none of some products.

Using the Bertrand formulation of downstream competition, Ordover, Salop and Saloner (1990) and Riordan (1997) have shown that vertical mergers may arise which reduce welfare. Our chapter is in this tradition and focuses on the incentives of a vertically-integrated firm to raise the costs of downstream rivals. In this same tradition are papers by Sibley and Weisman (1998a, 1998b), Mandy (2000), Economides (1998), Reiffen (1998) and Weisman and Kang (2001). These papers ignore the issue of whether a single vertical merger will take place and simply assume that it has done so. Given the existence of a vertically-integrated firm, these papers all deal with the incentives of that firm to discriminate against downstream rivals. They do so by assuming Cournot behavior downstream. Relative to the literature on raising rivals' costs, the contribution of the present chapter is to present and implement a test expression for discriminatory behavior when downstream markets are monopolistically competitive.

We have organized this chapter as follows. Section 10.2 presents an overview of market participants in the book industry, and provides a brief description of the nature of competition at the retail and wholesale levels. In section 10.3, we present a model of a vertically integrated firm's incentive to discriminate against its downstream (unintegrated) rivals. The modeling framework is used to simulate the competitive effects of the B&N/Ingram merger. Conclusions are presented in section 10.4. Appendix 1 presents the derivation of our test expression. Appendix 2 documents our calculation of retail market shares.

10.2. OVERVIEW OF MARKET PARTICIPANTS

10.2.1. Retail bookstores

A retail bookstore selects its own titles; places orders to wholesalers; carries a wide range of titles; and takes special orders from customers. In general, retail bookstores are stores whose principal business is the sale of books; however, some retail bookstores also derive substantial sales revenue from audio or video merchandise. Although consumers purchase books at other locations such as warehouse clubs (e.g., CostCo), mass merchandisers (e.g., Kmart and Walmart), food and drug stores (e.g. 7-Eleven), and through book clubs and mail order, these outlets are excluded from the definition of a retail bookstore because they

Table 10.1: Retail book sales (US$ millions).

	1994		1995		1996		1997		1998	
	Sales ($m)	Share (%)	Sales ($m)	Share (%)	Sales ($m)	Share (%)	Sales ($m)	Share (%)	Sales ($m)	Share (%)
Amazon.com	0	0.0	1	0.0	16	0.2	148	1.5	610	6.0
Barnes & Noble	1,623	20.2	1,977	22.0	2,448	25.3	2,782	28.1	3,006	29.8
Barnesandnoble.com	0	0.0	0	0.0	0	0.0	15	0.2	62	0.6
Books-A-Million	172	2.1	230	2.6	279	2.9	325	3.3	348	3.4
Borders	1,511	18.8	1,749	19.5	1,959	20.3	2,266	22.9	2,590	25.6
Borders.com	0	0.0	0	0.0	0	0.0	0	0.0	5	0.0
Crown	275	3.4	306	3.4	283	2.9	288	2.9	298	3.0
Independent bookstores and smaller chains	4,449	55.4	4,707	52.5	4,685	48.4	4,086	41.2	3,181	31.5
Total	8,030	100.0	8,970	100.0	9,670	100.0	9,910	100.0	10,100	100.0

Source. Company 10-K filings with the US Securities and Exchange Commission and historical SIC category sales data released by the US Census Bureau. Percentages may not total due to rounding. See Appendix 2 for derivation of figures.

carry very limited title lists, typically do not select their own titles, and do not take special orders. Specialty stores are also excluded because they do not carry a wide range of titles. Internet bookstores, such as Amazon.com, Inc. ("Amazon") and B&N's "online" unit, Barnesandnoble.com, are included in the definition of a retail bookstore.

Table 10.1 presents market shares for retail booksellers for the years 1994–1998. As shown in Table 10.1, nationwide B&N is the largest book retailer with a 29.8% market share in 1998. Borders Book Group, Inc. ("Borders") has the second largest market share, approximately 25.6%.[5] The drop in market share is precipitous going from the second to third largest firm, with Books-a-Million, Inc. having a market share of approximately 3.4%.[6] The combined market share of independent bookstores and small chains is approximately 31.5%. A noteworthy entry in Table 10.1 is the appearance of Amazon, a firm that captured a 6% market share in its first two years of operation.

At the retail level, competition depends on price to an important degree, but also on a number of non-price factors. For example, many independent store owners go to considerable lengths to purchase titles that appeal to local tastes and feature local authors. Community activities such as poetry readings and book signings are featured in many retail bookstores. When a large chain, such as B&N or Borders, locates in the same general area as a small independent bookstore, the latter survives by tailoring its title list carefully to local customers, often carrying books that the chain store does not carry. Thus, expert knowledge of books by the sales staff of the independent bookstore is important. Perhaps for this reason, independent bookstores owners claim to have been the first to spot many books that rise to the level of "best-sellers."

Because it is so important to tailor a book list to its locale, retail markets are considerably more localized than the wholesale market. Therefore, if a retailer were to impose a small but significant and nontransitory price increase, the extent to which demand would shift to other retail bookstores would depend, in part, on their proximity to the store in question.

10.2.2. Book wholesalers

A book wholesaler sells books to retail bookstores (as defined above); carries titles from many publishers; generally does not select titles; and takes special

---

[5] The subsidiaries of Borders Group, Inc. are Borders, Inc., Walden Book Company, Inc., Planet Music, Inc., Borders Properties, Inc,, and Waldenbooks Properties, Inc.

[6] The subsidiaries of Books-A-Million, Inc. are Books-A-Million, Books and Company, and Bookland.

orders from retail stores. This distinguishes a wholesaler from a "rack-jobber." A rack-jobber selects titles; purchases products from a variety of sources; packages and ships books for an individual location; and unpacks books and dresses racks. Rack-jobbers tend to serve mass merchants and supermarkets, which carry a limited selection of titles as a small adjunct to their business. A rack-jobber does not take special orders and carries a much smaller title list than would a book wholesaler. From the standpoint of a retailer, internal distribution centers are close substitutes for the wholesaler. Internal distribution centers only serve the retailers that own them.[7]

The threat and reality of large-scale backward integration by major retailers is a competitive check on the ability of wholesalers to increase price. The threat of backward integration also provides an incentive for wholesalers to improve service quality.

Retail bookstores obtain a large percentage of their newly-published books, so-called "front-list" books, direct from the publisher, usually at a discount off the suggested retail price of approximately 50%. The remaining newly-published books are obtained from book wholesalers. While the discount off the publisher's list price is larger when buying from a publisher as compared to a wholesaler, wholesalers tend to provide a superior distribution function. Retailers are concerned about the speed of delivery, and wholesalers can usually provide a book in two or three days, whereas publishers typically require a week or longer to provide a book. Wholesalers also carry a diverse number of titles from many publishers, whereas a publisher carries only its own titles. The large wholesalers, Ingram and Baker & Taylor, also provide additional support services, such as databases of books in print, suggestions about fast-moving titles, insurance, and

---

[7] The above wholesale market definition is motivated by the product market definition given in the US Department of Justice and Federal Trade Commission *Horizontal Merger Guidelines*. (See Department of Justice and Federal Trade Commission, 1992 *Horizontal Merger Guidelines*, at § 1.3 (revised Apr. 8, 1997), hereinafter "*Merger Guidelines*.") A proposed product market defined under the *Merger Guidelines* is accepted as correct if a price increase in the proposed market would not cause demand to shift to products outside the proposed market to such an extent as to dissuade a hypothetical profit-maximizing monopolist from imposing a "small but significant and nontransitory" price increase. Application of the *Merger Guidelines* eliminates book distribution by publishers from the wholesale market. Publishers typically carry only their own titles and do not provide books to retail bookstores as quickly as wholesalers. There have been attempts by publishers to perform the wholesale function (most notably by Random House); but these attempts have been small scale and unsuccessful as a substitute for a book wholesaler. Typical reasons provided for not switching are that publishers are not able to provide books to retailers in an acceptable period of time (whereas wholesalers do so routinely) and wholesalers have books from many publishers under "one roof," thereby eliminating the transaction costs resulting from multiple separate invoices with multiple publishers.

financing. Nearly all books in print for more than twelve months, so-called "back-list" books, are obtained from book wholesalers.

Among wholesalers, a key indicator of service quality is the "fill-rate." The fill-rate on an order from a retailer is simply the number of books provided by the wholesaler divided by the total number of books ordered by the retailer. For example, if a retailer ordered three copies of *Faust* and two copies of *Buddenbrooks* and the wholesaler supplied one copy of *Faust* and one copy of *Buddenbrooks*, the fill-rate is 40%.

A relevant geographic market is the area that encompasses firms that produce the relevant product such that the hypothetical monopolist of that product would find it profitable to raise the price by a small but significant amount for a non-transitory period. The geographic market for wholesale books is national, reflecting the fact that wholesalers are located throughout the United States and are usually able to get books anywhere in the country within a business week or less.

10.3. SIMULATING B&N'S INCENTIVE TO RAISE RIVALS' COSTS

10.3.1. The price effects of a vertical merger

When an upstream monopolist integrates downstream, the effects on the whole-sale price and retail price is not unambiguous. Consider, first, the effect on the wholesale price. Suppose that there are two downstream firms that do not compete with each other, perhaps due to different locations. If the upstream monopoly acquires one of the downstream firms, the upstream division of the merged firm sells to the downstream division at an effective price equal to the upstream marginal cost. It continues to sell to the remaining downstream firm, but may alter the price of the upstream input. Whether it raises or lowers the input price will depend on whether the elasticity of demand by the remaining downstream firm is higher or lower than the elasticity of the *aggregate* demand prior to the merger. Thus, if the elasticity of demand for the input after the merger is higher, the wholesale price will fall after the merger. Looking at retail prices, by integrating forward, the upstream monopoly solves a double markup problem, which lowers the retail price of the formerly independent downstream firm. The retail price of the remaining downstream firm will rise or fall with the wholesale price.

Now suppose that the two downstream firms are monopolistic competitors. Because an increase in the post-merger input price will cause the remaining firm to raise its retail price, this increases demand for the downstream division of the merged firm. Since prices of differentiated products are strategic complements, this will induce a retail price increase by the merged firm, further raising its profits. Therefore, an increase in the upstream price following the merger is more likely the more the merged firm competes with the remaining downstream firm. Still, the net effect of the merger on price is not clear a priori. Either outcome is possible (see Appendix 1).

To calculate directly whether prices will rise or fall following a vertical merger would require one to estimate and solve a full model of the upstream and downstream markets with and without the merger. This is usually a daunting task and unlikely to be feasible within the time constraints of a typical merger analysis. Therefore, we propose a test expression based on pre-merger data which will show the direction of the effect of the merger on the price of the input. Specifically, we calculate whether, at pre-merger prices and quantities, the merged firm will gain from an increase in the costs of its downstream rival. If so, then the post-merger upstream price will exceed the pre-merger price.

10.3.2. Model

The merger of B&N and Ingram could have raised the cost of unintegrated rivals in two ways. Ingram could price discriminate by raising the wholesale price that it charges retail competitors of B&N.[8] More subtly, the merged firm could raise its retail rival's costs by engaging in non-price discrimination. This could be accomplished by providing B&N superior access to best-selling titles, lowering the "fill rate" experienced by retail competitors,[9] and filling orders from competitors more slowly than it fills orders from B&N.

Actions taken by B&N to raise rivals' costs through Ingram do not unambiguously increase the profits of the integrated firm. Given some action by Ingram that would raise the costs of B&N's retail rivals, the first-order effect is that the rival will raise its retail prices in response. This will result in some retail customers not buying a book at all, some retail customers choosing to buy a less

---

[8] Because the integrated firm considers total profits, even if B&N's retail unit was charged the same wholesale price as its rivals, the wholesale price increase to B&N "cancels out" when the combined entity is considered. That is, the wholesale price appears as a cost to B&N but also as an offsetting revenue item for Ingram. Therefore, even if B&N did not instruct Ingram to raise the price charged to its retail rivals, those rivals would be paying more than the merged firm. Thus, the merged firm price discriminates against the retail rivals of B&N.

[9] As described earlier, the "fill rate" of a wholesaler equals the percentage of books requested by a retailer that the wholesaler is actually able to supply.

preferred book from the rival, and some retail customers switching to B&N or another competitor. From the standpoint of B&N, the net effect on demand depends on the fraction of the rival's lost customers that move to B&N. This fraction, δ, is known as the "diversion ratio."[10]

Thus, given an action by Ingram to raise rivals' costs (or withhold books), each unit of reduction in wholesale demand for Ingram costs the merged firm the wholesale price times Ingram's unit profit margin (given by the difference between price and marginal cost, divided by price). The beneficial effect on the B&N retail business is given by the B&N retail price times the retail unit profit margin multiplied by the diversion ratio; the retail unit profit margin is equal to the difference between the B&N retail price and B&N marginal cost, divided by the retail price. Denoting the wholesale price by w, the retail price by p and the unit profit margins in wholesale and retail by m_w and m_r, respectively, the change in total profit for each unit of reduced demand for Ingram, $\Delta\Pi$, is given by the following formula:

$$\Delta\Pi = wm_w(1-\delta) - pm_r\delta, \qquad (1)$$

where $\Delta\Pi$ is calculated at pre-merger prices and quantities.[11]

It is useful to solve for the diversion ratio that would make the merged firm indifferent between raising rivals' costs and not doing so (i.e., make the change in total profit equal to zero). This critical diversion ratio, $\hat{\delta}$, is given by the formula:

$$\hat{\delta} = \frac{(w/p_B)m_w}{m_r + (w/p_B)m_w}. \qquad (2)$$

If the actual diversion ratio exceeds the critical diversion ratio, then the merged firm can increase its profits by raising its rivals' costs. If it is lower than the critical level, then the incentive is not to raise rivals' cost.

10.3.3. Data requirements

Calculation of the critical diversion ratio requires information on (1) the contribution margins of the wholesale and retail units of the merged firm and (2) the relative prices of books sold at wholesale and retail. The correct measure of a firm's contribution margin equals the percentage difference between price and marginal cost. It is important to measure marginal costs properly. In particular,

---

[10] See, for example, Shapiro (1996).
[11] The derivation is presented in Appendix 1.

the time frame over which costs are measured must be taken into account. For example, if the diversion of sales is significant and is likely to be sustained, some capital costs may be included if the firm is facing capacity constraints. In practice, some analysts have adopted accounting gross margins.[12] However, the use of accounting gross margins assumes the only additional costs that will be incurred when sales are diverted to B&N are the costs of the books themselves. It omits other costs such as labor, taxes, insurance, and rent. Such an approach yields the correct conclusion about the profitability of discriminating only if the "true" *retail* margin differed from the accounting gross retail margin by precisely the same percentage amount as the "true" *wholesale* margin differed from the accounting gross wholesale margin.

For the purposes of illustrating our modeling approach we initially assume that the margins of B&N and Ingram, i.e., m_r and m_w, are 28.0% and 6.0%, respectively, and (w/p) equals 0.60.[13] Alternative simulations are then performed to examine the sensitivity of our findings to the underlying assumptions. Using the formula above, these initial assumptions imply a critical diversion ratio equal to 0.114. Thus, if the diversion ratio exceeds 0.114, there is an incentive for the merged firm to raise rivals' costs.

One approach to estimate the diversion ratio is to assume that once customers leave the rival retailers, they allocate themselves over other retailers in proportion to existing market shares. The use of market shares to calculate diversion ratios is supported by the random utility model.[14] Such a model is appropriate

---

[12] See, for example, Shapiro, C. (1996). This paper defines the term "gross margin" as "the percentage gap between price and incremental cost" (*Id.* p. 23). This definition, however, is not generally regarded as equivalent to "accounting gross margin" which is defined as sales revenue less costs of goods sold divided by sales revenue.

[13] B&N's reports a gross margin of approximately 28% for fiscal year 1998 (see Edgar Online, Inc., Barnes & Noble, Inc., Income Statement for Period Ending January 30, 1999). Information on wholesale margins is not publicly available as Ingram and other major wholesalers are not publicly traded companies. Lacking wholesale margin data, we assume wholesale gross margins are approximately 20% of retail margins and explore the sensitivity of our findings across a range of wholesale margins. With respect to the (w/p), as noted above, publishers typically provide a 50% discount from retail list prices for bulk purchases. We expect the discount offered by wholesalers is less to account for the added services wholesalers provide, e.g., databases of books in print, suggestions about fast-moving titles, insurance, financing, and delivery on short notice. To account for this added cost, we assume $(w/p) = 0.60$.

[14] For a discussion of the random utility model and its applications, see, for example, Domenicich, T. and McFadden, D. (1975). In the random utility model, the relative probability of choosing two existing alternatives is unaffected by the presence of additional alternatives. This is known as the independence-of-irrelevant alternative assumption ("IIA"). As an example, suppose a book purchaser is twice as likely to buy a book from Borders as compared to an independent bookstore and three times as likely to buy a book from B&N as compared to an independent bookstore. In this case, the

when some alternative sources of supply included in the analysis are not viewed as "closer" substitutes than others.[15] Diversion ratios are more likely to be proportionate to market shares in this case. Using this approach, if B&N were to raise the costs of all independents, the diversion ratio equals B&N's market share divided by the market shares of all retail outlets except independents. From Table 10.1, B&N's market share equals 29.8% and the market share of independents equals 31.5%. Thus, the diversion ratio using this method equals 0.435, i.e., $0.298/(1.0-0.315)$. This implies that approximately 44% of the independent bookstores' lost customers would be diverted to B&N. This value is significantly larger than the critical diversion ratio of 0.114.

To examine the sensitivity of this finding to the input values, we allow the values of the various input to vary over a reasonable range. In Table 10.2 below, possible values for the ratio of wholesale price to the retail price, (w/P_B), range from 0.5 to 1.0 (see column headings of the table). Ingram's price-cost margin, $(w - c)/w$, ranges from 0.04 to 0.40 (see row headings of the table). Given the estimated diversion ratio of 0.435, the entries in the table are the levels of the price-cost margin for B&N, $((P_B - \theta_B - w)/P_B)$, required for the merged firm to be indifferent between raising rivals' costs and not doing so, i.e., the critical retail margin. Thus, given the baseline estimates presented above, $w/P_B = 0.60$ and $(w - c)/w = 0.060$, B&N would require a retail price-cost margin of only 5% for the merged firm to have the incentive to raise rivals' costs. Because in our example the baseline margin is 28%, the incentive is to raise rivals' costs. In Table 10.2, the situations in which the baseline values would lead to

---

probabilities of buying a book from B&N, Borders, and an independent bookstore are 3/6, 2/6, and 1/6, respectively. Now suppose a new independent bookstore is added, differing from the first only in name. One would expect the probabilities of selecting B&N, Borders, Independent Bookstore 1, and Independent Bookstore 2 to be 3/6, 2/6, 1/12, and 1/12, respectively. Instead the random utility model produces probabilities 3/7, 2/7, 1/7, and 1/7, to preserve the relative probabilities.

[15] IIA is more likely to hold in this situation. Similarly, diversion ratios based on market shares go awry if some alternatives are viewed as "closer" substitutes than others. See Willig, R. (1991).

If data are available describing consumers' choice of bookstores and sets of available alternatives, econometric procedures are available to test for IIIA. See, for example, Hausman, J. and McFadden, D. (1984). Econometric procedures, such as the nested logit model, are also available to circumvent IIA if this assumption does not hold.

Store closing information can also be a value source of data for estimating diversion ratios. For example, companies often estimate the sales volumes of competitors and track the increase in their own sales following the closing of individual stores operated by competitors. Information of the type provides a natural experiment for estimating diversion ratios. For example, in 1998 Crown Bookstores declared bankruptcy and closed a number of stores. Using information on the annual sales of the individual Crown stores that closed and an estimate of the increase in sales at neighboring B&N's would yield a direct estimate of the diversion ratio.

Table 10.2:	Sensitivity analysis of the incentive to raise rivals' costs critical retail margin.

Wholesale margin $(w - c)/w$	Ratio of wholesale price to retail price (w/P_B)										
	0.50	0.55	0.60	0.65	0.70	0.75	0.80	0.85	0.90	0.95	1.00
0.04	0.03	0.03	0.03	0.03	0.04	0.04	0.04	0.04	0.05	0.05	0.05
0.05	0.03	0.04	0.04	0.04	0.05	0.05	0.05	0.06	0.06	0.06	0.06
0.06	0.04	0.04	0.05	0.05	0.05	0.06	0.06	0.07	0.07	0.07	0.08
0.07	0.05	0.05	0.05	0.06	0.06	0.07	0.07	0.08	0.08	0.09	0.09
0.08	0.05	0.06	0.06	0.07	0.07	0.08	0.08	0.09	0.09	0.10	0.10
0.12	0.08	0.09	0.09	0.10	0.11	0.12	0.12	0.13	0.14	0.15	0.16
0.16	0.10	0.11	0.12	0.14	0.15	0.16	0.17	0.18	0.19	0.20	0.21
0.20	0.13	0.14	0.16	0.17	0.18	0.19	0.21	0.22	0.23	0.25	0.26
0.24	0.16	0.17	0.19	0.20	0.22	0.23	0.25	0.26	0.28	0.30	0.31
0.28	0.18	0.20	0.22	0.24	0.25	0.27	0.29	0.31	0.33	0.35	0.36
0.32	0.21	0.23	0.25	0.27	0.29	0.31	0.33	0.35	0.37	0.39	0.42
0.36	0.23	0.26	0.28	0.30	0.33	0.35	0.37	0.40	0.42	0.44	0.47
0.40	0.26	0.29	0.31	0.34	0.36	0.39	0.42	0.44	0.47	0.49	0.52

Notes. Critical retail margin $= [(w/P_B)m_w][(1-\delta)/\delta]$. Values calculated for $\delta = 0.435$. Shaded areas represent critical retail margins

Table 10.3: Sensitivity analysis of the incentive to raise rivals' costs critical diversion ratios

Retail margin (%)	Wholesale margin (%)												
	4.0	6.0	8.0	12.0	16.0	20.0	24.0	28.0	32.0	36.0	42.0	44.0	46.0
4.0	0.38	0.47	0.55	0.64	0.71	0.75	0.78	0.81	0.83	0.84	0.86	0.87	0.87
6.0	0.29	0.38	0.44	0.55	0.62	0.67	0.71	0.74	0.76	0.78	0.81	0.81	0.82
8.0	0.23	0.31	0.38	0.47	0.55	0.60	0.64	0.68	0.71	0.73	0.76	0.77	0.78
10.0	0.19	0.25	0.32	0.42	0.49	0.55	0.59	0.63	0.66	0.68	0.72	0.73	0.73
12.0	0.17	0.23	0.29	0.38	0.44	0.50	0.55	0.58	0.62	0.64	0.68	0.69	0.70
14.0	0.15	0.20	0.26	0.34	0.41	0.46	0.51	0.55	0.58	0.61	0.64	0.65	0.66
16.0	0.13	0.18	0.23	0.31	0.38	0.43	0.47	0.51	0.55	0.57	0.61	0.62	0.63
18.0	0.12	0.17	0.21	0.29	0.35	0.40	0.44	0.48	0.52	0.55	0.58	0.59	0.61
20.0	0.11	0.15	0.19	0.25	0.32	0.38	0.42	0.46	0.49	0.52	0.56	0.57	0.58
22.0	0.10	0.14	0.18	0.25	0.30	0.35	0.40	0.43	0.47	0.50	0.53	0.55	0.56
24.0	0.09	0.13	0.17	0.23	0.29	0.33	0.38	0.41	0.44	0.47	0.51	0.52	0.53
26.0	0.08	0.12	0.16	0.22	0.27	0.32	0.36	0.39	0.42	0.45	0.49	0.50	0.51
28.0	0.08	0.11	0.15	0.20	0.26	0.30	0.34	0.38	0.41	0.44	0.47	0.49	0.50
30.0	0.07	0.11	0.14	0.19	0.24	0.29	0.32	0.36	0.39	0.42	0.46	0.47	0.48
32.0	0.07	0.10	0.13	0.18	0.23	0.27	0.31	0.34	0.38	0.40	0.44	0.45	0.46
34.0	0.07	0.10	0.12	0.17	0.22	0.26	0.30	0.33	0.36	0.39	0.43	0.44	0.45
36.0	0.06	0.09	0.12	0.17	0.21	0.25	0.29	0.32	0.35	0.38	0.41	0.42	0.43
38.0	0.06	0.09	0.11	0.16	0.20	0.24	0.27	0.31	0.34	0.36	0.40	0.41	0.42
40.0	0.06	0.08	0.11	0.16	0.19	0.23	0.26	0.30	0.32	0.35	0.39	0.40	0.41
42.0	0.05	0.08	0.10	0.15	0.19	0.22	0.26	0.29	0.31	0.34	0.38	0.39	0.40
44.0	0.05	0.08	0.10	0.14	0.18	0.21	0.25	0.28	0.30	0.33	0.36	0.38	0.39
46.0	0.05	0.07	0.09	0.14	0.17	0.21	0.24	0.27	0.29	0.32	0.35	0.36	0.38

Notes. Critical diversion ratio = $[(w/p_B)m_w]/[m_r +(w/p_B)m_w]$. Values calculated for $(w/p) = 0.60$. Shaded areas represent critical diversion ratios less than actual diversion ratio, i.e., combinations in which the incentive to raise rival costs is present.

anticompetitive behavior are shaded. In our example, the baseline values could be far from the assumed values (e.g., m_w could rise to approximately 0.20) without altering the conclusion that the merged firm will profit from raising rivals costs.

Table 10.3 examines the sensitivity of our findings by showing the critical diversion ratio for various combinations of wholesale and retail margins, assuming $(w/p) = 0.60$. For example, if Ingram's margin equaled 12% and B&N's margin equaled 28%, the critical diversion ratio would equal 0.204. As was the case in Table 10.2, the situations in which the baseline values would lead to anticompetitive behavior are shaded.

If non-price discrimination, or raising rivals' costs, is profitable for the merged firm, it follows that the incentive to simply raise the wholesale price is even stronger. An increase in the wholesale price not only increases the costs of a retail competitor, but also brings additional sales revenue to the wholesale business. Therefore, because when non-price discrimination is profitable for the combined firm, it must be true, a fortiori, that wholesale price discrimination will be even more profitable.

10.3.4. Reactions by other wholesalers

An important element that is left out of our test expression concerns the possible reactions of other wholesalers. In particular, even though Baker & Taylor is not oriented towards the retail market apart from libraries and schools, it does provide some competition to Ingram. Will it provide competition to Ingram that will deter the merged firm from engaging in anticompetitive behavior? The best way to characterize wholesale competition is monopolistic competition, since non-price service features such as fill rate, shelving services, trade credit, etc., are important features of the wholesale market.

This being the case, the prices of various wholesale suppliers are strategic complements.[16] Thus, if Ingram raises price or otherwise discriminates against independent retailers, the best response of Baker & Taylor will be to follow suit. Thus, even though the presence of Baker & Taylor would have constrained a post-merger Ingram, retailers' costs would have been higher post merger no matter which firm they bought from. It is necessary, however, to adjust our test expression to account for some diversion to competing wholesalers in order to see if there still remains an incentive to discriminate in the first place.

---

[16] See Church and Ware (2000).

One way to address this issue is to make an assumption regarding what percentage of Ingram's retail customers would have shifted to other wholesalers. This reduces the gains to discrimination, in our example, but it does not remove them. For example, assuming 30% of Ingram's retail customers will shift to other wholesalers leads to a diversion ratio of 0.305, i.e., 0.435×0.7. This value also exceeds the critical diversion ratio of 0.12. Therefore, our qualitative conclusions about the effects of the merger are unchanged. In our example, a loss factor for Ingram of 72% would be required for the estimated diversion ratio to fall below the critical level. This would appear to leave considerable scope for the profitable raising of rivals' costs.

10.4. CONCLUSION

The merger proposed between Barnes & Noble, Inc. and Ingram Book Company never took place. Nonetheless, the proposed merger provides an interesting vehicle to describe a technique for analyzing the incentives for price and non-price discrimination. Our test expression suggests the range of assumptions under which the proposed merger would have reduced competition and raised prices.

This analysis does not ask if the claimed benefits of the merger could have been achieved by some means other than a merger, such as a long-term contract. Inevitably, this question can only be answered in a case-specific way, using data that are often proprietary to the merging parties. In the case of B&N, Mr Riggio stated the US$600 million in cash and stock that was the purchase price for Ingram would be directed at "Plan B" investments which involved the expansion of its existing distribution center into a network with new warehouses that would provide warehouse space for the future.[17]

One possible improvement within our framework, though, is to formally model the reactions of upstream firms to vertical merger. We believe that the adjustments to our test expression presented above indicate that competitive reactions by Baker & Taylor, and other wholesalers would not have removed the merged firm's incentive to discriminate, in our illustrative example. However, desirable extension of the analysis would be to derive a test expression based on a formal model of competitive reactions by upstream firms.

---

[17] See Labatan and Carvajal (1999).

APPENDIX 1. DERIVATION OF TEST EXPRESSION

We model the post-merger book market as monopolistic competition between retail firms: one firm ("B&N") that is integrated backwards into wholesaling and a competitor. The retail rivals of B&N purchase books at wholesale from the wholesale of the integrated firm. We begin by defining the following terms:

P_c Competitor's retail price
P_B B&N's retail price
θ_c Competitor's retail marginal cost
θ_B B&N's retail marginal cost.
$q_B(P_c, P_B)$ Retail demand function for B&N
$q_c(P_c, P_B)$ Retail demand function for competitor
w Wholesale price
c Marginal cost of wholesale

The profit function for each firm after integration by B&N can be written as:

$$\Pi_B = (P_B - \theta_B - w)\, q_B(P_c, P_B) \tag{A.1}$$

$$\Pi_c = (P_c - \theta_c - w)\, q_c(P_c, P_B) \tag{A.2}$$

$$\Pi_B^I = (P_B - \theta_B - w)q_B(P_c, P_B) + (w - c)\,(q_c(P_c, P_B) + q_B(P_c, P_B)) \tag{A.3}$$

where Π_B^I is the profit function of the integrated B&N. In these expressions,

$$\partial q_B / \partial P_B < 0, \ \partial q_c / \partial P_c < 0, \text{ and } \partial q_B / \partial P_c > 0.$$

Rewriting equation (A.3) we have

$$\Pi_B^I = (P_B - \theta_B - c)\, q_B(P_c, P_B) + (w - c)\, q_c(P_B, P_c). \tag{A.4}$$

In this setting, the equilibrium upstream price may be either higher or lower after a vertical merger. Suppose that the downstream industry is a duopoly, where the demand curve facing the two downstream firms are given by:

$$q_i = a_i - P_i + \delta P_j, \qquad i, j = 1, 2.$$

Assume $c = 0$ and denote the upstream price by w^* prior to the merger and $\bar{w}$ after the merger. Assume that the upstream price is set before the downstream prices in both scenarios. It can be shown that

$$w^* \gtrless \bar{w} \quad \text{as} \quad \left(\frac{a_2}{a_1} - 1 \right) \left(1 - \frac{3}{2} \delta \right) + \delta^2 \gtrless 0 .$$

Thus, if $a_1 = a_2$ and $\delta > 0$, $w^* > \bar{w}$. However, if $\delta = 0.9$ and a_2/a_1 exceeds 2.32, then $w^* < \bar{w}$.

Given that both outcomes are possible, it is of some interest to derive a test expression to detect $\bar{w} > w^*$. To be useful, this test expression must be based on pre-merger data.

In order to understand the net effects of the merger on prices, it is instructive to evaluate $\partial \Pi_c / \partial P_B$ and $\partial \Pi_c / \partial w$ at the pre-merger prices denoted (w^*, P_B^*, P_c^*). Clearly, prior to the merger

$$\frac{\partial \Pi_i}{\partial P_i} = (P_i - \theta_i - w) \frac{\partial q_i}{\partial P_i} + q_i = 0, \quad i = B, C. \tag{A.5}$$

Furthermore, it is easy to show that $w^* > c$.

Now differentiate the integrated firm's profit function with respect to P_B and w and evaluate the derivative at (w^*, P_B^*, P_c^*):

$$\left. \frac{\partial \Pi_B^I}{\partial P_B} \right|_{(w^*, P_B^*, P_C^*)} = (w^* - c) + \left. \frac{\partial q_C}{\partial P_B} \right|_{(w^*, P_B^*, P_C^*)} \tag{A.6}$$

$$\frac{\partial \Pi_B^I}{\partial w} = q_C (P_B^*, P_C^*) + \left. \frac{\partial P_C}{\partial w} \frac{\partial \Pi_B}{\partial P_C} \right|_{(w^*, P_B^*, P_C^*)}. \tag{A.7}$$

From (A.6), as long as $w^* > c$, one effect of the merger is to raise P_B because by increasing the competitor's downstream output, q_c, upstream profits increase.

From (A.7), if w rises, upstream profits from the competing firm rise. However, calculating the expression $\partial \Pi_B^I / \partial P_c$ we have countervailing effects of the merger on the level of w:

$$\left. \frac{\partial \Pi_B^I}{\partial P_c} \right|_{(w^*, P_B^*, P_C^*)} = (w^* - c) \frac{\partial q_C}{\partial P_c} + (P_B^* - \theta - c) \frac{\partial q_B}{\partial P_c}. \tag{A.8}$$

By inducing an increase in P_c, an increase in w lowers the number of upstream units sold to the downstream competitor. However, the induced increase in the equilibrium level of P_c increases the integrated firm's profits from the retail market. The net effect is unclear. However, if we can show that (A.8) is positive, we will have established that the merged firm has an incentive to raise P_B and w slightly above the pre-merger levels.

The sign of (A.8) also determines the incentives of the merged firm to raise rivals' costs θ_c directly, even without an increase in w. To put (A.8) into a more usable form, we rewrite $\partial\Pi'_B/\partial P_C$ as

$$\left.\frac{\partial\Pi'_B}{\partial P_c}\right|_{(w^*,P_B^*,P_C^*)} \gtreqless 0 \quad \text{as} \quad \frac{w^*}{P_B^*}\left(\frac{w^*-c}{w^*}\right) \gtreqless \frac{(P_B^*-\theta_B-c)}{P_B^*}\,\frac{\partial q_B/\partial P_c}{-\partial q_c/\partial P_c} \quad (A.9)$$

with all variables at their pre-merger levels.

Defining the diversion ratio, δ, as $\delta \equiv (\partial q_B/\partial P_c)/(-\partial q_c/\partial P_c)$, we have (1) in the text.

The ratio, $(\partial q_B/\partial P_c)/(-\partial q_c/\partial P_c) \equiv \delta$, is sometimes called the "diversion ratio." It measures the number of customers of the competitor that would shift to B&N if the competitor's price rises, divided by the total number of customers that the competitor would lose. The denominator of the term equals the number of customers that shift to B&N plus the number of customers that stop buying altogether. Therefore, the diversion ratio, δ, cannot exceed unity. If δ was known, the test expression would be as follows:

$$\text{TE1:} \quad \frac{d\Pi'_B}{dP_c} \gtreqless 0 \quad \text{as} \quad \frac{w^*}{P_B^*}\,\frac{m_w}{m_r} \gtreqless \frac{\delta}{1-\delta}. \quad (A.10)$$

A difficulty with TE1 is that δ is not directly observable. However, as noted in the text a variety of methods are available to approximate δ.

APPENDIX 2. DERIVATION OF RETAIL MARKET SHARES

Annual sales figures for each of the companies listed by name in Table 10.1 — i.e., Amazon.com, Barnes & Noble, Barnesandnoble.com, Borders, Borders.com, Crown, and Books-A-Million — were retrieved from each company's Form 10-K filing with the US Securities and Exchange Commission.[18] The "Barnes &

---

[18] See Amazon.com, Inc., Form 10-K: Annual Report to Section 13 or 15(d) of the Securities Exchange Act of 1934, For the Year Ended December 31, 1998 (S.E.C. Mar. 5, 1999) (figures for 1994 measure sales from the company's inception on July 5, 1994 to the end of the year); Barnes & Noble, Inc., Form 10-K: Annual Report to Section 13 or 15(d) of the Securities Exchange Act of 1934, For the Fiscal Year Ended January 30, 1999 (S.E.C. Apr. 30, 1999); Borders Group, Inc., Form

Noble" category includes sales from the following stores: Barnes & Noble, B. Dalton, fifteen Doubleday Book Shops, eight Scribner's Bookstores, and seven other affiliated stores.[19] Similarly, the "Borders" category includes both Borders and Waldenbooks stores.[20]

Yearly totals for "Independent Bookstores and Smaller Chains," as well as total annual sales for the industry as a whole, were derived using data available from the US Census Bureau. Briefly, our methodology in doing so was as follows.

Since the 1930s, the United States government has employed a system of Standard Industrial Classification ("SIC") codes to "to promote uniformity and comparability of data collected and published by agencies within the US government, state agencies, trade associations, and research organizations."[21] The SIC code system "classified each establishment (defined as a single physical location at which economic activity occurs) according to its primary activity" and thus "covered the entire field of economic activities by defining industries in accordance with the composition and structure of the economy."[22] The US Census Bureau compiles and regularly releases data relating to most of the SIC categories; this data contains, among other things, sales and revenue figures for each industry segment. Annual sales figures for SIC category No. 5942 (retail

---

10-K: Annual Report to Section 13 or 15(d) of the Securities Exchange Act of 1934, For the Fiscal Year Ended January 24, 1999 (S.E.C. Apr. 26, 1999); Crown Books Corporation, Form 10-K: Annual Report to Section 13 or 15(d) of the Securities Exchange Act of 1934, For the Fiscal Year Ended January 31, 1998 (S.E.C. May 1, 1998); and Books-A-Million, Inc., Form 10-K: Annual Report to Section 13 or 15(d) of the Securities Exchange Act of 1934, For the Fiscal Year Ended January 30, 1999 (S.E.C. Apr. 29, 1999). Sales information for Barnesandnoble.com in 1998 (US$61.8 million) was provided by the following source: Hoover's Company Information, "Barnesandnoble.com, Inc. Company Overview," reproduced at http://cnniw.newsreal.com/ osform/NewsService?osform_template=pages%2FcnniwcoOverview.oft&ID=cnniw&found=1&by_name=barnesandnoble.com (citing Media General Financial Services, Inc. data).

[19] Barnes & Noble, Inc., Form 10-K: Annual Report to Section 13 or 15(d) of the Securities Exchange Act of 1934, For the Fiscal Year Ended January 30, 1999 (S.E.C. Apr. 30, 1999).

[20] Borders Group, Inc., Form 10-K: Annual Report to Section 13 or 15(d) of the Securities Exchange Act of 1934, For the Fiscal Year Ended January 24, 1999 (S.E.C. Apr. 26, 1999).

[21] In 1997, the United States government replaced the use of SIC codes with the newer North American Industry Classification System ("NAICS"). NAICS purports to improve upon the older SIC codes by providing a "production-oriented" system of categorization in which "[e]conomic units that use like processes to produce goods or services are grouped together." US Census Bureau, "Development of NAICS," http://www.census.gov/epcd/www/naicsdev.htm (Feb. 19, 1998). For the sake of consistency over the time period 1994 to 1998, however, we focus exclusively on sales figures for SIC category No. 5942, retail book sales.

[22] US Census Bureau, "Development of NAICS," http://www.census.gov/epcd/www/naicsdev.htm (Feb. 19, 1998).

"Book Stores") are available from the US Census Bureau for 1994 through 1998.[23] For these years, total sales in category 5942 were as follows: US$10.3 billion in 1994; US$11.5 billion in 1995; US$12.4 billion in 1996; US$12.7 billion in 1997; and US$13.0 billion in 1998.[24]

SIC category No. 5942 is comprised of three subcategories: general bookstores (SIC No. 594210); religious and specialty bookstores (SIC No. 594220); and college and university bookstores (SIC No. 594230). Complicating our analysis, however, is the fact that the Bureau publishes monthly and yearly sales figures only for the overall 5942 category. Information of college and university book sales was obtained from the Association of American Publishers, Inc. They estimate higher education book sales equaled US$2.9 billion in 1998.[25] Subtracting that value from the US$13.0 billion sales total for SIC category No. 5942 in 1998 produces total retail book sales (net of higher education) of US$10.1 billion in 1998, or 78% of SIC category No. 5942 total sales. Applying that same percentage to the annual totals for the overall retail bookstores category in previous years yields the following figures: US$8.03 billion in 1994; US$8.97 billion in 1995; US$9.67 billion in 1996; and US$9.91 billion in 1997.

In order to derive yearly sales figures for "Independent Bookstores and Smaller Chains," we subtract the sum of sales generated each year by Barnes & Noble, Borders, Crown, and Books-A-Million from our annual totals for SIC category No. 5492, net of the contribution of college and university bookstores. The results, which appear on Table 10.1, are approximately as follows: US$3.9 billion in 1994; US$4.1 billion in 1995; US$4.0 billion in 1996; US$3.5 billion in 1997; and US$3.2 billion in 1998.

The "total" sales figures for each year equal the sum of each of the outlets appearing in Table 10.1. That is, annual totals are equal to (1) the yearly sales totals for SIC category No. 5942 as given by the US Census Bureau, (2) minus

---

[23] The annual sales figures given by SIC category No. 5942 do not include sales made by Amazon.com, Barnesandnoble.com, or Borders.com; category 5942 does not include sales information for retailing books via electronic shopping, mail order, book clubs, or direct sale. These are instead subsumed under a separate SIC category, No. 5961. Nor does category No. 5942 include retail book sales via used merchandise, discount, or warehouse stores. Used book store sales are part of SIC category No. 5932, which also includes clothing consignment stores, flea markets, used furniture stores, and the like. Discount, warehouse, and other such retail establishments are similarly tracked by other SIC codes. *See generally* US Census Bureau, 1997 NAICS and 1987 SIC Correspondence Tables, http://www.census.gov/epcd/www/naicstab.htm (May 18, 1999).

[24] See US Census Bureau, Monthly Retail Trade Survey, http://www/census.gov/mrts/www/mrtshist. html (Apr. 17, 1999).

[25] See Association of American Publishers, Inc., 1998 Industry Statistics Report, http:/www. publishers.org/stats/index.htm (April 3, 2002).

our estimates of the portion of overall category 5942 sales attributable to college and university bookstores annually, (3) plus sales totals for Amazon.com, Barnesandnoble.com, and Borders.com. Individual shares were then calculated for each bookseller by dividing the company's annual sales by total bookseller sales for the year.

REFERENCES

Bianco, A. (1997). How the Ingrams built one of America's top private fortunes. *Business Week*, 29 September: 64.

Church, J., & Ware, R. (2000). *Industrial Organization: A Strategic Approach* (pp. 332–333). New York: Irwin McGraw-Hill.

Dixit, A., & Stiglitz, J. (1977). Monopolistic competition and optimum product diversity. *American Economic Review, 67*: 297–308.

Economides, N. (1998). The incentive for non-price discrimination by an input monopolist. *International Journal of Industrial Organization*: 271–284.

Hausman, J., & McFadden, D. (1984). Specification test for the multinomial logit model. *Econometrica, 52*: 1219–1240.

Hoover's Inc. (1999). *Hoover's Company Profile Database — American Public Companies*. Austin: Hoover's Inc.

Junnaker, S. (1998). Barnes & Noble buys Ingram Book. CNET News.com, 6 November 6 (reproduced at http://news.com.com/2100–1001–217609.html?legacy=cnet), accessed 2 April 2002.

Kühn, K.-U. & Vives, X. (1999). Excess entry, vertical integration and welfare. *Rand Journal of Economics, 30*(4): 575–603.

Labatan, S., & Carvajal, D. (1999). Book retailer ends bid for wholesaler. *New York Times*, 3 June, section C: 1.

Mandy, D. (2000). Killing the goose that may have laid the golden egg: Only data knows whether sabotage pays. *Journal of Regulatory Economics, 17*(2): 157–172.

Ordover, J., Salop, S., & Saloner, G. (1992). Equilibrium vertical foreclosure. *American Economic Review, 80*(1): 127–142.

Reiffen, D. (1998). A regulated firm's incentive to discriminate: A reevaluation and extension of Weisman's result. *Journal of Regulatory Economics, 14*(1): 79–86.

Riordan, M. (1997). Anticompetitive vertical integration by a dominant firm. *American Economic Review, 88*(5), 1232–1248.

Shapiro, C. (1996). Mergers with Differentiated Products. *Antitrust*: 23–29.

Sibley, D., & Weisman, D. (1998a). The competitive incentive of vertically integrated local exchange carriers: An economic and policy analysis. *Journal of Policy Analysis and Management, 19*(1), 74–93.

Sibley, D., & Weisman, D. (1998b). Raising rivals' costs: Entry of an upstream monopolist into downstream markets. *Information, Economics and Policy, 10*(4): 551–570.

US Department of Justice and US Federal Trade Commission, 1997, 1992 Horizontal merger guidelines, at § 1.3.

Willig, R. (1991). Merger analysis, industrial organization theory, and merger guidelines, *Brookings Papers on Economic Activity: Microeconomics*, 303–304.

Measuring Market Power
D. J. Slottje (editor)

CHAPTER 11

Mergers and Market Power

Estimating the effect on market power of the proposed acquisition by The Coca-Cola Company of Cadbury Schweppes' carbonated soft drinks in Canada

ANDREW ABERE,[a] ORAL CAPPS JR,[b]
JEFFREY CHURCH,[c]* and H. ALAN LOVE[b]

[a] *Princeton Economics Group, Inc., 707 State Road, Suite 223, Princeton, NJ, USA;*
[b] *Department of Agricultural Economics, Texas A&M University, College Station, TX 77810;*
[c] *Department of Agricultural Economics, University of Calgary, Calgary, Alberta, Canada, TJN 1N4*

Abstract

This chapter provides an economic analysis and assessment of the concerns raised by the Competition Bureau in Canada over the proposed acquisition by The Coca-Cola Company of Cadbury Schweppes' carbonated soft drinks. In the context of this transaction the chapter demonstrates the use of estimating demand systems in assessing competitive implications of mergers. The estimated demand systems were used to address two issues: (i) market delineation and (ii) estimating unilateral effects. In addition, the Bureau's concerns that the acquisition might lead to foreclosure and an increase in rivals' cost is critically assessed.

JEL classification: D11, D4, L12, L13, L4, L66, L22, L81
Keywords: unilateral effects, merger simulation, AIDS and Rotterdam demand systems, soft drinks, raising rivals' costs, market definition

---

* Corresponding author.

11.1. INTRODUCTION

In December of 1998 The Coca-Cola Company (TCCC) reached an agreement with Cadbury Schweppes plc (CS) to pay approximately US$1.85 billion for the acquisition of Cadbury Schweppes' international beverage business. Excluding the United States, France, and South Africa, the deal included the world-wide acquisition of approximately 30 beverage brands — including such well known carbonated soft drink brands as Canada Dry, Schweppes, Orange Crush, and Dr Pepper. The transaction attracted antitrust scrutiny from national competition authorities in more than 100 countries. Antitrust concerns led to the transaction being abandoned in a number of countries, including virtually all of Europe, Australia, Mexico, and Canada. In the summer of 2000, 18 months after the initial announcement of the acquisition, TCCC and CS announced that due to concerns raised by the Competition Bureau, Canada's antitrust authority, they were abandoning the transaction in Canada, thereby bringing the acquisition to a close. TCCC was able to acquire CS beverage business in approximately 160 countries for around US$1 billion.

The four of us provided economic consulting services to TCCC in its negotiations with the Competition Bureau over the acquisition of Cadbury Schweppes' beverage brands in Canada. The case is of interest to academics/practitioners involved in merger cases since the issue of market definition, following previous US experience involving soft drink mergers and the world-wide scrutiny the TCCC/CS transaction faced, played a prominent role. For instance, in two previous cases, the Federal Trade Commission concluded that nationally advertised branded carbonated soft drinks distributed directly by bottlers to retailers constituted a relevant product market.[1] Of particular interest is the key role that estimating a system of demand equations from grocery-chain scanner data played in assessing the competitive implications of the proposed transaction. The estimated demand systems were used to address two issues: (i) market delineation and (ii) estimating unilateral effects. The former is relevant to the traditional structural approach to determining the competitive implications of a merger; the latter is a more recent approach, which attempts to determine directly the competitive constraint each of the merging firms exerts on the other.

In addition, because the acquisition had vertical aspects — CS sold concentrate and licensed its brands in Canada to bottlers associated with both the Blue (PepsiCo) and Red (TCCC) distribution systems — the concerns of the Canadian

---

[1] See *In the matter of the Coca-Cola Company*, Docket no. 9207, June 13, 1994 ("Coca-Cola Decision"); and *In the matter of the Coca-Cola Bottling Company of the Southwest*, Docket no. 9215, August 31, 1994 ("Southwest Decision").

Competition Bureau were informed by, and reflected, recent theoretical developments in industrial organization. These developments suggest conditions under which firms may be able to enhance or create market power by raising the costs of their rivals. The possibility of foreclosure of input supply was given considerable weight by the Bureau in its analysis of the proposed acquisition.

The rest of this chapter is divided into nine sections. Section 11.2 provides an overview of the carbonated soft drink industry in Canada. Section 11.3 outlines the typical approaches taken to identify the competitive implications of a merger. Section 11.4 sets out the alternative demand systems (LA/AIDS and Rotterdam) estimated. Section 11.5 reports the estimates of the demand system for soft drinks in the Province of Ontario in Canada. In sections 11.6 and 11.7 we demonstrate the use of demand systems in merger analysis in assessing the competitive implications of the TCCC/CS transaction in Canada. Section 11.6 uses the estimated demand systems to implement the hypothetical monopolist test to antitrust market definition. Section 11.7 uses unilateral effects analysis to directly assess the effect of the acquisition on market power. In section 11.8 the Bureau's case theory is critically assessed. Concluding comments are made in section 11.9.

11.2. CSDs IN CANADA

The production and sale of carbonated soft drinks (CSDs) begins with the production and sale of concentrate to bottlers. The bottler adds carbonation, water, and a sweetener to the concentrate and bottles the finished product which is then sold for final consumption. Alternatively, the concentrate producer or the bottler supplies syrup for fountain dispensers. The syrup is then diluted with water and carbonation is added by the dispenser.

The Coca-Cola Company sells concentrate for its products and licenses trademarks for its brands in Canada primarily to Coca-Cola Bottling (CCB), a subsidiary of Coca-Cola Enterprises, the largest international bottler of TCCC products (in which TCCC has a significant ownership interest), through its Canadian subsidiary, Coca-Cola Limited (CCL). TCCC, CCE, their Canadian subsidiaries, and the few small independent bottlers that bottle TCCC brands are known collectively as the "Red system." Its leading brands are a cola and a lemon lime flavored CSD, Coca-Cola and Sprite respectively. Similarly PepsiCo's concentrate in Canada is supplied by Pepsi-Cola Canada (PCC) to its bottling network. PCC's leading brands in Canada are also a cola and a lemon lime flavored CSD, Pepsi and 7UP. Collectively we will refer to PCC and its bottlers as the "Blue system."

Cadbury Schweppes did not have any bottling facilities in Canada. Rather it supplied concentrate and licensed its various brands through its Canadian subsidiary — Cadbury Schweppes Beverages Canada Inc. (CBCI) — to the Red and Blue systems. Its key brands are two ginger ales — Schweppes and Canada Dry — and two orange flavoured CSDs — Orange Crush and C-Plus. Across Canada these brands were, and are, paired. In any geographic region one of these pairs is licensed to the Red system, the other to the Blue system. For instance in most of Ontario, the local Red bottler has the license to, and bottles, Canada Dry and C-Plus, while the local Blue bottler has the license to, and bottles, Schweppes and Orange Crush. Neither TCCC or Pepsi had a ginger ale or orange flavoured CSD of any signficance.

At the time of the proposed transaction, TCCC's share of CSD sales in Canada was almost 40%, Pepsi had approximately 34%, Cadbury just under 10%. Most of the remaining sales are private label brands of the main grocery chains manufactured by Cott Beverages (COTT).

As we will discuss extensively in section 11.8 the Bureau's concerns stemmed from the contractual arrangements between CBCI and Blue system bottlers to supply and license brands that TCCC would acquire. This would put TCCC in a position of being an input supplier to an important rival, with the possibility of it being either able to raise Blue bottlers' costs, or alternatively, enabling a greater degree of coordination and a collective increase in market power by both the Red and Blue systems.

Unable to negotiate a mutually acceptable remedy with the Competition Bureau, TCCC and CS agreed not to proceed with the acquisition in Canada. The rationale for abandonment appears to have been based on the following considerations: a change in management at TCCC; the small relative size of the Canadian market; and abandonment of the transaction in Canada — the last jurisdiction in which the legal status of the transaction was still up in the air — would finally bring to a close the transaction between TCCC and CS.[2]

11.3. APPROACHES TO IDENTIFYING AN SLC IN A MERGER

Section 92 of the *Competition Act* in Canada provides that the Competition Tribunal — a special court that presides over the non-criminal provisions of the *Act* and includes, typically, one economist — may block mergers that would substantially lessen, or prevent, competition. It is thus similar to Section 7 of the

---

[2] See Karen Jacobs, "Coke Won't Buy Cadbury Brands in Canada, Mexico," *Wall Street Journal*, 27 July 2000: C20.

Clayton Act in the United States that prohibits mergers that substantially lessen, or prevent, competition. In Canada, a substantial lessening of competition arises if the merger would result in a substantial increase in a firm's market power.

A firm's ability to exercise market power is constrained by consumers' ability to substitute to products supplied by competing firms. The extent of demand-side substitution depends on whether consumers can, and will, switch to other products in response to a price rise (or other manifestation of market power). The extent of supply-side substitution depends on whether consumers can find alternative suppliers of the same good in response to a price increase (or other manifestation of market power).[3] A firm can exercise market power if these possibilities for substitution are limited, and likely to remain so, for an extended period of time. Both substitution possibilities are summarized by a firm's elasticity of demand.

A merger may lead to an increase in market power if the effect of the merger is to eliminate a significant avenue of substitution. A unilateral effect arises if the products of the merging firms place significant competitive constraints on each other. If substitution to products produced by *B* constrains the market power of the brands produced by *A,* then by eliminating that constraint, the merger may lead to an increase in market power by the combined firm and a substantial lessening of competition. Alternatively, the merger might facilitate the interdependent exercise of market power if the elimination of a competitor facilitates the ability of the remaining firms in the market to coordinate their behavior in a manner that reduces competition and makes tacit collusion easier or more effective. Two analytical approaches for assessing the effects of a merger on market power and competition are the traditional structural approach and unilateral effects analysis.

11.3.1. The structural approach to merger analysis

The structural approach typically involves: (i) defining an antitrust market, (ii) determining the increase in concentration as a result of the merger, and (iii) assessing barriers to entry. If barriers to entry are high and the increase in concentration sufficiently large, the merger is *presumed* to lead to a substantial

---

[3] The *Merger Enforcement Guidelines* in the United States state that "A price increase can be made unprofitable by consumers either switching to other products or switching to the same product produced by firms at other locations." This corresponds to our distinction between demand- and supply-side substitution. The extent of supply-side substitution opportunities may depend on the ease of entry and product repositioning.

lessening of competition.[4] This approach makes the question of market definition virtually paramount in merger cases.

11.3.1.1. Antitrust market definition

The role of market definition is to enable market shares and statistics on concentration to be used as proxies for market power. Too narrow a market definition excludes demand-side substitutes that impose important competitive constraints. This results in high market shares that overstate market power. Too broad a market definition will lead to low market shares that understate market power, since the market includes products that are not close substitutes and do not exert significant competitive constraints. Antitrust markets are an attempt to define markets appropriately so that market shares are potentially reflective of market power: the objective of an antitrust market is to identify market power.

One method to determine the boundaries of antitrust markets is the hypothetical monopolist test. According to the Commissioner's Merger Guidelines:[5]

> Conceptually, a relevant market for merger analysis under the Act is defined in terms of the smallest group of products and smallest geographic area in relation to which sellers, if acting as a single firm (a "hypothetical monopolist") that was the only seller of those products in that area, could profitably impose and sustain a significant and nontransitory price increase above levels that would exist in the absence of the merger.

Similarly, the hypothetical monopolist test as set out in the Department of Justice and Federal Trade Commission's *Horizontal Merger Guidelines* is:[6]

> A market is defined as a product or group of products and a geographic area in which it is produced or sold such that a hypothetical profit-maximizing firm, not subject to price regulation, that was the only present and future producer or seller of those

---

[4] How large the increase in concentration must be before a presumption of an SLC depends, usually, on the prevailing, or pre-merger, concentration.

[5] Commissioner of Competition, *Merger Enforcement Guidelines, March* 1991: p. 7 (footnote omitted).

[6] US Department of Justice and Federal Trade Commission, *Horizontal Merger Guidelines,* 8 April 1997: Section 1.0.

products in that area likely would impose at least a "small but significant and nontransitory" increase in price, assuming the terms of sale of all other products are held constant. A relevant market is a group of products and a geographic area that is no bigger than necessary to satisfy this test.

In both jurisdictions the small, but significant and nontransitory increase in price (SSNIP) is typically defined to be 5% for one year.[7] The use of the hypothetical monopolist test insures that a firm with 100% of the market would be able to exercise market power, thereby providing some assurance that increases in concentration, though not necessarily to monopoly levels, will be indicative of an increase in market power.[8]

The key to implementing the hypothetical monopolist test is determining the costs and benefits from exercising market power. When the hypothetical monopolist increases its price, it gains increased revenues from a higher price on inframarginal sales — sales it continues to make — but loses profits on marginal sales — sales no longer made to consumers that substitute away and for which there was a positive margin over marginal cost. The question of whether the extent to which consumers can substitute is enough to constrain a profit-maximizing hypothetical monopolist to raise its price by less than the SSNIP depends on both the own price elasticity of demand and the price-marginal cost margin at prevailing prices. The own price elasticity of demand summarizes all substitution possibilities and determines the extent to which sales are lost at the margin, while the price-cost margin determines the implications for profits of the reduction in demand.

11.3.1.2. Critical elasticities of demand

The hypothetical monopolist test can be implemented by comparing the critical elasticity of demand with the prevailing elasticity of demand in the candidate,

---

[7] Notice that the US Merger Guidelines ask whether a profit-maximizing hypothetical monopolist "would" implement an SSNIP, the Canadian Guidelines whether it "could". "Would" reflects the correct perspective: the actual exercise of market power by the hypothetical monopolist. "Could" is the wrong question because it asks if the hypothetical monopolist's profits could increase with an SSNIP, not whether a hypothetical monopolist would actually do so. For instance, it may be profit maximizing for a hypothetical monopolist to raise prices by 3%, even though its profits would still increase relative to prevailing prices if it increased prices by 5%. However, the increase in profits from a 5% increase is less than from a 3% increase. The use of "would" correctly identifies that the hypothetical monopolist's market power is constrained by excluded products, while the use of "could" would inadvertently define the market to be too narrow.

or proposed, antitrust market. The critical elasticity of demand is defined as the elasticity of demand for which the profit-maximizing increase in price by the hypothetical monopolist just equals the SSNIP threshold. If the market elasticity is less than the critical level, then a profit-maximizing hypothetical monopolist would raise prices by more than the SSNIP. If the market elasticity is greater than the critical level, then a profit-maximizing hypothetical monopolist would raise prices by less than the SSNIP.

A profit-maximizing hypothetical monopolist would set p^m according to the familiar formula for profit-maximization:

$$m = \left(\frac{p^m - c}{p^m}\right) = \frac{1}{\varepsilon_{ii}(p^m)} \tag{1}$$

where $\varepsilon_{ii}(p^m)$ is the elasticity of demand at the monopoly price and c is marginal cost. We can rewrite (1) as

$$\varepsilon_{ii}(p^m) = \frac{1 + t}{m + t} \tag{2}$$

where t is the SSNIP and m is the prevailing Lerner index or price-cost margin. If the elasticity of demand is assumed to be constant, then the critical elasticity of demand is also given by (2).[9] Assuming that the elasticity of demand is constant — and thus that (2) is the critical elasticity of demand — will bias the results towards too narrow a market definition. As price rises, the elasticity of demand likely increases, resulting as Froeb and Werden (1992) observe, in a reverse cellophane fallacy. Because elasticity increases as price rises, the monopoly equilibrium elasticity will likely be greater than the prevailing elasticity of demand and use of the prevailing elasticity of demand will result in markets that are defined too narrowly and market shares will overestimate market power.

11.3.1.3. Diversion ratios and the next-best substitute

The relevant antitrust market is the smallest group of products for which a hypo-

---

[8] Of course, increases in concentration in a well defined antitrust market, while necessary are not sufficient for a finding of a substantial lessening of competition. At the very least there must also be sufficient barriers to entry that entry is not sufficient, timely or likely.

[9] See Church and Ware (2000, pp. 607–608) for derivation of the critical demand elasticity for a constant elasticity of demand curve. The concept originates with Werden (1998).

thetical monopolist would profitably impose an SSNIP. Conceptually, relevant antitrust markets are found by defining a sequence of candidate markets. A relevant antitrust market is defined for each of the products of both firms party to the merger by defining each product as an initial candidate market. A sequence of candidate markets for each product of the merging products is created by progressively adding to the market the next-best substitute. According to the *Merger Enforcement Guidelines* in Canada, the next-best substitute is the "product that would account for the largest percentage of the volume that would be lost by the hypothetical monopolist."[10] According to the *Horizontal Merger Guidelines* in the United States the next-best substitute "refers to the alternative which, if available in unlimited quantities at constant prices, would account for the greatest value of diversion of demand in response to a 'small but significant and nontransitory' price increase."[11] The relevant antitrust market is the first candidate market reached, i.e., the smallest, for which a hypothetical monopolist would find it profit-maximizing to implement an SSNIP.

Operationally, determining the next-best substitute involves determining measures of substitution — or diversion as they are called — by consumers away from a brand or product when its price increases. Two common diversion measures are the unit diversion ratio and the dollar diversion ratio. Both of these are measures of the extent of switching to substitutes. Unit diversion measures the increase in quantity of a substitute product. The unit diversion ratio normalizes this measure by dividing the unit diversion by the decrease in unit sales of the candidate market (product). The unit diversion ratio of product j from an increase in the price of product i is:

$$u_{ji} = \frac{\varepsilon_{ji} q_j}{\varepsilon_{ii} q_i} \tag{3}$$

where ε_{ji} is the cross-price elasticity of product j with respect to the price of i. The unit diversion ratio is equivalent to $\Delta q_j / \Delta q_i$ and is appropriate if products j and i are measured in the same units. If they are not, then the sales diversion ratio is appropriate.

Sales diversion measures the increase in the dollar sales of a substitute product. The dollar diversion ratio normalizes this measure by dividing sales diversion by the decrease in dollar sales of the candidate market. The dollar

---

[10] Commissioner of Competition, *Merger Enforcement Guidelines*, March 1991: p. 10 footnote 21.
[11] Department of Justice and Federal Trade Commission, *Horizontal Merger Guidelines,* April 1997: footnote 9.

diversion ratio measures the proportionate sales increase of substitute products relative to the change in the sales of the candidate market. The dollar diversion ratio to product j from an increase in the price of product i equals:

$$d_{ji} = \frac{\varepsilon_{ji} p_j q_j}{\varepsilon_{ii} p_i q_i}.$$ (4)

The dollar diversion ratio is equivalent to $p_j \Delta q_j / p_i \Delta q_i$.

Next-best substitutes should not be identified by ranking cross-price elasticities. To see this suppose that there is a high cross-price elasticity between products A and B. Product B still might not be a very close substitute for A, in the sense that when the price of A increases, the extent of substitution to B relative to the sales of A, is small. That is, while the percentage change in B is large, it represents a relatively small amount of the substitution away from A by consumers when the price of A increases.

The relevant antitrust market is the smallest number of products in the smallest geographic region such that a hypothetical monopolist of those products in that region would impose an SSNIP. Ignoring the geographic dimension, it is found by considering a sequence of candidate markets by iteratively adding to the set of products under the hypothetical monopolist's control, the next-best substitute. The question that then arises, is what is the product for which price increases are calculated? Are the candidate markets found by aggregating products such that the hypothetical monopolist is the sole supplier of a single aggregate product? Or is the hypothetical monopolist a multiproduct firm that is the sole supplier of each of the products in the candidate market? To see the difference consider a hypothetical monopolist of cola flavour carbonated soft drinks. To pass the hypothetical monopolist test must the hypothetical monopolist be able to raise the price of colas (the aggregate good) by the SSNIP? Or must it be able to raise the price of one — or is it all — of the individual brands that are included in the cola market, i.e. Coca-Cola, Pepsi-Cola, Royal Crown, etc.?

11.3.1.4. Implementing the hypothetical monopolist test

Directly implementing the hypothetical monopolist test requires information on the elasticity of demand, price-cost margins, and — to determine the next-best substitute via diversion ratios — cross-price elasticities. Estimating a demand system provides information on many of the relevant elasticities and can also provide, as we show below, information on prevailing price-cost margins.

11.3.1.5. Caveat: The difficulties of the structural approach when products are differentiated

The use of structural analysis — defining an antitrust market and using market shares to infer market power — when products are differentiated can be problematic. First, there is likely to be disagreement over market definition and determining what is in the market and what is out of the market. More fundamentally, the general approach of defining products to be "in" or "out" implicitly assumes that those "in" are equally effective competitors and those "out" provide no competitive constraint. Market shares do not account for competition at the margin between products "in" and "out" of the market and they do not provide any information regarding the nature of the competitive constraint and extent of competition between specific products when competition between products in the market is asymmetric. Thus the use of market shares which fail to distinguish between products that substitute in different degrees can lead to very misleading conclusions. For this reason, methods that statistically estimate directly the degree of market power and avoid market definition are particularly useful when products are differentiated. Unilateral effects analysis for differentiated products is considered in the next section.

11.3.2. Unilateral effects analysis for differentiated products

Recent theoretical developments in industrial organization, the dramatic decline in the cost of computing, and access to retail scanner data have resulted in the development of unilateral effects analysis which forgoes market definition and attempts to predict the price effect of mergers between producers of differentiated products through price or merger simulations. Early contributions are Hausman, Leonard, and Zona (1994) and Werden and Froeb (1994, 1996). There are two components to unilateral effects analysis. The choice of a demand system and its estimation is the "front-end" of a merger simulation (Werden 1997a). The "back-end" of a merger simulation assumes that pre-merger prices and market shares correspond to a (static) Nash equilibrium in prices and constant marginal costs. Given an estimated demand system, the expected price increase from a merger can be computed by forecasting the post-merger prices and comparing the pre- and post-merger prices. This is now a fairly well established methodology, used in both Canada and the United States.[12] The Federal Trade

---

[12] Recent surveys in the antitrust literature, which include examples of cases where unilateral effects analysis was used, are Hausman and Leonard (1997), Werden (1997b), and Csorgo and Sanderson (1999).

Commission recently announced a research project on unilateral effect analysis and identified a number of issues associated with its implementation and inter-pretation.[13] In this section we review merger simulation and discuss two candidate demand systems, the LA/AIDS implementation of the Almost Ideal Demand System (Deaton and Muellbauer 1980a) and the Rotterdam model (Barten 1977; Theil 1965).

11.3.2.1. Bertrand–Nash equilibrium and price simulations

The methodology to assess the unilateral price effects of a merger using the demand systems considered here was introduced by Hausman, Leonard and Zona (1994). In general, the possibility that product prices may rise, post-merger, results from removals of pre-merger competitive constraints created by demand side substitution. If pre-merger substitution by consumers of brand i to brand j limited the market power of the producer of brand i, then a merger between the producers of brands i and j will reduce this avenue of substitution. The merged entity will have an additional incentive to raise the price of both brands i and j: raising the price of product i will increase demand for product j and vice-versa. Post-merger, the cross-price effects are internalized and provide an additional incentive to increase prices.

If the product lines of the merging firms are weak substitutes, independent, or complements, this possibility does not exist. When the products of merging firms are weak substitutes, raising price for some products will result in most of the volume moving to suppliers of other closer substitutes. Consequently, the price effects of the merger will be marginal.

Hausman, Leonard and Zona's approach is based on four assumptions. First, firms are assumed to follow Bertrand–Nash price-setting behavior. Second, it assumes that there is no entry or product repositioning post-merger if prices rise. Third, the marginal production cost of each brand is assumed to be constant. Fourth, each brand's marginal production cost is assumed to remain unchanged from its pre-merger level.[14] Further, by assuming demand elasticities and product shares are unchanged post-merger, an approximate solution to post-merger price changes can be obtained that avoids the need to solve a system of nonlinear price equations.

---

[13] See the FTC News Release *Issues in Econometrics Analysis of Scanner Data* 5 December 2001 at URL: www.ftc.gov/be/econometrics.htm.

[14] However, it is possible to account for production efficiencies that stem from the merger by assuming that the constant unit costs post-merger are a fraction of pre-merger costs.

11.3.2.2. Duopoly of single brand firms

Consider first two single brand firms. Firm i's profit is given by:

$$\pi_i = (p_i - \lambda_i) q_i(p) \tag{5}$$

where π_i is the profit of firm i, p_i is brand i's price, λ_i is the marginal cost of brand i, $q_i(p)$ is the demand function for brand i, and p is the price vector (p_1, p_2). Profit maximization requires

$$\frac{\partial \pi_i}{\partial p_i} = q_i(p) + (p_i - \lambda_i) \frac{\partial q_i(p)}{\partial p_i} = 0 \tag{6}$$

for all i. The effect on profit of an increase in price is the sum of two terms in (6). The first is the increase in revenue and profit from inframarginal units, the second is the lost profit margin from units no longer sold as demand decreases from the price increase.

Equation (6) can be expressed in elasticity form as:

$$L_i = \frac{p_i - \lambda_i}{p_i} = -\frac{1}{\varepsilon_{ii}} \tag{7}$$

where ε_{ii} is the own price elasticity of demand of brand i and the left-hand is brand i's price-cost markup, or Lerner Index. In the Nash equilibrium each brand's pre-merger markup is equal to the negative of the inverse of its own-price elasticity of demand. Assuming that each firm produces one product, equilibrium requires equation (7) to be simultaneously satisfied for each brand.

Post-merger, both brands will be under common control. The profits of the firm will be

$$\pi = (p_i - \lambda_i) q_1(p_1, p_2) + (p_2 - \lambda_2) q_2(p_1, p_2). \tag{8}$$

Maximizing (8) with respect to p_i gives:

$$\frac{\partial \pi}{\partial p_i} = q_i(p) + (p_i - \lambda_i) \frac{\partial q_i(p)}{\partial p_i} + (p_j - \lambda_j) \frac{\partial q_j(p)}{\partial p_i} = 0. \tag{9}$$

The condition for profit-maximization post-merger, (9), differs from (6) by an extra positive term which reflects that there is an additional incentive to increase the price of brand i post-merger. Increases in p_i results in substitution by consumers away from brand i to brand j, increasing sales and profits of brand j. Equation (9) can be rewritten as

$$L_i^m = \frac{p_i^m - \lambda_i}{p_i^m} = -\frac{1}{\varepsilon_{ii}(p)} - L_j^m \frac{\varepsilon_{ji}(p)}{\varepsilon_{ii}(p)} \frac{w_j(p)}{w_i(p)} \tag{10}$$

where $w_i(p) = (p_i q_i)/(p_i q_i + p_j q_j)$ is the market share of brand i and L_i^m is the Lerner index for product i post-merger. Since the Lerner index for product j, $w_i(p)$, $w_j(p)$, and, assuming that the two goods are substitutes, $\varepsilon_{ji}(p)$ are all positive, the effect of the merger is to increase market power and prices of both products.[15] The merger eliminates a source of competitive discipline on the merged firms: the constraint on a firm's incentive to raise its price is substitution by consumers to other products. Post-merger that constraint is relaxed since the merged entity internalizes, or benefits from, the substitution to the other differentiated product, that is the merged firm benefits from the fact that raising the price of product i raises demand for product j. The greater the margin the merged firm earns on the other product, the greater the cross-price elasticity of demand, and the relatively more important the other product — the larger its expenditure share — the greater the exercise of market power post-merger relative to the pre-merger equilibrium.

Approximate solutions for the price increase can be obtained by assuming that market shares and elasticities are unchanged post-merger. Under this assumption (10) is a system of two equations in two unknowns (the post-merger Lerner Indices). Solving (10) the post-merger Lerner Index for brand $i = 1, 2$ is

$$L_i^m = \frac{\frac{w_j}{w_i} \varepsilon_{ji} - \varepsilon_{jj}}{\varepsilon_{ii} \varepsilon_{jj} - \varepsilon_{ji} \varepsilon_{ij}}. \tag{11}$$

Using (7) and (11) the approximate percentage increase in the price of brand i from the merger of the two firms and coordinated pricing of the two brands is

$$\frac{\Delta p_i}{p_i} = \frac{p_i^m - p_i}{p_i} = \frac{\varepsilon_{ij}\left(\varepsilon_{ij} - \varepsilon_{ii}\frac{w_j}{w_i}\right)}{\varepsilon_{ii}\left(\varepsilon_{ji}\left(\varepsilon_{ij} + \frac{w_j}{w_i}\right) - \varepsilon_{jj}(1 + \varepsilon_{ii})\right)}. \tag{12}$$

11.3.2.3. *Oligopoly with multibrand firms*

More generally we would expect that there would be more than two firms and that some, if not all, firms would produce more than one brand. Suppose that

---

[15] This claim assumes stability of the best-response functions.

there are M firms, which produce $K_1, K_2, \ldots, K_m$ brands. The pre-merger Nash equilibrium in prices requires that the following profit-maximizing condition be satisfied for each of the brands of firm i:

$$\left(\frac{p_k - \lambda_k}{p_k}\right) \varepsilon_{kk} w_k + \sum_{j \neq k}^{K_i} \left(\frac{p_j - \lambda_j}{p_j}\right) \varepsilon_{kj} w_j = -w_k \,. \tag{13}$$

Denote $s_k = w_k L_k$ as the product of the Lerner Index and expenditure share of brand k and let E define a block diagonal matrix

$$E = \begin{bmatrix} E_1 & & 0 \\ & \cdot & \\ 0 & & E_m \end{bmatrix}$$

with blocks $E_i = K_i \times K_i$ of own and cross-price elasticities for the products of firm i. If s is the vector of Lerner Index weighted shares then the pre-merger equilibrium is defined by the following system of equations:

$$E's = -w \tag{14}$$

where w is the vector of market, or expenditure, shares.

The post-merger elasticity matrix E^m differs from E by the deletion of the diagonal blocks for the two merging firms (i and j) and the addition of a new diagonal block of dimension $(K_i + K_j) \times (K_i + K_j)$ for the merged firm.

For instance suppose there are three firms in the industry pre-merger, and that firms 1 and 2 each produce a single brand, but firm 3 produces two brands. The pre-merger elasticity matrix is

$$E = \begin{bmatrix} \varepsilon_{11} & 0 & 0 & 0 \\ 0 & \varepsilon_{22} & 0 & 0 \\ 0 & 0 & \varepsilon_{33} & \varepsilon_{34} \\ 0 & 0 & \varepsilon_{43} & \varepsilon_{44} \end{bmatrix}.$$

If there is a merger between firms 1 and 2, the post-merger elasticity matrix would be

$$E^m = \begin{bmatrix} \varepsilon_{11} & \varepsilon_{12} & 0 & 0 \\ \varepsilon_{21} & \varepsilon_{22} & 0 & 0 \\ 0 & 0 & \varepsilon_{33} & \varepsilon_{34} \\ 0 & 0 & \varepsilon_{43} & \varepsilon_{44} \end{bmatrix}.$$

The post-merger equilibrium is defined by:

$$E^{m'} s^m = - w^m. \tag{15}$$

The approximate price increase from the merger is determined by assuming that expenditure shares and elasticities are unchanged post merger. These assumptions mean that systems (14) and (15) are linear. Inverting E' in (14) we have:

$$s = -(E')^{-1} w \tag{16}$$

and the pre-merger Lerner index for product k is $L_k = s_k / w_k$. Similarly using (15),

$$s^m = -(E^{m'})^{-1} w^m \tag{17}$$

and the post-merger Lerner index for product k is $L_k^m = s_k^m / w_k^m$. The percentage change in the price of a merging brand follows from L_k and L_k^m:

$$\frac{\Delta p_k}{p_k} = \left(\frac{1 - L_k}{1 - L_k^m} \right) - 1. \tag{18}$$

11.3.2.4. *Approximate versus exact price changes*

Equation (12), and more generally (18), are approximations of the price change expected from the merger. The approximation assumes that elasticities and market shares are unchanged by the merger. The value of the approximation depends on the change in the own and cross-price elasticities as the merged entity raises its prices. In general we would expect demand to become more elastic and the cross-price elasticities to increase as prices rise. In addition, we also expect that the prices of non-merging brands will change as well — under the approximation it is assumed that the prices of non-merging brands are unchanged.

Exact price increases can be found by substituting elasticity and share equations as a function of prices into (14), which is then solved numerically for the vector of marginal costs. Marginal cost, as well as the elasticities and share equations as a function of prices, are substituted into (15) and this system solved for the post-merger prices.[16]

---

[16] The advantage of using the approximations for the price change is that they can be easily computed and the standard errors of a merger between two single product firms estimated using the delta method. Solving for the exact price changes involves solving two sets of n non-linear equations in

11.4. DEMAND SYSTEMS

The implementation of either the hypothetical monopolist test or unilateral price analysis depends on information regarding own- and cross-price elasticities. Estimation of own- and cross-price elasticities requires specification of a demand system. There are three characteristics of a demand system which make it appropriate for merger analysis. First, it must be second-order flexible, the defining characteristic of which is that for each brand the cross-price elasticities of the demand system are estimated from the data. Second, the estimated elasticities cannot be constant, but must vary as prices change, typically rising as price increases.[17] Third, the demand system should allow for the imposition of restrictions derived from consumer demand theory (symmetry and homogeneity). Estimation and simulation results will be conditional on, and thus sensitive to, the functional form of the demand system.

Previous analyses of mergers and acquisitions have focused on the LA/AIDS demand specification (Hausman, Leonard, and Zona 1994; Hausman and Leonard 1997; Cotterill, Franklin, and Ma 1996; Peterson and Cotterill 1998; Rubinfeld 2000). However, many alternative functional forms are available and have been used in estimating demand systems. Another candidate demand system that can be used is the Rotterdam model. Use of the Rotterdam model is common in the estimation of demand systems from scanner data (Nayga and Capps 1994; Seo and Capps 1997; Capps, Seo, and Nichols 1997).

11.4.1. LA/AIDS

Letting i index the brands, the demand specification for brand i in the LA/AIDS models is:

$$w_i = \alpha_i + \sum_{j=1}^{N} \gamma_{ij} \ln(p_j) + \beta_i \ln(X/\bar{P}) \tag{19}$$

---

n unknowns, which must be done numerically. Estimation of standard errors of the price simulations is not possible with the delta method. Instead bootstrapping techniques must be used. See Capps, Church, and Love (2002) for details on performing exact price simulations and using bootstrapping to find the standard errors of the price simulations.

[17] See Crooke et al. (1999) for an analysis of the importance of the "curvature" of different specifications of demand for extrapolating post-merger prices. Here "curvature" refers to how quickly elasticity increases as price rises. A rapid increase in elasticity will quickly curtail price increases post-merger.

where there are N brands in the demand system, X is total expenditure in dollars on products in the demand system, p_i and q_i are the price and quantity of brand i, $w_i = (p_i q_i)/X$ is the expenditure share of i, and $\bar{P}$ is a price index defined as

$$\bar{P} = \alpha_0 + \sum_{j=1}^{N} \alpha_j \ln(p_j) + \frac{1}{2} \sum_{j=1}^{N} \sum_{i=1}^{N} \gamma_{ij} \ln(p_j) \ln(p_j) \,. \tag{20}$$

The parameter restrictions implied by demand theory are:

1 Adding up condition $\displaystyle\sum_{i=1}^{N} \alpha_i = 1, \ \sum_{i=1}^{N} \beta_i = 0, \ \text{and} \ \sum_{i=1}^{N} \gamma_{ij} = 0;$

2 Homogeneity condition $\displaystyle\sum_{j=1}^{N} \gamma_{ij} = 0 \,;$

3 Symmetry condition $\gamma_{ij} = \gamma_{ji}\,.$

The highly non-linear nature of $\bar{P}$ means that in practice when the AIDS model is estimated Stone's index (P) is used instead, where

$$\ln(P) = \sum_{i=1}^{N} w_i \ln(p_i). \tag{21}$$

When P is used instead of $\bar{P}$ the estimated demand system is known as the "linear approximate AIDS" or LA/AIDS model. Green and Alston (1990) provide the appropriate formula to compute the own-price and cross-price elasticities for the LA/AIDS model:[18]

$$\varepsilon_{ij} = -\delta_{ij} + \frac{\gamma_{ij} - \beta_i w_j}{w_i} \tag{22}$$

where $\delta_{ij} = 1$ when $i = j$ and 0 otherwise.

---

[18] See Capps, Church, and Love (2002) for an extended discussion of the appropriate elasticity formulas to use when the LA/AIDS model is estimated. They argue that the Green and Alston approximation based on the assumption of expenditure shares remaining constant is not appropriate, especially when exact price simulations are performed. The assumption of constant expenditure shares is consistent with the assumptions underlying approximate price simulations.

11.4.2. Rotterdam model

The demand specification for brand i for the Rotterdam model is:

$$w_{it} \, d \ln (q_{it}) = a_i + b_i \sum_{j=1}^{N} w_{jt} \, d \ln (q_{it}) + \sum_{j=1}^{N} c_{ij} \, d \ln (p_{jt}) \tag{23}$$

where $d \ln (q_{it}) = \ln (q_{it}/q_{it-1})$ and $d \ln (p_{jt}) = \ln (p_{jt} / p_{jt-1})$. The parameter restrictions implied by demand theory for the Rotterdam model are:

1 Adding up condition $\sum_{i=1}^{N} a_i = 0$, $\sum_{i=1}^{N} b_i = 1$, and $\sum_{i=1}^{N} c_{ij} = 0$;

2 Homogeneity condition $\sum_{j=1}^{N} c_{ij} = 0$;

3 Symmetry condition $c_{ij} = c_{ji}$.

The uncompensated own- and cross-price elasticities for the Rotterdam model are:

$$\varepsilon_{ij} = \frac{c_{ij} - w_j b_i}{w_i}. \tag{24}$$

11.5. ESTIMATION OF DEMAND SYSTEMS IN ONTARIO

In this section we discuss some of the issues associated with estimating demand systems from retail scanner data, econometric issues, and the estimated demand systems for soft drinks in the Province of Ontario in Canada.

11.5.1. The data

The focus of the analysis was on the largest province in Canada, Ontario, which is home to well over a third of all Canadians. Weekly data were available from A. C. Nielsen for the period February 10, 1996 to February 27, 1999, corresponding to 156 weekly observations. The beverages for which data were available were carbonated soft drinks (CSDs) and selected noncarbonated soft drinks (NCSDs). The NCSDs for which data were available correspond to ready-to-serve (RTS) fruit juices and drinks; sport drinks; and iced teas. Data were not

Table 11.1:   Average expenditure shares and prices for selected beverages in Ontario.

	Average expenditure shares	Average prices (US$/liter)
CCL	0.2011	0.7073
PCC	0.1279	0.7186
COTT	0.1114	0.5248
CBCI	0.0628	0.7385
AOB	0.0096	0.8105
Fruit juices and drinks	0.4590	1.2404
Sports drinks	0.0070	1.8710
Iced tea	0.0211	1.1911

available for powdered drinks, bottled water, or ready-to-drink coffee. The average aggregate expenditure shares and prices for carbonated soft drinks by concentrate supplier (CCL, PCC, COTT, CBCI and AOB) as well as aggregate averages for drink categories for which A. C. Nielsen data were available for Ontario are exhibited in Table 11.1.

Consumption of ready-to-drink products is almost split equally between RTS fruit drinks (46%) and CSDs (51%), with sports drinks and iced teas each having a relatively small market presence. Among concentrate suppliers of CSDs, CCL has a 20% share of all RTS drinks in the data set, and is the leading supplier of CSDs: its share of CSDs is 39.2%. CBCI, on the other hand, has just 6% of ready-to-drink products and 12.2% of the CSDs. The other two leading concentrate suppliers of CSDs in Ontario are Pepsi (24.9%) and private label formulated and bottled by COTT (21.7%).

A comparison of prices for CSDs and NCSDs in Table 11.1 reveals the following: (i) prices of noncarbonated drinks on a per liter basis are higher than prices of carbonated drinks; (ii) sport drinks have the highest prices per liter on average; (iii) prices of private label soft drinks (COTT) have the lowest prices per liter on average; and (iv) CBCI's soft drinks are on average priced higher on a per liter basis than the brands of the other two brandname producers.

Table 11.1, however, hides a great deal of information, because it aggregates over *both* brands and package formats. First CSDs are differentiated by flavour. There is a very large number of different flavours — cola, cherry cola, lemon lime, root beer, orange, ginger ale, etc — and for many of these flavours regular and diet versions are available. Within each flavour segment there is differentiation, for instance in the cola flavour segment Coca-Cola and Pepsi-Cola are not viewed by all consumers to be perfect substitutes. Second, the same brand is differentiated by package formats — 12-pack of cans, 24-case of cans, single serve bottle, 1 and 2 liter bottles etc. The total number of standard stock keeping units (SKUs) available from A. C. Nielsen just for CSDs produced by the four major producers was in excess of 500. Clearly estimation of a demand system in these circumstances, if not most, will require some mechanism to reduce the number of brands to a more manageable number.

11.5.2. Specification of the demand system: Aggregation and separability

One commonly used approach to reduce the number of brands in a demand system to a manageable number is multistage budgeting (Rubinfeld 2000; Hausman, Leonard, and Zona 1994). As Rubinfeld (2000, p. 173) observes this is "achieved by characterizing demand decisions according to a multilevel decision-making process, by aggregating individual brands into sensible aggregates, and by assuming that the demands for products in one "branch" or segment of the "tree structure" are separable from the demands of products in other branches." For instance at the first stage, or level, demand for total consumption of the "product" (for instance CSDs) is modeled as a function of the price index for CSDs, the price index for NCSDs, income, and other determinants of demand, e.g., demographic variables, time trend, etc. This stage determines total expenditure on CSDs, which is allocated in the second stage using the demand system chosen across flavour segments. In the third stage consumption within a flavour segment is allocated using the demand system across the brands in that segment.[19]

Rubinfeld (2000) discusses the implicit restrictions imposed on the estimated cross-price elasticities between brands included in different "nests" or segments at the third stage. By placing brands in different nests, or branches, at the lowest level the restriction imposed is that the brands across different segments are more likely to have relatively small cross-price elasticities. This is because the extent of substitution is forced to operate by reallocating expenditure between the different segments. If colas and lemon lime flavoured CSDs are in different flavour segments then a 1% increase in the price of Coca-Cola will result in a

---

[19] See Hausman, Leonard, and Zona (1994) for discussion and illustration using data on beer consumption in the United States.

less than 1% increase in the price of colas. This will result in a reallocation of expenditure away from colas to lemon lime flavoured CSDs — if they are substitutes — and that reallocation is determined by the cross-price elasticity between the two aggregates, colas and lemon lime flavoured CSDs. The increase in expenditures on lemon lime flavoured CSDs will then be allocated between the various brands that comprise the lemon lime flavour aggregate. The necessary and sufficient condition for treating the least aggregated stage in this manner is weak separability between the products in different segments at this level.[20]

Of considerable interest then is whether CSDs and NCSDs are separable. If they are separable then NCSDs can be excluded from the CSD demand segment. If they are not, then NCSDs should be included in the CSD segment or nest. Nayga and Capps (1994) provide the details of weak separability tests for the Rotterdam demand system. A necessary and sufficient condition for weak separability is that the intergroup off-diagonal terms in the Slutsky substitution matrix be proportional to the corresponding income derivatives of the goods in question. Let i and k be goods in group r and j be a good in group s. Then Nayga and Capps show that the restriction for weak separability is

$$\frac{\varepsilon^*_{ij}}{\varepsilon^*_{kj}} = \frac{N_i}{N_j} \tag{25}$$

for all i and k in r, and j in s, where ε^*_{ij} is the compensated cross-price elasticity and N_i is the expenditure elasticity of product i. The non-linear restriction implied by (25) on the parameters of the Rotterdam model is

$$\frac{c_{ij}}{c_{kj}} = \frac{b_i}{b_k} \tag{26}$$

where i and k are in group r and j is in group s.

The number of nonredundant weak separability restrictions for any partition of N products into S separable groups, with n_s products in group s, is

$$\frac{1}{2}\left[N^2 + N - S^2 + S - \sum_{s=1}^{n_s} (n_s + 1)\right]. \tag{27}$$

---

[20] A problem with the multistage approach is that it is only theoretically correct if the product at each stage has an income elasticity of one so that budget shares are independent of total expenditure. Neither the AIDS or Rotterdam system has this property. See Deaton and Muellbauer (1980b). See Edgerton (1997) on the estimation of elasticities in multistage demand functions.

The likelihood ratio test statistic is given by

$$\Psi = 2[LL_{UR} - LL_R] \tag{28}$$

which follows — at least asymptotically — a χ^2 distribution with degrees of freedom given by the number of restrictions and where LL_{UR} and LL_R are the unrestricted and restricted values of the log-likelihood function. Because of the known bias for restrictions in large demand systems to be rejected, we use the adjusted test statistic which compensates for degrees of freedom (Laitinen 1978; Byron 1970):

$$\Psi^* = \Psi + T\log\left(\frac{nT - p_1}{nT - p_0}\right) \tag{29}$$

where n is the number of equations in the demand system, T the number of observations, p_0 is the number of parameters with both the separability and classical restrictions imposed, and p_1 is the number of parameters to be estimated with only the classical restrictions imposed. Notice that $p_0 - p_1$ corresponds to the number of separability restrictions. We make a similar adjustment to the critical values (Moschini and Green 1991; Anderson and Blundell 1983; and Pudney 1981):

$$K^* = nT\log\left[1 + \left(\frac{p_1 - p_0}{nT - p_1}\right)F_{p_1-p_0,nT-p_1}\right]. \tag{30}$$

Details of the weak separability tests for ready-to-serve drinks in Ontario are found in Table 11.2. The Rotterdam demand system estimated consists of the following products: (1) the aggregate of all CCL CSDs; (2) the aggregate of all PCC CSDs; (3) the aggregate of all COTT CSDs; (4) the aggregate of all CBCI CSDs; (5) all other CSDs; (6) ready-to-serve fruit juices and drinks; (7) ready-to-serve sport drinks; and (8) ready-to-serve iced teas. The null hypothesis is that the three NCSDs for which data are available — ready-to-serve fruit juices and drinks, sport drinks, and iced teas — are separable from the five CSD aggregates. The test statistics indicate rejection of the hypothesis that CSDs and NCSDs are separable.

Our approach was to thus avoid imposition of a structure that might artificially limit the extent of substitution between CSDs and NCSDs and is not warranted based on the test for weak separability. Determination of the scope of the demand system, and determination of the number of brands was also complicated by line pricing.

Table 11.2:   Weak separability tests for CSDs and NCDSs in Ontario.

$\Psi = 2[LL_{UR} - LL_R] \sim \chi^2$ (test statistic)

LL_{UR} — log-likelihood function with classical restrictions only

LL_R — log-likelihood function with separability and classical restrictions

$\Psi^* = \Psi + T \log \left(\dfrac{nT - p_1}{nT - p_0} \right)$ (adjusted test statistic)

$K^* = nT \log \left[1 + \left(\dfrac{p_1 - p_0}{nT - p_1} \right) F_{p_1-p_0,nT-p_1} \right]$ (adjusted critical value)

n is the number of equations in the demand system (7)

T the number of observations (155)

p_0 is the number of parameters with both the separability and classical restrictions imposed (31)

p_1 is the number of parameters to be estimated with only the classical restrictions imposed (42)

$F_{p_1-p_0,nT-p_1} = $ 1.8032 at the 0.05 level
                        1.5825 at the 0.10 level

Ontario
$\Psi = 21.442^{[a]}$
$\Psi^* = 19.815^{[b]}$

Notes.
[a] significant at the 0.05 level.
[b] significant at the 0.10 level.

11.5.3. Line Pricing

Line pricing refers to the practice of retailers charging the same price for all soft drink brands of a particular size and package format from a given supplier. Consequently, if line pricing is in effect then all TCCC brands, for example Coca-Cola and Sprite, will have the same price for a given package type and size in a particular week. Similarly, Pepsi brands, for example Pepsi-Cola and 7UP, will have the same price for a given package type and size in a particular week if line pricing is in effect. If line pricing is practiced, estimation of a demand system that contains more than one product of a soft drink concentrate supplier will be impossible because of perfect collinearity. On the other hand, because of line pricing it makes it more acceptable to aggregate across the brands of a given CSD concentrate supplier.[21] Because of a high degree of line pricing for the products of the four soft drink suppliers, we found it necessary to aggregate products by concentrate supplier. Consequently, in the demand systems estimated, we focus on aggregates of all Coca-Cola (CCL) products, Pepsi (PCC) products, private label (COTT) products, and Cadbury Schweppes (CBCI) products.

A further important issue is that there is some evidence of line pricing between CBCI's brands and those of CCL and PCC. This is because Cadbury Schweppes' Canada Dry and C-Plus brands are distributed largely through Coca-Cola bottlers in Ontario, and if line pricing is in effect, they too will have the same price as CCL's brands. Further, as Cadbury Schweppes' Schweppes and CRUSH brands are distributed largely by the Blue system in Ontario, they will have the same price as Pepsi brands if line pricing is in effect. This means that the estimation of demand parameters governing the substitution between Cadbury Schweppes' and other concentrate suppliers' brands may be problematic. If line pricing were rigidly adhered to, then the price of Cadbury Schweppes' brands, on a store-to-store basis, would be a weighted average of the prices of CCL and PCC products. Exact linear dependency among prices would make it impossible to estimate a fully specified disaggregated demand system by brand. However, since prices used in the analysis include product promotion effects, prices of Cadbury Schweppes products may differ from those of either CCL products or PCC products. If departures from line pricing occur seldomly, and if store level product mix variations are minor, then brand prices will suffer from considerable collinearity. Demand parameter and elasticity estimates would then be subject to large standard errors and would be estimated imprecisely.

Because of concerns over line pricing we used the regressions diagnostics of Belsley, Kuh, and Welsch (1980) to test for degrading collinearity. The diagnostics used included variance inflation factors, condition indices, and variance proportions. The diagnostics indicated no degrading collinearity in the Rotterdam model. In the LA/AIDS model, there were two sources of degrading collinearity: (1) between the log of the price of CCL and the log of the price of sport drinks; and (2) between the log of the price of COTT and the log of the ratio of total

---

[21] Strict line pricing would result in pricing of all CSDs by a concentrate supplier moving in parallel, and as a result the composite commodity theorem of Hicks (1936) and Leontief (1936) will hold. See Deaton and Muellbauer (1980b, pp. 120–122) for details. A weaker test for aggregation has been proposed by Lewbel (1996). Recently Capps and Love (2002) have demonstrated the superiority of Lewbel's test for aggregation of scanner data.

expenditure to Stone's price index. To circumvent the collinearity problems, one potential solution is to impose the restrictions implied by demand theory, and indeed the effects of the degrading collinearity were dissipated when this was done.

11.5.4. Econometric considerations

For estimation the LA/AIDS (19) and Rotterdam (23) demand systems are augmented with quarterly dummies based on the calendar year and a random error term. The quarterly dummies are added to capture the possibility that there are seasonal shifts in demand. Both the LA/AIDS model and the Rotterdam model are estimated using an iterated seemingly unrelated regression (ITSUR) technique, with an allowance for serial correlation (AR(1)) in the disturbance terms of all equations (Berndt and Savin 1975).

Estimation of either the LA/AIDS or Rotterdam demand system raises concerns regarding identification since prices are included as independent regressors. The usual approach of finding cost-based instruments may be difficult if the demand system consists of a relatively large number of brands. A further difficulty with instruments is that they may not be available in the frequency of the scanner data. Hausman, Leonard, and Zona (1994) have suggested two alternatives. The first is that if scanner data are available from different geographic markets, then price data from one geographic region can be used as instruments for other regions.[22] The second is to observe that prices may in fact not be endogenous, but instead are set by retailers prior to consumers making their purchase decisions.[23] This assumption is consistent with the nature of scanner data: retailers set their price and at that price their supply is perfectly elastic. This is the implicit assumption we make.

11.5.5. Empirical estimates of the demand systems

The demand systems are estimated over the following eight products: (1) the aggregate of all CCL CSDs; (2) the aggregate of all PCC CSDs; (3) the aggregate

---

[22] This suggestion is appropriate if sales promotions and other local demand shocks for a brand are uncorrelated across geographic regions. The use of price data in other geographic markets is described in Hausman, Taylor and Zona (1994, pp. 164–165) and is an implementation of Hausman and Taylor (1981).

[23] The need to use instruments can be tested using Hausman's specification test (Hausman 1978). Using price data from British Columbia as instruments we found no endogeneity of prices.

of all COTT CSDs; (4) the aggregate of all CBCI CSDs; (5) all other CSDs; (6) ready-to-serve fruit juices and drinks; (7) ready-to-serve sport drinks; and (8) ready-to-serve iced teas. Goodness-of-fit measures and Durbin-Watson statistics, as well as estimated coefficients and tests of statistical significance of the coefficients for the Rotterdam and LA/AIDS models are exhibited in Tables 11.3 and 11.4. Goodness-of-fit measures suggest that both the Rotterdam and LA/AIDS specifications fit the data reasonably well over the sample period. The exceptions are for PCC in the LA/AIDS specification and sports drinks in the Rotterdam specification. More than half of the coefficients associated with the demand specifications are statistically different from zero at the 10% level of signficance.

In conducting demand systems analyses with A. C. Nielsen data, it is important to take into account serial correlation. In both cases, the serial correlation coefficient, rho, is statistically different from zero. This phenomenon is present in most time-series analyses. Serial correlation is attributable principally to the presence of dynamics, notably inventory adjustment or habit persistence; the omission of advertising and promotion effects; and possibly the omission of other beverages such as bottled water, milk, and coffee.

The corresponding own-price and cross-price elasticities are shown in Tables 11.5 and 11.6. For the Rotterdam model (Table 11.5) all own-price elasticities are negative and significant. Of the cross-price elasticities, 22 are positive and statistically significant (10% level of significance), while 6 are negative and statistically significant. Surprisingly, of the 12 cross-price elasticities involving a CSD, only two are positive and statistically significant — the two between COTT and CCL. Of considerable importance for the merger is that the two cross-price elasticities involving CBCI and CCL are negative and statistically significant. A similar pattern holds for CBCI and PCC.

For the LA/AIDS model (Table 11.6) all own-price elasticities are negative and significant. Of the cross-price elasticities, 16 are positive and statistically significant (10% level of significance), while 6 are negative and statistically significant. Again, of the 12 cross-price elasticities involving a CSD, only two are positive and statistically significant — the two between COTT and CCL. And once again, the two cross-price elasticities involving CBCI and CCL are negative and statistically significant.

The story told by the estimated demand elasticities is that the brands of CBCI and those of CCL and PCC are complements. There are two possible explanations for this. One is that it is correct and is driven by the fact that TCCC and Pepsi brands on the one hand and the CS ginger ales/mixers on the other hand are complements. No one will substitute Coke for tonic in making a gin and tonic if the price of tonic goes up! One can imagine people buying more of colas

Table 11.3:   Parameter estimates of the Rotterdam model for Ontario.

Parameter	Estimated coefficient	Standard error	*t*-ratio	*p*-value
A01	−0.107016E−02	0.185021E−02	−0.57	0.563
C11	−0.408664*	0.035604	−11.47	0.000
C12	0.047739*	0.024990	1.91	0.056
C13	0.108710*	0.023026	4.72	0.000
C14	−0.026926*	0.016367	−1.64	0.100
C15	0.267774*	0.024058	11.13	0.000
C16	0.769287E−03	0.459435E−02	0.16	0.867
C17	0.512022E−03	0.732757E−02	0.06	0.944
B1	0.312690*	0.014153	22.09	0.000
B01	0.101512E−04	0.215680E−02	0.00	0.996
C22	−0.267231*	0.031621	−8.45	0.000
C23	0.025713	0.020299	1.26	0.205
C24	−0.966796E−02	0.865769E−02	−1.11	0.264
C25	0.187457*	0.024397	7.68	0.000
C26	0.542774E−02*	0.254244E−02	2.13	0.033
C27	0.011309*	0.459952E−02	2.45	0.014
B2	0.153758*	0.016598	9.26	0.000
C01	−0.273740E−04	0.152871E−02	−0.01	0.986
C33	−0.222894*	0.027136	−8.21	0.000
C34	0.011711	0.948050E−02	1.23	0.217
C35	0.059848*	0.021122	2.83	0.005
C36	0.188170E−02	0.288137E−02	0.65	0.514
C37	0.011325*	0.520259E−02	2.17	0.029
B3	0.092853*	0.011658	7.93	0.000
D01	0.139789E−02*	0.613601E−03	2.27	0.023
C44	−0.080508*	0.016482	−4.88	0.000
C45	0.089031*	0.011130	7.99	0.000
C46	0.227325E−02	0.435705E−02	0.52	0.602
C47	0.015173*	0.642973E−02	2.35	0.018
B4	0.076667*	0.512736E−02	14.95	0.000
E01	0.643370E−03	0.237503E−02	0.27	0.786
C55	−0.619635*	0.033413	−18.54	0.000
C56	0.334237E−03	0.345668E−02	0.09	0.923
C57	0.663141E−02	0.612320E−02	1.08	0.279
B5	0.328703*	0.018368	17.89	0.000
F01	−0.196492E−03	0.159192E−03	−1.23	0.217
C66	−0.828822E−02*	0.273770E−02	−3.02	0.002
C67	−0.231279E−02	0.245441E−02	−0.94	0.346
B6	0.571784E−02*	0.136644E−02	4.18	0.000
G01	−0.631601E−03*	0.291760E−03	−2.16	0.030
C77	−0.039608*	0.497744E−02	−7.95	0.000

Table 11.3: *(continued)*

Parameter	Estimated coefficient	Standard error	*t*-ratio	*p*-value
B7	0.022564*	0.243495E–02	9.26	0.000
RHO	−0.320119*	0.029513	−10.84	0.000
D11	0.158902E–02	0.268532E–02	0.59	0.554
D12	0.249661E–02	0.260375E–02	0.95	0.338
D13	0.123016E–02	0.264107E–02	0.46	0.641
D21	0.169836E–02	0.312821E–02	0.54	0.587
D22	0.859266E–03	0.303640E–02	0.28	0.777
D23	0.816584E–03	0.307728E–02	0.26	0.791
D31	−0.924706E–03	0.221799E–02	−0.41	0.677
D32	−0.331595E–03	0.214965E–02	−0.15	0.877
D33	0.574084E–04	0.218033E–02	0.02	0.979
D41	−0.331260E–02*	0.892265E–03	−3.71	0.000
D42	−0.612109E–03	0.865372E–03	−0.70	0.479
D43	−0.224206E–02*	0.875379E–03	−2.56	0.010
D51	−0.259603E–03	0.345542E–02	0.07	0.940
D52	−0.609171E–02*	0.334173E–02	−1.82	0.068
D53	0.105317E–02	0.338828E–02	0.31	0.756
D61	0.215786E–03	0.232701E–03	0.92	0.354
D62	0.860256E–03*	0.225352e–03	3.81	0.000
D63	−0.111320E–03	0.226985E–03	−0.49	0.624
D71	0.694071E–03	0.424508E–03	1.63	0.102
D72	0.260175E–02*	0.414579E–03	6.27	0.000
D73	−0.901624E–03*	0.416302E–03	−2.16	0.030

Note. *Significant at the 0.10 level. $A_{01} = a_1$, $B_{01} = a_2$, $C_{01} = a_3$, etc., $B_i = b_i$, $C_{ij} = c_{ij}$.

Equation 1 — CCL   Durbin-Watson = 2.2816   R-squared = 0.9128

Equation 2 — PCC   Durbin-Watson = 2.7194   R-squared = 0.7350

Equation 3 — COTT   Durbin-Watson = 2.0896   R-squared = 0.5263

Equation 4 — CBCI   Durbin-Watson = 1.7545   R-squared = 0.8482

Equation 5 — FRU   Durbin-Watson = 2.1333   R-squared = 0.7773

Equation 6 — SPO   Durbin-Watson = 2.0740   R-squared = 0.2921

Equation 7 — TEA   Durbin-Watson = 1.7827   R-squared = 0.6422

Table 11.4:   Parameter estimates of the LA/AIDS model for Ontario.

Parameter	Estimated coefficient	Standard error	*t*-ratio	*p*-value
A1	−1.51713*	0.194822	−7.79	0.000
G11	−.226881*	0.033400	−6.79	0.000
G12	0.024552	0.023996	1.02	0.306
G13	0.071597*	0.022093	3.24	0.001
G14	−.022751	0.014187	−1.60	0.109
G15	0.142349*	0.023233	6.13	0.000
G16	−.200980E−02	0.405224E−02	−0.49	0.620
G17	0.502883E−02	0.693061E−02	0.73	0.468
B1	0.100402*	0.012093	8.30	0.000
A2	−.145586	0.252596	−0.58	0.564
G22	−.114424*	0.032700	−3.50	0.000
G23	0.606770E−02	0.019451	0.31	0.755
G24	−.013170*	0.753387E−02	−1.75	0.080
G25	0.084308*	0.025148	3.35	0.001
G26	0.435199E−02*	0.225306E−02	1.93	0.053
G27	0.944023E−02*	0.446148E−02	2.12	0.034
B2	0.013874	0.015651	0.89	0.375
A3	0.271610*	0.161452	1.68	0.093
G33	−.094421*	0.026392	−3.58	0.000
G34	0.132274E−02	0.873032E−02	0.15	0.880
G35	0.012209	0.020925	0.58	0.560
G36	−.193565E−02	0.272696E−02	−0.71	0.478
G37	0.365327E−02	0.533894E−02	0.68	0.494
B3	−.011560	0.999676E−02	−1.16	0.248
A4	−.200436*	0.063808	−3.14	0.002
G44	−.033222*	0.014748	−2.25	0.024
G45	0.059991*	0.010018	5.99	0.000
G46	0.371514E−02	0.389713E−02	0.95	0.340
G47	0.680692E−02	0.590430E−02	1.15	0.249
B4	0.013767*	0.397702E−02	3.46	0.001
A5	2.56816*	0.251756	10.20	0.000
G55	−.309778*	0.032870	−9.42	0.000
G56	−.109619E−02	0.322722E−02	−0.34	0.734
G57	0.826644E−02	0.615419E−02	1.34	0.179
B5	−.118138*	0.015816	−7.47	0.000
A6	0.030089*	0.017696	1.70	0.089
G66	−.102408E−02	0.241744E−02	−0.42	0.672
G67	−.202764E−02	0.220416E−02	−0.92	0.358
B6	−.133746E−02	0.111039E−02	−1.20	0.228
A7	−.035726	0.035004	−1.02	0.307
G77	−.026864*	0.476454E−02	−5.64	0.000
B7	0.409092E−02*	0.219094E−02	1.87	0.062

Table 11.4: *(continued)*

Parameter	Estimated coefficient	Standard error	*t*-ratio	*p*-value
RHO	0.86338*	0.016187	53.34	0.000
D11	0.351635E–02	0.721449E–02	0.48	0.626
D12	0.746392E–02	0.809444E–02	0.92	0.356
D13	0.011335	0.717068E–02	1.58	0.114
D21	−.01644*	0.929036E–02	−1.76	0.077
D22	−.665707E–02	0.010413	−0.63	0.923
D23	−.279816E–02	0.921649E–02	−0.30	0.761
D31	−.011357	0.594753E–02	−1.15	0.248
D32	−.014258*	0.670179E–02	−1.90	0.056
D33	−.011164*	0.592165E–02	−2.12	0.033
D41	−.631267E–02*	0.221144E–02	−2.85	0.004
D42	−.130912E–02	0.246903E–02	−0.53	0.596
D43	0.869459E–03	0.218926E–02	0.39	0.691
D51	0.027594*	0.91268E–02	3.02	0.002
D52	0.958259E–02	0.010239	0.93	0.349
D53	−.288633E–02	0.909183E–02	−0.31	0.751
D61	0.875263E–03	0.610502E–03	1.43	0.152
D62	0.138626E–02*	0.688153E–03	2.01	0.044
D63	0.101326E–02*	0.607055E–03	1.67	0.095
D71	0.213194E–02*	0.12275E–02	1.73	0.082
D72	0.343737E–02*	0.137967E–02	2.49	0.013
D73	0.340148E–02*	0.122956E–02	2.76	0.006

Note. *Significant at the 0.10 level. $A_i = \alpha_i$, $B_i = \beta_i$, and $G_{ij} = \gamma_{ij}$.

Equation 1 — CCL   Durbin Watson = 2.6937   R-squared = 0.6910

Equation 2 — PCC   Durbin Watson = 3.0912   R-squared = 0.2302

Equation 3 — COTT   Durbin Waston = 2.3216   R-squared = 0.7338

Equation 4 — CBCI   Durbin Watson = 2.1715   R-squared = 0.7557

Equation 5 — FRU   Durbin Watson = 2.5229   R-squared = 0.8661

Equation 6 — SPO   Durbin Watson = 2.1836   R-squared = 0.8312

Equation 7 — TEA   Durbin Watson = 1.4394   R-squared = 0.9492

Table 11.5: Uncompensated own-price and cross-price elasticity estimates at the sample means of the data for the Rotterdam model for Ontario.

		CCL	PCC	COTT	CBCI	FRU	SPO	TEA	AOB
CCL	Elasticity	-2.3455	0.0382	0.3679	-0.2317	0.6178	-0.007	-0.0304	0.0353
	Std error	0.1746	0.1225	0.1157	0.0818	0.1354	0.0229	0.0366	0.0137
	t-stat	-13.4365	0.3122	3.1798	-2.8345	4.5624	-0.3081	-0.8313	2.5820
	p-value	0.0000	0.7550	0.0010	0.0050	0.0000	0.7580	0.4060	0.0100
PCC	Elasticity	0.1314	-2.2402	0.0674	-0.1510	0.9124	0.0339	0.0629	-0.0173
	Std error	0.1964	0.2404	0.1612	0.0672	0.2237	0.0199	0.0363	0.0117
	t-stat	0.6690	-9.3194	0.4178	-2.2456	4.0794	1.7044	1.7321	-1.4713
	p-value	0.5040	0.0000	0.676	0.0250	0.0000	0.0880	0.0830	0.1410
COTT	Elasticity	0.8103	0.1244	-2.0987	0.0529	0.1549	0.0111	0.0842	0.0254
	Std error	0.2049	0.1786	0.2457	0.0854	0.2117	0.0260	0.0471	0.0154
	t-stat	3.9546	0.6965	-8.5408	0.6191	0.7319	0.4271	1.7897	1.6498
	p-value	0.0000	0.4860	0.0000	0.5360	0.4640	0.6690	0.0740	0.0990
CBCI	Elasticity	-0.6734	-0.3099	0.0508	-1.3571	0.8561	0.0276	0.2155	-0.0289
	Std error	0.2546	0.1349	0.1515	0.2639	0.1861	0.0694	0.1025	0.0420
	t-stat	-2.6443	-2.2969	0.3351	-5.1433	4.6005	0.3984	2.1026	-0.6884
	p-value	0.0080	0.0220	0.7380	0.0000	0.0000	0.6900	0.0350	0.4910

Table 11.5: *(continued)*

		CCL	PCC	COTT	CBCI	FRU	SPO	TEA	AOB
FRU	Elasticity	0.4393	0.3166	0.0508	0.1489	−1.6782	−0.0043	−0.0007	0.0118
	Std error	0.0512	0.0513	0.0462	0.0240	0.0833	0.0075	0.0134	0.0043
	t-stat	8.5723	6.1660	1.0990	6.2132	−20.1507	−0.5678	−0.0544	2.7282
	p-value	0.0000	0.0000	0.2720	0.0000	0.0000	0.5700	0.9570	0.0060
SPO	Elasticity	−0.0544	0.6708	0.1783	0.2737	−0.3277	−1.1911	−0.3481	−0.0193
	Std error	0.6434	0.3565	0.4132	0.6275	0.5040	0.3918	0.3516	0.1665
	t-stat	−0.0845	1.8816	0.4314	0.4362	−0.6501	−3.0400	−0.9901	−0.1159
	p-value	0.9330	0.0600	0.6660	0.6630	0.5160	0.0020	0.3220	0.9080
TEA	Elasticity	−0.1899	0.3973	0.416	0.649	−0.1759	−0.1166	−1.8914	−0.1532
	Std error	0.3394	0.2128	0.2461	0.3055	0.2972	0.1159	0.2353	0.0679
	t-stat	−0.5594	1.8670	1.6902	2.1246	−0.5920	−1.0056	−8.0368	−2.2562
	p-value	0.5760	0.0620	0.0910	0.0340	0.5540	0.3150	0.0000	0.0240
AOB	Elasticity	0.9069	−0.17200	0.3057	−0.1600	0.5570	−0.0135	−0.3327	−1.8286
	Std error	0.2808	0.1525	0.1783	0.2781	0.2116	0.1218	0.1506	0.1031
	T-stat	3.2304	−1.1277	1.7144	−0.5753	2.6329	−0.1112	−2.2087	−17.7311
	p-value	0.0010	0.2590	0.0860	0.5650	0.0080	0.9110	0.0270	0.0000

Table 11.6: Uncompensated own-price and cross-price elasticity estimates at the sample means of the data for the LA/AIDS model for Ontario.

		CCL	PCC	COTT	CBCI	FRU	SPO	TEA	AOB
CCL	Elasticity	-2.2290	0.0582	0.3007	-0.1446	0.4788	-0.0135	0.0144	0.0356
	Std error	0.1643	0.1174	0.1107	0.0707	0.1301	0.0202	0.0346	0.0132
	t-stat	-13.5705	0.4953	2.7166	-2.0438	3.6809	-0.6685	0.4170	2.6989
	p-value	0.0000	0.6200	0.0070	0.0410	0.0000	0.5040	0.6770	0.0070
PCC	Elasticity	0.1699	-1.9072	0.0353	-0.1096	0.6085	0.0332	0.0714	-0.0098
	Std error	0.1895	0.2483	0.1543	0.0582	0.2296	0.0176	0.0352	0.0113
	t-stat	0.8965	-7.6803	0.2290	-1.8822	2.6500	1.8825	2.0280	-0.8682
	p-value	0.3700	0.0000	0.8190	0.0600	0.0080	0.0600	0.0430	0.3850
COTT	Elasticity	0.6652	0.0679	-1.8382	0.0184	0.1576	-0.0167	0.0351	0.0146
	Std error	0.1972	0.1711	0.2383	0.0785	0.2086	0.0246	0.0482	0.0159
	t-stat	3.3741	0.3971	-7.7124	0.2350	0.7556	-0.6794	0.7272	0.9175
	p-value	0.0010	0.6910	0.0000	0.8140	0.4500	0.4970	0.4670	0.3590
CBCI	Elasticity	-0.4059	-0.2375	-0.0033	-1.5422	0.8536	0.0576	0.1036	-0.0449
	Std error	0.2217	0.1172	0.1390	0.2357	0.1687	0.0620	0.0940	0.0415
	t-stat	-1.8305	-2.0273	-0.0237	-6.5436	5.0598	0.9280	1.1018	-1.0834
	p-value	0.0670	0.0430	0.9810	0.0000	0.0000	0.3530	0.2710	0.2790

Table 11.6: *(continued)*

		CCL	PCC	COTT	CBCI	FRU	SPO	TEA	AOB
FRU	Elasticity	0.3618	0.2166	0.0552	0.1468	−1.5565	−0.0006	0.0235	0.0106
	Std error	0.0498	0.0529	0.0456	0.0216	0.0813	0.0070	0.0134	0.0044
	t-stat	7.2666	4.0910	1.2100	6.8137	−19.1527	−0.0837	1.7443	2.4224
	p-value	0.0000	0.0000	0.2260	0.0000	0.0000	0.9330	0.0810	0.0150
SPO	Elasticity	−0.2490	0.6469	−0.2556	0.5434	−0.0689	−1.1451	−0.2859	0.0056
	Std error	0.5699	0.3154	0.3902	0.5603	0.4779	0.3459	0.3156	0.1593
	t-stat	−0.4369	2.0511	−0.6551	0.9699	−0.1443	−3.3105	−0.9060	0.0350
	p-value	0.6620	0.0400	0.5120	0.3320	0.8850	0.0010	0.3650	0.9720
TEA	Elasticity	0.1985	0.4207	0.1509	0.3090	0.3014	−0.0970	−2.2716	−0.2049
	Std error	0.3221	0.2060	0.2522	0.2800	0.3033	0.1041	0.2252	0.0666
	t-stat	0.6161	2.0419	0.5986	1.1039	0.9938	−0.9322	−10.0879	−3.0771
	p-value	0.5380	0.0410	0.5490	0.2700	0.3200	0.3510	0.0000	0.0020
AOB	Elasticity	0.8720	−0.1031	0.1704	−0.2744	0.4451	0.0035	−0.4478	−1.5507
	Std error	0.2721	0.1472	0.1839	0.2739	0.2182	0.1165	0.1477	0.1078
	t-stat	3.2050	−0.7005	0.9268	−1.0020	2.0396	0.0304	−3.0318	−14.3869
	p-value	0.0010	0.4840	0.3540	0.3160	0.0410	0.9760	0.0020	0.0000

and mixers together for parties. While TCCC and Pepsi brands and CS brands are all technically "CSDs", it is likely that the ginger ales/mixers are not good demand substitutes for colas and fruit flavored CSDs.

The second explanation is that the negative cross-price elasticities between CBCI and PCC and CCL is an artifact of line pricing. When the prices of CCL products fall, then because of a common bottler and line pricing, so too do CBCI's products bottled by the Red system. Hence the cross-price elasticity estimated is in fact its own-price elasticity which we would expect to be negative. The diagnostic tests of Belsley, Kuh, and Welsch (1980) discussed earlier indicate otherwise, however.

11.6. IMPLEMENTING THE HYPOTHETICAL MONOPOLIST TEST

In this section we illustrate the role that estimation of a demand system from scanner data can play in implementing the hypothetical monopolist test. The Competition Bureau defined three relevant markets around CSDs. The three distinct CSD markets were distinguished by the mode of distribution and were (i) CSDs in the take home channel, (ii) CSDs in the impulse channel, and (iii) CSDs in the fountain channel. The take home channel corresponds to bulk purchases — typically in grocery stores — for consumption later, the impulse channel to single-servings in cans and bottles for immediate consumption, and the fountain channel to single-servings for immediate consumption out of a cup/glass at establishments with fountain dispensers.

11.6.1. Indirect evidence on market definition

When information on own- and cross-price elasticities is not available for possible candidate markets, indirect evidence is used to assess the demand-side substitution possibilities available for consumers. Sources of indirect evidence are described in the *Commissioner's Merger Enforcement Guidelines* in Section 3.2.2 as "Evaluative Criteria". Consideration of the four following evaluative criteria provides supporting evidence that CSDs cannot be the basis for defining relevant antitrust markets:

(i)   *Functional interchangeability.* CSDs, other non-carbonated soft drinks, and numerous other beverages are purchased to provide liquid refreshment. It is not easy on the basis of end use to distinguish between CSDs, other non-carbonated soft drinks, and other types of beverages.

(ii) *Physical and technical characteristics.* CSDs are differentiated by numerous tangible and intangible characteristics including flavour, colour, caloric content, packaging, and brand image. Non-carbonated soft drinks and other beverages are also differentiated by a wide variety of characteristics, some similar and some different than CSDs. Focusing on carbonation as the characteristic that defines the relevant market boundary is too simplistic and will ignore important competitive constraints provided by opportunities for consumers to switch from CSDs to other beverages.

(iii) *Trade views and behavior.* Brand owners and bottlers have recognized that non-carbonated soft drinks are a source of competition and an opportunity for significant growth from diversifying product lines. The emphasis on NCSDs is reflected in the broadening of product lines to include RTS juices/juice drinks, iced teas, sports drinks, and waters. The Red system has introduced Nestea Cool, Powerade, Fruitopia, Nestea, and Dasani. The Blue system has introduced Brisk, Lipton's Iced Tea, Fruitworks, Ocean Spray, Aquafina, and All Sport. It is becoming common to see non-carbonated beverages supplied by either Red or Blue bottlers available in grocery stores, coolers, fountain equipment, and vending machines along with CSDs. Over the period 1995 to 1999 the volume of CCB sales accounted for by non-CSD products doubled, with the annual growth rate of NCSDs almost five times as large as the rate of growth of CSDs in the late 1990s.

(iv) *Switching costs.* Costs to either consumers or retailers to switch from CSDs to non-carbonated soft drinks or even other beverages are negligible. Virtually everywhere that CSDs are sold, consumers can find non-carbonated beverages, and increasingly broad selections to choose from. Retailers of any type can also easily switch their product mix between CSDs and non-carbonated beverages.

11.6.2. Direct evidence on market definition

Our approach to implementing the hypothetical monopolist test directly using estimated demand systems was not strictly in accordance with the approach suggested by the merger enforcement guidelines of either Canada or the US. Rather than start with every CBCI and CCL brand and apply the hypothetical monopolist test to a sequence of candidate markets, we instead applied the test to CSDs to determine whether they were, as posited by the Bureau, an antitrust market. In addition we used the estimated demand system to provide evidence on the next-best substitutes to CCL's and CBCI's CSDs. However, because of data limitations the analysis is only directly applicable to the take-home channel.

We found that both of these exercises point to a broader market definition than all CSDs. Diversion ratios suggest that the next-best substitute to CCL's and CBCI's CSDs are ready-to-drink fruit juices, not other CSDs. This suggests that a candidate market defined to include only all CSDs would never be reached in a correctly defined sequence of candidate antitrust markets. Direct application of the hypothetical monopolist test to CSDs also raises considerable doubts that all CSDs are an antitrust market. The profitability of an SSNIP by a hypothetical monopolist is questionable.

11.6.2.1. Next-best substitutes for CCL and CBCI brand CSDs

Table 11.7 shows the unit and dollar diversion ratios obtained from the Rotter-dam and LA/AIDS models for CBCI brands. Recall that the unit diversion ratios relate the change in the quantity of the other soft drink due to a one unit change in the quantity of CBCI products and that the dollar diversion ratio weighs the changes in quantities by prices. For substitute (complementary) products the diversion ratios are negative (positive). The sum of diversion ratios is not, in general, 1.

The largest diversion ratios are for ready-to-serve fruit juices and drinks. Because of a price increase in Cadbury Schweppes' products, a 1 liter decrease in these products would result in a 0.40 to 0.46 liter diversion to ready-to-serve fruit juices and drinks. The next largest unit diversion ratios are for ready-to-serve iced tea. These ratios vary from -0.04 to -0.10. Private label products (COTT) and ready-to-serve sport drinks are the third and fourth best alternatives respectively. However, all negative diversion ratios except for ready-to-serve fruit juices and drinks are statistically insignificant at the 5% level.

The importance of RTS fruit juices and drinks as an avenue of sales diversion is not determinative because of the aggregate nature of the RTS fruit juice and drink data. The high diversion ratios arise because of its large market share and relatively high cross-price elasticity with CBCI. However, the large diversion ratios are yet another indication that NCSDs might well be an important source of competitive constraint on the pricing of CSDs, especially those of CBCI.

Table 11.7: Unit diversion ratios and dollar diversion ratios for CBCI from the proposed acquisition by TCCC of CSDs in Canada.

		Unit diversion ratios		Dollar diversion ratios	
		Rotterdam	LA/AIDS	Rotterdam	LA/AIDS
CCL	Estimate	0.5710	0.3135	0.5469	0.3002
	Std error	0.2966	0.1927	0.2841	0.1846
	t-stat	1.93	1.63	1.93	1.63
	p-value	0.054	0.104	0.054	0.104
PCC	Estimate	0.2337	0.1493	0.2273	0.1453
	Std error	0.1135	0.0836	0.1104	0.0813
	t-stat	2.06	1.79	2.06	1.79
	p-value	0.040	0.074	0.040	0.074
COTT	Estimate	−0.0936	−0.0287	−0.0665	−0.0204
	Std error	0.1528	0.1220	0.1086	0.0867
	t-stat	−0.61	−0.24	−0.61	−0.24
	p-value	0.540	0.814	0.540	0.814
FRU	Estimate	−0.4646	−0.4032	−0.7808	−0.6776
	Std error	0.0915	0.0693	0.1538	0.1165
	t-stat	−5.08	−5.82	−5.08	−5.82
	p-value	0.000	0.000	0.000	0.000
SPO	Estimate	−0.0088	−0.0155	−0.0224	−0.0392
	Std error	0.0204	0.0163	0.0518	0.414
	t-stat	−0.43	−0.95	−0.43	−0.95
	p-value	0.665	0.344	0.665	0.344
TEA	Estimate	−0.1029	−0.0431	−0.1660	−0.0695
	Std error	0.0527	0.0396	0.0850	0.0639
	t-stat	−1.95	−1.09	−1.95	−1.09
	p-value	0.051	0.276	0.051	0.276
AOB	Estimate	0.0161	0.0244	0.0177	0.0268
	Std error	0.0281	0.0244	0.0309	0.0269
	t-stat	0.57	1.00	0.57	1.00
	p-value	0.566	0.319	0.566	0.319

11.6.2.2. *Applying the hypothetical monopolist test to CSDs*

To apply the hypothetical monopolist test to CSDs, we estimated the Rotterdam specification over five product groups: (i) the CSDs of CCL, PCC, CBCI, and COTT; (ii) all other carbonated beverages (AOB);[24] (iii) ready-to-serve fruit juices; (iv) sports drinks; and (v) iced teas. Evaluated at the sample mean, the own-price elasticity for CSDs is 1.99. However, consistent with the increased importance of NCSDs, the estimated demand elasticity evaluated at the average values for the first three months of 1999 is 2.12.

Using the formula for the critical demand elasticity and the estimated demand elasticities, it is possible to solve for a critical cut-off margin. This is done by solving (2) for *m*:

$$m = \frac{1 + \varepsilon}{\varepsilon} - t. \tag{31}$$

This margin can then be compared to estimates of actual margins to provide evidence on whether CSDs are a hypothetical monopoly, i.e., a relevant antitrust market. Margins above the cut-off margin mean that the indicated SSNIP is not profit-maximizing, while margins below the cut-off margin mean that the indicated SSNIP or a greater increase in price is profit-maximizing.

The advantage of estimating the demand elasticity and calculating critical margins is that it focuses not on whether there is a distinct segment of the population that will purchase CSDs for relevant price increases — so called infra-marginal consumers — but on the number of consumers who will substitute — marginal consumers. It is the number of marginal consumers that determines market power. Table 11.8 shows the critical cut-off margins as a function of the two estimates for the elasticity and the SSNIP.

The objective of market definition is to define markets so that market shares are reflective of market power. This then permits structural analysis to identify mergers that potentially create or enhance market power. In particular, the point of market definition is to facilitate the identification of horizontal mergers between firms which produce products that exert competitive constraints on each other's pricing. The rationale for the hypothetical monopolist test is that if a hypothetical monopolist could not raise prices, then a merger within that market could not (even if it was a merger to monopoly) create market power.

The choice of the threshold SSNIP is very important in applying the hypothetical monopolist test. Too low an SSNIP will exclude substitutes, and in these

---

[24] The market share of AOB is 1.9%.

Table 11.8:   Critical cut-off margins based on critical elasticity formula and indicated elasticity: hypothetical monopolist test.

| SSNIP | Critical cut-off margin | |
| | Elasticity | |
	1.99	**2.12**
5%	0.478	0.445
10%	0.453	0.419
20%	0.403	0.366
30%	0.354	0.313

circumstances because it will result in very narrow markets, could easily result in a failure to identify horizontal mergers. Too high an SSNIP will include too many weak substitutes and fail to identify horizontal mergers that would create market power. The choice of an SSNIP in any particular case should be based on considering whether the resulting market definition accurately identifies the implications for market power of a merger.

In this case there are three reasons why the commonly used value of 5% for the SSNIP is likely a poor choice. First, the smallest market principle identifies the smallest group of products for which a hypothetical monopolist would prof- itability impose an SSNIP as the relevant antitrust market. The use of the smallest market principle and small SSNIP potentially biases the hypothetical monopo- list test to markets that are too narrow (Werden 1983, p. 551).

Second, uncertainty over the "best-guess" of the price increase of a hypo- thetical monopolist suggests that a larger SSNIP be used to avoid errors that the real price increase might be less than the SSNIP (Werden 1983, p. 549). The uncertainty regarding the best-guess of the price increase by a hypothetical monopolist depends on the estimates of the elasticity of demand and the hypo- thetical monopolist's margin. The estimates of the demand elasticity are biased downwards for the following two reasons:

(i)   The demand elasticity is underestimated because of omitted substitutes and the absence of expenditure effects. The estimated demand system excludes some substitutes and corresponds to the second stage of a two-stage budgeting exercise. This means that the estimates are conditional on holding expenditures constant and the elasticities do not reflect that an increase in the price of CSDs would lead to a reallocation of expenditure away from CSDs to other products as the price of CSDs increase.

(ii) As price rises, the elasticity of demand increases, resulting as Froeb and Werden (1992) observe, in a reverse cellophane fallacy. Because elasticity increases as price rises, the monopoly equilibrium elasticity will likely be greater than the prevailing elasticity and its use will result in an over-estimate of market power, leading to markets that are defined too narrowly.

Third, the average price of branded CSDs over the sample used to estimate the demand elasticity is US$0.72/liter, so a 5% increase in price corresponds to a 3.6 cent increase per liter. A 10% price increase corresponds to an increase in price of just over 7 cents per liter. The *Commissioner's Merger Enforcement Guidelines* observe that in these circumstances it is possible that an SSNIP greater than 5% should be used because the 5% threshold might fail to recognize a horizontal relationship. The *Guidelines* recognize that for very small absolute price changes demand might be very inelastic, but that for larger price increase it might be quite elastic.

For all of these three reasons, using an SSNIP of 5% could result in a failure to identify a horizontal relationship between CSDs and other soft drinks, and suggests that price increases greater than 5% more likely constitute an appropriate SSNIP.

The estimated demand system from section 11.5.5 provides an estimate of the own-price elasticity of demand for each family of CSDs. If pre-merger the firms prices are consistent with a Nash equilibrium in prices, then according to (7) the inverse of the own-price elasticity provides an estimate of the firm's Lerner Index or margin. Table 11.9 shows the average price and implied marginal cost and margin for each of the eight products in the demand system. The weighted average margin for CSDs (CCL, PCC, COTT, and CBCI) from the Rotterdam estimates is 0.4849. Regardless of the SSNIP and the estimated elasticity this estimated margin exceeds the critical cut-off margins in Table 11.8. A hypothetical monopolist would not find it profit-maximizing to raise its price by the SSNIP: the high margin makes it particularly costly.

Application of the hypothetical monopolist test raise significant questions over whether CSDs in the take-home channel are an antitrust market. The direct and indirect evidence, while perhaps not definitive given the limitations of the data, is certainly strongly indicative of a broader market definition than CSDs. Empirical work in the United States using a related approach reaches a similar conclusion (Higgins et al. 1995).

Table 11.9: Calculated gross margins and marginal costs (Ontario).

	Average price	Rotterdam		LA/AIDS	
		Margin	**Marginal cost**	**Margin**	**Marginal cost**
CCL[a]	0.71	0.43	0.41	0.45	0.39
PCC[b]	0.72	0.45	0.40	0.52	0.34
COTT[c]	0.52	0.48	0.27	0.54	0.24
CBCI[d]	0.74	0.74	0.19	0.65	0.26
FRU[e]	1.24	0.60	0.50	0.64	0.44
SPO[f]	1.87	0.84	0.30	0.87	0.24
TEA[g]	1.19	0.53	0.56	0.44	0.67
AOB[h]	0.81	0.55	0.37	0.64	0.29

[a] *CCL* — Coca-Cola products
[b] *PCC* — Pepsi products
[c] *COTT* — private label products
[d] *CBCI* — Cadbury Schweppes products
[e] *FRU* — ready-to-serve fruit juices and drinks
[f] *SPO* — ready-to-serve sport drinks
[g] *TEA* — ready-to-serve iced tea
[h] *AOB* — all other carbonated beverages

11.6.3. Distribution channels as separate antitrust markets

The Bureau considered that there might be three CSD markets on the basis of distribution channels. The A.C. Nielsen data used in the previous section comes primarily from sales in the grocery channel. Hence it is not directly applicable to whether or not the separate channels identified by the Bureau are indeed antitrust markets. The single serve/impulse channel and fountain channel both typically involve single serve formats, though they clearly differ from each other in some physical and economic characteristics. However the physical characteristics of the single serve/impulse channel product can be virtually identical to that of a product available in the grocery channel — the cans/bottles purchased from a cooler for immediate consumption are generally the same as those purchased for later consumption from a grocery store except for temperature and quantity.

11.6.3.1. Single serve/impulse channel

The Bureau's assertion that CSDs in this channel are a separate antitrust market is not convincing. It is subject to attack on two fronts: competition from NCSDs and, to a lesser extent, arbitrage of CSDs from the take home channel.

The antitrust market analysis in section 11.6.2 suggested that in the take home channel at least three types of non-carbonated soft drinks were important competitive constraints on the pricing of CSDs. While the necessary data are not readily available to estimate demand systems in the impulse/single serve channel, the importance of substitution to NCSDs is likely to extend to the impulse/single serve channel — indeed it might even be more important when appropriate consideration is given to the nature of demand, functional interchangeability, and switching costs. Demand in this channel is for immediate consumption of a cold beverage and a large variety of non-carbonated soft drinks are increasingly found side-by-side with CSDs in retailers' coolers. As of the late 1990s, non-carbonated beverages in the single drink package format accounted for more than a third of some bottlers sales in the single drink package format.

Competition between CSDs and NCSDs in this channel is also suggested by the extent of price correlation. While the use of price correlations on their own is problematic in defining antitrust markets, they can provide some indication of substitution.[25] A high price correlation between two products can arise because of significant cross-price elasticities. In response to an increase in the price of product *A*, buyers switch to product *B*, increasing demand for, and the price of, *B*. However, if the two goods are in different markets then the cost and demand fluctuations that change the price of *A* will not affect the price in *B* and the two prices would not move together — their fluctuations would be independent and their correlation would be low.

The *Commissioner's Merger Guidelines* in Section 3.2.2.6 observe that "a high correlation in the price movements of products A and B is often indicative of significant competition between products." We demonstrated, using CCB data for single serve formats, that the price correlations between the average price per liter of CSDs, iced teas, and fruit drinks were high and increasing over the period January 1996 to August 1999. The correlation coefficient for the period January 1998 to August 1999 was well above 0.80 for iced teas and above 0.90 for fruit drinks.

A final limit on the ability of a hypothetical monopolist of CSDs in the impulse/single serve channel to raise prices is the possibility of arbitrage by

---

[25] See the discussion in Church and Ware (2000, pp. 613–616) for the limitations on the use of price correlations to identify antitrust markets.

retailers. They can substitute bulk purchases if the price of single serve supply is increased. It is easy for retailers to purchase cases of 12 or 24 cans in the take home channel (e.g. from a price-aggressive mass merchandiser or major grocery retailer), "unbundle" the cans and resell them from a cooler as single serve. Prices in the take home channel — constrained by NCSDs — should exert some constraint on pricing of CSDs in the impulse channels.

11.6.3.2. The fountain channel

While not as obvious, as in the single serve/impulse market, competition from CSDs in the take home and NCSDs, as well as CSDs in the single serve/impulse channel likely do constrain the pricing of CSDs at the fountain. Retailers could substitute NCSDs and both CSDs/NCSDs in cans/bottles in response to an increase in the price of CSDs at the fountain. In many instances, retailers can, and do, serve both fountain and cold single serve CSDs/NCSDs.

11.7. PRICE SIMULATIONS

In this section we use the estimates of our demand systems from scanner data to identify unilateral effects associated with the TCCC/CS carbonated soft drinks transaction. The computed average simulated price changes at retail from the acquisition by TCCC of CS CSD brands in Canada are shown in Table 11.10. The respective models correspond to the demand system specifications previously described. Owing to the negative cross-price elasticities of CCL brands and CBCI brands, the simulated price changes from the various demand systems analyses are negative. The price changes for CCL for the two demand systems are similar, a decrease of between 5% and just over 7.5%. The simulated price effects on the price of CBCI brands is materially larger, a decline of just over 26% is the estimate from the LA/AIDS demand system and an estimate of almost 45% based on the Rotterdam demand system.

Since the estimated elasticities are random, so too are the estimated price effects of the acquisition, and based on the precision of the estimated elasticities we can ask how precise are the calculated price simulations. The standard errors of the price simulations can be approximated using the delta method. These standard errors, along with information on the statistical signficance of the price simulations are shown in Table 11.10. The simulated price reductions are statistically significant at the 10% level for both demand systems, except for the price decrease for CBCI using the LA/AIDS demand system. The unilateral

Table 11.10:   Simulated average price changes from the proposed acquisition of TCCC of CS CSDs in Canada.

	Rotterdam Model				LA/AIDS Model			
	Estimate %	Std error	t-stat	p-value	Estimate %	Std error	t-stat	p-value
CCL	−7.6612*	3.3424	−2.29	0.022	−5.1241*	2.9473	−1.73	0.082
CBCI	−44.0025*	24.9583	−1.76	0.078	−26.3148	16.5562	−1.59	0.112

Note. *Significant at the 0.10 level.

effects analysis does not support concerns that this transaction would lead to a substantial lessening of competition in Canada. Quite the contrary, it indicates that the internalization of a complementary relationship would lead to significantly — both statistically and economically — lower prices for CCL and CBCI's CSD brands.

11.8 THE BUREAU'S CASE

The Bureau's concerns were two-fold. First, while the Bureau acknowledged the role of effective remaining competition in the take home market channel for CSDs from the Blue system and COTT (private label), in preventing an increase in the unilateral exercise of market power post-acquisition by the Red system, it expressed concerns that a raising rivals' costs strategy might result in a substantial lessening of competition post-acquisition in the impulse and fountain channels. In these two distribution channels for CSDs, the competition both pre- and post-acquisition was perceived by the Bureau to be only from the Blue system. Thus if the acquisition of TCCC and CS CSD reduced the effectiveness of remaining competition from the Blue system in the fountain and impulse channels, it could make it possible for the Red system to exercise a materially greater degree of market power in these channels.

The second concern of the Bureau was that the transaction would facilitate the ability of the Red and Blue systems to exercise significantly greater market power interdependently. Post-acquisition, the extent of coordination between the two major suppliers could increase. This interdependent theory was raised as an issue in all three Bureau defined markets.

Of course neither of these theories will stand up if CSDs are not the appropriate product dimension of the relevant antitrust market. The analysis of section 11.5 raises substantial doubts regarding the merits of excluding NCSDs from the market.

11.8.1. Raising rivals' costs

In the Bureau's view the only two effective competitors in the two single serve channels both pre-and post-acquisition were the Red and Blue systems. For the acquisition to lessen competition substantially in either of these two markets, the acquisition of the Blue CBCI brands by the Red system must change the competitive interaction between the Red and Blue systems in such a way that the market power of the Red system increases. The Bureau suggested that the acquisition by TCCC of CS CSD brands could affect competition between the Red and Blue systems in these two "markets" by raising costs of Blue system bottlers, and thereby reducing the competitive constraint of Blue system bottlers on Red system bottlers.

The Bureau's concern was that the Red system would foreclose access to the Blue system of its CBCI brands. The Red system would no longer supply concentrate or license its existing trademarks to the Blue system. The alleged reduction in the competitive constraint posed by the Blue system arises because of the Bureau's assumption of a portfolio effect: retailers in the two systems demand a full range of flavours and the inability of the Blue system to provide a full range of products if it loses its CBCI brands reduces its demand and increases the demand for the Red system, allowing the Red system to charge higher prices for its CSDs. Alternatively, foreclosure could take the form of either raising the price of concentrate, including a reduction in direct marketing funding, or by imposing additional costs on the Blue system through discrimination in the supply of CBCI brands to Blue bottlers. Discrimination in the supply of other CBCI brands to the Blue system versus supply of CBCI brands to the Red system could occur by CCL over-zealously exercising its contractual rights to monitor quality, restrict package format, etc.

11.8.1.1. Foreclosure in the fountain channel

A convincing foreclosure theory by the Red system requires demonstration and evidence that two conditions will hold. These are[26]

---

[26] See Church and Gandal (2000) for discussion and citations to the literature.

(i) *An incentive to foreclose*: assuming that there is no retaliation, the benefits of foreclosing must exceed the cost of foreclosing. Foreclosure involves a trade-off between upstream and downstream profits: it creates profits down-stream — in the sale of CSDs — for the integrated firm, but because it does so by reducing the competitive constraint of buyers of the input — concen-trate — the demand for the input decreases and so too do profits from sales of the input. There is no free lunch: in foreclosure theories there is typically a cost associated with raising the costs of rivals.

(ii) *No avenue or incentive to adopt defensive strategies*: the foreclosed firm must not have the means and incentive to mitigate or avoid the effects of the foreclosure, for instance through self-supply or vertical merger.

In our view neither of these two conditions seemed very likely.

The alleged portfolio effect in the fountain channel rests on the assumptions that retailers in this channel usually deal exclusively with one CSD supplier and that fountain demand at the wholesale level depends not only on the relative number of flavours that a bottler can offer, but that demand depends on the key CBCI brand flavours (orange and ginger ale/mixers). If the demand effect is significant, then elimination of the Blue system's orange and ginger ale/mixer could put it at a material competitive disadvantage. The effect of foreclosure by CCL would be to increase the price and volume of Red fountain CSD sales and decrease both the price and volume of Blue fountain CSD sales.

However, the extent of these price effects, the competitive disadvantage of the Blue bottlers, and the incentive for CCL to foreclose depends on the importance to demand of the Blue bottlers maintaining a full portfolio of flavours that includes their present CBCI flavours. If this effect is small then it is not likely that CCL will have an incentive to foreclose Blue bottler access to these trade-marks/brands: the increase in profits on Red system CSD fountain sales does not make up for its lost margin on foregone sales of concentrate to Blue bottlers.

The size of the demand effect depends on the extent to which consumers will switch to other retailers or reduce their consumption of all beverages if a retailer does not have CBCI flavours. Ginger ale/mixer and orange share of CSD sales (total, and especially fountain) suggest that these flavours are not determinative of retailer choice by consumers. The choice between two pizza parlors is unlikely to depend on which has an orange fountain drink or the brand of its orange foun-tain drink.

However, if the effect was important enough that CCL would find it profitable to foreclose, then retailers will find it in their interests to maintain their own sup-ply of oranges and ginger ale/mixers in bottles/cans or to source from more than one fountain CSD supplier, including private label suppliers. The relatively small volumes of these flavours and the relatively limited number of establishments where particular CBCI flavours in the fountain have limited substitutes and are important (primarily ginger ales/mixers for use in preparation of alcoholic beverages) suggests the feasibility of maintaining a supply of these flavours in bottles.

To demonstrate this possibility, we estimated total CBCI fountain sales of ginger ale/mixers and the price differential per liter between the take home channel and the fountain channel for ginger ales/mixers. We then multiplied this differential by the volume of ginger ales/mixers sold by CBCI. Dividing this by the volume of Red System fountain sales indicated that a rough upper bound on the price increase of fountain sales would be well below half a cent a liter. This price ceiling is small because the volumes of fountain ginger ale/mixer are, on a relative basis, very small.

Perhaps more importantly, the Blue system may be able to respond by introducing its own replacement brands or licensing third party brands, and it will clearly have a strong incentive to do so if oranges and/or ginger ales/mixers have an important effect on fountain demand. The profitability of this strategy depends on the incremental costs of developing, marketing, and producing replacement brands:

(i) *Development costs:* The costs of developing a new flavour either in house or through a flavour house appear to be relatively insignificant relative to the size of the market. The Blue system also has the flexibility to introduce replacement brands that already exist in other countries owned by Pepsi (e.g., Slice, an orange flavour CSD) or by others (e.g., Seagrams ginger ales and mixers[27]). For these brands there are no development costs.

(ii) *Production of concentrate:* Production of concentrate is not capital intensive and does not appear to be characterized by significant and sustained production scale economies.[28]

(iii) *Marketing:* In the case of fountain drinks, the costs of marketing depend on the importance of brand awareness for consumers. The importance of brand preference for orange and ginger ale/mixers is not suggested by CBCI's share of national media advertising, which is well below its share of CSD sales. In general it is not the case that fountain retailers advertise brands available in the orange or ginger ale/mixer flavour segment. Indeed for those that are most likely to require a specific CBCI flavour segment replacement — bars for ginger ale/mixers — there is often no on-premise

---

[27] Seagrams ginger ales and mixers were subsequently acquired by TCCC.

[28] See *In the Matter of the Coca-Cola Company* 1990 FTC Lexis 469 at paragraphs 243–252 for a discussion of the ease of entry into concentrate and fountain syrup production.

advertising or identification of the ginger ale/mixer brands available. Indeed the largest fountain retailer in Canada sells both an unbranded orange and root beer, and the orange soda supplied by CCB, the largest fountain supplier in Canada, is a brand that is not advertised or available in the take home channel.

The Bureau suggested that even if consumers do not care directly about the brand of orange or ginger ale/mixer served from the fountain, they might care about the overall quality of the brand. The Bureau suggested that the perception of the quality of the retailer depends on it having nationally recognized CSD brands: in other words there is a "halo effect" from the quality of a retailer's CSD brands to consumers' perceptions of the retailer's quality. The Bureau asserts that the perception by consumers of the quality of a CSD brand depends on national advertising and the availability of the brand in the take home channel.

The halo effect is similar to theories of branded ingredient strategies (BIS). Under a BIS, the manufacturer of a defining input encourages downstream manufacturers to identify the presence of its input in their product. BIS are not widely observed in practice: notable examples are NutraSweet (aspartame), Intel (microprocessors), Du Pont (teflon), and Heinz (ketchup). The requirements for a BIS are that the quality of the final output depends on the quality of a defining input. The performance or quality of the defining input determines the quality/performance of the final product. Though an empirical matter, the suggestion by the Bureau that the quality of an orange or ginger ale fountain drink would determine the quality of most retailers in the fountain channel in any significant manner appears tenuous at best: consumption of orange and ginger ale/mixer fountain beverages does not typically define the consumption experience.

While a halo effect might suggest why an entrant without any established brands might encounter difficulties, it does not explain why Pepsi, with its established reputation for quality and its flagship brands, would have difficulty introducing replacement brands. If there is a halo effect it likely derives from the retailer carrying Pepsi or CCL brands in general.

Recognition of the profitability and ease with which the Blue system could respond with replacement brands limits the ability of CCL to foreclose or otherwise raise the costs of the Blue system. Such a response would result in a loss in margins from concentrate sales to the Blue system without any off-setting advantage in the sale of Red system CSDs.

In fact, it is doubtful that the *Blue system* would have difficulties introducing replacement brands *even into* the take home channel. In this respect it is important to differentiate between an established flavour segment and new flavour segments. It is true that there have been failures or disappointment associated with brands that attempt to pioneer new flavour segments such as cherry colas and Cherry 7UP where demand failed to materialize as expected. However, the relevant entry in this case is in established flavour segments against brands that do not have anywhere near the same level of brand capital, reputation and, by extension, brand loyalty as Coca-Cola or Pepsi-Cola.

The experience in the root beer segment is instructive. Both CCL and PCC successfully introduced their own root beer brands within a year of each other. Previously they had each supplied a CBCI branded root beer; A&W and Hires, two brands that consumers were familiar with because of the age of the brand and their availability in the take home channel, but which had limited national advertising. Both systems were able to seamlessly replace their root beers with brands licensed from TCCC (Barq's) and PepsiCo (Mug) using relatively small national advertising campaigns. In the process they revitalized sales of root beer in Canada. The clear implication is that effective brand management and relatively small investments in national brand capital can result in tremendous expansion in flavour segments like root beer.

11.8.1.2. Impulse/single serve channel

The portfolio effect alleged to disadvantage Blue bottlers in this channel is more subtle than in the fountain channel. The reason is that in most instances retailers do not enter into exclusive supply arrangements with bottlers.[29] Instead there is often multiple sourcing. In the event of foreclosure post-acquisition, a full range of flavours could be obtained by sourcing both Red and Blue bottlers. However, the Bureau raised concerns over "integer effects" which could occur if a Blue bottler's loss of the CBCI brands resulted in insufficient brands to adequately

---

[29] The exceptions are retailers that enter into exclusive arrangements for supply of cans/bottles either through their outlets or by having only Red or Blue vending machines. The advantages of being exclusive to retailers appear to be much less in this channel as compared to fountain. In particular the costs of being non-exclusive are less and the demand advantages greater. Retail exclusivity would result in a retailer foregoing substantial sales in the single serve/impulse channel, but not in the fountain channel. This means it is much easier for retailers to choose not to be exclusive. This substantially limits the market power that any portfolio effect might create for the Red system over retailers who have chosen exclusive arrangements in this channel. In response to a price increase, those retailers can easily choose to source CSDs from multiple suppliers.

stock Blue bottler coolers, resulting in their replacement by Red bottler coolers. The unarticulated underpinning of this argument was that the loss of the CBCI brands lowers the profitability to the retailer of a Blue bottler cooler below the profitability of a replacement Red bottler cooler, reducing the competitive constraint of the Blue bottler on the Red bottler, i.e., allowing the Red bottler to profitably charge retailers in this channel a higher price.

The magnitude of this effect clearly depends on the importance of bottler-owned coolers. If retailers only have their own coolers ("generic" coolers), then the integer effect and concerns about it vanish. Whether the integer effect will have any material effect on the Blue system and creates market power for the Red system depends on the prevalence of retailers that have, and wish to continue to have, only bottler-owned coolers.

Even assuming a retailer that only has bottler-owned coolers, the integer argument requires the following to be true:

(i) The Blue bottler is not able to replace the volume represented by CBCI brands with similarly profitable — for the retailer — alternative brands, either non-carbonated, carbonated in other flavour segments, or replacement brands in the same flavour segments as the CBCI brands. The Blue bottler could of course also augment the number/volume of brands in its cooler by permitting retailers to include third party brands, i.e., non-Blue and non-Red system brands.

(ii) The profitability of an additional Red cooler must exceed the profitability of the displaced Blue cooler, stocked with replacement brands or a generic cooler, stocked with whatever mix of products and brands the retailer finds most profitable, including Blue system brands.

The first necessary condition is problematic for the following reasons:

(a) As noted above, the sunk costs to the Blue system of introducing replacement brands across the three channels to establish brand capital (awareness or identity) equivalent to those of the CBCI brands is not likely prohibitive. Indeed, given the profitability of this channel it appears that entry barriers to brands in this channel may well be less than in the other channels and a national brand identity is not necessary. For instance, Brio Industries Inc. distributes and bottles a number of boutique sodas marketed cold in single serve package formats. These included — in various parts of the country — Virgin Cola and Sodas, Hansen's Signature Sodas, Natural Sodas and Smoothies, Red Devil Power Colas, and Stewart's Fountain Classics. Of course if Blue bottlers are able to respond with new brands, then the profitability of the Red system foreclosing is reduced since it foregoes profits of concentrate on the CBCI brands sold to the Blue system and is not able to raise prices of its CSDs to retailers in this channel.

(b) There is not a shortage of flavours, especially given the possibilities and innovation in non-carbonated beverages. This is a weak link for the Bureau with regard to market definition as well as its raising rivals' costs theory. The Bureau relies on differences in (i) buyers' views, strategies and behavior; (ii) functional interchangeability; and (iii) physical and technical characteristics to distinguish the three channels as separate markets. However, in the impulse channel the same three criteria suggest that CSD cannot be distinguished from many non-carbonated soft drinks. Non-carbonated soft drinks in this channel are purchased cold-serve for immediate consumption and many are in package formats similar to the CSD products with which they share coolers.

(c) In most coolers, CBCI brands occupy a small volume and have a small number of facings — visible shelf space.

The second necessary condition is also problematic since it requires that the reduction in profits on the small volume of CBCI brands lost to the retailer on Blue system products be sufficiently large that the retailer would find it profitable to replace the Blue cooler with a Red cooler. In doing so the retailer loses the profits on all of the Blue brand volume in the replaced cooler. Its gain is the profits on the replacement Red brand volume. However, the profitability of the lost Blue brands is likely larger than the profitability of the added Red brands because of diminishing marginal returns.

Consider an outlet that presently has two Red and two Blue coolers and after foreclosure of the CBCI brands is, according to the hypothesis of the Bureau, considering replacing one of its Blue coolers with a Red cooler. To understand that it is very unlikely that the retailer will replace a Blue cooler with a Red cooler, consider why it initially had equal numbers of Red and Blue coolers. The reason is that the profitability of the second Blue cooler must be greater than the profitability of a third Red cooler (and vice versa). This reflects estimates of relative sales in this channel: approximately equal. It also underpins why retailers are non-exclusive: forgoing either the Red or Blue system would be very costly in terms of lost sales and profits.

Removal of the small number and facings of the Blue CBCI brands impacts only marginally on the profitability of the second Blue cooler, while removal of all of the other Blue brands/volumes in that second cooler likely results in a considerable reduction in profits. Given the small volume of the CBCI brands, the lost sales of the Blue brands are likely greater than the replacement Red brands. Displaced will be Blue brands that are very likely more profitable than the Red brands that are replacing them. Why? Because the second Blue cooler profitability was greater than the third Red cooler and the impact of the CBCI brands on the profitability of the second Blue cooler is not likely significant.

And even if there is an integer effect, the more likely response by a retailer may be to introduce its own cooler. It could then continue to maintain its selection, volume and profits from the Blue brands.

Thus in neither channel did we find it convincing that the acquisition would result in foreclosure raising the costs of the Blue system, and allowing the Red system to exercise more market power.

11.8.2. Interdependency concerns

The Bureau also expressed concerns that the proposed transaction, rather than facilitating an increase in market power of the Red system by reducing the competitive constraint of the Blue system, could instead lead to an increase in the ability of both to collectively exercise market power. According to the Bureau, an increase in interdependency or cooperative behavior post-acquisition could arise either because of structural changes in the industry or because it changes the ability of firms to discipline rivals who depart from cooperative outcomes.

The structural change that occurs as a result of the acquisition is that CCL becomes a supplier to Blue bottlers if it continues to license CBCI brands to Blue bottlers. The possibility arises that the interaction of CCL with Blue bottlers could provide an avenue for explicitly collusive behaviour. Under this hypothesis CCL becomes an information conduit between Red and Blue system bottlers. The ability to explicitly discuss the nature and extent of competition could remove important impediments to reaching a more cooperative outcome, characterized by a reduction in price and non-price competition.

As well, the Bureau was concerned that a more collusive outcome might be supported because the Red system is able, as a result of the acquisition, to more effectively discipline the pricing of the Blue system. The idea appears to have been that the profits from the Blue CBCI brands that used to be earned by the Blue system bottlers and CBCI will now be earned by the Red system, either in whole or in part, depending on whether the Red system continues to supply CBCI brands to Blue bottlers, and these profits provide the Red system with additional financial resources that enable it to more aggressively punish the Blue system should it lower prices. Alternatively, if the Red system continues to supply CBCI brands to the Blue system, it can enforce a more cooperative outcome by disciplining Blue bottlers for low prices by raising their costs, either by discriminatory provision of concentrates/syrups or by raising their prices/reducing marketing support.

In what follows we critically assess each of these possibilities.

11.8.2.1. Structural change

If the vertical relationship is to facilitate collusion — by making an agreement easier to reach — the Bureau must establish that communication and coordination is likely to occur and that it would lead to a substantial lessening of competition. There are two difficulties: (i) the communication may not occur and (ii) even if it does, it may not be effective.

The explicit coordination hypothesis of the Bureau would require the active and conscious participation of CCL and CCB, plus multiple bottlers in the Blue system. This type of behavior is criminal under Section 45 of the Canadian Competition Act. The Bureau must show, on the balance of probabilities, that the moral and criminal sanctions of price fixing are insufficient to deter possible communication and coordination. The wider the alleged coordination — the greater the participation by Red and Blue bottlers, Pepsi, and CCL — the more difficult coordination and the more likely that the conspiracy will be detected. Presumably the increased fines and stepped-up enforcement of Section 45 have a role to play in deterring communication of the sort considered by the Bureau.

In any event, even if the communication did occur, there are a number of factors in this industry that militate against effective collusion or even enhanced coordination and that the ability to communicate explicitly with one another is unlikely to overcome. Reaching an agreement will be complicated because of asymmetries between the Red and Blue system in product offerings, relative sales, costs, and multiple franchised Blue system bottlers. Agreements will not be effective unless they limit non-price competition as well as price competition. Limiting price competition alone is insufficient since if it is successful, firms will fight for profitable sales through non-price competition: advertising, new product introductions, innovation in packaging, etc. Moreover, non-price competition makes cooperative pricing more difficult to sustain because it can often be more difficult to detect, or even define, non-price competition that increases sales as a deviation from a cooperative agreement.[30]

---

[30] See Chapter 10 in Church and Ware (2000) for an extended discussion of the factors that make an industry susceptible to enhanced coordination.

The profitability of increased coordination depends on the elasticity of demand of the firms party to the agreement. This depends, in turn, on market demand and the number of suppliers not included in the agreement. The Bureau's own analysis indicates the important competitive constraint provided by private label brands in the take home channel. In addition, the elasticity of demand facing CSDs is enhanced by the possibility of substitution by consumers to non-carbonated soft drinks.

To test the incentives for enhanced coordination, we estimated Rotterdam and LA/AIDS demand systems defined over the following brands: (i) CCL, PCC, and CBCI brands; (ii) COTT; (iii) ready-to-serve fruit drinks; (iv) iced teas; (v) sport drinks; and (vi) all other CSDs. This demand system yields an estimate of the price elasticity of a hypothetical monopolist of all CBCI, CCL, and Pepsi brands based on A.C. Nielsen data in Ontario. The estimated elasticities are 2.12 for the LA/AIDs system and 2.36 for the Rotterdam system.

These conservative estimates of the own-price elasticity for a monopolist of brandname CSDs can be used to assess the market power implications of relaxing price competition between the Red and Blue systems. If the elasticity of the "cartel" is sufficiently high, relative to their margins, then coordinated pricing will not be profitable. Attempts by the Red and Blue systems to raise prices will be frustrated by consumer substitution to private label CSDs and other non-carbonated beverages. Whether coordinated pricing would be profitable depends on the trade-off between the increase in revenues on inframarginal units for which the higher price is received and the lost margin from units no longer sold because the higher price induces consumers to reduce their demand and substitute to other products.

Again we can use (31) to calculate a critical margin that makes a given price increase by a "cartel" of Red and Blue bottlers just profit-maximizing. If prevailing margins exceed the critical margin, then the price increase is not profitable because of the lost margins as consumers substitute away. If prevailing margins are less than the critical margin, then the price increase is profitable — the profits forgone on sales lost from the price increase are insufficient to offset the increased profitability of inframarginal sales.

Table 11.11 shows the critical margins for the two different demand systems. Again we can use the relationship implied by profit maximization between the estimated elasticities of demand in section 11.5.5 and the Lerner index to estimate actual margins. Using Table 11.9 the weighted average margin for branded CSDs (CCL, PCC, and CBCI) for the Rotterdam estimates is 0.4600. The estimated average margin for branded CSDs using the LA/AIDS estimates is 0.4818. Regardless of the SSNIP and the estimated elasticity the relevant estimated margin exceeds the critical cut-off margins in Table 11.11. A cartel of

Table 11.11: Critical cut-off margins based on critical elasticity formula and indicated elasticity: incentive for collusion.

	Critical cut-off margin	
Price increase	Elasticity	
	2.12 (LA/AIDS)	2.36 (Rotterdam)
2%	0.461	0.412
5%	0.445	0.394
10%	0.419	0.366

the brandname CSDs would not find it profit-maximizing to raise price by the indicated amount. In the take home channel, effective competition from retailer brands and NCSDs appears to be more than sufficient to eliminate concerns regarding any increase in market power from enhanced interdependency or coordination.

While Cott's competitive constraint in the impulse or single serve channel is not as significant as in the take home channel, the effectiveness of enhanced coordination in the impulse channel will be constrained by competition from NCSDs and some opportunity for arbitrage by retailers, especially those with small volumes.

The potential for the acquisition to enhance interdependent behavior and create market power in the fountain channel is not only complicated by asymmetries between the Red and Blue system and non-price competition. In the fountain and other channels, price transparency can also be an issue since transaction prices are not public. Without public pricing, firms cannot monitor cooperative agreements and discipline firms that deviate. Moreover, it may be difficult to infer transaction prices based on publicly available retail prices because of complicated contractural terms, involving rebates based on volume thresholds and marketing support. This inference problem is even more of an issue, however, in the fountain channel for two reasons. First, because accounts are typically exclusive, inference of supply prices from public retail prices is complicated because it is not as easy under exclusivity for the firm without the account to estimate the costs of the retailer. Second, the inference in fountain is more difficult because the cost of fountain syrup generally accounts for a relatively small percentage of the price of the finished product. This lack of transparency in the fountain channel is complicated by the fact that a relatively small handful of national accounts/contracts represent significant volumes, thereby contributing to relatively infrequent transactions of large value. And since these accounts are typically exclusive, coordination on price is unsufficient. Firms would also have to have either a customer allocation scheme, side payments, or both to maintain the agreement. These conditions — non-public pricing, small numbers of large accounts, and exclusivity — all suggest that the fountain channel is not conducive to successful coordination.

11.8.2.2. Relaxation of price competition

The factors in this industry that militate against enhanced coordination identified in determining the impact of the structural change are just as relevant for assessing the possibility of a relaxation of price competition. It seems unlikely that any increase in the ability to discipline the Blue system as a result of the acquisition will overcome these factors. More importantly, it is unclear how the increase in financial resources or the ability to raise the costs of the Blue system will lead to an increase in the ability of the Red system to discipline pricing by the Blue system.

The contention that all that prevents an increase in interdependent behavior that would lead to a substantial lessening of competition is insufficient financial resources, we termed the deep pocket theory. If the Red system simply had more money to lose, it could more effectively discipline the Blue system. Of course whether it has the money to lose or not does not determine whether it has an incentive to discipline the Blue system. If the incentive does exist, it is simply incredible that it is only the lack of the additional financial resources associated with the small volumes of the CBCI brands that prevents the Red system from acting on that incentive. Moreover the deepening of the Red system's pockets does not create the incentive to discipline, or increase the profitability of disciplining the Blue system.

The raising rivals' cost version of the discipline theory is similar. Under this theory, the Red system would raise the cost of access to the Blue system CBCI brands — by raising price or otherwise discriminating against the Blue system — not to maximize its profits, but to punish the Blue system for deviating from cooperative behavior. The problem with this theory is that the Red system could incur those losses now and effectively punish the Blue system for deviations through its own pricing. The Red system does not have to acquire all of the CBCI brands and raise the costs of the Blue system to effectively discipline Blue system pricing deviations.

11.9. CONCLUSION

This chapter provided a summary of our analysis of the proposed transaction between TCCC and CS in Canada. We estimated demand systems from scanner data and used the estimated elasticities to assess market definition and simulate the price effects of the acquisition. In addition, we also provided a critical assessment of the Bureau's theory of the case. Our main conclusions were:

(i)   The hypothetical monopolist test, dollar and unit diversion ratios to determine next-best substitutes, and indirect structural criteria all suggest a relevant antitrust market that is broader than CSDs in the take home channel. While the evidence is less clear, there are also indications that the other two CSD channels are not antitrust markets. Significant substitution possibilities between CSDs across the channels exist, as do substitution possibilities between CSDs and non-CSDs within and across channels.

(ii) Unilateral effects analysis suggests that the CCL and CBCI brands do not exert strong competitive constraints on each other.

(iii) Competition between the Red and Blue systems within the fountain and single serve channels would not be significantly affected by the transaction. In the fountain channel it is unlikely that complete foreclosure of the CBCI brands would have a material impact on Blue system demand from a portfolio effect and, even if it would, fountain retailers could respond by sourcing brands in the take home channel or by sourcing multiple fountain suppliers; and more importantly, the Blue system would have the incentive and capability to easily introduce replacement brands. In the single serve/impulse channel, the allegation that integer effects might result in a substantial lessening of competition is tenuous because it assumes the Blue system cannot replace the small volume and facings of its CBCI brands and that the replacement of a Blue cooler by yet another Red cooler will be profitable for retailers.

(iv) The transaction is also unlikely to increase the ability of the Red and Blue systems to exercise a greater degree of market power interdependently. The case theories are unpersuasive because they ignore important characteristics that make it difficult for the Red and Blue systems to coordinate their behaviour. In addition the structural change theory requires explicit illegal communication, while the relaxing competition hypothesis founders because it is not clear how the transaction enhances incentives for the Red system to discipline the Blue system or relaxes a binding pre-acquisition constraint limiting the ability of the Red system to discipline the pricing of the Blue system.

REFERENCES

Alston, J., Foster, K., & Green, R. (1994). Estimating elasticities with the linear approximate almost ideal demand system: Some Monte Carlo results. *Review of Economics and Statistics*, *76*: 351–356.

Anderson, A., & Blundell, R. (1983). Testing restrictions in a flexible dynamic demand system: An application to consumers' expenditures in Canada. *Review of Economic Studies*, *50*: 397–410.

Baker, J. (1997a). Contemporary empirical merger analysis. *George Mason Law Review 5*: 347–361.

Baker, J. (1997b). Unilateral competitive effects theories in merger analysis. *Antitrust, 11*: 21–26.

Barten, A. (1977). The systems of consumer demand functions approach: A review. *Econometrica, 45*: 23–51.

Belsley, D., Kuh, E., & Welsch, R. (1980). *Regression Diagnostics Identifying Influential Data and Sources of Collinearity*. New York: John Wiley & Sons.

Berndt, E., & Savin, N. (1975) Estimation and hypothesis testing in singular equation systems with autoregressive disturbances. *Econometrica, 43*: 937–957.

Blanciforti, L., & Green, R. (1983). An almost ideal demand system incorporating habits: An analysis of expenditures on food and aggregate community groups. *Review of Economics and Statistics, 65*: 511–515.

Buse, A. (1994). Evaluating the linearized almost ideal demand system, *American Journal of Agricultural Economics, 76*: 781–793.

Byron, R. P. (1970). A simple method for estimating demand systems under separable utility assumptions. *Review of Economic Studies, 37*: 261–274.

Capps Jr, O., Church, J., & Love, H. A. (2002). Specification issues and confidence intervals in unilateral price effects analysis. *Journal of Econometrics* (forthcoming).

Capps Jr, O., & Love, H. A. (2002). Econometric considerations in the use of electronic scanner data to conduct consumer demand analysis. *American Journal of Agricultural Economics, 84*: 267–276.

Capps Jr, O., Seo, S. C., & Nichols, J. P. (1997). On the estimation of advertising effects for branded products: An application to spaghetti sauces. *Journal of Agricultural and Applied Economics, 29*: 291–302.

Church, J., & Gandal, N. (2000). Systems competition, vertical merger, and foreclosure. *Journal of Economics and Management Strategy, 9*: 25–52.

Church, J., & Ware, R. (2000). *Industrial Organization: A Strategic Approach*. San Francisco: McGraw-Hill.

Cotterill, R. W., Franklin, A. W., & Ma, L. Y. (1996). Measuring market power effects in differentiated product industries: An application to the soft drink industry. Food Marketing Policy Center.

Crooke, P., Froeb, L., Tschantz, S., & Werden, G. (1999). Effects of assumed demand form on simulated postmerger equilibria. *Review of Industrial Organization, 15*: 205–217.

Csorgo, L., & Sanderson, M. (1999). Differentiated products mergers: Recent experience in Canada and the U.S. In: B. Graham (ed.) *Annual Fall Conference on Competition Law* (pp. 133–152). Ottawa: Canada Bar Association.

Davidson, R., & MacKinnon, J. (1993). *Estimation and Inference in Econometrics*. New York: Oxford University Press.

Deaton, A., & Muellbauer, J. (1980a). An almost ideal demand system. *American Economic Review, 70*: 312–326.

Deaton, A., & Muellbauer, J. (1980b). *Economics and Consumer Behaviour*. Cambridge: Cambridge University Press.

Edgerton, D. (1997). Weak separability and the estimation of elasticities in multistage demand systems. *American Journal of Agricultural Economics, 79*: 62–79.

Efron, B. (1979). Bootstrap methods: Another look at the jackknife. *Annals of Statistics, 7*: 1–26.

Efron, B. (1982). *The Jackknife, the Bootstrap and Other Resampling Plans*. Philadelphia: Society for Industrial and Applied Mathematics.

Freedman, D. A., & Peters, S. (1984). Bootstrapping a regression equation: Some empirical results. *Journal of American Statistical Association, 79*: 97–106.

Froeb, L., & Werden, G. (1992). The reverse *Cellophane* fallacy in market delineation. *Review of Industrial Organization, 7*: 241–247.

Green, R., & Alston, J. (1990). Elasticities in AIDS models. *American Journal of Agricultural Economics, 72*: 442–445.

Hausman, J. (1978). Specification tests in econometrics. *Econometrica, 46*: 1251–1271.

Hausman, J., & Leonard, G. (1997). Economic analysis of differentiated products mergers using real world data. *George Mason Law Review, 5*: 321–346.

Hausman, J., Leonard, G., & Zona, J. D. (1994). Competitive analysis with differentiated products. *Annales d' Economie et Statistique, 34*: 159–180.

Hausman, J., & Taylor, W. (1981). Panel data and unobservable individual effects. *Econometrica, 49*: 1377–1398.

Hicks, J. (1936). *Value and Capital*. Oxford: Oxford University Press.

Higgins, R., Kaplan, D., McDonald, M., & Tollison, R. (1995). Residual demand analysis of the carbonated soft drink industry. *Empirica, 22*: 115–126.

Laitinen, K. (1978). Why is demand homogeneity so often rejected? *Economics Letters, 1*: 187–191.

Leontief, W. (1936). Composite commodities and the problem of index numbers. *Econometrica, 4*: 39–59.

Lewbel, A. (1996). Aggregation without separability: A generalized composite commodity theorem. *American Economic Review, 86*: 525–543.

Moschini, G., & Green, R. (1991). Separability in demand analysis: Untested assumption or tested hypothesis? S-216 Regional Committee Symposium, Washington, D.C.

Nayga Jr, R. M., & Capps Jr, O. (1994). Tests of weak separability in disaggregated meat products. *American Journal of Agricultural Economics, 76*: 800–808.

Peterson, E. B., & Cotterill, R. W. (1998). Incorporating flexible demand systems in empirical models of market power. Food Marketing Policy Center.

Pollak, R. A., & Wales, T. J. (1991). The likelihood dominance criterion: A new approach to model selection. *Journal of Econometrics, 47*: 227–242.

Pudney, S. (1981). An empirical method of approximating the separable structure of consumer preferences. *Review of Economic Studies, 48*: 561–577.

Rayner, R. (1990). Bootstrapping p values and power in the first-order autoregression: A monte carlo investigation. *The Journal of Business and Economic Statistics, 8*: 251–263.

Rubinfeld, D. (2000). Market definition with differentiated products: The Post/Nabisco cereal merger. *Antitrust Law Journal, 68*: 163–182.

Scheffman, D. (1992). Statistical measures of market power. *Antitrust Law Journal, 60*: 901–919.

Seo, S. C., & Capps Jr, O. (1997). Regional variability of price and expenditure elasticities: The case of spaghetti sauces. *Agribusiness: An International Journal, 13*: 659–672.

Theil, H. (1965). The information approach to demand analysis. *Econometrica, 33*: 67–87.

Theil, H. (1980). *The System-Wide Approach to Microeconomics.* Chicago: University of Chicago Press.

Werden, G. (1983). Market delineation and the justice's merger guidelines. *Duke Law Journal, 3*: 514–579.

Werden, G. (1997a). Simulating unilateral competitive effects from differentiated products. *Antitrust* (Spring): 27–30.

Werden, G. (1997b). Simulating the effects of differentiated products mergers: A practical alternative to structural merger policy. *George Mason Law Review, 5*: 363–386.

Werden, G., & Froeb, L. (1994). The effects of mergers in differentiated products industries: Logit demand and merger policy. *Journal of Law, Economics, & Organization, 10*: 407–426.

Werden, G., & Froeb, L. (1996). Simulation as an alternative to structural merger policy in differentiated products industries. In: M. Coates and A. Kleit (eds), *The Economics of the Antitrust Process* (pp. 65–88). Boston: Kluwer Academic Publishers.

Measuring Market Power
D. J. Slottje (editor)

CHAPTER 12

Geographic Market Limits
for Yellow Pages Advertising
in California

JON M. RIDDLE[a] and WILLIAM S.
COMANOR[b]*

[a] University of California, Los Angeles, CA 90095–1477;
[b] Santa Barbara, UCBS, CA 93106–9210

Abstract

In this chapter, we find that the geographic market limits for Yellow Pages advertising in California are local areas within which one or more competing Yellow Pages directories are distributed. In reaching this conclusion, we employ price-based concepts that are consistent with the price uniformity requirements that must be satisfied within a relevant geographic market. We use analysis of variance and non-parametric procedures to test the proposition that the variability of prices within a relevant market will be smaller compared to the variability of prices prevailing outside a market area. In conducting this analysis, we use price and circulation data on over 200 Yellow Pages directories distributed throughout California in 1996.

JEL classification: D4, L11, L82
Keywords: Geographic market definition, Yellow Pages advertising

---

* Corresponding author.

12.1. INTRODUCTION

This paper describes the concepts, methods, and data sources used to delineate geographic markets for Yellow Pages advertising in California. It rests on a report used in recent litigation, where that issue was important for the outcome of the case. On other grounds, we had already found that Yellow Pages advertising is a separate product market from other advertising media.

12.2. THE CROSS-PRICE ELASTICITY STANDARD

Determining the geographic scope of a market hinges on the extent to which transactions in one area are highly substitutable for the same product or service available in other areas. In this instance, we sought to determine the extent to which ads placed in Yellow Pages directories that are distributed in one location are sufficiently distinct from ads placed in directories distributed elsewhere.

The answer to this question depends on the magnitude of the relevant cross-price elasticities of demand, which of course are critical for market definition issues. Specifically, geographic market boundaries depend on the cross-price elasticity of demand for ads placed in directories distributed in a particular area as compared with those placed in different directories. If these elasticities are relatively high, then advertisers in one area will switch to ads published elsewhere in response to small rate changes. A fairly low cross-price elasticity, on the other hand, indicates that advertisers will not move their ads to different directories in response to small changes in advertising rates. Two or more directories are thereby in the same geographic market where the cross-price elasticities of demand among them are relatively high, but occupy separate and distinct geographic markets when these elasticities are low.

12.3. THE *MERGER GUIDELINES* STANDARD

In the *Merger Guidelines*, the Department of Justice and the Federal Trade Commission suggest an alternate standard for determining the geographic parameters of a market. That standard defines the relevant geographic market as a region such that a hypothetical monopolist, that is the only present and future producer of the relevant product can profitably impose a small but significant and non-transitory price increase, holding constant the terms of sale for all products supplied elsewhere. As the *Guidelines* note, if consumers find products produced outside the hypothesized region sufficiently attractive at their existing terms of trade, then any attempt by this monopolist to impose a price increase would result in lost sales sufficient to make the price increase not profitable. In that case, the hypothesized geographic area boundaries are too narrow and should be redrawn to include firms supplying the product in these outlying areas (US Dept. of Justice 1992).

In the case of Yellow Pages advertising and applying this alternate standard, we start with a specific directory or directories distributed in a particular area. The geographic boundaries of this candidate market are limited by the neighborhoods in which the directory or directories are distributed. We then consider the effect on advertising placements when a hypothetical monopolist, publishing all of the relevant directories, imposes the requisite "small but significant and non-transitory" price increase. If advertisers would not switch to directories distributed in other areas, then this neighborhood or neighborhoods is a distinct geographic market. If, on the other hand, advertisers would shift their ads to directories circulated in adjacent areas, then the hypothetical monopolist would suffer eroding revenues and the price increase would not prevail.

12.4. USING PRICES TO DELINEATE GEOGRAPHIC MARKETS FOR YELLOW PAGES ADVERTISING

Both standards turn essentially on the willingness of buyers and sellers to switch transactions in response to a new set of prices. *That response underlies the Guidelines test as much as it affects the relevant cross-elasticities of demand and supply.* It is not surprising therefore that data on actual prices should be a critical factor in applying both standards. Insofar as the cross-price elasticity standard is applied, the ideal procedure would be to estimate a system of advertising demand equations. From the estimated parameters, one could then infer the scope of the product market. However, that avenue is often closed. Sufficient data is rarely available. We are typically faced with the recognition that cross-price elasticities of demand and supply cannot be directly determined.

As a result, there is a need to develop less data-intensive criteria that also shed light on market boundaries. In this case, we applied price-based tests to determine market boundaries. We thereby follow Areeda and Turner, who concluded that "price relationships are clearly the best single guide to geographic market definition . . . and in many if not most cases they will be quite sufficient" (Areeda and Turner 1978). Procedures relying on prices charged for ads placed in competing directories provide useful indicators of the geographic markets for Yellow Pages directories in California.

Where advertisers believe that the advertising messages inserted in different directories, but serving the same locale, are highly substitutable, they are not willing to pay more for advertising placed in one directory than in another. In that case, competing directory publishers are unable to charge more for ads in one directory than in another; and prices will tend to uniformity across competing directories. On the other hand, where advertisers view advertising in alternate directories as non-substitutable, perhaps because they reach different groups of consumers, advertisers do not readily switch among rival directories in response to price differences. As a result, prices may differ for the same advertising in different directories, which depends on the distinct supply and demand conditions faced by the publishers of each directory. An important indication of market boundaries is therefore the variability or the absence of variability of prices across directories.

So central is this issue of price variability to the economic concept of a market that this factor is sometimes mentioned as providing the basic construct of a market. Thus, Nobel Laureate George Stigler wrote: "a market for a commodity is the area within which the price tends to uniformity, allowance being made for transportation costs" (Stigler 1942). More recently Stigler and Sherwin summarize this position as follows:

> If there is a single price (allowing for transportation costs) over a given area, that must mean that either buyers or sellers (or both) can and do consider transactions at any point within the area to be an excellent (in the limit, a perfect) substitute for transactions at other points within the area. Hence the market area embraces the buyers who are willing to deal with any seller, or the sellers who are willing to deal with any buyer, or both.
>
> (Stigler and Sherwin 1985, pp. 555–556)

These authors thereby suggest that a single price prevails in a well-defined market, which is represented as the Law of One Price.

However, as these authors also acknowledge, within geographic markets, prices can differ because of factors other than transportation costs. These other factors may include transitory shifts in the various determinants of supply and demand, and also minor quality differences among products. Few products are perfectly homogeneous, so we cannot require perfect price uniformity as a condition for including different areas in the same geographic market. The relevant question is not whether observed prices within the boundaries of a proposed market area are precisely equal, which is rarely the case, but rather whether there is a substantial tendency towards equality within proposed boundaries of particular markets.

12.5. PRICE-BASED TESTS OF GEOGRAPHIC MARKET
   BOUNDARIES

To identify the geographic areas in California within which there is a substantial tendency towards price uniformity, we collected a cross section of price and circulation data for all 209 Yellow Pages directories published in California in 1996 by the three leading publishers, Pacific Bell, GTE, and the National Directory Company. The latter distributes the Donnelly Directories. We gathered these data from a Yellow Pages Publishers Association volume entitled *Rates and Data,* which is publicly available. We did not include information from specialized Business-to-Business or Hispanic community directories.

Since there are numerous advertising formats from which advertisers can choose, we selected a sample of five ad configurations that represented those that advertisers typically purchase.[1] These representative ads include bold listing (BLN), double quarter column (DQC), double half column (DHC), full page (FP), and bold listing with art work (HSA). The first ad looks like the typical residential listing, except that the business' name is printed in large, boldface type. The second ad is two columns wide and typically includes logos and other graphics. The double-half column ad is two columns wide and a half page tall. It also typically includes logos and other graphics. The full-page ad spans the whole page of a directory. The final ad incorporates a business logo into the bold listing ad.

Rates and Data reports list prices, but these are the typical transaction prices paid by advertisers as there is relatively little discounting. Furthermore, the *Rates and Data* prices reflect the dollar costs per year for a particular ad. Ultimately, an advertiser cares about the number of consumers who potentially can read his Yellow Pages advertisement. We therefore determine circulation-based prices by dividing list prices by a particular directory's circulation. Thus, the relevant price used in our analysis is stated on a per-home basis. Specifically, our ad prices express the annual price per year per thousand directories distributed.

We report summary data and descriptive statistics for the 209 California directories in Table 12.1. Based on total distribution, Pacific Bell published approximately 60% of the 31.7 million Yellow Pages directories distributed throughout California in 1996, while GTE and National distribute about 24% and 16%, respectively.[2] While GTE distributes more directories throughout

---

[1] Our representative sample is drawn from a review of the ads published in Yellow Pages directories serving the Mid-Cities area of Los Angeles (a Pacific Bell directory) and Santa Barbara (a GTE directory).

[2] The corresponding state-level Hirschman-Herfindahl Index of concentration is 4432.

Table 12.1: California Yellow Pages directory descriptive statistics 1996.

Publisher	Number of directories	Total distribution	Average distribution	Average price per 1,000 circulation (US$)					
				BLN	DQC	DHC	FP	HSA
GTE	106	7,692,504	82,715	2.71	23.71	39.73	163.00	14.30
Pacific Bell	83	19,031,016	229,289	1.84	8.82	21.58	101.58	5.07
National	20	4,995,840	312,240	0.62	5.56	10.61	39.94	—
All directories				2.16	15.80	29.01	133.87	9.95
Highest price				42.31	234.31	469.42	1265.08	171.66
Lowest price				0.18	3.19	4.28	14.58	1.48
Range				42.13	231.12	465.14	1250.50	170.18
Standard deviation				4.61	20.69	39.55	116.46	14.99
Coefficient of variation				2.13	1.31	1.36	0.87	1.51

the State, its typical directory is distributed to a smaller audience as compared with those of the other two publishers.

Even though it accounts for the smallest share of total directories distributed throughout California, National's directories feature the largest average circulation. Its distribution is limited to the five large counties of Los Angeles, Orange, Riverside, San Diego and Ventura in Southern California. Throughout the balance of California, GTE and Pacific Bell face no competition from National.

The statewide average prices and standard deviations reported in Table 12.1 suggest that the State of California is too broad to represent a geographic market. For example, the difference between the highest and lowest price for each ad is substantial. For the bold listing in particular, the highest price is 235 times the lowest. The range is similarly large for the other ad prices.

As indicated by the coefficient of variation, which is the standard deviation divided by the average, advertising rates vary greatly statewide. For example, for the bold listing type ads, the standard deviation of ad rates is more than twice the average price of US$2.16 per thousand of circulation indicating a wide distribution of prices throughout California. Except in the instance of full-page ads, where the coefficient of variation is 0.87, the standard deviation of ad rates exceeds the respective mean values. We conclude that the substantial variation in prices across the various directories indicates that different supply and demand conditions prevail in different areas in California. This substantial variability in ad prices indicates that The Law of One Price is not satisfied at the state level. For this reason, the geographic dimensions of these markets are likely to be smaller than the entire state.

The critical issue for setting geographic market boundaries is whether the distribution of prices within hypothetical boundaries reflects a larger statewide market, or whether it reflects the supply and demand conditions unique to each particular market. In other words, the central empirical question is: do the Yellow Pages advertising rates show a greater tendency towards uniformity within hypothesized market boundaries as compared to the statewide distribution? If we find that advertising rates within certain boundaries are more distinct than prices overall, that result suggests that there are separate and distinct geographic markets.

To answer this question, we employ two statistical tests using the *Rates and Data* prices. The first is an analysis of variance (ANOVA), which tests the null hypothesis that average prices within each hypothesized market are equal, so there is no effect due to any proposed market boundaries. The alternative conclusion is that grouping directories into hypothesized market boundaries explains more of the variability in ad prices. Rejecting the null hypothesis provides evidence that the proposed market boundaries do influence average prices, and that there is more variation across the proposed market boundaries than within them.

In conducting the ANOVA, we consider three different hypothetical market boundaries. First, we hypothesize that geographic markets for Yellow Pages advertising are defined by county boundaries. Using distribution maps for individual directories, we assigned the 209 directories to 51 counties. Second, we hypothesize that geographic markets for Yellow Pages advertising are defined by the Census Bureau's metropolitan statistical areas (MSA). Using the same distribution maps, we assigned the 209 directories to 25 MSAs. And third, we hypothesize that the geographic markets for Yellow Pages advertising are defined by contiguous market area (CMA) boundaries. We define a CMA as a region in California in which one or more directories are distributed. In many cases, there is only one directory distributed to residents. In these cases, the boundaries of the directory's distribution and the boundaries of the CMA coincide. Where more than one directory is distributed to residents, the combined distribution area of all overlapping directories is considered as the relevant CMA. CMAs are mutually exclusive in that their boundaries are drawn where there is no further overlapping distribution of Yellow Pages directories.

In the upper panel of Table 12.2, we report the computed F-statistics for separate analyses of variance for the alternative market definitions across the five different ad prices. As indicated, only two of the five test statistics are statistically significant for the county boundaries case. When Yellow Pages markets are defined as MSA boundaries, the ANOVA finds statistically significant results for four of the five ad prices. However, when markets are defined to be CMAs, we can reject the hypothesis of equal prices in all instances. Based on the ANOVA test, we find that contiguous market areas are the most likely relevant markets for Yellow Pages in California. By finding in favor of the smallest geographic market area, we are following the "smallest market" standard suggested by the Department of Justice and the Federal Trade Commission (US Dept. of Justice 1992).

The analysis of variance requires certain distributional assumptions that could affect the validity of the tests and the conclusions inferred from them. Specifically, the ANOVA requires that prices within each proposed market area be normally distributed and that the distribution of prices within each market share a common variance. The common variance requirement is potentially an issue because some of the proposed geographic markets show no price variability since only one directory is distributed within the proposed market. Therefore, we perform a second set of tests using the Kruskal-Wallis procedure. This procedure is a non-parametric alternative to the ANOVA test that requires less from the underlying data. Specifically, the Kruskal-Wallis test requires only that ad

Table 12.2: Computed F and chi-squared statistics.

Proposed market boundaries	Number of markets with		Ad type				
	At least 1 directory	2 or more directories	BLN	DQC	DHC	FP	HSA
I. Analysis of variance test (F statistic)							
County	51	26	1.22	2.05*	1.56	1.27	1.77*
Metropolitan statistical area	25	17	1.62	3.18*	2.31*	1.90*	2.76*
Contiguous market area	70	21	2.23*	2.07*	1.90*	1.81*	1.78*
II. Non-parametric test (chi-squared statistic)							
County	51	26	57.85*	40.12*	39.59*	30.82	33.84
Metropolitan statistical area	25	17	45.89*	42.40*	40.19*	23.05	29.14*
Contiguous market area	70	21	44.92*	42.64*	43.06*	37.68*	36.81*

Note. * Indicates statistical significance at the 5% confidence level.

rates used to test the hypothesized market boundaries result from independent random sampling. To implement this procedure, we rank ad prices from lowest to highest and then test if prices within each hypothesized market share adjacent rankings.

In the lower panel of Table 12.2, we report the computed Chi-square statistics for the three hypothesized market definitions across the five different ad prices using this second test. As indicated, only three of the five test statistics are statistically significant if Yellow Pages markets are defined by the county boundaries case. When Yellow Pages markets are defined as MSA boundaries, the Kruskal-Wallis test finds statistically significant results for four of the five ad prices. However, when markets are defined as CMAs, we reject the hypothesis of equal prices for all five prices. In other words, prices tend towards equality within CMAs but tend to be different across CMAs. As these nonparametric test results generally match our findings from the ANOVA, we conclude that the 70 CMAs constitute the relevant geographic markets for Yellow Pages advertising in California.

Coefficients of variation provide additional corroborating evidence that CMAs describe the relevant markets. In Table 12.3, we report coefficients of variation for selected CMAs in which two or more directories are circulated. These 17 markets fairly represent the entire state, comprising approximately 70% of all directories circulated in California in 1996. A striking feature of these results is that there are relatively few instances where the coefficient of variation exceeds unity. In fact, the coefficients of variation average from 0.56 to 0.76 across these markets. Furthermore, these values contrast with the coefficients of variation of 0.87 to 2.13 for all of California, as reported in Table 12.1. These results demonstrate that, while there is substantial variability in ad prices at the state level, this variability declines substantially within CMAs. Overall, the empirical results indicate that prices within contiguous market areas have a greater tendency towards uniformity, suggesting that these boundaries denote separate relevant geographic markets.

12.6. CONTIGUOUS MARKET AREAS AND THE *MERGER GUIDELINES* STANDARD

The boundaries of the CMAs also satisfy the requirements of the *Merger Guidelines* standard. To verify this result, consider the following counter-argument. Suppose that in response to an exogenous cost shock, a publisher serving a particular CMA raises its ad prices. In response, advertisers move their listings to an adjacent CMA where ad prices are now relatively lower.

Table 12.3: Coefficient of variation for ad rates within selected contiguous market areas 1996.

CMA	Number of publishers	Number of directories	Coefficient of variation				
			BLN	DQC	DHC	FP	HSA
North Coastal	2	4	0.57	0.76	0.97	0.76	0.71
Antelope Valley	2	6	0.81	1.00	0.67	0.41	0.95
East Los Angeles	3	22	0.95	0.60	0.61	0.52	0.60
Los Angeles	3	30	0.81	0.83	0.80	0.77	0.83
San Fernando Valley	3	14	1.06	0.74	0.57	0.53	0.76
Ontario–Pomona	2	3	0.42	0.48	0.33	0.26	0.44
Marin & Sonoma County	2	4	1.78	1.65	1.65	1.40	1.74
Orange County	3	14	1.30	1.04	1.02	0.98	1.14
Riverside	3	6	0.60	0.55	0.55	0.62	0.51
Palm Springs– Indio	2	3	0.22	0.33	0.34	0.01	0.03
San Bernardino	2	3	0.64	0.67	0.66	0.58	0.71
Modesto–Stockton	2	3	0.14	0.20	0.14	0.25	0.19
San Luis Obispo	2	2	0.25	0.41	0.36	0.27	0.41
Santa Barbara	2	3	1.20	1.03	0.98	0.97	1.11
Los Gatos	2	4	0.77	0.59	0.56	0.44	0.69
Sunnyvale	2	2	0.36	0.30	0.25	0.22	0.22
Ventura	2	3	1.10	0.94	0.91	0.87	1.03
North San Diego County	3	5	0.70	0.63	0.61	0.34	0.64
San Jose	2	7	0.66	0.49	0.47	0.51	0.59
Fowler, Sanger & Reedley	2	4	0.85	0.84	NA	0.59	0.87
Average			0.76	0.70	0.66	0.56	0.71

Table 12.4:   HHIs for the California Yellow Pages advertising markets 1996.

	Number of markets	Approximate distribution	% of distribution
3000 < HHI < 5000	5	16,794,155	60%
5000 < HHI < 10,000	12	5,187,560	19%
HHI = 10,000			
GTE	18	458,910	2%
Pacific Bell	33	5,547,305	19%
National	0	0	0%
Combined	51	6,006,215	21%
Total	68	27,987,930	100%

Competition among publishers serving the two CMAs will tend to equalize ad prices. However, the results of our statistical tests found that Yellow Pages advertising rates are in fact different across the various CMAs. It would then be the case that a hypothetical monopolist serving an individual CMA could profitably impose a small but significant and non-transitory price increase.

12.7.   CONCENTRATION AND MARKET POWER

Having established the product and geographic boundaries of California Yellow Pages advertising markets, we now examine concentration levels. Using our contiguous market area boundaries, we calculate each publisher's market share within each of these markets. Using these market shares, we then construct each market's Herfindahl-Hirschman Index (HHI) of market concentration.[3] As shown in Table 12.4, the typical Yellow Pages advertising market is highly concentrated. In no instance is the HHI less than 3000, a number far greater than the *Merger Guidelines* benchmark of 1800 for a highly concentrated market. Furthermore, 75% of the markets are monopolized by either GTE or Pacific Bell. While these 51 monopolized markets account for only 21% of Yellow Pages

---

[3] *Rates and Data* did not report distribution data for a few of the directories included in our sample. Accordingly, we were unable to calculate market shares and HHIs for several of the CMAs.

directory distribution in 1996, virtually all of them are located outside the three major population centers in the San Francisco Bay, Los Angeles-Orange County, and San Diego areas of the state.

A closer examination of market shares and HHIs finds a geographic concentration in markets monopolized by Pacific Bell and GTE. For example, all but three of the markets monopolized by Pacific Bell are located in Central and Northern California. On the other hand, most of the markets monopolized by GTE are located in Central and Southern California.

12.8. CONCLUDING COMMENTS

Although the two standards used to define geographic markets focus on the ability of buyers and sellers to switch among products in response to price differences, there is frequently insufficient data to examine this issue directly. Alternative approaches are therefore required. Many commentators have suggested that price data should be used to help define markets. This chapter suggests a means of using available price data for these purposes.

REFERENCES

Areeda, P., & Turner, D. (1978). *Antitrust Law*, vol. II. Boston: Little-Brown, p. 357.

Stigler, G. (1942). *The Theory of Competitive Price*. New York: Macmillan, p. 92.

Stigler, G., & Sherwin, R. (1985). The extent of the market. *Journal of Law and Economics, 28*: 555–585.

United States Department of Justice and Federal Trade Commission. (1992). *Horizontal Merger Guidelines*. Washington, DC: US Department of Justice, pp. 15–17.

Yellow Pages Publishers Association. (1996). *Rates and Data*, vol. G–Z. Troy, MI: Yellow Pages Publishers Association.

Measuring Market Power
D. J. Slottje (editor)

CHAPTER 13

Market Power in the US Airline Industry

JESSE C. WEIHER,[a] ROBIN C. SICKLES,[b]* and JEFFREY PERLOFF[c]

[a] FDIC Division of Research and Statistics, 550 17th St., NW, Washington, DC 20429;
[b] Rice University, Department of Economics – MS22, Houston, TX 77005–1892;
[c] University of California, Berkeley, Department of Agricultural and Resource Economics, 207 Giannini Hall, Berkeley, CA 94720–3310.

Abstract

Using data from the US Department of Transportation (1979–1992), we calculate the marginal cost of air travel. We then use this estimate of marginal cost to directly calculate the degree of market power in the airline industry. We show that the degree of market power varies with market structure.

Keywords: Airline industry, market power, cost, panel data
JEL classification: L40, L10

* Corresponding author.

13.1. INTRODUCTION

Do airlines exercise market power? If so, does that power vary with market structure? In recent years, most empirical industrial organization economists have tried to answer questions such as these by estimating complex structural models. However, using an unusually detailed data set, we can directly determine marginal cost and use that to calculate (rather than estimate) the degree of market power.

Many important public policy decisions turn on these questions. Since the wave of mergers that followed deregulation, these concerns have dominated the debate on regulating this market.[1] Because mergers may increase efficiency and increase market power, the net effect on price is theoretically ambiguous.[2]

Most previous research on the effects of market structure on this industry has used national level data or has focused on a few specific markets. We examine collusion on a market-by-market basis for the entire United States.

Moreover, most previous studies focus on trips between origin and destination *airports*. However, doing so neglects the competition that airlines face from carriers that fly from different airports within the same city. For instance, people who fly from Houston to Chicago have four combinations of airport pairs to choose from: Bush Intercontinental/Chicago O'Hare, Bush Intercontinental/Chicago Midway, Houston Hobby/Chicago O'Hare, and finally Houston Hobby/Chicago Midway. If the flight were round trip, they have four more airport combinations for the return trip. United and American have a considerable share of flights from Bush Intercontinental to Chicago O'Hare because O'Hare is a hub for those two carriers. However, Southwest Airlines has many flights between Houston Hobby and Chicago Midway. Studies that define a route as being between airport pairs would ignore that Southwest competes with United

---

[1] Many papers have discussed the effects of mergers in the airline industry, including Hergott (1977), Carlton, Landes, and Posner (1980), Knapp (1990), Borenstein (1990), Beutel and McBride (1992), Kim and Singal (1993), and Singal (1996). Using case study data from several markets, Brock (2000) reported that the airline industry is becoming increasingly concentrated through mergers and through strategic alliances and that tacitly collusive, non-competitive pricing strategies are becoming more prevalent.

[2] When United Airways sought to buy USAir in a 4.3 billion dollar deal in May of 2000, CIBC Oppenheimer analyst Julius Maldutis said he expected the airlines to have a "good case" before US regulators because there was no substantial overlap in route structures between the two firms. (Sidel, Robin, "UAL to Buy US Airways in $4.3 Billion Deal," Reuters Press, May 24, 2000.) Mr Maldutis assumed that US regulators were primarily concerned about reducing competition in any given set of markets, but were not concerned about an expansion of the number of markets serviced by any one firm. However when airlines compete on an increasing number of routes, their ability to sustain collusion may increase.

and American on flights between Houston and Chicago. Consequently, we examine trips between origin and destination *cities*.

We start by carefully constructing marginal cost estimates.[3] We then use these estimates to construct measures of the price markup over marginal cost, $(p - MC)/MC$, where p is the price and MC is the marginal cost. This approach is a relatively agnostic method of determining market power in any static model.[4]

Our results indicate that routes dominated by one or two firms, which are virtually all the markets in the United States, have much larger markups than do other routes. Markets dominated by one firm have larger markups than those dominated by two firms.

13.2. DATA

Our primary data source is the Department of Transportation (DOT) DB1A data set, which includes a one in ten sample of all tickets issued from January 1979 through December 1992. All tickets with the same fare, airlines, and plane changes in a given quarter are aggregated. Because of this aggregation, we cannot identify the date and time of day, flight number, and equipment type. The only fare information that is consistently available over time is whether the ticket is first class or coach and whether any restriction was placed on the ticket. That is, we do not have detailed information on the type of restriction such as whether the airline required an advance purchase or Saturday night stay or would not offer refunds.

Before they eliminate information on time of day and date of travel, DOT uses this information to identify trip breaks, and consequently identifies the traveler's ultimate destination. In some cases, this identification is unambiguous. If the trip had two flight segments and the second ended where the first began, then the ticket was for a round trip. If there are three trip segments, interpreting the information is more difficult. The ultimate destination is likely to be the location with the longest break. On the other hand, such a ticket could be associated with travel where both the city at the end of the first segment and the city at the end of the second segment were destinations. Over the time period of the study, the DB1A

---

[3] Brander and Zhang (1990, 1993) calculated a marginal cost measure and then used it to test for market structures in a structural model. We construct marginal cost using a much more detailed and presumably more accurate approach then they did.

[4] We are working on a dynamic structural model of this market, which is a generalization of the structural dynamic oligopoly model in Karp and Perloff (1993). Alam et al. (2001) provide evidence of dynamic strategic behavior in the airlines market using a time-series analysis. Brander and Zhang (1993) estimate a supergame/trigger-price model for airlines.

data set reported tickets with up to 23 segments. In some cases, these complicated trips are listed simply as round-trip tickets. Because we have less information than DOT had to make judgments about what the ultimate trip purpose was, we cannot modify the classification of these tickets. Still, leaving multi-destination tickets in the sample would seriously compromise the study, since they represent sales in more than one market. Thus, we use only tickets that can be clearly classified as either one-way or round trips with a single destination. Up to six total segments are allowed for the flight (a five stop, one-way ticket or a round trip ticket with two stops per leg of the trip). Including only one way and round trip tickets with no more than six total segments eliminates only a little more than 1% of the sample.

When a consumer purchases a ticket, the ticket consists of "coupons" that correspond to flight numbers. Each time the itinerary involves a change in flight numbers, an additional coupon is added. Consequently a coupon segment covers that part of the itinerary for which the flight number remains unchanged. If a stop leads to a change in flight number, then that stop leads to a change in coupon segments. Such a change certainly occurs if the passenger changes planes, but it may also occur even if the passenger stays on the plane and the airline changes the flight number. Unfortunately, this last possibility may introduce an error when we estimate marginal costs and the impact of the number of stops on price.

There are clearly other variables that many have attempted to incorporate into modeling the demand side of long distance travel. These include factors that are weather related, such as mean temperature difference, in an attempt to capture vacation travel in the winter months. Others have included variables that attempt to capture the demand for business travel such as the number of white-collar jobs in an area. The model for this paper assumes that these factors are either very slow to change or that they are strongly correlated with other factors in the model. These slowly moving factors are captured with fixed route specific effects that describe the origin-destination pair. There are approximately 99,000 route effects in the data. These route effects have been controlled for in earlier analyses in which the price indices utilized in this study were constructed.[5]

13.3. COSTS[6]

We can use the DOT data set to construct various cost measures, including marginal cost. We start by describing the available cost data. Then we describe how we construct our cost measures.

---

[5] The price data are based on the work of Good, Sickles, and Weiher (2001).

[6] Ila Alam, David Good, and Robin Sickles constructed the cost data. See Good, Nadiri and Sickles (1997) and Alam and Sickles (2000) for relatively new analyses of the cost data.

13.3.1. Cost data

DOT's airline production data set (based on Form 41/T100) includes four inputs: labor; energy; flight capital; and a residual category, materials, that includes supplies, outside services, and non-flight capital. The data set includes two output measures: scheduled and non-scheduled revenue passenger-miles. Quantity and price data were constructed using the multilateral Tornqvist-Theil index number procedure. The data set also includes two network characteristics: stage length and load factor.

Flight capital is described by four aircraft attributes: the average size (measured in seats); the average age; and the separate proportions of aircraft in the fleet that are jet powered or wide-bodied designs. The data set includes information for the 14 largest US air carriers that were operating at the time of deregulation and their descendant airlines: American Airlines (AA), Allegheny Airlines (AL), Braniff International, Eastern Airlines (EA), Continental Airlines (CO), Delta Airlines (DL), Frontier Airlines (FL), Northwest Airlines (NW), Piedmont Airlines (PI), Republic Airlines (RC), Southwest (WN), Texas International (TI), TransWorld Airlines (TW), and United Airlines (UA).

The data set provides nearly total coverage of quarterly, air carrier specific scheduled air traffic. We restricted our attention to the traditional certificated carriers because routine data reporting for those carriers was well established at the time of deregulation.[7] This data set is the largest, cleanest data set available on the production of scheduled US passenger air transport.

13.3.1.1. Labor

The labor inputs are an aggregation of 93 separate labor accounts into five major employment classes (flight deck crews, flight attendants, mechanics, passenger/cargo/aircraft handlers, and other personnel). We could not correct for differing utilization rates because we lack information on the number of hours worked by the various employment classes. Expenditures in these five subcomponents are constructed from the expenditure data in DOT Form 41 Schedules P5, P6, P7, and P8. The expense per person quarter and the number of person quarters were calculated using this expense and head count information.

---

[7] New entrants could be added to this data set with some difficulty. However, these carriers have little experience in providing the often burdensome reporting required by DOT Form 41. Noncompliance results in virtually no sanctions. Consequently, new entrant data tend to be of significantly lower quality.

13.3.1.2. Energy

We want an energy input that only captures aircraft fuel. However, the material index also includes fuel that is used for ground operations and electricity. Our energy input was constructed by combining information on aircraft fuel gallons used with fuel expense data per period. Aircraft fuel cost in dollars comes from Schedule PS, account 5145.1. Gallons of aircraft fuel is listed in Schedule T2, account Z921. This input has undergone virtually no change because these accounts remained substantially unchanged over the span of the data set.

13.3.1.3. Materials

The materials input consists of 69 separate expenditure accounts aggregated into 12 broad classes of materials or other inputs that did not fit into the labor, energy, or flight capital categories. Carrier-specific price or quantity deflators for these expenditure groups were unavailable. Instead, industry-wide price deflators were obtained from a variety of sources.

13.3.1.4. Flight capital

The number of each different model of aircraft that a carrier operated was collected from DOT Form 41, Schedule T2 (account Z82O). Data on the technological characteristics for the approximately 60 types of aircraft in significant use over the period 1970 through 1992 were collected from *Jane's All the World's Aircraft* (1945 through 1982 editions).

We constructed the average number of aircraft in service for each quarter by dividing the total number of aircraft days for all aircraft types by the number of days in the quarter. This construct provides a gross measure of the size of the fleet (number of aircraft).

This measure of flight capital was adjusted by the average equipment size as measured by the highest density single-class seating configuration listed in *Jane's* for each aircraft type. We weighted the fleet-wide average by the number of aircraft of each type in service. In some cases (particularly with wide-bodied jets), the actual number of seats was substantially less than described by this configuration because the airline used first-class and business-class seating. Our adjustment reflects the physical size of the aircraft rather than how carriers chose to use or configure them.

Our fleet vintage measure is the average number of months used since the FAA's type-certification of aircraft designs. Our assumption is that technological innovation in an aircraft does not change after the design is type-certified.

Consequently, the measure of technological age does not fully capture the deterioration in capital and increased maintenance costs caused by use. This measure does capture retrofitting older designs with major innovations, if these innovations were significant enough to require recertification of the type.

Finally, the conversion to jet aircraft was the major innovation during the 1960s and 1970s. While many carriers had largely adopted this innovation prior to our study period, this conversion was by no means universal. Many of the local service airlines used turboprop aircraft as a significant portion of their fleets. We control for a carrier's mixture of planes by including measures of the proportion of aircraft in the fleet that are jet powered and the proportion of widebodied aircraft.

13.3.1.5. Output

We use the most commonly used measure of carrier output, revenue ton-mile. The data set provides this measure as well as measures of revenue output that are disaggregated into scheduled and nonscheduled output. Nonscheduled output includes cargo and charter operations. Revenue and traffic data were available from DOT Form 41. These data allowed construction of price and quantities for seven different outputs produced by the typical airline. We calculated the price per unit (passenger-mile or ton-mile) of the relevant service by dividing the revenue generated in the category by the physical amount of output in that category. In cases where a carrier offered only one type of service (called "first class" by convention), the service was redefined to be coach class. The reporting of revenue and traffic charter operations between cargo and passenger service was very sporadic. These two outputs were combined into a single category with passenger-miles converted to ton-miles, assuming an average weight of 200 pounds per passenger (including baggage). Changes in DOT Form 41 in 1985 led to the elimination of the distinction between express cargo and air freight. Consequently, these two categories were also collapsed. Three different price and quantity index pairs are generated. The first is total revenue-output and uses the multilateral Tornqvist-Theil index number procedure on all the revenue-output categories. The second used the Tornqvist-Theil index number procedure on the two passenger categories. The third results from the use of the index number procedure on mail, cargo and charter services.

The capacity of flight operations is also provided in this data set. This describes the total amount of traffic generated, regardless of whether or not it was sold. While it is possible to distinguish between an unsold coach seat and an unsold first-class seat (they are of different sizes), such distinctions are not logically possible in the case of cargo operations (mail and cargo could be carried in the same location). Consequently, the measure of airline capacity includes only three broad categories: first-class seat-miles flown, coach seat-miles flown, and nonscheduled ton-miles flown. With the change to T100 as the primary database for airline traffic in 1990, carriers are no longer required to report available seat-miles, revenue seat-miles, or revenues by the level of passenger service. Instead, these amounts are aggregated with revenues supplied as account 3901 on Schedule P1 after 1990.

The convention that passenger along with baggage is 200 pounds (one-tenth of a ton) is used to construct the nonscheduled ton-miles. Potential revenues that could be collected, if all services were sold, are constructed assuming that the prices for each of these categories remain the same as for output actually sold. In other words, the price for first-class revenue passenger-miles flown is imputed to first-class available seat-miles flown.

Two important measures of the carrier's network are also generated. The first is a passenger load factor. This is found by dividing revenue passenger-miles by available seat-miles. This measure is generally related to flight frequency with a lower number indicating more frequent flights and consequently a higher level of service. Other definitions of load factor are possible, such as dividing the total passenger revenue collected by the total that would be collected were the planes flown full (derived from the passenger capacity output times passenger capacity price). Stage length also provides an important measure of carrier output. Generally, the shorter the flight, the higher the proportion of ground services required per passenger-mile and the more circuitous the flight (a higher proportion of aircraft miles flown is needed to accommodate the needs of air traffic control). This generally results in a higher cost per mile for short flights than for longer flights. Average stage length is found by dividing total revenue aircraft miles flown by total revenue aircraft departures.

13.3.2. Cost measures

We assume that the individual cost functions are Cobb-Douglas:

$$
\begin{aligned}
\ln \text{Cost} = \ &\beta_1 \text{ Revenue Passenger Miles} + \beta_2 \ln \text{Enplanements} + \\
&\beta_3 \ln \text{Cargo Ton Miles} + \beta_4 \ln \text{Cities} + \beta_5 \ln \text{Load Factor} + \\
&\beta_6 \ln \text{Average Stage Length} + \beta_7 \ln \text{Labor Price} + \\
&\beta_8 \ln \text{Fuel Price} + \beta_9 \ln \text{Materials Price} + \beta_{10} \ln \text{Capital Price} + \\
&\sum_{i=1}^{\text{number of airlines}} \delta_i \text{ Airline}_i .
\end{aligned}
$$

Revenue Passenger Miles are the sum of the miles traveled by paying passengers. Enplanements are the sum of the passengers on all flights.[8] Cargo Ton Miles are the number of cargo ton miles per flight.

The Cities variable provides a measure of the network size for a carrier. Caves, Christensen, and Tretheway (1984) suggest that network size is an important reason why airline costs differ. As the number of cities increases, the density of traffic on the carriers network, holding number of passenger miles constant, tends to decrease. Incorporating Load Factor into the model allows us to consider the effects of changes in revenue passenger miles, while holding the number of available seat miles constant. One would expect that increasing revenue passenger miles while holding available seat miles constant would have a very low cost since it involves simply filling up an otherwise empty seat.

For a cross-sectional, time series model, this regression fits well ($\bar{R}^2 = 0.79$) and is globally regular. The estimated scale elasticity is 1.018, which is not statistically different from 1 at conventional significance levels. Using these estimates, we calculate various carrier- and time-specific marginal costs for the passenger's flight:

$$\text{Terminal Costs} = MC_{\text{Enplanements}},$$

$$\text{Per Mile Cost} = MC_{\text{Revenue Passenger Miles}},$$

$$\text{Total Segment Cost} = MC_{\text{Enplanements}} + MC_{\text{Revenue Passenger Miles}} \times \text{Miles Flown.}$$

For multi-segment trips, the cost of a particular itinerary is the sum of the cost for the individual trip segments.

These estimates were based on data for the entire US system and not for specific city-pair routes because cost data for individual routes are not available. However, we believe that by incorporating information on the specific number of enplanements, and the specific distance of particular flights, the marginal cost estimates are reasonably accurate. Indeed, these estimates correspond very well with published Standard Industry Fare Level (SIFL) values.

After estimating marginal costs, we construct a data set with four variables: carrier, date, $MC_{\text{Enplanement}}$, and $MC_{\text{Revenue Passenger Miles}}$. Next, we merge this data set segment-by-segment with the DB1A data. We merge segment-by-segment because itineraries may involve more than one carrier due to code sharing.

---

[8] Passengers on a flight are not considered to have enplaned if their flight involves a stop. If the passengers' itineraries require that they change flights then they would have a second enplanement for that trip.

We want to allocate the appropriate costs to each carrier for every segment rather than assign the costs to the carrier whose name happens to be on the ticket. We calculate the Total Itinerary Cost as

Total Itinerary Cost =

$$\sum_i^{\substack{\text{number of} \\ \text{segments}}} MC^{i,\text{carrier}_i}_{\text{Enplanement}} + MC^{i,\text{carrier}_i}_{\text{Revenue Passenger Miles}} \times \text{Distance}_i,$$

where i indexes segments and carrier_i is the carrier for segment i.

13.4. MARKET POWER MEASURES

Typically, one uses Lerner's Index, $(p - MC)/p$, where p is price and MC is marginal cost, to measure market power. Our usual presumption when using Lerner's Index is that price is at least as great as marginal cost. However, many airline tickets have a price that is well below marginal cost.

Figure 13.1 shows that the distribution of price per mile is skewed to the left. Nearly a third of the entire sample (31%) is below our estimates of marginal cost.

Prices may be below marginal cost for at least four reasons. First, firms may engage in predation or price wars.[9] Second, firms may lower prices on one route to encourage use of other higher-markup routes (loss leader).

Third, some observations may be very low price tickets reflecting price discrimination. Our marginal cost measure reflects the marginal cost of a flight rather than the marginal cost of the last few seats, which may be essentially zero.

Fourth, many fliers travel on zero coupon (price) tickets. The majority of zero coupon tickets are obtained using frequent flyer miles. American Airlines introduced the first frequent flyer program in 1981. Other airlines quickly followed. These programs were designed to increase customer loyalty to a particular airline by providing frequent travelers with free trips at a later date.

---

[9] Using case study data from several markets, Brock (2000) reported that major firms are responding to smaller firms with increasing episodes of predatory pricing. Busse (2001) tests whether the probability that a firm initiates a price war depends on its financial conditions. She uses DB1A data from 1985 until 1992. Ingeniously, she uses *Wall Street Journal* articles to identify when a price war occurs and which carrier initiated and which ones participated in the price war. She models the probability of a firm entering a price war as being a function of demand (which she estimates separately), financial indicators and control variables. Her results indicate that firms whose financial measures are in the lowest third of the distribution are 5 to 8 percentage points more likely to start a price war.

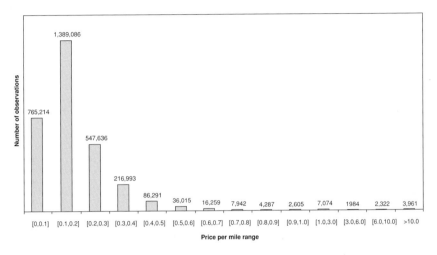

Figure 13.1: Histogram of real prices per mile (US$1978).

A Lerner Index cannot be constructed for each individual ticket because zero coupon tickets will have a Lerner Index of negative infinity. To reduce the problem of a zero or very low price, we aggregate the data to the route level in a given quarter. However, even when we do that, many average route prices are below average route marginal cost.

To further reduce the problem associated with below-marginal cost prices, we use $(p - MC)/MC$ as our measure of market power. By dividing by marginal cost instead of price, we put less weight on below-marginal cost prices. The lowest value this measure can reach is -1 (whereas the Lerner can approach negative infinity). Because we are interested in averages of these indexes, normalizing using the marginal cost instead of price leads to more reasonable results (one very large negative Lerner measure could swamp many positive measures, which are constrained to lie between zero and one).

13.5. MARKET POWER BY MARKET STRUCTURE

We use our estimated marginal cost measures to calculate the price markup over marginal cost, $(p - MC)/MC$. We report the average markups by market structure in Table 13.1.

Table 13.1:   Summary statistics by market structure.

Type of market	$(p - MC)/$ MC	$P < MC$ (%)	HHI	Observations	Share (%)
All	1.08	31	4,903	3,087,669	100
Monopoly	2.32	26	10,000	554,619	18
Dominant firm	2.06	23	6,554	1,228,838	40
Dominant pair	0.24	24	3,347	1,300,856	42
Duopoly	1.19	26	7,450	582,845	19
Dominant firm	1.31	25	7,858	431,846	14
No dominant firm	0.48	31	5,058	142,576	5
Triopoly	0.75	26	6,425	486,525	16
Dominant firm	0.91	24	7,172	271,253	9
No dominant firm	0.30	31	4,339	215,108	7
Quadrapoly	0.82	27	5,739	393,473	13
Dominant firm	1.17	23	6,851	172,619	6
Dominant pair	0.28	33	4,010	220,849	7
Neither	1.09	N/A	4,369	5	~0
Five or more firms	0.28	33	4,010	1,078,799	35
Dominant firm	2.50	23	6,221	353,120	11
Dominant pair	0.39	39	3,244	722,323	23
Neither	0.05	52	1,128	3,356	0.1

The first row of Table 13.1 reports the results for the entire sample of 3,087,669 route/months. Across all market structures, the average markup of price over marginal cost is 1.08. That is, the difference between price and marginal cost is 108% of marginal cost — price is more than twice as large as marginal cost. On average, the Herfindahl-Hirshman Index (HHI) is 4,903. That is approximately the HHI we would get with two equal size firms (5,000).[10]

---

[10] This markup over marginal cost corresponds to a Lerner Index of 0.519. With two identical Cournot firms, that would correspond to a market elasticity of about -0.963 and a demand elasticity facing each firm of -1.926.

Nearly a third of the sample (31%) has a price less than our estimated marginal cost. (Zero coupons are 3.3% of all tickets.)

The remaining rows show comparable results for various other market structures. The first column identifies the market structure. The second row covers monopoly routes. As the last column shows, monopolies are 18% of all route/month observations. Other rows report that duopolies are 19%, triopolies are 16%, quadrapolies are 13%, and five or more firms 35%.

Although 64% of routes have three or more firms, one or two firms dominate virtually all routes. In the table, we call a carrier a dominant firm if it has more than a 60% market share but is not a monopoly. We call a pair of carriers a dominant pair if they collectively have more than 60% of the market but neither firm is individually a dominant firm. Monopolies (18%) and dominant firms (40%) are 58% of the sample. These types of firms along with dominant pairs (42%) constitute nearly the entire sample. The only remaining category is 3,361 (5 of the quadrapoly and 3,356 of the five or more firm observations) out of 3,087,669 total observations, or approximately 0.1% of the total sample.

The percentage markup is 232% for monopolies and 206% for dominant firms. In contrast, over our sample period, the average price is only 24% above marginal cost for dominant pairs.[11] The average HHI (see the third column of the table) for a dominant firm market is 6,554. In contrast, the HHI is only 3,347 for dominant pairs (approximately equal to the HHI for three equal size firms).

Examining the various rows in Table 13.1, we find that the percentage markup depends much more on whether there is a dominant firm or dominant pair than the total number of firms in the market. If there is a dominant pair, whether there are four or five firms, the markup is between 28% for a quadrapoly and 39% for five or more firms. If there is a dominant firm, the markup is 131% for duopoly, 91% for triopoly, 117% for quadrapoly, and 250% if there are five or more firms. We are relatively unsure what the markup would be on routes with neither a dominant firm nor a dominant pair, because this situation is true for only about a tenth of 1% of the sample.

The share of tickets where price is less than marginal cost ranges from 23% to 39% (ignoring the last row with relatively few observations). For only about a quarter of the tickets is price less than marginal cost on routes where there is a dominant firm. In contrast, roughly a third have price less than marginal cost in markets with a dominant pair.

---

[11] Cf. Barla (2000) who examined firm size inequality and market power in the airline industry. Evans and Kessides (1993) concluded that airport dominance leads to market power.

13.6. CONCLUSIONS

The nation's policy makers have been concerned about market power in the US airline industry ever since it was deregulated in 1978. By carefully constructing a relatively accurate measure of marginal cost, we can calculate the degree of market power without having to make the strong parametric assumptions used in empirical industrial organization estimates of market power based on structural models.

In general, firms exercise substantial market power on average. Across all flights, the average markup of price, (price − marginal cost)/marginal cost, is 108%.

Further, we find that virtually all routes have a monopoly, a dominant firm (a non-monopoly firm that has over 60% of the market), or dominant pair of firms (that have over 60% of the market yet neither is a dominant firm). On the 18% of monopolized routes, the average markup is 232%. On the 40% of routes with a dominant firm, the markup averages 206%. On the 42% of routes with a dominant pair, the typical markup is 24%.

Apparently, avoiding having a single dominant firm can greatly lower the markup. Even if two firms dominate the market, the markup is relatively small.

REFERENCES

Alam, I. M. S., Ross, L. B., & Sickles, R. C. (2001). Time series analysis of strategic pricing behavior in the US airline industry. *Journal of Productivity Analysis, 16(1)*, July: 49–62.

Alam, I. M. S., & Sickles, R. C. (2000). Time series analysis of deregulatory dynamics and technical efficiency: The case of the US airline industry. *International Economic Review, 41*: 203–218.

Armantier, O., & Richard, O. (2000). Exchanges of cost information in the airline industry. Mimeo.

Barla, P. (2000). Firm size inequality and market power. *International Journal of Industrial Organization, 18(5)*, July: 693–722.

Borenstein, S. (1990). Hubs and high fares: Airport dominance and market power. *American Economic Review, 80*: 400–404.

Beutel, P. A., & McBride, M. E. (1992). Market power and the Northwest-Republic airline merger: A residual demand approach. *Southern Economic Journal, 58(3)*, January: 709–20.

Brander, J. A., & Zhang, A. (1990). Market conduct in the airline industry: An empirical investigation. *Rand Journal of Economics, 21*: 567–583.

Brander, J. A., & Zhang A. (1993). Dynamic oligopoly in the airline industry. *International Journal of Industrial Organization, 11*: 407–435.

Brueckner, J. K. (1997). The economics of international codesharing: An analysis of airline alliances. Working paper, University of Illinois at Urbana-Champaign Office of Research.

Busse, M. R. (2001). Firm financial condition and airline price wars. Mimeo, Yale, March.

Carlton, D., Landes, W., & Posner, R. (1980). Benefits and costs of airline mergers: A case study. *Bell Journal of Economics, 11*: 65–83.

Caves, D., Christensen, L., & Tretheway, M. (1984). Economies of density versus economies of scale: Why trunk and local service airlines costs differ. *Rand Journal of Economics, 15*: 471–489.

Evans, W. N., & Kessides, I. N. (1993). Localized market power in the US airline industry. *Review of Economics and Statistics, 75*(1), February: 66–75.

FAA. FAA historical chronology, 1926–1996. http://www.faa.gov/docs/b-chron.doc.

Good, D., Nadiri, M. I., & Sickles, R. C. (1997). Index number and factor demand approaches to the estimation of productivity. In: M. H. Pesaran and P. Schmidt (eds.), Chapter 1 of the *Handbook of Applied Econometrics*, Volume II – Microeconometrics (pp. 14–80). Oxford: Basil Blackwell.

Good, D., Sickles, R. C., & Weiher, J. (2001). On a new hedonic price index for airline travel. Mimeo, Rice University.

Hergott, M. J. (1997). Airport concentration and market power: An events study approach. *Review of Industrial Organization, 12*(5–6), December: 793–800.

Jane's Publishing. (1945–1982). J. Taylor (ed.), *Jane's All the World's Aircraft*. London: Jane's Publishing.

Karp, L. S., & Perloff, J. M. (1993). Dynamic oligopoly in the rice export market. *Review of Economics and Statistics, 71*: 462–470.

Kim, E. H., & Singal, V. (1993). Mergers and market power: Evidence from the airline industry. *American Economic Review, 83*(3), June: 549–69.

Knapp, W. (1990). Event analysis of air carrier mergers and acquisitions. *Review of Economics and Statistics, 72*(4), November: 703–707.

Singal, V. (1996). Airline mergers and competition: An integration of stock and product price effects. *Journal of Business, 69*(2), April: 233–268.

Index